D1127555

"WHO HAS THE YOUTH, HAS THE FUTURE"

"WHO HAS THE YOUTH, HAS THE FUTURE"

THE CAMPAIGN TO SAVE YOUNG WORKERS IN IMPERIAL GERMANY

DEREK S. LINTON
Hobart and William Smith Colleges

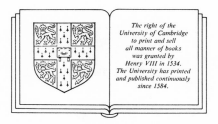

The right of the
University of Cambridge
to print and sell
all manner of books
was granted by
Henry VIII in 1534.
The University has printed
and published continuously
since 1584.

CAMBRIDGE UNIVERSITY PRESS

CAMBRIDGE

NEW YORK   PORT CHESTER   MELBOURNE   SYDNEY

Published by the Press Syndicate of the University of Cambridge
The Pitt Building, Trumpington Street, Cambridge CB2 1RP
40 West 20th Street, New York, NY 10011, USA
10 Stamford Road, Oakleigh, Melbourne 3166, Australia

First published 1991

Printed in the United States of America

Library of Congress Cataloging-in-Publication Data
Linton, Derek S.
"Who has the youth, has the future" : the campaign to save young
workers in imperial Germany / Derek S. Linton.
p.   cm.
Includes bibliographical references and index.
ISBN 0–521–38537–7
1. Youth – Employment – Germany – History.   2. Youth – Germany
– Social conditions.   3. Germany – History – 1871–   I. Title.
Hd6276.G4L56   1991
331.3′4′0943 – dc20   90–44209
                                                                    CIP

British Library Cataloging-in-Publication Data applied for

ISBN 0-521-38537-7 hardback

Contents

v

Tables

vii

Acknowledgments

Since the turn of the century various discourses on the "youth problem" — whether on delinquency, educational deficiencies, rebelliousness, or lack of adequate vocational skills — have never ceased to flow from the tongues and pens of welfare workers, sociologists, and public officials. This book traces the original construction of young laborers as an official social problem in Imperial Germany around 1900. It explores the ways that middle-class social reformers and government officials labeled young workers a social problem and then set about erecting a new institutional framework that would encompass these youth and embody a new disciplining and socializing regime. Also examined are the manner in which the reformers implemented their policies and the effectiveness of the new discourses and institutions in achieving their goals.

This book grew out of a dissertation. I embarked on research almost a decade ago in an attempt to resolve a central debate in German labor history, the debate over the degree of integration of workers, especially Social Democratic workers, in the Wilhelmine polity. This debate arose from conflicting evaluations of the German Social Democratic party's decision to support the Imperial state by voting for war credits in August 1914. Was this vote a heinous betrayal of the party's previously principled opposition to militarism, as leftist critics have maintained, or did it simply register the patriotic sentiment widespread in the German working class, as the party's defenders have replied? I expected to approach the problem of the "nationalization of the masses" by investigating the socialization of young workers in the prewar era and their responses to the war itself.

In the course of research, however, the focus of investigation changed. Although the question of social and political integration continued to loom large, the central focus gradually shifted from the youth themselves to the campaign and institutions designed to make them loyal and productive mainstays of the Empire. In part this shift was prompted by practical considerations. A moral crusade conducted by articulate and literate clergy, public officials, and teachers had churned out mounds of documentation, whereas young laborers had little opportunity or inclination to express their loyalty or opposition to the Empire directly. Their positions can only be inferred from faint traces usually recorded by others. In part, however, focusing on young workers' responses to the outbreak of the war increasingly struck me as overly constraining, since these responses proved to be incomprehensible without a broader examination of age and social relations in the prewar era. Youth savers had designated young laborers an official social problem well before the war. Moreover, many of the institutions founded as a result of the battle for youth outlasted the war. To have made the entire research project converge on the war as a kind of inevitable terminus ad quem would have meant stressing the militarization of youth policy and youthful radicalization, exceptional moments in a long-term process, rather than the process itself. As the focus of investigation changed, so, too, did my intellectual commitments. Although a spirit of theoretical and methodological eclecticism still presides over the work, the proportions in this eclectic mixture have changed, with larger measures of Weber and Foucault and a smaller measure of Gramsci than in the earlier dissertation.

Like all books that began their lives as dissertations, however radically transformed they might be, this one could not have been brought to completion without substantial assistance from numerous individuals and institutions. First, thanks go to Arno J. Mayer, who supervised the dissertation and offered both constructive criticism and encouragement. I would also like to thank the members of my dissertation committee, including John Gillis, David Abraham, and Michael A. Bernstein, all of whom provided excellent counsel on how to convert a ramshackle edifice into a publishable monograph. If I have often failed to heed their valuable advice, it has largely been due to a lack of time and resources. I am also extremely grateful for the careful reading given the manuscript by the outside readers for Cambridge University Press, James C. Albisetti and an anonymous reviewer. Both saved me from a number of embarrassing mistakes and suggested a number of well-conceived revisions. Needless to say, all earlier readers are absolved for any errors or shortcomings remaining in the final text.

Most of the archival research for this book was undertaken in the Lower Rhine and Ruhr regions of the Federal Republic of Germany during 1979–81. Few scholars who have worked in German archives can fail to be impressed by the competence, hospitality, and efficiency of their staffs. I would like to thank the staff of the Haupstaatsarchiv Düsseldorf (Zweig Kalkum) and those of the municipal archives in Essen and Solingen. Special thanks to Dr. Weidenhaupt and the staff of the Stadtarchiv Düsseldorf for making a lengthy period of research both productive and pleasant. Several religious archives made their collections available, including the Historisches Archiv des Erzbistums Köln and the Evangelische Kirche im Rheinland in Düsseldorf. Thanks to the staffs of the Stadtbibliothek MönchenGladbach, the Archiv des deutchen Gewerkschaftsbundes in Düsseldorf and the library of the CVJM (the German YMCA) in Wuppertal, who made it possible for me to read through many of the pamphlets on youth policy collected by the Volksverein für das katholische Deutschland, the periodicals of the Arbeiterjugendbewegung, and the press of various Protestant youth groups. The industrial archives of the Krupp firm (Werkarchiv Krupp–Villa Hügel) and Mannesmann in Düsseldorf cordially placed their collections at my disposal. Research and reference librarians at Düsseldorf, Bielefeld, Bonn, Köln, Princeton, and Cornell Universities were unfailingly helpful in tracking down obscure references, books, articles, conference papers, and tracts, as were the librarians at the New York Public Library. Initial funding came from an eighteen-month predoctoral grant from the German Academic Exchange Service (DAAD), funding that made the entire project possible. When piggybacked on a Fulbright seminar in Germany, a small Hewlett Mellon research grant administered by Hobart and William Smith Colleges permitted me to conduct two additional weeks of archival research during the summer of 1986, and a Hewlett Mellon writing grant from the same source enabled me to take a ten-week leave from teaching in order to write during the fall of 1987. An earlier version of Chapter 8 appeared as an article entitled "Between School and Marriage, Workshop and Household: Young Working Women as a Social Problem in Late Imperial Germany," in *European History Quarterly*, 18, no. 4 (October 1988). I am grateful to SAGE Publications for permitting me to make use of and recast this earlier article.

Geneva, New York   *Derek S. Linton*

1

Introduction: the natural history of a social problem

"Who has the youth, has the future!" At the turn of the century this shibboleth, sometimes attributed to Luther, became the battle cry of a nascent campaign launched by middle-class reformers to capture the hearts and minds of young urban German workers. Soon male laborers between the ages of fourteen and twenty, or "between primary school and barracks" in the then current phrase, became the cynosure of public debate and policy. The campaign was undertaken to protect them from a host of ostensible moral dangers associated with urban life, to save them from the unpatriotic influence of the Social Democratic party (SPD), and to better their health and upgrade their industrial skills as means of promoting national efficiency, both in the economic and military spheres.

Dating with exactitude the origin of the youth salvation campaign that was to sweep late Imperial Germany is impossible. Like most moral crusades, it germinated slowly before erupting forcefully into public consciousness. Although there was no sense of a generalized problem with young workers in the 1870s, one can certainly discover examples of the concerns and rhetoric adopted by the turn-of-the-century youth salvation campaign. Thus, in 1878 Fritz Kalle, a Saxon factory owner and well-known advocate of popular education, in a speech before the Social Policy Association (Verein für Sozialpolitik), an association of influential government officials and academics opposed to Manchester liberalism and committed to state financed social reform, denounced the spread of youthful wildness (Verwilderung) and loss of moral restraint that, he believed, were results of the decline of the artisanal order and the rise of the factory system.[1] Reformers periodically voiced concerns about the physical and moral well-being of young workers, not only those in the Social Policy Association, but also those in reform organizations like the liberal Society for the Propagation of Popular Education (Gesellschaft für Verbreitung von Volksbildung), the government-supported Central Association for the Welfare of the Working Classes (Centralverein für das Wohl der arbeitenden Klassen), and the Association of Catholic Industrialists and Friends of Labor (Arbeiterwohl).[2] As the historian Jürgen Reulecke has shown, during the 1870s and 1880s such reform associations sporadically pressed for measures like the extension of protective legislation for young factory workers, the institution of factory savings deposits for young workers to encourage thriftiness, and instruction in useful household handicrafts to strengthen ties between youths and their families.

But it was only in the 1890s that the notion that something was amiss with the nation's young laborers, that they were becoming a palpable threat to the social order gained a powerful grip on the imaginations of the educated middle class and officialdom. In 1890 Johannes Corvey of the Central Association for the Welfare of the Working Classes expressed alarm at the radicalization of young workers; their militancy, their hatred of employers, their uprootedness and dissociation from all family bonds.[3] Pamphlets like the one by Ernst Floessel entitled "What Is Wrong with Our Laboring Youth?" began to appear. Public discussion of craft protection highlighted the educational deficiencies of apprentices. Debates in the Reichstag over the family law provisions of the Imperial Civil Code drew attention to neglected and wayward youth. In a speech before the Reichstag in 1899, War Minister von Gossler warned of a dangerous upsurge in juvenile delinquency, claiming that the number of convicted youths had increased 82 percent between 1882 and 1897. The same year, in an attempt to bridle the flight from the land, the Prussian legislature considered a law that would have forbidden youths from migrating to large cities from rural districts without written consent from their parents or guardians. The Prussian House of Lords recommended that the government prohibit youths under seventeen from visiting taverns and that communities set up recreational facilities that would enable young workers to spend their Sundays and holidays enjoying wholesome and ennobling recreations.[4]

By 1900 the belief that young working males constituted a pressing and distressing social problem that demanded remedial welfare measures was becoming widespread among municipal bureaucrats and social reformers. As one urban official proclaimed, "Welfare [*Fürsorge*] for post-school-age youth is a modern problem. It is even in a certain sense the newest among the social problems that the modern world poses for the activity of private associations and state and communal agencies."[5] Pastor Albert Fritsch, a Protestant minister associated with the Inner Mission in Berlin, was happy to relate that "the conviction of the necessity of such welfare measures has penetrated ever wider circles...."[6] The officially sanctioned Center for Workers' Welfare Institutions, which vetted government social policies and proffered advice on reform, and the Protestant Social Congress, an association of Protestant ministers and laypersons founded in 1890 to formulate a Christian social policy, made young male laborers the central theme of their annual conventions in 1900, and in the case of the Center in 1901 as well. In spring of 1900 the Royal Academy of Useful Knowledge in Erfurt announced a prize essay contest on the question, "What is the best way to educate our male youth for the good of civil society between leaving primary school and entering the army?"[7]

Even the phrasing of this question signaled the new way of conceptualizing young workers that was solidifying at the turn of the century. Whereas prior to this, criteria for age categorization had been haphazard and arbitrary, with different definitions of "youth" inscribed in civil law, criminal law, and the Industrial Code, by 1900 standard terms like *schulentlassene Jugend* (youth released from school) or *gewerbsthätige Jugend* (industrially active youth) were acquiring a more univocal sense. Although certainly closely related to puberty (*Entwicklungsalter*, *Uebergangszeit*), when the young not only completed their physiological development but were also supposedly vulnerable to extreme psychological lability (frequent oscillations in self-esteem, intense shifts in mood and judgment) and to the dangers attendant upon the awakening of sexual impulse and fantasy (masturbation, precocious sexual relations), these terms were not synonymous.[8] Instead, *schulentlassene Jugend* was steadily coming to designate young male workers in the dangerously unconstrained period between entering the labor force at age fourteen and induction into the army at age twenty, the years institutionally bounded by primary school and barracks.

The conferences held in 1900 and 1901 provide evidence of the social and organizational anchorage of the accelerating campaign for youth salvation. Attending the conferences of the Center for Workers' Welfare Institutions were official representatives from the Imperial Naval Office, the Insurance Office, various Prussian ministries, the states of Baden, Württemberg, Saxony, and Bavaria, and most major cities, as well as Catholic and Protestant clergymen, school superintendants, and a few doctors and businessmen. Over half of the 399 participants in the assembly of the Protestant Social Congress in 1900 were pastors, theology students, or church administrators, but civil servants, teachers, and practitioners of various free professions were also represented. The Erfurt essay contest, won by the Munich school superintendant Georg Kerschensteiner, attracted seventy-five entrants, among them nineteen primary school teachers, sixteen municipal school officials, sixteen Protestant ministers, and a handful of writers, businessmen, technicians, army officers, and jurists.[9]

These events faintly heralded the subsequent scope and scale of youth salvation activities as the campaign burgeoned into a nationwide crusade. Over the next eighteen years there was an unsurveyeable flood of books, pamphlets, articles, and tracts on youth welfare. City and state governments, the churches, and various reform associations organized countless parleys, meetings, and seminars on young laborers. The Center for Workers' Welfare Institutions and its successor, the Center for Popular Welfare, held three more conferences devoted to this subject. The Society for Social Reform, with an executive board that boasted eminent Wilhelmine reformers, such as the previous Prussian commerce minister, Freiherr von Berlepsch, the National Liberal Party chair, Ernst Bassermann, the National Social leader, Friedrich Naumann, the economist and liberal social theorist, Lujo Brentano, and the chairman of the People's League for Catholic Germany, August Pieper, staged an important conference on young male workers in 1911.[10]

Attendance at such conferences expanded prodigiously during the late Imperial period; by 1912 regional conferences with several thousand participants had become common. Although youth work would partially feminize, especially after 1911, when young working women began to be treated as a social problem in their own right, the social profile of participants remained practically unchanged between 1900 and the war. Most youth savers were part of the *Bildungsbürgertum,* the educated middle classes: municipal administrators, primary and continuation school teachers, clergy, businessmen, and other urban professionals, such as doctors, lawyers and journalists.[11] Thus a regional youth welfare conference in Düsseldorf in October 1913 packed the municipal concert hall with 2,060 youth savers, slightly over half of whom were women. Teachers (1,000) formed the largest single occupational group, followed by contingents of business people (238), clergy (200), and urban officials (163).[12] In general, youth savers obviously belonged to professions that regularly came into contact with young male workers, and their participation in the campaign should be viewed as a rather natural extension of professional concerns. Evidence on political affiliation is available for only a few prominent youth savers, but extrapolations from this small sample suggest that youth savers largely backed the centrist parties: the National Liberal Party, the various left liberal groupings, or the Cologne (middle-class) or Mönchen-Gladbach (populist social Catholic) tendencies of the Catholic Center Party.[13] All were advocates of further welfare legislation that would primarily serve to strengthen the national state, which they accepted uncritically as the preeminent focus of loyalty and identity. They also shared middle-class anxieties over the gathering strength of the Social Democratic party and the supposed disorder of urban life. Both these commitments and these anxieties would be reflected and expressed in their programs. Because of the central place occupied by many youth savers in municipal governments and the churches, they would also be remarkably successful in implementing and embodying their programs in new or revamped institutions like the industrial continuation schools and church-sponsored youth associations. Thus the movement for youth salvation was urban in locus, middle-class professional in composition, and strongly nationalist and social liberal in political orientation. Indeed, the history of the youth salvation campaign is an important part of the history of the *Bildungsbürgertum* in the late Empire and, at least in the case of Protestant youth savers, reveals much about the shift from individualist to social liberalism at the turn of the century.

Positions taken in this campaign became Rorschach tests indicating orientations toward a series of issues central to the self-definition and status aspirations of the Wilhelmine educated middle class: socialism, urbanization, family values, crime, secularization, mass culture, large-scale industry, and Germany's place in the international arena. Such issues overshadowed the putative aims of the youth salvation campaign to such a degree at times that it would be difficult to deny the assertion by Günther Dehn, a Protestant pastor in a working-class district in Berlin, that the contenders in the battle for youth were often more interested in controlling the future than they were in fostering the welfare of young workers.[14]

Because of the political dimensions of the youth salvation campaign, a survey of its development provides a somewhat oblique but nonetheless excellent vantage point from which to approach the historiographical controversies that have swirled around Imperial Germany. Since the youth salvation campaign was in part conceived as a way of integrating young workers into the Wilhelmine polity and social order, and since antisocialism bound together the disparate strands of this campaign, an examination of the campaign's results can increase our understanding of the degree of national integration.[15] A discussion of the SPD's ambivalent responses to various aspects of the campaign can also help to clarify the position of the party within the political order, and an account of Socialist attitudes toward young workers and the appeals to them by the Socialist youth movement will enable us to map some of the jagged boundaries between the culture of the labor movement and the culture of the working class, a mapping recently proposed by Richard J. Evans. Finally, placing the youth savers amid the political, social, and religious crosscurrents of the Empire and evaluating their achievements and failures, will contribute to an assessment of the capacity of Wilhelmine Germany for substantive reform, a point of dispute between historians extremely critical of the Empire, such as Hans-Ulrich Wehler, and those, such as Thomas Nipperdey, who are more favorably disposed toward the Kaiserreich.[16]

This book, then, examines the campaign to save young workers in late Imperial Germany. It explores the way in which young laborers became stamped as an official social problem and designated objects of social policy. It attempts to answer questions including, Why did young workers become problematic? Who were the youth savers? How did they portray the problem of young workers? What sorts of policies did they recommend? How were these policies implemented and to what effect? What does the youth salvation campaign signify about social relations in Wilhelmine Germany? What does the battle for hegemony over young laborers tell us about the nature of the Wilhelmine polity? Thus, this book reconstructs the "natural history of a social problem." As the sociologists Richard C. Fuller and Richard R. Myers declared in their classic article of that title:

Social problems do not arise full-blown, commanding community attention and evoking adequate policies and machinery for their solution. On the contrary, we believe that social problems exhibit a temporal course of development in which different phases or stages may be distinguished. Each stage anticipates its successor in time and each succeeding stage contains new elements which mark it off from its predecessor. A social problem thus conceived as always being in a dynamic state of "becoming" passes through the natural history stages of awareness, policy determination and reform.[17]

Although the stages postulated by Fuller and Myers cannot be so neatly and schematically differentiated, the advantage of such a "natural history" approach is that it denaturalizes the development of "social problems," which themselves are rendered problematic and regarded as contingent outcomes of specific historic conjunctures and political controversies.

Hence this book treats the campaign surrounding young laborers, rather than being intended primarily as a social history of these youths, although, obviously, both histories are inextricably intertwined. Although this book makes no attempt to recreate the life worlds of young laborers, I certainly hope that readers committed to *Alltagsgeschichte* will find much that intersects with their interests in the following pages.[18] To the degree that this work does deal with "youth and history," it differs from some of the major works in this field in several key respects, some conceptual, some substantive.

Probably the most striking conceptual difference is the minimal place assigned to "generation" either as a descriptive or analytical category.[19] Given that Karl Mannheim and other sociologists fashioned the concept of "generation" and its closely related correlate, "generational conflict," into social scientific instruments during the 1920s, immediately after the period covered in this book, this absence requires an explanation. Certainly Mannheim's notion of "generational location," a notion derived by analogy from social class location, could be applied to young urban laborers in late Imperial Germany. Their social backgrounds, educational levels, and position in the labor force certainly limited these youths "to a specific range of potential experience, predisposing them for a certain characteristic mode of thought and experience and a characteristic type of historically relevant action." In short, "generational location" is equated with an age- and class-specific structure of opportunity. One could possibly even extend Mannheim's concept of "actual generation" to young laborers in Germany between 1900 and 1918 since they "were exposed to the same social and intellectual symptoms of dynamic destabilization." Young workers had to adjust to rapid economic change, the sensory bombardment of the large city, new forms of mass culture, such as films and sports, the bombastic patriotism that accompanied Germany's growing international power, and debates over socialism. They would also confront a new institutional nexus that included continuation schools and adult-sponsored youth associations. They would generally be subject to the same labor protection laws and moral policing. To some degree, they would all experience the disillusion and deprivation resulting from Germany's failures during the Great War. In part it was clearly this common generational location of young manual laborers that enabled middle-class reformers to define them as a social problem and to construct a new institutional framework to encompass them.

Youth savers were quite aware, however, of significant distinctions within this social stratum. Moreover, it can be plausibly argued that insofar as young laborers composed a generation, to the degree they did have "an experience of generational affiliation and conflict," it was the institutions created by the youth savers that inadvertently supplied much of the basis of this commonality. Although I certainly do not wish to reject the notion of generation entirely or to eschew all generalizations about laborers between the ages of fourteen and twenty, I doubt that Mannheim's web of conceptual distinctions really captures anything very fundamental about young laborers at the turn of the century. Like their adult counterparts, young laborers were divided by skill level, trade, religion, political orientation, and gender. Even among young laborers there were a variety of "generational units," as Mannheim called broad groups that reconstructed their common experience in different specific ways and an even greater variety of formal and informal organizations, or "concrete" groups, in Mannheimian terminology, which crystallized these generational units, for example, the Workers' Youth Movement, Catholic youth sodalities, the Young Germany League. Generational tools have been most applicable and effective when analyzing formal organizations or well-defined, if informal, coteries with extensive networks of social communication, rather than birth cohorts.

What then of generational conflict? Certainly, as in all societies, one can easily marshal numerous examples of antagonism between old and young in Imperial Germany. Age-related hostilities were evident, whether in the villas of Berlin's tony West End or in the rent barracks of proletarian Wedding, albeit with different tonalities. The revolt of middle-class sons against authoritarian fathers and repressive schools had even become a modish theme for critical German authors at the turn of the century. Recent historians have echoed such themes by portraying the middle-class youth movement as an important catalyst hastening the autumn of the patriarch.[20] But to the degree that this study can be said to treat generational conflict, it is largely concerned with generational conflict conditioned by the class fissures of Wilhelmine society. Or as the political economist Wilhelm Troeltsch described this sort of conflict to the Protestant Social Congress in 1900, it was antagonism suffused by the strong prejudices that arise "when one social stratum [*Schicht*] judges the younger generation of another and vice versa."[21] Above all, the battle for young laborers would assume the form of a political class struggle waged in the future tense, a battle by professional groups within the propertied and educated middle class, each one wanting to shape the future in accordance with its own vision by securing hegemony over young laborers.

The emphasis on the concepts of generation and generational conflict, especially when coupled with the proposition that "youth makes its own history," although unexceptionable in and of itself, has not merely served as a heuristic device, but has had the effect of channeling research on youth in Imperial Germany into quite specific directions. It has led to an inordinate amount of research being devoted to the middle-class *Wandervogel* movement, which has been marmorealized as the first movement by and for youth themselves.[22] Whether its members have been celebrated and romanticized as prototypes of adolescent rebels with a cause, champions of nature against the stony urban deserts, camaraderie and charismatic leadership against bureaucratic hierarchies, simplicity against the dessicated conventions, stuffy routines, and meaningless rituals of bourgeois life, or whether, instead, on the basis of their *völkisch*-tinged nationalist metapolitics and their organizational forms, they have been criticized and condemned as somewhat naive and inadvertent progenitors of Nazism, their paramount importance has been accepted as incontrovertible.

But the nature of this supposed importance has never been spelled out very clearly. Walter Laqueur, in *Young Germany,* advanced three claims for the importance of the *Wandervogel,* all of which have been repeated by later authors, such as Peter Stachura, covering the same terrain, but none of which is especially compelling or convincing. The first two are to be found in the assertion that

... the youth movement in its way was a microcosm of modern Germany. Few are the political leaders, and even fewer the intellectual leaders among the generations born between 1890 and 1920, who were not at one time or another members of the youth movement, or influenced by it in their most impressionable years. And even perhaps more important than this personal element is the fact that all the great issues of the time are reflected in the history of the movement. At the outset it was non-political in character, or rather it wished to be so, yet it was gradually drawn into a confrontation with the dominant issues of the age.[23]

Although the passage certainly contains a number of ambiguities, Laqueur's two major claims are clear enough. The first is that the *Wandervogel* influenced Germany's intellectual and political leaders born within a thirty-year period. Yet few major figures are actually cited, and the nature of this ostensible influence is left unexplored. Second, Laqueur claims that the movement was a reflection of its age or, as implied later in the book and argued more explicitly by George Mosse or Hermann Giesecke, that it made manifest the dilemmas and weaknesses of Germany's Protestant middle class.[24] The same sort of claim, couched in slightly different terms, is advanced by John Gillis in his pioneering survey of European age relations, *Youth and History*. There, Gillis avows that "the ultimate importance of the *Wandervogel* lay not in its myriad organizational forms, but in the historical social reality that it reflected," a historical social reality that soon turns out to be congruent with German middle-class concerns.[25] But even if one concedes that the *Wandervögeln* did reflect uncertainty about personal, sexual, political, and social identity common among the educated middle class, this claim is fundamentally weak. After all, it has never been asserted that the *Wandervögeln* were somehow uniquely representative of their age or that an analysis of these student groups yields pregnant insights about Wilhelmine society not apparent from studying other middle-class life reform movements.

The third claim is that

The vast majority of German boys and girls were enrolled in confessional organizations, not in the autonomous youth movement. And yet in some respects the impact of the youth movement on the mass organizations inside Germany, and even outside her borders, was decisive. The youth movement introduced new ingredients and a new style which, by the late nineteen twenties, had spread widely among the younger generation in Germany and other European countries. Both the Hitler youth and, later on, the Free German Youth of East Germany adopted many of its outward trappings.[26]

But even assuming we accept that the *Wandervogel* exerted this decisive influence, this passage still begs the question of significance. Why are we to attribute such importance to the widespread adoption of outer trappings and superficial stylistic imitation? Gillis's analogous, if more carefully supported, claim is this:

Not so much in terms of numbers but in the way it shaped the approach to adolesence in Germany, it remained the most influential of the youth movements, leaving its mark on the civil as well as the social status of youth for several decades to come.[27]

In the end, according to Gillis:

Ironically, the most notable contribution of the *Wandervogel,* a social-historical movement associated with rebelliousness, was a new kind of conformity which was institutionalized in schools and extracurricular organizations as meeting the supposed needs of adolescents. The image of dependence and immaturity gradually became the operating principle for all state and voluntary agencies concerned with the education and care of that age group. By 1933 the dependent status of those 14 to 18 was taken for granted; and the Nazi declaration of that year, officially requiring the association of all youth with the Hitler Youth only completed a trend toward compulsory supervision already well underway.[28]

Gillis was assuredly right to emphasize the image of dependency and the trend toward compulsory supervision of youth, but as this study will demonstrate, that image was already regnant among middle-class reformers, who decried the newfound autonomy of unskilled young employees in the labor market and large cities at the turn of the century and set about curbing that independence with no reference to the *Wandervogel*. If such claims for the centrality of the *Wandervogel* have been accepted almost without challenge, it is only because relatively little research has been carried out on young laborers, religious youth groups, or such institutions as the continuation schools. Undoubtedly, the *Wandervogel* phenomenon and the related cult of youth did express some of the tensions and insecurities in middle-class life in Imperial Germany, tensions rooted in outmoded authority relations in the household and higher schools. Undoubtedly the *Wandervogel* did have a major impact on pedagogical theorizing. But it is difficult to shake the suspicion that the importance of the *Wandervogel* has been much exaggerated and inflated because of the assiduous efforts of a loyal and dedicated coterie of former members who founded archives, subsidized and conducted research, and lovingly cultivated a nostalgic afterimage.

Apart from a tradition of East German research on the Socialist youth movement, calculated to legitimate the policies of the SPD's left wing in the age of imperialism and to trace a dubious teleology from Workers' Youth Movement in the early twentieth century to the government-controlled Free German Youth of the late 1940s, interest in the middle-class youth cult and youth myth associated with the *Wandervogel* continues to motivate much of the writing on youth in Imperial Germany.[29] As younger historians more critical of traditional German historiography have entered West German academic life in recent decades, however, there has been something of a broadening of research to working-class youth as well. Such research has often made use of the sociological concepts of "social control" and "social discipline" or Foucauldian-inspired notions of the "carceral" and "normalization."[30] As a result, even writers hiking along the well-worn

Holzweg, "from the *Wandervogel* to the Hitler Youth," have begun to strike out on byways and forage for material on the Socialist youth movement and state-directed "youth cultivation" (*Jugendpflege*).[31] This book is closely related in both theme and approach to some of the newer literature concerned with young laborers. Therefore, it is appropriate at the outset to trace its affinities to and differences from some of these recent studies.

One early attempt to lay the foundations for a social history of a working-class youth problem was a 1982 article on "Large City Youth in Germany Before 1914" by the Munich labor historian Klaus Tenfelde.[32] In this article Tenfelde sought to unearth the demographic bases underlying the creation of an urban youth problem in Germany at the turn of the century. He primarily reconstructed the age pyramid of industrial centers and charted the migration of young workers to various types of cities. According to Tenfelde, such migration resulted in a "cumulatively increasing youthfulness" of German metropolitan areas. Tenfelde compiled much valuable information on the changing age structures of major German cities and made some useful comparisons between urban and rural Germany, as well as international comparisons with Great Britain, the United States, and France. However, he sometimes overstated the significance of the differences shown by these comparisons, and unfortunately, the value of the article is somewhat vitiated by the extraordinary elasticity of his concept of "youth." Rather than reworking the data from German statistical offices, Tenfelde simply reproduced them, a procedure that at times left him with broad-gauge ranges that extended from fifteen years of age to thirty. Although he wished to relate this increasing youthfulness to such phenomena as juvenile delinquency, specific forms of youth protest, and the formation of a working-class youth movement, because of its methodological weaknesses, in the final analysis the article is more suggestive than convincing, perhaps as the author intended. Furthermore, it is doubtful that such a purely demographic approach can provide an adequate understanding of the structural preconditions of an urban youth problem unless supplemented by an account of the changing position of young workers in the labor force.

Closest in theme to the present work is a survey article by Jürgen Reulecke on middle-class social reformers and young workers in Imperial Germany, which also appeared in 1982.[33] There, Reulecke argued that the concern of middle-class social reformers with young workers was an indication of their especially sensitive reaction to the massive changes German society underwent at the turn of the century. His article was at its strongest in presenting the activities of social reformers in the 1870s and 1880s, for example, attempts to protect the health and foster the family sense of young workers, before a generalized working-class youth problem emerged. For the period after 1890, when reformers began to regard young workers as a menace to the social order, Reulecke discusses changes in middle-class perceptions of young workers, albeit as though changing perceptions followed a linear pattern from negative perceptions to more positive ones, and provides an overview of several of the religiously affiliated youth associations that reformers launched to tame ostensible youthful wildness. Although correctly underlining the importance of the adult-sponsored youth association, however, he barely mentions the other key institution of the youth salvation campaign, the industrial continuation school. Moreover, he fails to discuss some of the new reform efforts after 1900, such as those designed to suppress penny dreadfuls. Despite his promise to handle the meaning of the concrete social reform measures for the daily lives of young workers, the article remains largely at the level of the public pronouncements of youth savers. Finally, because of the unsatisfactory state of previous research, Reulecke is perforce somewhat inconclusive about the ultimate effects of the middle-class youth salvation campaign. While leaving open alternative possibilities, he provisionally concludes that the reformers' efforts to mediate between the classes were ineffectual and that they were overrun by developments like the militarization of youth work in the prewar era, conclusions that certainly stand in need of revision and modification.

Plans and proposals for this militarization of youth work before the Prussian Youth Cultivation Edict of 1911 and their subsequent implementation have already been treated in a thoroughly documented article by Klaus Saul on "The Struggle for Youth between Primary School and Barracks," which appeared in 1971, accompanied by a large selection of representative archival documents pertaining to military youth work.[34] Within the rather restricted horizon of his research program, Saul's article is unquestionably definitive, but his monocular focus on the military side of youth cultivation means that he completely excludes its civil side. Consequently, he misinterprets the significance of the continuation schools and underestimates the very real influence of Georg Kerschensteiner's subtle strategy for combatting the Socialists among young workers. Since youth cultivation for young males did become one-sidedly militaristic during the war, Saul's later article, which takes up the premilitary training of youth between 1914 and 1918, "Youth in the Shadow of War" is potentially less misleading.[35]

In addition to these articles, several books published in the Federal Republic of Germany take up specific aspects of the youth salvation campaign. Two works in the history of education have investigated the industrial continuation schools *(gewerbliche Fortbildungsschulen)*, which, as already suggested, after 1900 became the paramount public socializing institutions for young male workers "between primary school and barracks." The more recent of these, Klaus Harney's book, examines the relegation of vocational schools to inferior status within the increasingly differentiated and hierarchical educational system in nineteenth-century Prussia and considers the problems of educational legitimation this inferiority brought in its wake.[36] Despite his narrow perspective and his compulsive tendency to state the obvious in jargon-laden prose, Harney adds some interesting observations about the debates over making these schools obligatory for young male artisans and workers, the symbolic function of the pedagogical program advanced by Kerschensteiner, and the failure of the continuation school law introduced in the Prussian Diet in 1911. Slightly older but considerably more rewarding is the work by Wolf-Dietrich Greinert, "Schools as Instruments of Social Control and Objects of Private Interests," subtitled "The Contribution of Vocational Schools to the Political Education of the Lower Classes."[37] Especially valuable is his close analysis of the image of society and social relations sketched in continuation school textbooks. Like much of the work written in the 1970s under the influence of the Fischer School, which accented continuities between the Empire and Third Reich, Harney tends to magnify the reactionary tendencies within the Empire. Consequently, he ascribes a decisive role to the artisanate and conservative forces in molding these institutions and overlooks much of the reformist impulse embodied in their curriculum. Despite my reservations about some of his specific interpretations, however, Greinert's book offers a serious and well-researched effort to evaluate the civic education purveyed in these once vitally important, but now virtually forgotten, mass vocational schools. Surprisingly, however, both books tend to play down the actual vocational instruction in these schools and to neglect their extensive extracurricular programs.

Although better known for his research on youth in the Weimar Republic and nonconformity and resistance of youth in the Third

Reich, Detlev Peukert has also made an important contribution to understanding the constitution of a specific lower-class youth problem in Wilhelmine Germany. Drawing on the works of Michel Foucault, Norbert Elias, and Jürgen Habermas, his book on the "limits of social discipline" uses "the rise and crisis of German youth welfare from 1878 to 1932" to illuminate some of the "pathologies of modernity."[38] Although a brief section dealt with Prussian youth cultivation after 1911, Peukert was chiefly engaged in comprehending the process by which delinquent and wayward youth became the objects of pedagogical and legal discourses that labeled them as deviants to be normalized, reeducated, and rehabilitated, rather than punished. He was interested in outlining the limits of this discourse, which became apparent in the late Weimar Republic. The book's forte is its handling of the development of these professional discourses rather than in an investigation of the "microtechnics" of power instantiated in reformatories or welfare institutions.

The present book certainly builds on this research, but in many respects it also diverges from and goes beyond it. First, rather than confining myself to one aspect of the youth cultivation campaign (for example, the continuation schools, adult-sponsored youth groups, reform programs, or delinquency), I have attempted to assemble and arrange the various panels into a more comprehensive portrait. I hope that the resulting design is more complex and colorful, if also more ambiguous and contradictory, but such judgments will have to be left to the reader. Second, in contrast to the other works mentioned, I have also brought in young working women.[39] The inclusion of young working women as part of the generalized problem of post-school-age youth was both belated and distinctive. Although the Prussian government recognized young female workers as an official problem in 1913, the extension of youth cultivation to these youths was not fully completed until the Weimar Republic. Nonetheless, the way in which young women were finally converted into an officially recognized social problem, recapitulating in a highly compressed sequence the natural historical stages of awareness, policy determination, and reform, is both an interesting and important episode in its own right and casts considerable light on the overall nature of the youth salvation campaign. Third, previous research has been far too little concerned with the actual implementation of the youth savers' programs, the manner in which programmatic statements or ministerial decrees were translated into institutional practices that affected the everyday life of young workers. To overcome this deficiency, I have carried out substantial research at the local and regional levels, largely in Düsseldorf and the old Prussian governmental district of Düsseldorf.

The advantages of examining the implementation of youth-saving measures in this region, which covered the Lower Rhine and Ruhr and presented a microcosm of the Empire, were numerous. Apart from making research manageable, the geographical narrowing enabled me to examine a wider variety of programs and institutions in situ, to trace the affiliations among them and follow their development over time. The diversity of the Düssseldorf district meant that every tendency in the battle for youth was present. The district was highly urbanized, with a chain of large and dynamic cities boasting a broad array of industries and handicrafts that employed thousands of young workers – the machine and metallurgical industries of Düsseldorf, the Krupp steel mills and coal mines of Essen, the textile plants of Mönchen-Gladbach or Elberfeld and Barmen, the cutlery and metal-wares trades of Solingen. Second, most of the major fissures and conflicts that divided Imperial Germany and that determined the alignments in the battle for youth – whether economic, political, social, ideological, or religious – found expression in this heterogeneous district. It contained a large Catholic population and several centers of Catholic social thought and action, such as Mönchen-Gladbach, as well as a number of old Protestant strongholds, such as Elberfeld and Barmen. Düsseldorf and several other of the major cities were confessionally mixed. Within the Düsseldorf region, the Social Democratic party, Catholic Center party, and National Liberals all contested for votes and influence, although as a result of Prussia's three-class electoral system, the National Liberals maintained a stranglehold on urban governments, frustrating their Socialist and Catholic adversaries. Antagonisms between workers and management, as well as more muted conflicts of interest between artisans and industry, were endemic to the region and often flared into the open. Third, a number of central and influential figures in the youth salvation campaign resided in the district and through their initiatives were able to transform cities like Düsseldorf or Essen into laboratories for experiments in youth cultivation. Consequently, I frequently move back and forth among the national, regional, and local levels in a way that I hope will not be overly confusing. However, on occasion I have not hesitated to enlist sources from states other than Prussia and cities other than those in the Düsseldorf district, for example, Munich and Hamburg, in order to illustrate particular points, especially in those rare instances when

Prussia, Germany's largest and most powerful state, was not in the forefront of the youth salvation campaign. These forays outside the Düsseldorf district and Prussia also serve as checks on the general reliability of my conclusions.

The structure of the book is as follows. Chapter 2, which is heavily statistical, recasts Tenfelde's problematic and demonstrates the structural foundations and objective preconditions for the youth salvation campaign. It analyzes the position of young workers in Germany's urban population, these workers' rapidly changing roles in the labor force, and their legal status. With Chapter 3 the youth savers and youth salvation campaign come into focus as the natural history stages of awareness and policy determination are examined. This chapter explores the image of young laborers sketched by the youth savers, the concrete social ills they addressed, and the remedies they proposed. The next two chapters switch to the institutional nexus in which the youth savers' reform programs were realized: the part-time industrial continuation schools and religious youth associations. For several reasons, including the fact that the industrial continuation schools were closely associated with the Munich school superintendant and educational theorist Georg Kerschensteiner and the Munich continuation schools became prototypes for similar institutions throughout Germany, in Chapter 4 I compare the schools in Düsseldorf with those in the Bavarian capital. Chapter 5 contrasts the youth work of the Protestant and Catholic churches and discusses the difficulties that both churches encountered in trying to win young workers. Antisocialism was always one of the ideological underpinnings, not only of religious youth activity but also of the efforts of the entire middle-class youth salvation campaign. This antisocialism acquired considerably greater importance with the formation of a Socialist youth movement in 1904. The genesis of this movement and its relations with the Imperial authorities and the youth salvation campaign are the subjects of Chapter 6. The growth of the Socialist youth movement prompted the Prussian government to become increasingly involved in coordinating, centralizing, and militarizing the youth salvation campaign, thereby ushering in a new, more intense, and more politicized phase. This phase was announced in 1911 with the Youth Cultivation Edict of the Prussian Minister of Education and Religious Affairs. The characteristics of this new phase and their consequences are the topics explored in Chapter 7. It was only after this edict that women social reformers were finally able to ensure that young female workers were recognized as an official social problem and accorded roughly equal treatment within the official youth cultivation campaign. The inclusion of young females in the salvation campaign is the theme of Chapter 8. The war completed the militarization of the youth salvation campaign for males and had a profound impact on the situation of young workers of both sexes. After the initial phase of domestic peace, the battle for youth assumed even sharper contours as German society polarized. Young workers and youth cultivation in war are the subjects of Chapter 9. In Chapter 10 conclusions are drawn about the significance of the battle for young workers in Imperial Germany, and some questions are raised about lines of continuity between the youth policy of the Empire and the policies of the Weimar Republic and Nazi Germany.

In general, I have proceeded topically and chronologically within topics. At times, however, topical treatment has necessitated flashbacks or short preliminary discussions of issues that subsequently receive more elaborate and comprehensive development. Again, I have tried not to disorient the reader overmuch with such temporal leapfrogging, but some cutting back and forth has proven unavoidable. I can only ask for the reader's patience and forbearance.

2

Young laborers in the population, labor force, and industrial law: structural preconditions of the youth salvation campaign

The emergence of the youth salvation campaign at the turn of the century was certainly conditioned by middle-class perceptions of young workers' heightened visibility in Germany's flourishing urban centers and of their ever-greater indispensability as a major component of the Empire's economically vital industrial labor force. Young workers became both symbols and symptoms of the rapid social and economic modernization that Germany was undergoing: the massive migration from rural settlements and small towns to large cities, the shift from employment on farms and in handicraft workshops to wage labor in factories and offices, the transformation of Germany from an agrarian to an industrial state.[1] Thus an analysis of youth as a sector of the population and as part of the work force during the late nineteenth and early twentieth centuries forms a necessary prerequisite for comprehending the anxieties, aspirations, and demands of the youth savers. In this context, it is also worthwhile to examine the legal provisions applying to youth in the Industrial Code. There are several reasons for doing so. First, since factory and apprenticeship regulations determined matters like the length of the workday and safety precautions, they concretely affected the physical and material well-being of young workers. Recognizing this, youth savers could propose amendments to the laws that would, for example, improve the health of young workers, thus safeguarding their fitness for military service or motherhood, as the case might be. Second, the laws embodied widely shared middle-class assumptions about the degree of autonomy youth should have from their families, the role of adults as moral overseers and preceptors, and the nature and importance of learning to labor. These moral beliefs constituted a shared horizon

for most youth savers that established the limits of their vision. Thus
the Industrial Code confronted young workers as an objective phenomenon directly impinging on their work experience, while youth
savers would regard labor law as an instrument for the realization of
their national priorities and the exercise of their moral authority.

Between 1871 and 1911, as the population of Germany spiraled
from 41,059,000 to 64,992,000, a 58 percent increase, the youth population, defined as young people between the ages of fifteen and
twenty, more than held pace, growing from 3,746,000 to 6,285,000,
almost 68 percent.[2] During these forty years, youth as a percentage
of the total population climbed from 9.1 to 9.7 percent. If fourteen-
and twenty-year-olds were also counted, as they frequently were by
various state and municipal statistical bureaus and in civil law, then
by 1910 almost 12 percent of the population of the Reich belonged
to this age group. But given that youth salvation would be a municipal
project and most youth reform would have an urban focus, it is most
important to survey youth as a sector of the urban population, especially in Germany's rapidly expanding large cities, that is, those with
populations over one hundred thousand.

Census statistics of Germany's major cities show that in most me-
tropolises youth composed almost the same proportion of inhabitants
as they did of the Empire's total population (see Table 2.1). In Altona,
outside Hamburg, in 1911, 11.7 percent of the population ranged
between fifteen and twenty-one, while in the Wuppertal textile center
Elberfeld slightly over 12 percent of the population was made up of
post-school-age youths. Youths were slightly underrepresented in the
burgeoning coal-mining towns of the Ruhr, however, because of the
demographic bulge created by the influx of twenty- to thirty-year-old
male newcomers. Hence in the Ruhr mining and metallurgical city of
Bochum, 11.5 percent of the population was between fifteen and
twenty-one, 10.9 percent in Gelsenkirchen, and 10.6 percent in Hamborn. This underscores the importance of migration. It was in the
age range between fifteen and twenty that young workers began migrating on their own and that consequently sex ratios in German cities
began diverging significantly, since certain industries preferentially
hired either males or females. The sex ratio discrepancies also suggest
that the intercity migration rates of young workers were high. Thus
11,594 young women in the fifteen-to-twenty-one age group were
living in Elberfeld, where textile firms were the major employers,
whereas only 8,987 young males resided there.[3] In Gelsenkirchen, by
contrast, where coal was king, young males outnumbered young fe-

Table 2.1. *The youth population of selected German cities, 1910*

City	Youths >15–<21 yr[a]	Urban population	Percent youths
Altona			
M	9,802	84,487	
F	10,444	88,141	
M + F	20,246	172,628	11.73
Berlin			
M	109,707	994,206	
F	121,715	1,077,051	
M + F	231,422	2,071,257	11.17
Bochum			
M	8,243	70,894	
F	7,592	66,037	
M + F	15,735	136,931	11.49
Düsseldorf			
M	20,388	179,703	
F	21,240	179,025	
M + F	41,628	358,728	11.60
Elberfeld			
M	8,987	80,153	
F	11,594	90,042	
M + F	20,581	170,195	12.09
Essen			
M	16,575	152,102	
F	15,825	142,551	
M + F	32,400	294,653	11.00
Frankfurt am Main			
M	21,684	201,144	
F	25,419	213,432	
M + F	47,103	414,576	11.86
Gelsenkirchen			
M	10,043	88,374	
F	8,412	81,139	
M + F	18,455	169,513	10.89
Hamborn			
M	7,216	58,452	
F	3,604	43,251	
M + F	10,820	101,703	10.64
Hamburg[a]			
M	41,393	461,221	
F	45,421	469,814	
M + F	86,814	931,035	9.32[a]
Leipzig[a]			
M	29,230	287,412	
F	31,544	302,438	
M + F	60,774	589,850	10.30[a]

Table 2.1. (*cont.*)

City	Youths >15–<21 yr	Urban population	Percent youths
Munich[a]			
M	24,897	284,007	
F	28,680	312,460	
M + F	53,577	596,467	8.98[a]
Stuttgart[a]			
M	14,432	139,399	
F	15,403	146,819	
M + F	29,835	286,218	10.42[a]

[a]"Youth" was defined as >15 years to <20 years in non-Prussian cities.
Source: Compiled from *Statistisches Jahrbuch deutscher Städte* (Breslau, 1914), pp. 78–82.

males by 10,043 to 8,412. Although confirmatory statistical material on the age of urban in- and out-migrants is relatively sparse, municipal records attest to the fact that young workers of both sexes were extremely mobile. In Berlin between 1907 and 1909, 26,816 of the 154,672 newcomers to the capital, or more than 17 percent, had been born between 1888 and 1892, and 15,981 of the 126,244 males leaving the city, or 12.7 percent, were born between these years.[4] Although far fewer females were mobile in all other age ranges than males, during their late teen-age years young women in the capital, if not elsewhere, were apparently slightly more likely to migrate. Thus 27,869 of the 119,016, or 23 percent, of the young females recorded as arriving were born between 1888 and 1892, and 18,623 of the 100,462 females, or 18.5 percent, of those departing from this metropolis. Only young adults in their twenties were more geographically mobile than post-school-age youth. Hence we can conclude that labor demand played an important role in shaping the migration patterns of young workers, the total number of youth living in a city, and the urban sex ratios of this age group.

Demand for youthful labor was clearly mounting during the last decade of the nineteenth century and the first decade of the twentieth, as evidenced by the rising number of firms employing young laborers, the increasing rates of labor force participation, and the growing percentage of youth employed in various branches of industry. From 1892 to 1908 the number of factories, that is, workshops employing more than five laborers, with young workers on payroll skyrocketed from 35,284 to 91,888, a 260 percent increase.[5] By the latter year over one-third of all German factories employed young workers. During the twelve years separating the censuses of 1895 and 1907 the percentage of all males between the ages of fourteen and eighteen who were gainfully employed edged forward from 79.0 to 82.6 percent, and the increase was from 91.4 to 93.0 percent for males between eighteen and twenty (see Table 2.2). Moreover, by 1907 the degree of participation varied only slightly among the federal states. This uniformly high rate of participation meant that virtually every male in this age group who was not a student or institutionalized found employment, indicating that demand for youthful male labor probably outstripped supply. Labor force participation rates for young females, by contrast, remained consistently lower but were advancing far more rapidly. The rate rose from just over 40 percent of all young females between the ages of fourteen and eighteen in 1895 to just over 50 percent in 1907, a substantial gain of almost 25 percent, although if domestic servants were included, participation rates at both dates would be approximately 12 percent higher.[6] For young women between the ages of eighteen and twenty the participation rate shot up from 48.4 percent in 1895 to 56.6 percent in 1907. Although the trend toward greater participation rates held across Germany, the variation was considerably greater from state to state than for males as a group. The south German states, with their high concentrations of textile manufacture and their more important agrarian sectors, invariably registered a higher percentage of young women working than did Prussia. It should be added, however, that in most of Germany's major cities labor force participation rates of both male and female youth lay slightly below the national average, since urban centers contained larger populations of students, internees in medical and penal institutions, or youths who were simply nonemployed.[7]

In terms of the absolute numbers of youth working, the expansion between 1895 and 1907 was also substantial. Whereas in 1895 there were 2,592,430 economically active males, in 1907 the figure had risen to 3,047,722, a net gain of over four hundred thousand (Table 2.2). The corresponding figures for young women moved from 1,367,717 at the former date to 1,890,422 at the latter, an even more impressive gain of over five hundred thousand jobs. This overall expansion was accompanied by a major displacement in youth employment among the three major sectors of the economy: agriculture, industry, and commerce (see Table 2.3). As can be ascertained from the table, not only the relative number but the absolute number of young males

Table 2.2. *Economically active youths in the German Empire and the larger states, 1895 and 1907*[a]

	Number and percent of economically active youths in entire resident population			
	14–18 years		18–20 years	
Area	1895	1907	1895	1907
German Empire				
M	1,651,441	1,966,701	940,989	1,081,021
	(79.0)	(82.6)	(91.4)	(93.0)
F	857,443	1,226,384	510,274	664,038
	(40.5)	(50.2)	(48.4)	(56.5)
M + F	2,508,884	3,193,085	1,451,263	1,745,059
	(60.0)	(66.2)	(69.6)	(74.7)
Prussia				
M	975,085	1,206,113	563,751	683,119
	(76.2)	(81.3)	(90.2)	(93.0)
F	442,213	702,310	272,212	382,775
	(34.7)	(46.0)	(43.1)	(52.2)
M + F	1,417,298	1,908,423	835,963	1,065,894
	(55.5)	(63.4)	(66.4)	(72.6)
Bavaria				
M	199,567	211,025	107,117	101,524
	(83.6)	(85.0)	(92.3)	(92.3)
F	137,296	161,196	76,271	83,852
	(56.3)	(64.8)	(64.0)	(70.6)
M + F	336,863	372,221	183,388	185,376
	(69.8)	(74.9)	(78.8)	(81.3)
Saxony				
M	130,472	158,718	71,625	80,601
	(88.4)	(87.3)	(93.7)	(93.5)
F	88,152	110,925	53,075	64,528
	(58.2)	(58.4)	(67.0)	(67.6)
M + F	218,624	269,643	124,700	145,129
	(73.1)	(72.5)	(80.5)	(79.9)
Würrtemberg				
M	78,505	77,200	37,811	37,105
	(89.8)	(88.6)	(94.5)	(93.9)
F	40,513	55,045	21,921	24,981
	(44.5)	(63.1)	(51.2)	(64.9)
M + F	119,018	132,245	59,732	62,086
	(66.7)	(75.8)	(72.2)	(79.7)

Table 2.2. (*cont.*)

| | Number and percent of economically active youths in entire resident population | | | |
| | 14–18 years | | 18–20 years | |
Area	1895	1907	1895	1907
Baden				
M	64,090	65,167	34,197	35,476
	(86.7)	(84.2)	(92.9)	(91.2)
F	44,233	48,365	23,049	24,428
	(57.8)	(63.4)	(60.9)	(66.3)
M + F	108,323	113,532	57,246	59,904
	(72.1)	(73.8)	(76.7)	(79.0)

Percentages given in parentheses.
^aExcludes household servants.

Percentages given in parentheses.
[a]Excludes household servants.
Source: "Pflege der schulentlassenen weiblichen Jugend," *Schriften der Zentrallstelle für Volkswohlfahrt*, Heft 9 (Berlin, 1913), pp. 6–7.

employed in the agricultural sector declined between 1895 and 1907, a labor statistical vindication of conservative laments about flight from the land. Moreover, the decline became steepest after the eighteenth year, when young males were most inclined to migrate. At the same time, young rural females were clearly less likely to leave the countryside, and as a result the farm labor force was steadily feminizing. By 1907 the absolute number of females under twenty actually surpassed the number of young males laboring on the land, making the agricultural sector the only one in which young women predominated. Sectoral analysis also demonstrates the much more rapidly rising demand across the board for young female employees. Despite the relatively small contribution of the service sector to total jobs, growth of youthful female employment was somewhat more pronounced there than in industry. The service sector included hotels and restaurants as well as commercial firms that hired young female shop assistants and sales clerks. Demand for young males was ascending most rapidly in mining, industry, and construction, where employment of males between the ages of fourteen and twenty rose 21 percent between 1895 and 1907, although even in the industrial sector the employment of young women advanced more rapidly. By contrast, agricultur-

Table 2.3. Youths employed in major sectors of the German economy, 1895 and 1907[a]

	14–16 years			16–18 years			18–20 years			Σ 14–20 years		
	1895	1907	% Δ	1895	1907	% Δ	1895	1907	% Δ	1895	1907	% Δ
A. Agriculture, gardening, and livestock												
M	319,504	333,218	+ 4.3	324,823	316,829	− 2.5	307,039	283,310	− 7.7	951,366	933,357	− 1.9
F	232,733	332,759	+43.0	268,757	343,637	+28.0	260,055	313,318	+20.0	761,545	989,714	+30.0
M + F	552,237	665,977	+21.0	593,580	660,466	+11.0	567,094	596,628	+ 5.2	1,712,911	1,923,071	+12.0
B. Industry, mining, and construction												
M	369,191	469,594	+22.0	478,896	575,264	+20.0	495,644	580,137	+17.0	1,343,731	1,625,995	+21.0
F	97,364	147,901	+52.0	155,748	207,798	+33.0	173,473	199,758	+15.0	426,585	555,457	+30.0
M + F	466,555	617,495	+32.0	634,644	783,062	+23.0	669,117	779,895	+16.5	1,770,316	2,180,452	+23.0
C. Commerce and transport												
M	54,781	65,809	+20.0	78,939	86,228	+ 9.0	87,368	89,273	+ 2.2	221,088	241,310	+ 9.0
F	23,785	38,632	+62.0	45,381	61,076	+35.0	54,148	67,122	+24.0	123,314	166,830	+35.0
M + F	78,566	104,441	+33.0	124,320	147,304	+18.0	141,516	156,395	+10.5	344,402	408,140	+18.5
Σ A–C												
M	743,476	868,621	+16.8	882,658	978,321	+10.8	890,051	952,720	+ 7.0	2,516,185	2,799,662	+11.3
F	353,882	519,292	+46.7	469,886	612,511	+30.3	487,676	580,198	+19.0	1,311,444	1,712,001	+30.5
M + F	1,097,358	1,387,933	+26.4	1,352,544	1,590,832	+17.6	1,377,727	1,532,918	+11.2	3,827,629	4,511,663	+17.9

[a]This table excludes not only domestic servants, but also the self-employed, technical office personnel, and unclassified wage laborers.
Sources: Detlev J. Peukert, Grenzen der Sozialdisziplinierung (Cologne, 1986), p. 321, Table 2; Waldemar Zimmermann, "Die Erwerbsarbeit der Kinder und Jugendlichen," Handbuch für Jugendpflege (Langensalza, 1913), p. 204.

Table 2.4. *Male factory workers in Germany, ages 14–16, 1894–1912[a]*

Branch	1894 No.	1900 No.	1900 %Δ	1906 No.	1906 %Δ	1912 No.	1912 %Δ
Mining	18,623	28,435	+ 31.2	33,258	+ 16.9	42,976	+29.2
Quarry	20,068	29,235	+ 45.6	30,397	+ 3.9	29,130	− 4.2
Metal	20,806	35,768	+ 67.1	42,789	+ 23.7	59,858	+39.9
Machine	19,294	41,155	+113.3	51,220	+ 24.5	76,487	+49.3
Chemical	2,124	1,568	− 26.2	3,765	+140.0	4,403	+16.9
Heating and lighting	339	778	+ 95.0	1,151	+ 47.9	1,434	+24.6
Textiles	21,503	24,961	+ 16.1	29,190	+ 16.9	33,801	+15.8
Paper and leather	5,910	8,194	+ 38.6	10,335	+ 26.1	13,433	+30.0
Wood	8,364	13,516	+ 61.6	19,953	+ 47.6	28,387	+42.3
Food	10,865	25,124	+131.0	18,729	+ 25.4	29,539	+57.7
Clothing and cleaning	2,950	4,779	+ 62.0	6,957	+ 45.6	10,158	+46.0
Printing	7,071	10,824	+ 53.1	12,496	+ 15.4	14,575	+16.6
Construction	n/a	6,661	—	7,484	+ 12.4	13,450	+79.7
Other	1,414	241	—	605		641	—
Total	139,391	231,807	+ 66.3	268,329	+ 15.8	358,327	+33.5

[a] Includes firms with ten or more workers.
Sources: Compiled from *Vierteljahrhefte zur Statistik des deutschen Reiches:* 1895, IV.45; 1900, IV.276; 1907, IV.248; 1913, IV.41.

al employment of young males was plunging. The tertiary sector also opened an above-average number of positions for fourteen- to sixteen-year-old males, probably a sign of the swelling army of messenger and delivery boys in major cities and within large firms. But revealing though they are, such highly aggregated statistics also conceal much about the real nature of youth employment. In order to secure a better grip on that, it will be necessary to examine the structure of youth employment in various branches of industry, in specific crafts, and by level of skill for both males and females.

The expansion of industrial labor for youth meant that new entrants to the work force were having to prepare for new types of jobs in a swiftly shifting labor market. This can be seen from Table 2.4, which records shifts in the factory employment of fourteen- to sixteen-year-old males in various branches of industry at six-year intervals between 1894 and 1912. Since this table was compiled from statistics collected by factory inspectors, who only reported on firms with ten or more workers, in part it indexes the larger scale and concentration of German industry after the 1890s. But although these statistics omit small artisanal shops, nonetheless, this table clearly points to some of the major trends and directions in the employment of youth after the mid-1890s. The first thing to be noted is the enormous increase in the total factory employment of post-school-age males, the 66 percent increase in total employment between 1894, a recession year, and 1900, as the stop-and-go tendencies of economic growth characteristic of the preceding two decades finally yielded to the sustained boom of the late 1890s.[8] This rapid increase in total employment also went hand in hand with a realignment among branches. Whereas in 1894 textile factories employed the largest number of post-school-age males, followed closely by the metal-processing firms, quarries, machine manufacturers, and mines, by 1900 the machine industry had surged into first place as the most significant employer of post-school-age males, with metal processing, quarry work, and mining lagging behind. Textiles no longer even placed among the first five, having been overtaken and supplanted by the food-processing industry. (The wildly erratic fluctuations in the numbers of youth supposedly working in the food-processing industry arouse suspicions, however. They may in part reflect seasonal patterns within this branch, as may the absence of youth listed in the construction trades in the statistical data for 1894.) By 1912 the machine industry had secured its lead as the branch recruiting the most young males, employing over 20 percent of young males engaged in factories, while the metal-processing industry remained in second place. Between them, these two branches accounted for almost 40 percent of employment of fourteen- to sixteen-year-old male factory workers. Next among major employers came mining, with textiles, food processing, quarry work, and the woodworking industry each offering positions to almost thirty thousand young males. The last of these, the woodworking industry, had gone from being a rather modest employer of young laborers in 1894 to being a quite substantial one by 1912. Thus a male completing primary school and entering the labor force in 1912 was far more likely to work in an enterprise involved with some aspect of metal processing or machine manufacture than had been his counterpart eighteen years earlier. By contrast, fewer jobs had opened in branches, such as textiles and quarrying, that had previously ranked among the foremost employers of male youth. Thus, the types of occupations available for youth changed quite substantially after the mid-1890s.

Not only were the types of occupation changing, but so was the skill composition of the youth labor force. This can be demonstrated at the local level. Table 2.5A illustrates the post-1900 development of

Table 2.5A. *Changes in the skill composition of the male youth labor force in Düsseldorf, 1903–13[a]*

	1903		1908		1913	
Training type	No.	% Σ	No.	% Σ	No.	% Σ
A. Factory apprentices	524	23	1,128	30	1,994	29
B. Craftshop apprentices	888	39	1,316	35	1,672	24
C. Total skilled (A + B)	1,412	62	2,444	65	3,666	54
D. Total unskilled	864	38	1,318	35	3,173	46
Total Σ (C + D)	2,276		3,762		6,839	

Table 2.5B. *Factory apprentices in machine building in Düsseldorf, 1903–13[a]*

Year	No.	% Δ
1903	524	
1908	901	+172
1913	1,278	+142

[a]The figures for 1903 and 1908 include fourteen- to sixteen-year-old males. Those for 1913 include seventeen-year-old males as well.
Source: Compiled from *Verwaltungsbericht der Stadt Düsseldorf 1914–18*, pp. 126–7.

skill composition for young males in Düsseldorf, a key center for the metal-processing and machine industries on the lower Rhine. The trajectory of development in Düsseldorf paralleled the national trend. During the first decade of the twentieth century the percentage of unskilled laborers in the total youth labor force rose markedly. The rate of growth of unskilled jobs, 367 percent between 1903 and 1913, far exceeded the overall growth rate in employment of fourteen- to seventeen-year-olds in industry (300 percent). In part, however, the city's exponential increase in young unskilled laborers between 1908 and 1913 was an artifact of the incorporation of a number of industrial suburbs with steel mills, which recruited an army of untrained manual laborers. A more detailed report on youth occupations from 1909 provides a far more differentiated portrait of the variety of jobs performed by unskilled youth.[9] Of the 1,477 unskilled males between the ages of fourteen and sixteen in Düsseldorf in 1909, 310 (21 percent) worked as messenger or delivery boys; 269 (18.2 percent) held jobs as helpers in iron or steel mills, moving raw materials and finished goods, packing crates, or tending machines; 388 (26.3 percent) labored as helpers in woodworking, textile, enamelware, or other sorts of factories; and the remainder carried out a host of diverse tasks or else were unemployed. (Even among youth the unskilled were much more vulnerable to seasonal or conjunctural bouts of unemployment than the skilled.[10]) Although the relative importance of craft apprenticeship also receded markedly in Düsseldorf during this decade, the number of factory apprenticeships advanced quite appreciably, especially in the machine industry (Table 2.5B), again, a trend in keeping with the nationwide pattern. But although youthful school leavers who filled out job preference forms in major German cities would continue to choose handicrafts over unskilled labor, often by a margin approaching three to one, it is clear from such data on shifts in skill composition that chances of ending up a craft apprentice were diminishing and steadily growing numbers were destined to join and remain in the ranks of the unskilled.[11] A variety of factors could slate a school leaver for an unskilled position: failure to complete the upper form of primary school, physical handicaps, mental defects, family poverty (since unskilled jobs initially paid higher wages than apprenticeships), lack of suitable openings, the termination of an incompatible apprenticeship, or a combination of several of these factors.[12] Eliminating the factors that slotted youths into such positions would be a project dear to youth savers.

Despite the declining importance of craft apprenticeship, in general, as we shall see, youth savers would adopt its time-honored traditions as the normative standard for the young worker. Thus, as soon as a young male finished primary school, his father was expected to conclude a multiyear contractual arrangement with a master artisan who presided over his own small shop. During the period specified in the contract, which usually lasted three to four years, the artisan would instruct the youth thoroughly in the skills required to ply his trade. In return for this training, the youth agreed to live under the master's roof as part of his family and to submit willingly to his master's paternal authority and commands while receiving at most a little pocket money as compensation for his labor. Although such arrangements certainly remained prevalent, especially in many small towns and traditional crafts, by the turn of the century they were no longer the norm. As the ranks of unskilled labor continued to swell, craft apprenticeship was becoming less crucial as a form of industrial training. Moreover, the institution of apprenticeship was far from being static. Instead, it was altering quite significantly, becoming both less

Table 2.6. *Male apprentices employed in major sectors of the German economy, 1895 and 1907*

Shop size	1895	1907	% Δ
A. Agriculture, gardening, livestock, and forestry			
1–5	5,580	6,285	+ 14.7
6+	3,818	4,295	+ 12.5
Total	9,398	10,580	+ 12.6
B. Industry, mining, and construction			
1–5	331,196	287,435	− 13.2
6+	234,539	331,251	+ 41.2
Total	565,735	618,686	+ 9.4
C. Commerce and transport			
1–5	32,278	31,974	− 1.0
6+	27,214	35,624	+ 30.9
Total	59,492	67,598	+ 13.6
All sectors			
1–5	368,954	325,694	− 11.7
6+	265,571	371,170	+ 39.8
Total	634,525	696,863	+ 9.8

Sources: Compiled from "Uebersicht 12: Die verheirateten Arbeiterinnen und die Lehrlinge in den Jahren 1907 und 1895," *Statistik des deutschen Reiches*, Band 220/221, *Berufs- und Betriebszählung vom 12 Juni 1907* (Berlin, 1914), pp. 156–7.

personal and more formal as it switched to large shop or factory settings.

The course of some of these shifts can be followed by examining the data on apprenticeships of males presented in Table 2.6. The absolute decline in the number of youth serving their apprenticeships in small industrial shops, that is, shops with fewer than five workers, and the rapid increase in apprentices engaged by medium and large shops, that is, those with between five and twenty or with more than twenty workers, stand out in bold relief. Thus, after the turn of the century, the old-style master artisan who owned and managed his workshop, assisted by a journeyman, and supervised one or two apprentices had ceased to be the major trainer of skilled labor. The relative decline of the patriarchal small-shop apprenticeship arrangement is also indicated by the fading importance of room and board as part of the apprenticeship arrangement.[13] Whereas over 80 percent of apprentices in shops with one to five employees still lived with their masters in 1895, the percentage sank to 48.5 percent in shops with between six and twenty employees, and in firms with more than twenty-one employees it dwindled to a mere 5.3 percent. Whereas approximately 90 percent of youths apprenticed to traditional craftsmen, such as bakers, butchers, smiths, or cobblers, still received room and board, this was true of under 30 percent of youths apprenticed to tool and instrument makers, book printers, machine builders, and craftsmen in the building trades. In the case of machine builders fewer than seven of every hundred apprentices dwelled with their masters' families. Thus in large firms – and for that matter in large cities as well – the receipt of room and board, a standard feature of traditional apprenticeship, was falling into desuetude. Another aspect of the diminishing significance of apprenticeship emerges when Tables 2.3 and 2.6 are compared. If we make the highly plausible assumption that the vast majority of apprentices ranged between the ages of fourteen and eighteen, then although still a majority, apprentices made up a decreasing proportion of the total number of youthful male employees, having dropped from about 66 percent of the total in 1895 to around 59 percent in 1907. Even the figures in Table 2.6, however, overstate the significance of training in the small-shop craft sector, since many young workers were victimized by "apprentice breeding"; that is, they were being exploited by struggling or unscrupulous artisans as cheap hands, without benefiting from systematic training or other compensation in return. Apprentice breeding was apparently much more commonly an urban phenomenon rather than a rural or small-town one, and according to the Prussian factory inspectorate, it was not found in factories.[14]

In a carefully researched report written in 1900, based on industrial census data from 1895, Andreas Voigt, an official in Frankfurt am Main, concluded that, despite legal prohibitions, apprentice breeding was widely practiced in several major trades.[15] In such trades the number of apprentices bore no realistic relation to the forseeable number of potential openings; skilled workers faced relatively high rates of unemployment and as a result were forced to seek other occupations. Among the worst practitioners of apprentice breeding he numbered the owners of bakeries and confectionery shops. Close to 41,000, or 19.4 percent of all employees in such firms, were apprentices; the unemployment rate for bakers approached 4 percent, and many bakers were abandoning their trade for unskilled positions. Worse still were barbershops, where 12,691, or 22.47 percent of employees, were serving apprenticeships, while the unemployment rates for trained barbers exceeded 3 percent. A third trade that exhibited the signs of widespread apprentice breeding, Voigt noted, was book printing. In this trade 14,454 of the 58,878 employees, or 24.55 percent of the total, were apprentices. Although unemployment rates for skilled book printers, which stood at 2.67 percent, certainly averaged below those for bakers and barbers, they nonetheless surpassed the average rate for all trades, 2.27 percent. Voigt also conjectured that many butcher shops were breeding apprentices. Although the percentage of apprentices, at 16.03 percent, was appreciably lower in this trade than the level in bakeries or barbershops, the unemployment rate among accredited butchers, which hovered around 4 percent, stood even higher than in those crafts. This was an ominous portent for the prospects of aspirant butchers.

Although somewhat overly schematic, as Voigt readily admitted, another index of apprentice breeding was the presence of more apprentices in a shop than the number of skilled workers.[16] He surmised that under such circumstances the training of apprentices would be more likely to be somewhat neglected. If, despite its limitations, this index were applied, then 12.6 percent of all masters were open to the charge of contracting more apprentices than they could probably instruct adequately, and 22.1 percent of all apprentices worked for shops committed to training an excess number of apprentices. In some trades, however, the percentage of apprentices employed in shops where trainees outnumbered the skilled far overtopped this average. Thus 61 percent of all mechanic (*Schlosser*) apprentices worked in such shops, 40.2 percent of all book printer apprentices, 35 percent of all barber apprentices, and 34.8 percent of all confectioner apprentices. The high correlation between the trades in which maintaining excess apprentices was commonplace and other evidence of widespread apprentice breeding implies that Voigt's index may well have been broadly reliable. Such quantitative measures, however, suffered from serious drawbacks, as Voigt clearly recognized. It was impossible to infer with certainty that artisans were undertaking apprentice breeding purely on the basis of a high percentage of apprentices among the total employees in a trade, or even by the presence of more apprentices than skilled workers in many shops. In some instances, a large contingent of apprentices might signify that a host of youth were clamoring to enter a dynamic and unusually attractive trade.

This, according to Voigt, was the case with mechanic apprentices (*Schlosser, Maschinenbauer, Elektrotechniker*).[17] Citing statistical evidence that only considered specialized mechanical workshops (*Schlosserei*), critics of the decay of apprenticeship usually condemned these mechanic trades as flagrant practitioners of apprentice breeding since apprentices appeared to make up over 34 percent of total employees. But Voigt pointed out that many mechanics found employment in other types of workshops and that if these other firms were taken into account, the percentage of apprentices fell to just under 17.5 percent. After reordering available data on this trade, Voigt arrived at the result that, if anything, too few apprentices were being trained to cover demand, a conclusion that accords with the enormous expansion of employment for youth in the machine-building and metal-processing branches shown in Table 2.4. Indeed, after the turn of the century one of the standard complaints raised by small handicraft workshops in trades like metalwork or electrical repair was that large-scale factories were getting a free ride. The giants were siphoning off newly trained journeymen, thereby recruiting a highly skilled work force without contributing anything to training costs.[18] Whatever the validity of this accusation, many factories in the machine, electrical, and metal-processing industries were launching or had already instituted their own instructional programs for apprentices.

As suggested by Tables 2.5 and 2.6, after 1900 the number of factory apprentices made a prodigious leap forward. This growth kept pace with the expansion and technological transformation of the metal and machine industries, in which factory apprentices were concentrated. Already by 1903, 5,219 of 7,154 apprentices employed in factories with more than ten workers in the Düsseldorf governmental district labored in these two branches of industry.[19] To be sure, before 1900 most industries did hire their skilled laborers from among craft-trained journeymen. Only in extreme cases of skilled labor shortages would large firms like Krupp instruct their own apprentices, fearing that competitors would lure away their trained workers.[20] Factory apprenticeships were usually feasible in sections of the plant that corresponded to craft analogues – the mechanical, lathe, smith, and repair shops. Such workshops were common in factories, however, since most German metal and machine firms essentially remained amalgamated craft shops. Factory apprenticeship was largely informal. As the apprentice acquired knowledge and dexterity, the master or older workman to whom his training was entrusted gave him more difficult pieces and taught him more complicated techniques.[21] From the outset, the apprentice learned by working on actual parts in the flow of production. Although in large plants one foreman usually coordinated the training of apprentices, few masters were pedagogically prepared, and since they earned little extra pay for instruction time, they had slight incentive to take this task seriously.[22] In most major respects, training in factories differed little from that imparted in small craft shops, and as in such shops it tended to transmit conservatism of techniques.

However, at the turn of the century as the German metal-processing and machine industries began facing stiff competition from technologically sophisticated and efficiently organized U.S. rivals, they embarked upon a systematic rationalization of their firms.[23] A key part of this wave of industrial reorganization, this rationalization before the more famous rationalization movement of the 1920s, was the institutionalization of the separate apprentice workshop with a system of formal instruction.

Although such separate apprentice workshops spread among major firms during the first decade of the twentieth century, often as part of a more comprehensive plan for upgrading and modernizing facilities, they were still confined to a small and innovative minority.[24] Only five of eighteen major machine firms with large contingents of apprentices queried in 1912 had established separate workshops. In Düsseldorf, Germany's third-ranking center of machine production, only three of the sixteen major firms had set up apprentice shops before the war.

Apart from meeting demand for highly skilled workers, several considerations prompted managers to introduce separate training shops. First, some managers believed that the skills of workers trained in small craft shops were woefully inadequate for new and more complex machines.[25] Such workers were unable to adjust rapidly since they lacked sufficient knowledge about machinery, materials, and the reasons for various operations. To overcome these inadequacies, managers promoted training programs that integrated formal knowledge with practical experience. Second, as the rate of technological change quickened, managers desired less specialized workers.[26] A lathe operator who could also set up and operate a variety of milling machines was obviously preferable to one who couldn't, since greater versatility offered managers greater flexibility in deploying labor. Both of these considerations, integrating formal knowledge with practical experience and training more versatile skilled workers, were incorporated in the educational programs of the new workshops. Critics argued that these workshops unnecessarily raised training costs; moreover, since apprentices lost contact with the imperatives of the production process, they would also fail to develop a sense for the necessity of speed and economical procedures.[27] Advocates countered by claiming that only the first year or two would be spent in a separate workshop and that apprentices would then rapidly become accustomed to the shopfloor. Moreover, higher initial expense would be more than offset by the enhanced productivity that resulted from a more secure base of knowledge about machines and materials.[28]

To provide this more secure base of knowledge, the apprentice workshop supervisor, generally a skilled metalworker or engineer with teaching experience in a technical school, ensured that apprentices received a thorough basic training during their first year.[29] He introduced new apprentices to the factory and its facilities, safety precautions, and the importance of clean and orderly methods. Apprentices also learned about the properties of iron and steel and the correct use of hand tools, lessons they were expected to apply to simple practice pieces that they ground, filed, drilled, and so forth. In the second year apprentices began to specialize. A fitter apprentice, for example, would begin filing and assembling machine parts. Instructors emphasized precision and orderliness, rather than speed, however, since they believed that speed would come naturally with proficiency. Despite incipient specialization, apprentices continued to acquire familiarity with other workshops and processes. Thus, the apprentice lathe operator might pass several weeks in the filing shop. In the third year apprentices progressed to more difficult pieces and would usually begin working in the shops to which they would be permanently assigned. By the final year of their apprenticeships they would be working for piece rates at the same tasks as adult skilled workers. At the conclusion of the contractual period each apprentice had to complete a journeyman's piece, displaying competency in the techniques of his trade, a piece that had to be approved by the shop foreman or an engineer, who would then administer an oral examination before certifying the graduate apprentice a journeyman.

Throughout the apprenticeship period, classroom instruction complemented workshop training. Some large machine factories, such as those merging into DEMAG or the Loewe Machine Factory in Berlin, set up their own schools, which met municipal requirements for continuing education.[30] In-plant classes saved time and facilitated closer linkage of practical and theoretical knowledge. Classroom examples could be selected directly from the shopfloor experience. Thus Loewe used diagrams of lathe cuts to teach apprentices to read and draw blueprints. Some plants devoted one day weekly to classroom education. Such theoretical instruction, the more formal character of the training, and the initial separation of the apprentice from the production process distinguished these factory apprenticeships from those in small craft shops.

Since factory apprenticeships unlocked the gates to the best-paying, most interesting, and most secure manual trades, they were much desired. Hence companies could be quite selective. Many favored the sons of their skilled workers, and almost all demanded good primary school grades and a record of excellent health.[31] Apprentices could be fired for a variety of reasons, ranging from insubordination to divulging company secrets, although warnings, fines, or notifying parents of delicts were more commonly invoked sanctions.[32] After 1900 apprentices were generally paid between three and five marks weekly the first year, six to eight the second, and eight to ten the third. In the fourth year, they received ten to twelve marks; this could be supplemented by piece rates. These wages were considerably below those of unskilled youth, whose weekly wages usually started at ten marks per week the first year, probably the major inducement to enter unskilled positions, and rose two marks every year until they reached a plateau of between twenty-four and twenty-eight marks in the twenty-first year. In addition to such minimal wages, however, many firms gave employees successfully concluding their apprenticeships bonuses that varied between thirty and one hundred twenty marks, although one Düsseldorf machine firm awarded a thousand mark stipend to its ablest apprentice to enable him to attend a technical school. Although few apprentices broke their contracts, such bonuses offered an incentive to serve out their final year when they had already mastered most of the techniques of their trades and could probably earn more elsewhere. Factory apprenticeships certainly manifested some continuities with traditional small-shop craft training, but after the turn of the century the new, more formalized factory apprenticeships were beginning to diverge considerably from the craft model.

Hence, it is clear that every aspect of employment for young males was metamorphosing at the turn of the century: the types of occupations, the size of the workshops, the skill composition of the youthful labor force, and the training procedures for apprentices. Much the same was true of the working world of females between the ages of fourteen and twenty, who by 1907 made up almost 30 percent of the entire female labor force. However, household servants and domestic workers were excluded from the Industrial Code and not counted in the occupational census. Despite this official exclusion, no account of the position of post-school-age females in the labor force would be adequate without discussing domestic service, even though its importance was gradually waning at the turn of the century. In 1895, 16.6 percent of all females between the ages of fourteen and eighteen worked as household servants, and 19.4 percent of those between the ages of eighteen and twenty. In 1907 the percentages for these two age categories had fallen to 14.7 and 17.3 percent, respectively.[33] In some of Germany's more prosperous cities and upper-middle-class suburbs, however, the proportion of young females serving as domestics soared considerably higher. Thus in Schöneberg in 1907, 33.2 percent of all employed females between the ages of sixteen and eighteen were domestic servants, 31.7 percent in Charlottenburg, 27.5 percent in Hamburg, and 23.1 percent in Dresden. In working-class quarters or purely industrial areas, by contrast, the percentages fell far below the average. In the Berlin industrial suburb Neukölln, for example, under 10 percent of sixteen- to eighteen-year-old females held such positions. Several surveys of female factory employees conducted after the turn of the century suggest that younger ones were far less likely to have spent several years as domestic servants after leaving school than were older ones. Of 510 married women factory workers surveyed in Bremen, 43 percent had entered domestic service after schooling, whereas 38.8 percent had immediately taken factory work.[34] Among single factory workers surveyed, however, 61 percent had obtained factory work immediately upon leaving school. Such fragmentary statistics can be buttressed by the impressions of Rosa Kempf, a former student of the liberal social reformer Lujo Brentano at the University of Munich and pioneer empirical investigator of the lives of young female factory laborers, who claimed in 1913 that less than a third of domestic servants in large cities were natives.[35] Moreover, most of these natives stemmed from petit bourgeois rather than working-class backgrounds and viewed domestic service in the homes of the well-to-do as a kind of finishing school. But most domestic servants were young female migrants from farms or small towns. According to Kempf, fewer urban working-class girls were looking for positions as domestics because their parents feared that service in the houses of the wealthy would stimulate overblown social expectations and foster proclivities to profligacy. Moreover, wealthy householders preferred rural girls both because of their more robust physical constitutions and because of their greater docility. Be that as it may, in 1907 over 560,000 young women between the ages of fourteen and twenty were still serving as domestics, almost half the total.

Instead of finding jobs as servants young urban women were increasingly moving into manufacturing jobs. This is documented in

Table 2.7. *Female factory workers in Germany, ages 14–21, 1894–1912*[a]

Branch	1894 No.	1900 No.	%Δ	1906 No.	%Δ	1912 No.	%Δ
Mining	8,209	7,645	− 6.9	8,639	+ 13.0	8,334	− 4.5
Quarry	17,404	27,896	+ 60.3	32,318	+ 15.9	34,829	+ 7.8
Metal	18,649	24,501	+ 31.4	33,699	+ 37.5	43,916	+30.3
Machine	5,189	10,688	+105.9	18,522	+ 73.3	34,642	+87.0
Chemical	5,677	5,736	+ 1.0	9,319	+ 62.5	12,912	+38.6
Heating and lighting	1,724	3,434	+ 99.2	4,043	+ 17.7	5,076	+25.6
Textiles	150,870	166,499	+ 10.4	184,096	+ 10.6	208,663	+13.3
Paper and leather	22,599	30,499	+ 35.0	38,151	+ 25.1	46,744	+78.3
Wood	6,898	9,622	+ 39.5	12,750	+ 32.5	16,584	+30.1
Food	43,035	59,494	+ 38.2	68,049	+ 14.4	83,685	+23.0
Clothing and cleaning	29,421	52,164	+ 77.3	141,144	+170.1	193,822	+37.3
Printing	9,802	15,413	+ 57.2	19,890	+ 29.0	23,008	+15.7
Construction	n/a	160		133		186	
Other	1,536	482		772		962	
Total	321,013	414,233	+ 29.0	571,525	+ 38.0	713,363	+24.8

[a] Includes firms with ten or more workers.
Sources: Compiled from *Vierteljahrhefte zur Statistik des deutschen Reiches:* 1895, IV.45; 1900, IV.276; 1907, IV.248; 1913, IV.41.

Table 2.7, which traces the changes in the factory employment of young women between the ages of fourteen and twenty-one at six-year intervals between 1894 and 1912. Apart from the massive growth in total female youth employment during these eighteen years, an overall advance of 122 percent, the most notable feature brought out by the table is the enormous expansion of employment opportunities for young women in several major branches of industry. To be sure, from 1894 to 1912 the textile industry held its place as the leading employer of young female workers, but whereas this branch grew at a steady rate, employment prospects for young females in the clothing industry increased exponentially, especially during the late 1890s and the early years of the new century. By 1912 the clothing industry had attained almost as great a significance as textiles as an employer of young women. (Because of considerable domestic employment, the number of young women in the clothing industry may well be understated. Moreover, as more protective legislation was introduced for women and youths, employers either evaded these laws or else turned increasingly to this form of employment, although home workers were more likely to be older married women.)[36] The food-processing branch, the second most important source of employment for young women in the early 1890s, although dropping to third place by 1906, nonetheless almost doubled the size of its young female labor force, reaching over 83,000, during these eighteen years. Much of this work may have been both semirural and seasonal, however, since country girls often took temporary work in sugar beet factories or other processing plants during lulls in farm operations.[37] Although certainly not in the same league in terms of the provision of to-tal employment, the machine industry was consistently the fastest-growing creator of new jobs, moving up from eleventh position as an employer in 1894 to seventh by 1912, another sign of the meteoric rise of this branch in Germany. Undoubtedly many of the new open-ings available in both the metal and machine industries were clerical and secretarial positions, as contemporary observers testified.[38] But a more detailed breakdown of employment within these industries that would enable one to chart the takeoff of office work is unavailable.[39]

According to Kempf, one seldom encountered urban girls of the lower classes in skilled crafts.[40] To be sure, a few entered into ap-prenticeships with seamstresses or milliners, "but without a regular-ized contract and without the intention of years-long training. The little enough that is learned in such 'apprenticeships' makes possible only poorly paid positions as assistants or as home workers for com-mon wares." In 1912 Frau Levy Rathenau, the director of the Female Employment Office of the League of German Women's Associations decried the lack of competence of many of the seamstresses who took on apprentices and concluded that many of the young female ap-prentices paid a high apprentice fee only to be exploited.[41] Despite the growing number of apprenticed young females between 1895 and 1907, growth probably attributable in large measure to more clerical apprenticeships in offices, in comparing Tables 2.6 and 2.8, one is struck by the relative insignificance of this institution for post-school-age girls in comparison with its importance for boys. A mere 16 per-cent of the number of apprenticeships were filled by girls in 1907 as were held by boys, and as Kempf affirmed, apprenticeships for young females were probably distinguished from those for males by quali-tative differences as well. Undoubtedly the all but complete neglect of formalized industrial training for young women was a function of the widespread perception that wage labor was a temporary situation that would be instantly terminated upon marriage, a perception that, however, was slowly forfeiting its purchase on reality.[42]

Table 2.8. *Female apprentices employed in major sectors of the German economy, 1895 and 1907*

Shop size	1895	1907	% Δ
A. Agriculture, gardening, livestock, and forestry			
1–5	102	127	+ 24.5
6+	136	260	+ 91.2
Total	238	387	+ 62.6
B. Industry, mining, and construction			
1–5	23,404	31,389	+ 34.1
6+	21,386	39,593	+ 85.1
Total	44,790	70,982	+ 58.5
C. Commerce and transport			
1–5	9,522	13,600	+ 42.8
6+	11,976	25,477	+112.7
Total	21,498	39,077	+ 81.8
All sectors			
1–5	33,028	45,116	+ 36.6
6+	33,498	65,330	+ 95.0
Total	66,526	110,446	+ 66.0

Sources: Compiled from: "Uebersicht 12: Die verheirateten Arbeiterinnen und die Lehrlinge in den Jahren 1907 und 1895," *Statistik des deutschen Reiches*, Band 220/221, *Berufs- und Betriebszählung vom 12 Juni 1907* (Berlin, 1914), pp. 156–7.

Although young females were seldom found in the skilled trades, a variety of urban handicrafts depended heavily on their labor. Females under the age of twenty were considerably overrepresented in various trades, constituting between 25 and 40 percent of their total work forces in the mid-1890s.[43] Reckoned among the trades with such youthful and feminized work forces were manufacturers of steel pens, artificial flowers, corsets, neckties and suspenders, toys, tobacco products, tin wares, needles, and hairbrushes. Young women also made up a significant component of the labor force in confectionery shops and among bookbinders and seamstresses. Apart from industry and trades, however, young women were also increasingly drawn to jobs in the tertiary sector. As is evident from Table 2.3, by 1907 just under one hundred thousand female employees under the age of eighteen were already earning their livelihoods in restaurants and retail trade.

In the late 1920s the sociologist Paul Lazarsfeld reported that in the aggregate, the freely expressed occupational choices of youth were likely to correspond to the occupational structure of the city in which they lived, with some correction for the business cycle and for the age-specific predilections of school leavers.[44] In general, this empirical rule seems to have held for female students in late Imperial Germany. Thus of 2,213 upper-form primary and middle school girls replying to a questionnaire on occupational preferences in Düsseldorf in early 1914, 495 (22.4 percent) wished to become seamstresses, 441 (20 percent) favored clerical, sales, or commercial employment, 422 (19.1 percent) expected to look for positions as domestic servants, and 100 (4.5 percent) were predisposed to take a host of miscellaneous jobs as flower binders, ironers, general factory workers, and so on.[45] Slightly over 17 percent remained undecided, and another 17 percent intended to assist their mothers at home for a few years, a common practice in working-class households, which in part explains the relatively lower rates of labor force participation among post-school-age females compared to males. Clearly girls completing school were aware of the improving prospects for finding pink-collar positions and had a fairly good grasp of the structure of the labor market, even if they collectively overestimated their chances of becoming seamstresses and showed a marked disinclination for unskilled factory labor. Thus young women were also trying to accommodate to rapidly and radically changing employment opportunities in late Imperial Germany.

Having briefly shown some of the effects of the structural transformation of youth employment in late Imperial Germany, it is time to turn to the place of youth in labor law, for reasons mentioned at the outset of the chapter. Young workers were encompassed by a variety of statutes, ordinances, factory codes, and supplementary laws passed by a variety of bodies: the Imperial Parliament, the Federal Council, state parliaments, city councils, employers' liability insurance associations, and factory owners in conjunction with workers' committees. Although a few of these measures covered all working minors, most applied only to those in the fourteen-to-sixteen age group. Apart from a few rather inconsequential exceptions, workers over eighteen were treated as adults.[46] Moreover, except for a small number of general provisions in the new Imperial Civil Code of 1896, such as the one belatedly eliminating the general right of employers in the household and agriculture to administer corporal punishment or the one requiring adequate living quarters, young domestic servants and agricultural workers were expressly omitted from protective ordinances, as were young workers, although not apprentices, in most firms that regularly employed fewer than ten workers.[47] The justifications advanced for these omissions testify to some of the functions assigned to youth labor regulations. Legislators contended that in households, on farms, and in small shops, a patriarchal relation bound master and servant, with the master assuming responsibility for the physical and moral well-being of his young charge. Protective legislation was only deemed necessary in larger industrial firms, where impersonal labor relations prevailed and youths were likely to attain greater independence. Some commentators admitted, however, that small shops had also been exempted because of the costs entailed by complying with protective legislation. But basically youth legislation was conceived as a functional surrogate for declining patriarchal relations, as a way of compelling large-scale employers to adopt an attitude of solicitous paternalism toward their young workers and to remind the youth themselves of their continuing subordination to and dependence on employers and parents.

The most important legal provisions covering young workers were contained in the Imperial Industrial Code of 1871, although these provisions were subsequently modified on numerous occasions. Many of these amendments were added in the early 1890s as Kaiser Wilhelm II briefly sought to play the people's emperor and to win over workers by persuading them of his deeply felt social compassion.[48] A few of the general provisions of the Code applied without exception to all young workers under the age of twenty-one. Most important of these general rules in practical terms was the one mandating that a youth acquire a work book as a prerequisite for employment. Local police departments could issue work books only with the consent of the youth's parents or legal guardians and upon proof that primary school requirements had been completed and that no previous work book had been dispensed. Upon being hired, the youth handed the book over to his or her employer, who retained it until employment ceased, at which time he returned it either to the youth or to his or her parents if the employee was still under sixteen. The employer wrote only the dates of employment in the work book, and was legally interdicted from making any judgments, whether positive or pejorative, in reference to the youth's work performance or deportment. Such judgments could be recorded, however, in a certificate presented either to the young laborer or the youth's parents at the conclusion of the employment period. If the youth failed to fulfill his or her contractual obligations, the employer could keep the work book until these obligations were met, he had received satisfactory compensation, or he had agreed to nullify the contract. Without the work book, the youth would be unable to take another job. If an employer's right to hold a work book were challenged, the dispute could be settled by an industrial court, guilds (*Innungen*), or the communal authorities. As Karl Bittmann, one of the foremost experts on youth labor law observed, work books and the rules governing them served the purpose of "control and supervision by the legal representative of the minor, the employer and the officials" and they "essentially restricted the self-determination of the underaged worker...."[49]

Other general provisions of the Industrial Code that converged toward similar goals were those touching on the payment of wages. Employers had to fill out wage books for all youthful employees, in which the amounts being paid out were to be recorded each payday. Not only were such books intended to prevent conflicts over payments, but as Bittmann pointed out, they enabled the youth's legal representative to stay informed about the youth's earnings. Another provision of the Code empowered communities to pass statutes whereby wages could be paid directly to the parents or guardians of youthful employees, rather than to the youths themselves. Clearly these ordinances would have allowed parents to establish complete domain over their children's earnings.[50] To the dismay of conservatives who hoped that this law would be a powerful instrument for reasserting parental authority, communities generally proved reluctant to take advantage of this legal possibility, presumably because of the demands on parental time and resentment among youth that such an indirect system of payment would have engendered. Nor did such wage provisions exhaust the disciplinary features of industrial legislation for youth. Factories with at least twenty workers could impose rules calculated to regulate the behavior and morality of the underaged worker outside working hours and away from the shopfloor, such as forbidding visits to bars, dance halls, or other places of pleasure.[51] Such rules, legally impermissible for adult workers, could be introduced by factory owners after consulting with a standing committee of employees and securing their assent. Nor were minors entitled to any voice or representation on such committees. Few factories instituted such rules, however, probably because of both their obvious unenforceability and the hesitancy of adult workers to approve such restrictively paternalistic practices.

A second set of general rules was designed to protect the health and morals of young workers under the age of eighteen.[52] Among these was Article 106 of the Industrial Code, which shielded young workers from employers with serious criminal records by debarring adults who had been deprived of their citizenship rights from hiring youths under eighteen. Another general article admonished employers to safeguard the health and morals of their young workers, although the only concrete stipulation contained in this article was one that disallowed youths under eighteen from producing articles associated with sex, for example, printing sexually explicit literature or manufacturing sexual aids. Most important of the general rules for youths under eighteen and one that would assume considerably greater significance after the turn of the century was the one obliging employers to allow their young workers and apprentices sufficient time off to attend continuation schools when further education beyond the primary level was required by a local statute. As part-time municipally sponsored industrial continuation schools proliferated after 1900, this law would both provide a legal foundation for such schools and become a focus for disgruntled artisans who were loath to release their apprentices during working hours.

A third set of articles in the Industrial Code helped to maintain the health of fourteen- to sixteen-year-old workers by limiting work time.[53] Fourteen- to sixteen-year-olds could work a maximum of ten hours daily, their workday was not to begin before 5:30 A.M. or end after 8:30 P.M., they were to enjoy uninterrupted rest of at least eleven hours between consecutive workdays, and they were to be free from employment on Sundays, holidays, and during times designated for catechism, confirmation, or communion instruction. Young laborers working a full ten-hour day were guaranteed at least an hour for lunch and at least half an hour for breaks, both in the morning and in the afternoon. When possible, these breaks were to be spent in the open air. If conditions precluded outdoor activity, however, breaks were to passed in a room away from the work area. In case of emergency or special circumstances, the Federal Council (Bundesrat), the national legislative body composed of representatives of the federal states, had the power temporarily to rescind these limitations on work time.

After 1891 the Federal Council was also armed with the power to ban the employment of youth in branches of industry or in occupations that posed especially serious dangers to their health or morals, a power that the Council occasionally exercised.[54] The Council extended to young males a number of measures that had originally been legislated to preserve the health of adult women workers. For example, owners of factories that primarily made lead products were denied permission to employ young males, as were firms involved in grinding or storing slag from Thomas process steel. Nor were young workers to be assigned a dangerous task like firing the kiln in brick-yards. Various industrial enterprises, including book-printing shops, type foundries, rubber-vulcanizing factories, cigar-rolling shops, and glass factories among others, were subject to some restrictions on their employment of youth. Similar but less general protective regulations were agreed to by employers' liability insurance associations, presumably because of prohibitive insurance premiums.[55] For example, the Saxon-Thuringian Iron and Steel Liability Association forbade using youth under eighteen to tend lathes in the machine-building and small ironwares industries. The Liability Association of Chimney Sweep Masters of the German Reich proscribed having unsupervised apprentices clean smokestacks of steam engines or central heating units. Literally hundreds of such highly specific rules were in effect throughout Germany, although these insurance regulations varied considerably from region to region.

Whereas these rules, laws, and ordinances pertained to young industrial workers, several sections of the Industrial Code specifically governed relations between masters and apprentices.[56] These articles required the apprentice to subordinate him- or herself to the paternal authority of the master and obligated him or her to obedience, loyalty, diligence, and upright behavior. In turn, the master was duty bound to devote the necessary time to instructing his apprentice, to ensure that his apprentice was industrious and upheld good morals, to allow the apprentice time to go to church on the sabbath, and to protect the apprentice against abuse by other employees of his shop or members of his household. The law also stipulated a few more well-defined protective measures for apprentices. Masters could not force apprentices to perform household chores unless they were receiving room and board, nor could masters inflict immoderate, humiliating, or health-endangering punishments on their apprentices. If a master violated these stipulations or neglected the moral or trade instruction of the apprentice, the apprentice could unilaterally void the contract. He could also break the contract if his parents decided that he would learn another trade. The master in turn could cancel the contract unilaterally if the apprentice consistently failed to carry out his duties or regularly failed to attend continuation school. If an apprentice ran away from his master without sufficient grounds, however, the police could return him forcibly at the master's request, or instead the master might demand compensation in lieu of unfulfilled contractual obligations. Article 128 of the Industrial Code explicitly prohibited apprentice breeding, and municipal authorities could deprive masters of their training rights if they repeatedly took on more apprentices than they could train adequately. Although the Industrial Code was strongly biased in favor of masters, it certainly did provide apprentices with some modicum of legal protection. But as many commentators understood, given the number of craft apprentices in small shops and the few inspectors, it was virtually impossible to oversee effective enforcement of these regulations, a point that should already be obvious from the previous discussion of widespread apprentice breeding in urban trades.[57]

Thus by the 1890s a well-developed body of industrial laws and regulations covering young workers already existed, embodying norms for preserving the health and ensuring the safety of youths as well as for overseeing and controlling their morals and behavior. Furthermore, the Industrial Code implicitly acknowledged a right to industrial training and education beyond the elementary level, since it enabled communities to require young workers to attend continuation schools, institutions that would become pivotal for the youth savers. At the turn of the century, youth savers would also take up the enforcement, extension, and reform of industrial law to bring it in accord with the transforming world of industrial labor and to remedy perceived deficiencies in military fitness, demographic vitality, and economic efficiency. Recognition of the tectonic shifts in the position of youth in Germany's population and labor force would undergird the justification for major youth policy initiatives and substantial legal reform. Existing industrial law would provide a solid foundation upon which to erect this reformed framework.

3

Youth savers and youth salvation: the image of young workers and institutional reform

As mentioned in Chapter 1, in terms of the "natural history" of the youth problem, the conferences of the Center for Workers' Welfare Institutions and Protestant Social Congress and the Erfurt essay contest in 1900 began the progression from the stage of awareness to the stages of policy determination and reform. The conferences and writings of the reformers served three fundamental purposes. First, they traced the origins of the working-class youth problem in order to determine its elements and measure its dimensions. Second, they explored in detail particular facets of the youth problem that they considered most serious: the deteriorating health of young workers, the declining morals of urban youth, and the rising rate of juvenile delinquency, among others. Third, they attempted to hammer out programs of legislation, institutional reform, and officially sanctioned and financed activities that could ameliorate, if not eradicate, the youth problem. Behind these endeavors lay an image of young workers that would be sketched at these conferences and would persist through the war, albeit with some minor retouching.

Many of the binary oppositions that are standardly used to characterize the "Great Transformation" originated in the social thought of Imperial Germany: Ferdinand Tönnies's "community" versus "society," Max Weber's contrast between traditional and rational action. The rapidity of Germany's industrialization and urbanization in the last half of the nineteenth century gave rise to a widespread sense of displacement and estrangement that prompted numerous German thinkers to grapple with the meaning of modernity. Although certainly not as theoretically sophisticated as Tönnies or Weber, the reformers' accounts of the genesis of the youth problem placed it within the context of the sharp transition from a traditional to a modern

48

social order. They invoked a diremption between a preindustrial Germany of small, tightly knit, closely supervised, hierarchical communities with stable and time-honored work routines and a modern, rapidly changing Germany of large cities, in which mobile, uprooted, denatured, and historyless individuals labored and lived. Whereas the characteristic enterprise of the old order had been the small shop supervised by the highly skilled master craftsmen, the dominant enterprise of the new Germany was the large-scale factory with its demand for unskilled labor. The transformation of Germany from an agrarian to an industrial state, from a land of villages and small towns into a nation with numerous large cities, had destroyed old social relations and profoundly altered the life cycle of the young.[1] Although few youth savers believed that a restoration of past relations was either possible or desirable, fewer still could entirely escape from harboring some degree of nostalgia for this supposedly simpler and more orderly past.

As the Frankfurt official Andreas Voigt explained to the conference of the Center for Workers' Welfare Institutions in 1900, the road to independence for the young had previously been long and arduous.[2] After school, the young male had been contracted to apprenticeship under the watchful eye of a master in whose house he also lived. Young females had usually begun domestic service. Although Voigt disclaimed any desire to idealize past relations, since as he admitted, there had been bad masters and wayward youth, nonetheless, "in the old order of things every young person was directed to his fixed place, and his path through life proceeded within its foreordained limits." This was no longer the case. The large factory required vast numbers of unskilled laborers who underwent no apprenticeship and hence had no reason to remain in the same shop. Moreover, early wages permitted early independence. Soon after completing school, young workers "cast loose from their families in order to enter an independent contract in a strange locality, rent a sleeping place [*Schlafstelle*], take care of their own food and clothes, and spend the rest of their wages as they see fit." A decade later the Berlin jurist Alfred Kühne would summarize the same process, placing greater emphasis on the new roles of youth in the labor force:

The patriarchal relation between master and apprentice is no longer common. Certainly, it still exists in small and medium-sized towns, but in large cities it is the exception even in the crafts for an apprentice to receive room and board from his master. That is even more true for the growing number of factory apprentices and especially the so-called unskilled workers.... As messengers and laborers, they carry out all kinds of auxiliary labor in the plants, earn comparatively high wages, and hence become independent of the parental home too soon. The increasing roughness and the rising criminality of youth point to the serious dangers for the entire life of our people.[3]

As these passages suggest, the youth savers tended to criticize urban working-class family life and new industrial relations in terms of their deviation from a nostalgic ideal of small-town family life and preindustrial craft apprenticeship, which they accepted as norms. Moreover, their critique of modern conditions would be couched largely in moral terms, rather than in economic or social ones.

Whereas the youth savers regarded the family lives of farmers, rural laborers, and craftsmen as healthy, they portrayed the urban working-class family, not as a distinctive form of kinship association conditioned by the new economic relations, but rather as a degenerate and dissolving institution. For these solidly middle-class reformers for whom well-regulated family life and parental authority were sacrosanct, the loose bonds of the urban working-class family were alarming.[4] Because of long work hours and resulting fatigue, fathers had little contact with or control over their children. Many working-class fathers passed their evenings drinking in the *Kneipen* (saloons), which the Hamburg youth minister Walther Classen regarded as the graveyard of family life. On Sundays these men recuperated from their exhausting work week by sleeping. From their earliest years urban children grew up running wild in the streets, unobserved by their mothers, who were busily performing chores on the upper floors of multistoried tenements. Common family meals, even on Sundays, were becoming a rarity, a matter of complete indifference to the young. Moreover, children attending urban primary schools were often better educated than their parents. Nor were parents able to offer much guidance on employment, since they were unfamiliar with the urban job market and newly developing skills. The early earnings of the young factory worker, sorely needed to sustain the household, enabled him to play master in his parents' house. If not completely forfeited, parental authority was at the very least diminished by the concatenation of social factors.

Of course, both the timing of youthful independence and the degree of parental authority partly depended on the young worker's trade. Far from considering young laborers as an undifferentiated mass, most youth savers, who were keen, if moralizing, observers of urban working-class youth, distinguished carefully among the various strata. They usually stratified these youth into craft apprentices, whether in factories or artisanal shops, the unskilled and the "half-strong" (*Halbstarken*), although they sometimes introduced more refined classificatory schemes as well. Although youth savers commonly recognized that certain types of white-collar positions, for example, scribes (*Schreiber*), were recruited largely from blue-collar backgrounds and that such workers lived in proletarian neighborhoods, these office employees were usually treated separately. Even when their living standards and life chances approximated those of young factory workers, they supposedly maintained social distance: riding in different sections of streetcars, eating in different restaurants, visiting different bars, dressing in the high collar and tie of the office worker, and defining themselves as a distinct social group.[5] Distinctions among groups of young workers not only signified various levels of skill and earning power, but also ostensibly connoted deep-rooted psychological, moral, and behavioral dispositions, although it is doubtful that the distinctions were quite as sharply defined as youth savers believed or hoped. Whatever their accuracy, however, such typologies revealed much about the values and moral universe of the youth savers themselves, including their attitudes toward work, authority, and urban mass culture.

Most favored by the youth savers were the craft apprentices, those who were "learning something" and who most closely resembled the artisanal apprentices of old.[6] This stratum would replenish the ranks of skilled labor. Although these apprentices could no longer expect to become independent masters, they could aspire to becoming foremen with a pension and the security of the new middle class. According to several prominent youth savers, unlike the old apprentices, modern ones lacked a specific craft consciousness, a pride in being a toolmaker or mechanic, but they did nurture a general pride in their labor and considered themselves superior to the unskilled. The modern apprentice was also intellectually alert, with a willingness to learn new things, and therefore was the ideal continuation school student, assiduous and eager for extra courses. In the workshop he learned discipline, goal-oriented behavior, and modesty. He was willing to suffer dressing-downs or cuffs for his mistakes since he recognized that the master and journeymen knew more than he. Moreover, with his minimal *Kostgeld*, he was debarred from indulging in the pleasures of the large city. Apart from a few marks pocket money, he turned his meager earnings over to his parents, on whom he continued to depend and to whom he continued to look for counsel. This lack of autonomy also made him the most likely candidate for membership in youth associations. Only when he was eighteen and had mastered his trade would he finally attain greater independence. Thus the hard-working, sober, self-improving, goal-oriented, disciplined, and dependent artisanal or factory apprentice was the youth savers' model young worker.

In contrast to their positive image of the skilled, their portrait of the unskilled was largely negative. The unskilled, a third of all young employees, were regarded with considerable suspicion and apprehension.[7] Although white-collar employees like scribes and office boys were sometimes numbered among the unskilled, *ungelernte* was usually applied to the innumerable messenger and delivery boys who were such an inescapable element of the urban scene and to the army of young factory handymen who moved materials and finished goods, polished machines, and cleaned workshops. A variety of factors might destine young lower-class males for such positions: poor school performance; family economic difficulties that put a premium on initial high wages; a failed apprenticeship, terminated because it in no way corresponded to the physical abilities or personal inclinations of the school leaver; or some combination of these factors. By whatever routes youths arrived in such dead-end positions, these occupations were fraught with dangers. First, the work itself was unengaging and unchallenging drudgery. At the age when a lad was still capable of learning, he acquired no skills. Employers took no interest in his further development, his capacity for intellectual growth atrophied, and he became stultified. The youth could neither take pride nor derive inner satisfaction from his work. His work was simply a job, a means to earn money. Second, because of this instrumental relation to his labor, he was inclined to instability. The youth had no reason to stay with one firm and was therefore likely to float from one workplace to another in accordance with fluctuating labor demand or his own fickle humor. Finally, the gravest dangers arose from the relatively high wages earned by unskilled youths, which allowed them to attain far greater independence from their families than could the young apprentice. High earnings also enabled them to become precocious consumers of urban pleasures. It was the young unskilled worker who was the typical cinema patron and reader of penny dreadfuls, with their lurid themes of crime, suicide, and adultery. It was the young unskilled worker who was prematurely sexually active and who could be found smoking and drinking in the bars. This susceptibility to urban vices was exacerbated by the working conditions of many unskilled young workers. Most at risk were the messengers and delivery boys, who plied their trades on the streets without supervision.[8]

Youth employed on the streets often shaded off into the *Halbstarken*, degenerate, disorderly, often physically malformed, and maladapted spawn of the worst urban environments, offspring of negligent and alcoholic fathers.[9] Disruptive in school, they made little progress. From early childhood they committed petty crimes and thus became known to ministers, welfare workers, and the police, who despite their good intentions and well-meaning efforts were unable to stop the youths' slide into perdition. Unable to keep a regular job, these youths drifted from one form of casual labor to another, working as porters or coal handlers. Each stint of employment was punctuated by a longer period of unemployment. According to the Hamburg youth minister Clemens Schultz, whose 1912 pamphlet virtually defined these youths and traced their "natural history," the *Halbstarken* were largely nocturnal creatures, habitués of the commonest bars and bordellos, inhabitants of the borderlands of petty criminality, carriers of venereal disease. The Berlin minister Günther Dehn graphically depicted these youths as encountered in the bars of proletarian districts.

There they sit in heaps, dirty playing cards or greasy sausage wrappers in hand, or they stand around on street corners or in entryways, sports caps on the head, cigarette in the corner of the mouth, hands buried in the pockets, around the neck a scarf tied into a "revolver knot," which represents a collar and tie. If a riot or brawl breaks out anyplace, there they are. There they shoot up like mushrooms from the earth. In their pockets are stones, by chance a slingshot. With their fingers they bring forth a piercing whistle; from ambush the revolution is made with cries and howls. But if one proceeds energetically against them, they disappear like rats into their holes, since these people are cowardly.[10]

The vividness and emotional timbre of such writing, with its cathected images of filth, rodents, and revolution, leave little doubt that these hooligans and rebels appeared to the youth savers as highly disturbing urban types: the counterimage of all they considered orderly, healthy, normal – a condensed symbol of degeneracy and disorder.

Thus the youth savers were united in believing that the release of the young from the constraints of the parental home was contributing to the breakdown of order and morality. Moreover, since modern labor was devoid of expressive potential and hence unfulfilling, young workers, especially the unskilled, were inclined to seek fulfillment in hedonistic pleasure seeking (*Genusssucht*). Bad conditions and long

hours provided further inducements to pursue instantaneous gratification, a pursuit facilitated by their relatively high wages and various
features of the urban environment: enticing store displays and advertisements that touted the acquisition of material goods; pervasive
cheap entertainment in the bars, dance halls, and cinemas; cramped
working-class flats where youths learned about sex early and from
which they escaped by congregating on the streets.[11]

Symptoms of both bad working conditions and loss of moral restraint were numerous. Although some doctors doubted that the
health of young workers was steadily declining, other physicians using
much the same evidence concluded that the physical condition of
young urban workers was demonstrably deteriorating. The most commonly cited statistic, and one that applied to middle-class gymnasia-
educated males as well, was the growing percentage of youth declared
unfit for military service on medical grounds.[12] Thus between 1902/
3 and 1907/8 the percentage of urban-born males accepted by the
army had dropped from 53.8 to 49.7 percent, whereas the corresponding drop for rural youth was from 59.7 to 57.2 percent. Some
health officials were quick to point out, however, that the drop was
slight and could be interpreted in various ways. They suspected that
because of a larger draft pool, resulting from a demographic bulge,
army physicians had become somewhat more selective than in the
past. Whatever the truth about the rates of fitness for the military,
there were less equivocal signs of serious health problems among
urban adolescents.

The mortality rate in large cities among males between the ages of
fifteen and twenty had inched upward from 4.0 to 4.3 per thousand
between 1900/1 and 1905/6, and the German death rates for male
fourteen- to eighteen-year-olds surpassed the English rates by more
than 20 percent.[13] Local medical insurance offices showed that young
workers in some occupations suffered from staggeringly high rates
of accident and injury. During every year between 1905 and 1908, at
least 70 percent of all youths employed in the Ruhr coal industry
missed some days of work because of medically confirmed illness. In
some years the rate reached 80 percent. In several large rolling and
hammering mills in the iron industry such average annual sickness
frequencies for fifteen- to nineteen-year-olds ranged between 75 and
111 percent, compared with an industry average of 56 percent for all
age groups. In the metal-finishing industries, the largest branch of
employment for young males, the annual sickness rate over a seven-
year period was 53.6 percent, considerably lower than in iron works

but still somewhat higher than the 49.4 percent rate for adult metal finishers between the ages of twenty and forty. Over a third of the days lost by youth in metal finishing resulted from industrial accidents.

On the basis of such statistical material culled from various health studies and the reports of local health insurance offices, J. Kaup informed the Society for Social Reform that there was sufficient evidence to warrant the conclusion that industrial employments were imperiling the health and vitality of youth independently of other living conditions. He also stressed, however, that good nutrition, adequate ventilation, and the prevention of alcohol abuse, bar visits, stimulating reading matter, and sexual activity were necessary for the proper physical development of young workers. Wilhelm Martius, a municipal physician in Munich, warned the Central Agency in 1900 of the rampant increase in youthful alcoholism, which he attributed to the dust, heat, and long hours of the workplace, the lack of alternatives to bars for socializing, and the bad example set by older workers, who considered emptying a glass of schnapps in one draft a sign of manliness.[14] Another symptom of the loss of moral restraint with consequences for public health was the rapid spread of venereal disease among youth.[15] Since both working conditions and free-time usage were endangering the health and fitness of youth, Germany's potential military strength was being sapped and its industrial productivity diminished.

For many youth savers, however, the upward spiral of delinquency, at a time when the rate of adult crime was decreasing slightly, was the most unsettling sign of moral breakdown.[16] Between 1882, the first year when separate figures on youthful offenders were kept, and 1898 the number of youths convicted rose from 31,000 to 48,000, or from 5.68 per thousand youths to 6.97. By the turn of the century, 5.6 percent of all males had been charged with crimes by their eighteenth birthday. Moreover, recidivism rates of youth were relatively high in comparison to those of adult offenders. Although the majority of juvenile delinquents were convicted of petty theft or vandalism, serious offenses like assault and arson were becoming far more common. Recent research has discounted the notion of any simple or direct linkage between increasing juvenile delinquency and either industrialization or urbanization in Imperial Germany.[17] Moreover, the historian Detlev Peukert has cautioned that because of the "dark figures" and the regionally divergent law enforcement procedures of police departments and conviction policies of the courts, Imperial Germany's youth criminal statistics should be taken *cum grano salis*.

But although they may well have been wrong, many youth savers certainly strongly believed that specifically urban conditions and forms of entertainment contributed to rising youth crime.

The Hamburg youth minister Clemens Schultz thought that sensationalist films and penny dreadfuls could only trigger wrongdoing by making manifest previous dispositions toward criminality. Clever juvenile delinquents used their reading matter as mitigating explanations in court. Catholic newspapers, however, often ran stories about youth impelled into heinous crimes by reading lurid penny detective stories.[18] The Berlin jurist and leading juvenile crime expert Paul Köhne, who considered social milieu and greater opportunity more conducive to youth crime than individual failings, advanced five reasons for the rising crime rate among young males.[19] First came the more frequent breakup of families and the consequent neglect of children in the modern urban environment. Second was the overloaded nervous systems of modern urban youth, constantly bombarded by traffic noise, advertisements, and other shocks to their sensory systems that induced nervousness, hysteria, neurasthenia, and psychopathic constitutions. Third was the poor quality and crowded urban housing where from their earliest years children became familiar with prostitution and sex. Fourth was the eclipse of religion as a result of the triumph of the natural sciences. Fifth came competing political parties that were trying to drag youth prematurely into public controversy, thus damaging "the necessary sense of modesty and love of truth of a growing youth. . . . " All of these factors, according to Köhne, seriously weakened moral inhibitions.

Although he carefully avoided mentioning the SPD by name, Köhne's reference to political parties that appealed to unripe boys clearly indicated that, like other youth savers, he regarded the Socialists as both a catalyst and by-product of the collapse of restraint and moral order.[20] Both Socialists and juvenile delinquents were viewed as different manifestations of the modern rejection of authority and the untrameled desire for instantaneous gratification. Already in 1878 Fritz Kalle had asserted to the Social Policy Association that the pleasure seeking and the drive for independence of young factory workers propelled them into the Socialist ranks, where they soon lost the last vestiges of shame and respect for authority. Such moral critiques of the SPD resurfaced in the youth discourse at the turn of the century. Wilhelm Martius of Munich objected to young workers being able to visit bars, not only because it injured their health, but also because it was there that Socialists recruited them and taught them "fundamental discontent, demanding arrogance, and contempt for frugality, modesty, and obedience." Andreas Voigt of Frankfurt held that by claiming that individual saving was no solution to the workers' economic difficulties, the SPD was encouraging youths to be spendthrifts. Walther Classen, the Hamburg youth minister, maintained that the new generation of Socialists lacked the idealism, ethical standards, drive for knowledge, and courage of the older generation that sprang from rural and small-town roots and that had steadfastly carried the party through the years of Bismarckian repression. By contrast, the new generation of Socialists was materialistic, not in the philosophical but in the economic sense. Younger Socialists were a mindless mass filled with slogans, utterly lacking in any sense of responsibility and individual conscience. Georg Kerschensteiner, the Munich school superintendant and winner of the Erfurt essay contest, also regarded the SPD as a symptom of greater wealth and pleasure seeking. With its lack of religious and patriotic sentiment, its gospel of class hatred, and its demagogic promises, he felt the SPD was reinforcing the base egoism of the young. Although several recent histories of Wilhelmine education have treated the primary schools as effective instruments of social control that turned out well-disciplined and obedient subjects for the Empire, Kerschensteiner, like many of the youth savers, feared that Germany's system of elementary education was just sufficient to make the young vulnerable to the blandishments of eloquent orators and inadequate to enable them to see through the hollow rhetoric of these demagogues.[21]

But Kerschensteiner hoped that in time the SPD might be converted to Fabian gradualism and that the trade unions might serve as schools of public virtue. Such beliefs were common among liberal reformers who recognized the failure of Bismarck's anti-Socialist exceptional laws in the 1880s and who had opposed attempts to pass draconian new anti-Socialist legislation during the "Stumm era," 1894–99, when the kaiser abandoned his earlier support of reconciliatory social policy. Such reformers were conversant with English affairs and looked forward to an eventual lib-lab alliance in Germany, a position made credible by the rise of revisionism in the SPD and the growing moderation of the Free Trade Unions. Thus Hugo Blitz, a Protestant minister from Lüneburg whose essay placed second in the Erfurt contest, questioned whether the entire SPD was still revolutionary and doubted that the entire work of the youth savers should be directed entirely toward combatting the Socialists. At the conference of the Protestant Social Congress in 1900 political economist Wilhelm

Troeltsch, the keynote speaker, assailed the SPD as a menace to German polity and society. Nonetheless, he warned against proposing discriminatory legislation against young workers, since this would embitter the SPD and trade unions and thus preclude cooperation on jointly supported youth reforms. Although the youth reformers were consistently and stridently anti-Socialist and vigorously criticized what they held to be the morally deleterious consequences of the SPD's influence on youth, many envisaged their youth programs as means of bridging Imperial Germany's deep political and class divisions.

One of the reasons some reformers could plausibly hope for limited cooperation with the SPD was that they, like the Socialists, accepted the irreversibility of Germany's transformation from an agrarian to an industrial state and the concomitant changes in relations of authority. By contrast, many conservatives, including a minority in the Protestant Social Congress, were willing to countenance forceful measures to slow migration of youths to the city and to restore a patriarchal order. Among these measures were corporal punishment for juvenile delinquents, restrictions on the rights of youth to change jobs and move freely from place to place, and direct payments of minors' wages to their parents.[22] Although many reformers sympathized with conservative jeremiads against moral degeneration, most repudiated such draconian and anachronistic methods, which would have drastically curtailed broadly accepted rights. Instead, they advocated a series of piecemeal reforms to address specific problems and the establishment or modification of institutions that could act as functional substitutes for the supervisory agencies of the old order.

Such social reforms, as Detlev Peukert has argued, were far from being purely defensive, but rather were aimed at a "comprehensively rational restructuring of the modes of life in industrial society," a reordering that included a "normalization of the course of life."[23] As the youth savers moved from policy determination to reform, their proposals covered four areas. First were those reforms that were calculated to improve the occupational situation and associated health problems of young workers. Second came reforms that were designed to alter those features of the urban setting that impinged on the moral development of youth. Third was reform of the juvenile justice system, a part of what Peukert has called the "pedagogisation of deviant behavior." The final area of reform involved the establishment of institutions that would reimpose restraints on young male workers between primary school and barracks.

Youth savers called for three types of reforms that would affect youth employment: systematic vocational counseling, more stringent enforcement of the youth provisions of the Industrial Code, and new restrictions on the employment of young workers.

By the turn of the century youth savers were convinced that occupational counseling was necessary before youths entered the labor force. Given the extraordinary complexity of the urban division of labor and the school leaver's consequent lack of orientation, job selection was all too often haphazard and based on hearsay or mere chance. Inappropriate selection soon led to discontent, changes in occupation, and frequent job turnover, all of which impaired economic efficiency.[24] Despite the strong case for institutionalized vocational counseling, in most cities its development was slow. To take Düsseldorf as an example, the first sign of interest in counseling appeared in the late 1890s, when the private Association for the Promotion of Workers' References began handing out to boys completing primary school flyers that extolled the moral and economic advantages of acquiring a skilled trade.[25] But rather than offering concrete advice on how to proceed, the flyers simply admonished school leavers to bear in mind the economic insecurity prevailing among the unskilled and the fact that such laborers were accorded no respect. In 1908 the city administration adopted a practical course by requesting that the Chamber of Commerce and Chamber of Handicrafts assist with job placement of primary school graduates. The impact of this request proved to be minimal, however, since neither of these public corporations worked closely with the city's schools. By 1913 city officials and teachers had come to recognize the limited success of this previous policy and therefore drew up plans for a comprehensive program of job counseling and placement closely linked to the primary schools. As part of its policy of wooing artisans for a new conservative coalition, the Prussian government was willing to provide subventions for placement programs that would channel boys into the handicrafts, thus relieving the labor shortages about which many artisans were grousing. Düsseldorf's proindustry administrators do not appear to have been especially enthusiastic about this use of placement services, but government aid at least made such an extensive counseling program feasible. The war broke out, however, before the new program could be implemented, and the dislocations caused by the war economy rendered previous plans irrelevant.

Attempts to introduce occupational counseling and placement in Munich were far more successful. There, city officials encouraged young workers who were searching for entry-level positions or who were unemployed to register at the municipal labor exchange. Beginning in 1904 teachers distributed questionnaires to students in the upper class of primary school about their occupational preferences and plans.[26] Students could then bring these completed forms to the municipal labor bureau to seek an appropriate job. Such experiments with vocational placement were indications of the new importance ascribed to placing youths in employments that corresponded to their aptitudes and inclinations in order to enhance labor satisfaction and maximize economic efficiency. By 1913 a vocational counselor in Halle estimated that somewhere between 130 and 140 counseling centers were available for school leavers and about 30,000 youths were receiving counseling annually – still a small minority, however.[27]

Occupational counseling was only one area of concern about the employment of youth. Many youth reformers deplored the inadequate enforcement of the amendments to the Industrial Code of 1891, which limited the working day of youths under sixteen to ten hours, abolished night work, and prohibited employers from assigning young workers to sections of plants with dangerously high temperature or gas levels. Therefore, reformers pressed for more vigorous and rigorous enforcement. Some physicians also advanced a battery of novel extensions to protective legislation for youth. Among the measures recommended were obligatory two-week annual vacations to be spent in the countryside; three half workdays weekly, with the other half day given over to education in continuation schools and to sports; and periodic medical examinations of continuation and technical school students in order to ascertain occupationally related diseases and disorders.[28]

Housing reform constituted a bridge between concerns about the health of young workers and the state of youthful morals in the large cities. For single youths not living with parents or masters, reformers proposed erecting publicly and privately funded dormitories. Such proposals resulted from worries about the young urban newcomer jointly renting part of a mattress at minimal cost in the apartment of a poor worker, the notorious *Schlafstelle*.[29] The number of such renters, or *Schlafgänger,* had multiplied exponentially in the late nineteenth century, from 9,604 to 22,897 in Leipzig between 1880 and 1900 and from 1,196 to 7,851 in Essen during those decades. Berlin alone counted 100,000 *Schlafgänger* in 1900, a figure that clearly included many young female as well as male factory laborers. This mode of existence was regarded as especially dangerous for fifteen- to nineteen-year-olds, who were likely to fall in with morally suspect companions or to have precocious sexual relations. Such a system of subtenantry also facilitated the spread of infectious diseases, including scabies and tuberculosis. Apart from building dormitories, cities instituted regular inspections of *Schlafstellen* to counteract these perils.

Another aspect of the campaign to safeguard the morals of urban youth was the attack on penny dreadfuls — short, cheap, badly written booklets with brightly colored covers, whose action-packed stories were filled with the daring deeds of detectives, bandits, or cowboys. Not only did this attack tap the energies of clergymen and teachers in primary and continuation schools, who often founded committees to suppress this literature, but it also received considerable support from the Prussian government and even the Krupps.[30] Many youth savers clearly agreed with the pamphlet of the Center for Popular Welfare that avowed that "the struggle against penny dreadfuls is itself a struggle for youth."[31] Penny dreadfuls captivated the lively fantasy, desire for adventure, and hero worship of inexperienced youth. These seductive adventures supposedly not only threatened traditional German culture, but also poisoned young minds and planted the seeds of immorality and criminality. Although most youth savers and characteristic cultural organizations of the educated and nationalist middle class like the Dürerbund preferred positive, if ineffectual, steps, such as publishing reading lists of approved books, some pressured shopkeepers into eliminating penny dreadfuls from their shelves and even called for censorship or police control of sales.[32] Claimed the pamphlet of the Center for Popular Welfare, "[I]t is less bad that a harmless book is forbidden than that a hundred ruinous books find their way to the broad masses."

Simultaneously, youth savers conducted an intense, analogous campaign against films, the newest manifestation of what they perceived as a threatening mass urban culture. In Düsseldorf, for example, by 1910 nine cinemas were operating. According to the police, they competed for viewers by displaying increasingly sensational advertisements and showing ever more depraved films.[33] Colorful placards, reminiscent of the covers of penny dreadfuls, depicted scenes of horror, violence, and sex. Such posters entranced schoolchildren and young workers, luring them into the darkened cinema halls. Once they were inside, the screen vamp Asta Nielsen would tempt them into lives of crime and degradation, just as she wrecked the lives of the male screen protagonists. At very least, most films, with their scenes and episodes from the demimonde of large cities, their murders, robberies, adulteries, and suicides, would overstimulate the nerves of pubescents. Moreover, the police feared that since some films portrayed public officials as laughing stocks, they might undermine respect for law and the state. In response to such concerns, many city administrations appointed film censorship boards. In this campaign, too, however, positive measures resonated more than repressive ones, since many police officials, clergy, and teachers believed that film also had potential educational benefits.[34] The Catholic Church and People's League for Catholic Germany filmed several theologically impeccable Passion plays; teachers considered many documentaries and newsreels praiseworthy, and the government, convinced of the propagandistic value of motion pictures, brought pressure to bear on the German film industry to produce more commercially attractive patriotic films. But all these concerted efforts seem to have had little effect on the reading habits or viewing tastes of young workers, who loyally stood by Nick Carter and Asta Nielsen despite official disapproval.

Of course, fear of rising juvenile delinquency was one of the initial stimuli setting the entire youth salvation effort in motion, and reducing youthful crime was one of the major objectives of the attack on penny dreadfuls and immoral films. Because of their desire to curb delinquency, youth savers were also committed to reforming juvenile law and such closely associated institutions as the courts and reformatories. Debates over the treatment of juvenile delinquents and wayward youth can be traced back to the 1870s. An amendment to the Imperial Criminal Code in 1876 made it easier for officials to take wayward and neglected children away from their families and place them in public institutions.[35] Although this change was minor, it inaugurated a new discourse about wayward youth that was concerned with policing the lower-class family. Jurists soon added another strand to this new discourse. As Detlev Peukert argued in his history of youth welfare and social discipline:

Whereas on the one side the number of such pedagogues and welfare workers grew, who above all denied the competence of the lower-class family in industrial society to carry out normal childrearing in the sense of contemporary models and thereby in terms of social policy placed the primacy of family childrearing in question, there arose among jurists, on the other side, a similarly directed movement in terms of results that was convinced of the inefficacy of the previous system of criminal law, especially for juvenile delinquents, and that therefore demanded more scope for an educational reaction to norm-violating behavior.[36]

Prominent jurists like Franz von Liszt called for concentration on the young offender, not on the offense, for more attention to be paid to the sociological conditions and biological constitutions of young offenders. They also believed that it was essential to separate supposedly congenital young criminals from the improvable, to render the former harmless and to educate the latter. Such a "paradigm shift" in criminal law, a shift toward the pedagogization of youth criminal law, resulted, as Peukert claims, from a complex interaction among "social reform concerns, changes in the human sciences, and a general crisis of the hitherto liberal legal thought."[37]

Debates over the new Imperial Civil Code of 1896 and the Prussian Welfare Education Law of 1901 pushed juvenile delinquents and wayward youth into the forefront of public attention and hence gave new impetus to the newer social and pedagogical currents.[38] Many of the reformers were disappointed with the new Civil Code, however, since its protection of the rights of families against governmental interference struck them as a retreat to older liberal juristic concepts of the minimalist state. To be sure, the new code contained a clause that allowed an adoption court to place a minor with a suitable family or to enter a minor in to an educational institution or reformatory when a father neglected or abused the minor's mental or physical well-being or when the minor was threatened with complete moral ruin. The interpretation of the highly elastic phrase "complete moral ruin" unleashed much controversy.[39] When the Imperial Civil Code was first debated, this restriction had been introduced by Socialists and Catholic Centrists, who were worried that the law would be applied in a discriminatory fashion against parents with unpopular political or religious views. On pragmatic grounds jurists were generally satisfied with the clause, since they feared that if evidentiary requirements to demonstrate parental neglect were relaxed, the welfare education system would be overwhelmed. But many teachers and other youth savers dismissed earlier fears about political and religious abuses of the law as purely theoretical and instead lamented that the courts were lax and the law toothless. Speakers at a conference of the Center for Youth Welfare held in Berlin in 1906 cited supposedly hair-raising examples of children of prostitutes and pimps who regularly witnessed grossly immoral acts. But despite repeated complaints, judges ostensibly refused to deprive such parents of their children. Hence speakers called for strengthening the law so that prophylactic measures could be taken before the minor was completely ruined and embarked on a life of crime. Prussia's Welfare Education Law and those of several other states, including Hamburg, Baden, and Bavaria, which were passed immediately after the new Civil Code, were in part meant to offset the deficiencies that the reformers found in the Civil Code. But although these new laws generally extended broader powers to the adoption courts, they were nontheless constrained by the Imperial Code. Still, the replacement of the term "forced education" (*Zwangserziehung*) with "welfare education" (*Fürsorgeerziehung*) and the transference of jurisdiction over wayward youth from criminal courts to adoption courts illustrate the shift in conceiving and treating both neglected and delinquent youths. Both categories of youth, which often overlapped, were now considered unfortunate products of unfavorable social circumstances, to be reformed by pedagogical action.

Increasingly the cases of accused juvenile delinquents were turned over to special juvenile courts, based on U.S. experiments.[40] Such courts had been discussed at the German Jurist Conventions of 1903 and 1904, and in 1905 the Berlin administrative court councillor Paul Köhne explained the U.S. juvenile court system to the Berlin Jurist Society and had published a proposed law to institute such courts. By 1908 juvenile courts were operating in Frankfurt am Main and Cologne. The Prussian Justice Ministry soon backed this movement toward special juvenile courts and by 1912 almost 40 percent of all German administrative courts had set up some sort of distinct juvenile justice system. Juvenile courts ensured that young defendants would be treated more mildly than adults and that publicity would be minimized so that youths wouldn't be labeled criminals for life. One reason for the rapidity of the spread of juvenile courts was that high youthful recidivism rates persuaded judges that such traditional punishments as warnings, fines, and jail sentences were often counterproductive.[41] A warning had little effect, fines often only harmed the youth's family, and jail terms put the young offender in the company of hardened and habitual criminals and permanently damaged his future prospects by marking him as a convict. Moreover, despite some protests from conservatives and theologians who deplored the elimination of a notion of sin, young offenders were increasingly seen as products of demoralized families and wretched urban milieus, a disease of the social body requiring therapeutic care, rather than as willfully depraved individuals. This shift in perspective from emphasis on individual responsibility to social causation, already foreshadowed in the 1880s and 1890s by Franz von Liszt, reflected the shift from individualism and Manchester liberalism to social and statist liberalism. It was even lauded by the Socialists as a revolution against individualism in legal thought.[42]

In keeping with this new social and medical image of the young offender, judges began soliciting reports on youths' social environment and moral development from teachers, psychiatrists, and welfare workers, the last sometimes employed directly by the juvenile courts.[43] Such reports, as well as advice from the local welfare committees composed of teachers, clergy, local officials, and other professionals, were de facto accepted as evidence in juvenile court proceedings. Thus the delinquent was becoming the ward of welfare professionals, themselves often key figures in promoting the youth salvation campaign. Youths under eighteen, who were absolved from moral responsibility for their crimes because they were deemed to lack sufficient insight into the criminal nature of their acts, almost 9 percent of young defendants in Berlin, could either be released or handed over to an adoption court for placement in welfare education.[44] Even when youths were judged to be criminally liable and convicted, juvenile justices had considerable power to exercise discretion in meting out punishment. The youth might well be sentenced to a prison term, but if he agreed to welfare education, he would be pardoned or his sentence commuted.[45] Conservatives deplored the emphasis on welfare education, which they thought was weakening individual responsibility and deterrence. But proponents of the new system replied that since the youth remained under surveillance and without liberty until his twenty-first year, many delinquents found the new system more punitive than a shorter jail term under the old one.

Coupled with this reform of the juvenile justice system was an attempt to remove any stigma from the welfare education system and to eliminate the most glaringly penal features of reformatories and institutes for wayward youths. In keeping with the youth savers' family values and notions of the close connection between the temptations of urban streets and juvenile delinquency, they considered it best if youths assigned to welfare education were placed with families, especially the families of artisans or farmers, in small towns or the countryside, where they might learn a useful trade in a more wholesome environment.[46] Care had to be taken, however, to guarantee that the motives of families applying for welfare education internees were not purely mercenary and that their youthful charges actually would acquire skills that suited them and would enable them to support themselves, rather than being used as cheap hands or working for masters in declining trades, who could no longer find regular apprentices.

When family placement proved impossible, youths remained in welfare education institutes or reformatories, whether under government, church, or private auspices. But the directors of such institutes were now supposed to strive to make their establishments communities with educational, religious, and economic functions, communities of families with inmates housed in small units under the paternal care of a housefather.[47] Such a concept of a familylike milieu that would work on the ethical character of the internees and compensate for their lost bonds to family and community can be traced back to the foundation of Rauhen Haus in Hamburg by the Protestant minister Johan Wichern in Hamburg in 1833.[48] But it would only be with the youth salvation campaign in Imperial Germany that Wichern's ideas, which had stressed social bonds and responsibilities against the individualism of early liberalism, would come to fruition.

A jaillike atmosphere was undesirable, since it just engendered mistrust and resistance. Certainly, the milder regime meant that some older and rough juvenile criminals escaped. Several cases of arson and assaults on directors had been made into journalistic sensations.[49] Such incidents could be decreased, it was thought, if internees were categorized and sorted more carefully, the younger and less vicious separated from the older and more refractory. Directors were also advised to divide out the psychopaths and feeble-minded, who could be placed under the supervision of psychologically trained personnel. More homogeneous institutions would allow directors to individualize the treatment of their internees to a greater degree. But whatever the state of the inmates, according to the Protestant pastor L. Platz, director of the educational home in Zehlendorf, love, trust, and freedom, not walls and bars, were indispensable for fulfilling the primarily educational mission of these institutions.

Similar sentiments were apparently shared by the Prussian Education and Interior ministries, which jointly promulgated an order limiting corporal punishment of welfare education internees in Prussian reformatories.[50] Only the director of the institution was empowered to administer corporal punishment, except under extraordinary circumstances, and only in accordance with written institution regulations. An accurate record of punishments had to be kept, and it was open to examination by government inspectors. Punishment by isolation in a darkened cell was stringently restricted. The new model of discipline was to be that ordinarily practiced in the family or work-shop, not the penitentiary.

Instead of punitive measures, after the turn of the century, voca-tional training in useful crafts or gardening was emphasized, along with the practice of cooperation and sociability through sports, hikes, or the theater. Such activities would enable the internee to be rein-tegrated into society as a useful member upon attaining his majority.[51] According to Pastor Platz, in the past reformatory labor had often been far from edifying or ennobling. Such previously common ex-ploitative labor as the manufacture of tin buckets or matches under factory conditions had prompted revulsion from work. Instead of being condemned to such drudgery, internees needed to learn han-dicrafts and to acquire a thorough grounding in materials, tools, and techniques. Both crafts and sports were defended in terms adapted from Kerschensteiner's writings on civic education in continuation schools, which will be analyzed below. Again, conservative critics were highly suspicious of the new turn. They warned that reformatories and welfare education institutes should not be made so attractive that youths leaving them would be unsuited for the harsh world outside. It is doubtful that they had sufficient reason to fear since clearly most institutions fell far short of newly prescribed programmatic norms. Many of the penal features of the old "forced education law" persisted. Nor should the gray, monotonous, barrackslike character of refor-matories be underestimated.[52] Nonetheless, the youth law reform movement and the new legislation at the turn of the century inau-gurated a new phase in the treatment of juvenile delinquents and wayward youth. Now these youthful subjects of the judicial system were conceived of as being as conditioned by social and psychological causation rather than of being willfully depraved or sinful. A softer pedagogical model that stressed joyful labor and education to socia-bility within a familial community was replacing a harsher penal order enforced in jaillike surroundings. If a deep chasm undoubtedly yawned between program and practice, practice was slowly approach-ing the programmatic norms advanced by the youth savers.

Although youth savers expended considerable energy on stiffening protective legislation for young workers, safeguarding the morals of urban youth and revamping the juvenile justice system, most of their initiatives centered on creating or reshaping institutions that could perform the same disciplinary and controlling functions as those of the old patriarchal order while accommodating to the demands of a modern economy and liberalized polity. The two institutions best fulfilling these requirements would be the adult-supervised youth association and the mandatory industrial continuation school. Although both the Catholic and Protestant churches had been working with youth at the parish level for decades before 1900, neither had devoted much sustained or systematic attention to this area of work. Moreover, most of these parish groups professed strictly religious goals, reached via lectures on religious topics, Bible reading, and prayer. In his essay, which placed second in the essay contest of the Erfurt Academy in 1900, Hugo Blitz disparaged the previous youth work of the churches for its lack of imagination and inspiration.[53] As a model for what could be achieved, he outlined a pedantically detailed program for new obligatory youth associations. The goal of such associations was to raise "idealistically minded German citizens dedicated to the community." Municipalities were to set up well-accoutered youth centers with libraries, game rooms, lecture halls, gyms, and refreshment bars. Every young male who had completed primary school was to be required to spend at least one evening weekly at the center and every other Sunday. Good novels and nonfiction would be available, but no newspapers because of their often sensational content. Not only could youth read there, but they could also play board games, join the fife and drum corps or brass ensemble, sing in the choir, do gymnastic exercises, or learn handicrafts. Lectures on German art and literature would be held regularly. Youths could even buy carefully dispensed quantities of beer, and those over eighteen would be permitted to smoke. Occasionally the centers would hold well-chaperoned and properly chaste dances. Such centers were to be administered by the "natural authorities in the community – city councillors, clergymen, teachers, doctors, and elders," in conjunction with master artisans, fathers of members, and even representatives elected by the youths themselves. Thus Blitz's model associations were to appeal to youth by partially incorporating the pleasures of the bar and dance hall, albeit in highly regulated and watered-down forms, while simultaneously fostering those recreations that youth savers wholeheartedly approved. Youthful members would be granted a simulacrum of self-administration, while the reins of authority would remain firmly in the hands of middle-class adults. No single youth group or municipality ever adopted all of these suggestions, but Blitz's essay was nonetheless significant since it drew a prototype of the youth centers and associations organized under religious, private, secular, and municipal auspices that would proliferate throughout Germany over the next fourteen years.

The second institution most widely promoted by the youth savers was the mandatory industrial continuation school, an institution closely identified with the school superintendant of Munich, Georg Kerschensteiner. In 1900 Munich became the first city outside Saxony to mandate such part-time trade schools for all young males who had completed primary school. This extension of required education was carried through by the able and energetic Kerschensteiner, a former mathematics and science teacher, whose writings and lectures would soon establish him as one of the foremost youth savers and pedagogical thinkers of the period, not only in Germany, but throughout Europe and the United States.[54] His first-prize Erfurt essay, "Civic Education," which was reissued in numerous editions over the next decade and was probably the most frequently quoted document of the youth salvation campaign, was a lengthy exposition legitimating the continuation school and endowing it with a mission.

Kerschensteiner maintained that the modern constitutional state, with its broad array of civil rights, needed citizens dedicated to the general good if it was to survive in the intensified struggle among nations for existence.[55] He doubted, however, that modern civil society, with its clash of petty interests, produced selfless and self-limiting citizens. Instead, it was more likely to incubate narrow and self-serving egoists. Here lay the task for educators. Kerschensteiner's concrete proposals for the curriculum and programs of the continuation schools were designed to guide young workers by almost imperceptible steps from their egoistic interests in bettering their occupational skills to an altruistic concern for the community and the welfare of the state.

The school was to be mandatory for apprentices and workers between the ages of fourteen and seventeen.[56] Eight or nine hours of instruction would be scheduled weekly, preferably during daytime hours, when students were more alert. Initially instruction should concentrate solely on imparting industrial skills by acquainting students with the tools and materials most commonly used in their trades. Where possible, such workshop instruction should be taught by experienced artisans rather than by ordinary teachers. Such practical training was to be complemented by courses familiarizing students with bookkeeping and other common business procedures, courses that were obviously most relevant for students destined to become independent artisans. Whenever possible, instructors would interweave material in these courses relating the students' trades to the broader stream of German history. In industrial regions, teachers could insert the history of industrial labor or the rise of the British unions, whose bread-and-butter approach appeared to Kerschensteiner, as to many social liberals, such as the Munich economist Lujo Brentano, to be preferable to the class struggle and socialist orientations of German labor. Through such unforced linking of the individual's occupation with history, the student would begin to perceive himself as connected to a larger totality and begin to acquire a sense of civic responsibility. As the educational historian Wolf-Dietrich Greinert has argued, one of the major reasons for the success of Kerschensteiner's essay was that it combined an educational program based on the importance of the artisanal trade that was in keeping with government efforts to preserve the independent *Mittelstand* "with a pedagogical political program that exactly corresponded to the interests of civil [*bürgerliche*] society in an industrial state caught in the throes of rapid development."[57]

For Kerschensteiner, as for many educators at the turn of the century, moral development took precedence over intellectual attainments. Not only were continuation schools supposed to train students' minds and hands, they were also to meet students' needs for physical fitness, recreation, and sociability.[58] Kerschensteiner thought that gymnastics would be especially suitable for meeting these needs since it not only steeled the body, but when practiced in group formations, demanded precision, discipline, and cooperation. He also recommended regular evenings of entertainment, already held in the continuation school in Leipzig under the direction of Oskar Pache, the other major advocate of continuation schools. Such evenings should commemorate historical anniversaries and celebrate famous men with songs, declamations, and gymnastic routines performed by the students. Continuation schools were additionally charged with fostering a variety of voluntary clubs that would shape a sense of collective identity and common achievement. To demonstrate the ways in which voluntary associations nurtured public virtues, Kerschensteiner pointed to the relation between vibrant club life and pervasive civic spirit among the English. Private educational and athletic associations, among them the German Gymnasts, the largest nationalist sports association, were to be drawn into the recreational work of these schools. This would give middle-class associations the opportunity to reach young workers and thereby begin to dismantle class barriers. When conjoined with classroom instruction, such extracurricular activities would contribute to weaning students from personal, trade, and class egoism and winning them to supraindividual projects and communally oriented altruism.

As Kerschensteiner recognized, however, his entire program depended on the initial assumption that the student possessed trade egoism, that he was vitally interested in improving his skills.[59] When such interest was absent, even the best-organized continuation school would confront insuperable impediments. In Munich, where almost 13 percent of the students were unskilled messengers, delivery boys, and day laborers whose relation to labor was purely instrumental, the school was virtually powerless to elicit their active participation. When faced with the unskilled, the schools encountered the limits of educability. For such unfortunate youths, Kerschensteiner proposed alternative forms of social disciplining. He especially believed that paramilitary formations modeled after the British Boys' Brigades might prove useful in accustoming these youths to order and discipline. Moreover, such brigades would be officered by middle- and upper-class adults, whom he hoped these youths would come to respect and rely upon. But even such paramilitary formations, with their drills, uniforms, and exercises, were merely means to achieve religious and ethical ends. The fact that in Britain the drills of the Boys' Brigades were preceded by a sermon and closed with a hymn and that the Brigades were attached to parish churches received his warm praise. Through such paramilitary dressage, Kerschensteiner hoped that those whom he regarded as potentially dangerous young outcasts might be transformed into free and ethical citizens who would ultimately voluntarily support the state. But for liberal youth savers like Kerschensteiner, whose model of man and citizen presupposed self-determining, self-disciplined individuals, unskilled workers would constitute a corrosive problem, constantly gnawing at the foundations of their optimistic assumptions. As Kerschensteiner's program for the unskilled also suggests, fear of the disorderliness of unskilled youth would make many youth savers very susceptible to supporting the militarization of youth work.

In 1901, when the Center for Workers' Welfare Institutions held its annual convention in Munich and once again made young workers the topic of its sessions, participants spent one afternoon visiting the city's refashioned continuation schools.[60] Following this tour, several speakers cautioned against prescribing continuation schools as a panacea for the youth problem, but most apparently concurred with Voigt, who noted that these schools were the only institutions that could encompass and permanently influence all young workers and hence should be made obligatory in all German cities. As we shall see in the next chapter, by 1910 such schools had become virtually universal in major German cities.

This introduces the final point about the early stage of the youth salvation campaign. During the decade after 1900, most of the impetus propelling youth salvation programs would be generated in the municipalities and would largely be underwritten by urban governments in cooperation with the churches and various private agencies. It was urban civil servants like Andreas Voigt or Georg Kerschensteiner and urban pastors like Hugo Blitz or Walther Classen who would formulate youth policy and spearhead the campaign. To be sure, they received some welcome assistance and funding from state governments. The Prussian ministries of Trade, the Interior, and Education issued joint circulars in January 1900, November 1901, and November 1905, pressing administrative officials to encourage teachers and clergy to become active in developing programs for recreation and welfare that could guard young males against moral dangers and ensure that they used their free time rationally between leaving primary school and entering military service.[61] The circular sent in 1900 designated the youth work of the Protestant ministers Walther Classen and Clemens Schultz in Hamburg and the Catholic Kolping Societies for journeymen as examples to be emulated. But apart from the inspirational and facilitating roles of praising effective youth welfare work and providing some financial supplements for continuation schools, state governments undertook relatively little. Officials seem to have had little sense of urgency about youth saving, as evidenced by the fact that the joint circular of the Prussian ministries of 1901 requested a follow-up report on the development of programs for youth only after two years. Thus although conferences and writings like those discussed in this chapter would forge a consensus, shape common perceptions and rhetoric, and result in considerable uniformity in the programs espoused by youth savers, the youth salvation campaign was decentralized, and there was considerable leeway for local variation and experimentation. Nonetheless, by 1901 the struggle to save Germany's young male workers from pernicious urban dangers had begun in earnest and rapidly assumed nationwide scope.

4

Vocation and civics: the continuation school in practice

As Georg Kerschensteiner, Oskar Pache, and the other youth reformers had advocated after the turn of the century, mandatory industrial continuation schools became the paramount municipally sponsored socializing agencies for young urban working-class males who had completed elementary school and entered the labor force. Although playing down the controversy these schools generated in Germany, in 1907 M. E. Sadler, an English historian of education in Manchester, concisely summarized the combination of concerns about national competitiveness and moral policing, of urban anxieties and schemes for reasserting discipline that inspired the decisive transformation of these schools:

> The view that technical training following upon a good general education has become indispensable to the industrial and commercial success of a nation commands the unreserved assent of the German people.... And therefore as soon as it was realized that modern conditions of industry and commerce threatened to deprive young people of the educational care that was previously provided through apprenticeship, the idea of compulsory attendance at suitable continuation schools rapidly grew in favour among the workpeople and, though more slowly, among the mass of employers also. But it was not to economic interests alone that the growth of this opinion was due. Moral considerations supported it. Fears were felt that the moral welfare of the nation would suffer if no measures were taken to counteract the deteriorating influences of town and city life during the first years of a youth's freedom from the discipline of day school life.[1]

Although it was only around 1900 that mandatory industrial continuation schools spread throughout Germany, they had a long prehistory, and their legal foundation had been laid during the early years of the Reich. German educators often traced the origins of the continuation school back to the sixteenth century, when in the wake

73

of the Reformation, the churches instituted obligatory Sunday schools for young people who had been confirmed.[2] But a more plausible and proximate origin could be discovered in responses to nascent factory competition with traditional crafts during the first decades of the nineteenth century. Between 1820 and 1840 many states and cities, often in conjunction with the guilds, created voluntary Sunday or evening schools for the further education of artisanal apprentices. Such schools, which in many respects resembled the mechanics institutes in England, concentrated on general education and technical drawing, the sort of instruction that appealed to diligent and self-improving apprentices and journeymen. With the abolition of the guilds during the 1850s and 1860s, the heyday of Manchester liberalism in Germany, continuation schools languished. These schools were given new impetus, however, by the movement for educational reform that accompanied the founding of the Reich.

Both the Industrial Code of Bismarck's North German Confederation in 1869 and the almost identical Industrial Code of the new Reich contained provisions enabling communities to make continuation schools mandatory for youths under eighteen years of age and requiring employers to release their young employees to attend such schools during working hours.[3] In Prussia and several other German states these statutes would provide the legal basis for obligatory continuation schools until the 1920s. In many of the other states, however, the schools received a more secure legal underpinning when educational ministries remodeled their educational systems in the early 1870s, usually along lines favored by the dominant liberals, with considerations of promoting industrial development and fostering national loyalty figuring prominently. In Saxony, Hesse, and Baden, for example, by 1874, as part of a broader educational reform that included the introduction a more modern curriculum in the primary schools, continuation schools were made obligatory for males between the ages of fifteen and eighteen having only elementary educations. These schools were assigned the tasks both of reviewing the lessons in German and arithmetic learned and often immediately forgotten in the primary schools and teaching general skills, such as mechanical drawing, which were useful in a variety of trades and industrial employments. Indeed, until the turn of the century these schools had an indistinct mission, since they oscillated between general education, supplementing the program of the primary schools, and craft-oriented vocational education.

During the 1870s a number of voluntary associations, such as the

Society for the Propagation of Popular Education (Gesellschaft für Verbreitung von Volksbildung), and economic pressure groups, such as the Association of Middle Rhenish Industrialists (Mittelrheinische Fabrikanten Verein) proposed extending such schools to the entire Reich. The Society for Popular Education, whose members included liberal notables, such as the supporter of artisanal cooperatives, Hermann Schultze-Delitsch, and the future Prussian finance minister, Johannes von Miquel, as well as prominent educators, was especially active in this area.[4] Its members viewed these schools as a means for preserving the artisanate, fostering nationalism, and countering the Socialists. The case for extension was put forward by the Saxon manufacturer and leading member of the Society for the Propagation of Popular Education, Fritz Kalle, at the 1878 plenum of the Social Policy Association.[5] There, Kalle decried the decay of industrial competence, the moral confusion, and the growth of socialism, which he considered by-products of the disintegration of the artisanal order and the patriarchal apprenticeship relation. To offset loosening institutional constraints on young males and improve industrial skills, he championed mandatory continuation schools. Such concerns about the deficit in secondary socialization would remain central to all discussions of continuing education. But most of the German states, including the largest, Prussia, ceded the right to decide whether to support continuation schools to the municipalities, although state ministries framed guidelines for such schools.

In Prussia the continuation schools gained a new lease on life during the economically depressed 1880s as a facet of social protectionism calculated to preserve the artisanate and of official concern over the competitiveness of German arts and crafts with those of France.[6] In accordance with requests from reconstituted guilds (*Innungen*) of Berlin, in 1883 Bismarck transferred the affairs of continuation and trade schools (*Fachschulen*) from the Education Ministry (*Kultus*) to the Prussian Ministry for Commerce and Industry (*Handel und Gewerbe*), a transfer of administrative jurisdiction that was supposed to ensure that such schools would develop in tandem with the needs of industry and the handicrafts.[7] As a token of its new role, the Trade Ministry soon made provision to assist Prussia's 664 local continuation schools in upgrading drawing instruction.[8] At the same time, many guilds required attendance by their apprentices, thus providing these schools with a stable constituency. The previously informal bond between trade and continuation schools and the artisanate was further strengthened by the Handicrafts Law of 1897, which mandated continuing education for apprentices of craftsmen belonging to official craft bodies like the guilds and chambers of handicrafts.

On the basis of such evidence, educational historians like Herwig Blankertz have concluded that craft education became normative for these schools, precluding specifically industrial forms of training, and that the character of the continuation schools in Wilhelmine Germany was stamped by reactionary preindustrial forces.[9] Although issues of craft preservation certainly loomed large in the development of the continuation schools during the last decades of the nineteenth century, such a judgment is open to question. Most educational reformers maintained that the crafts could be preserved only if the training of artisans was significantly reformed, only if artisans were willing to adjust to modern business methods and to adopt new techniques.[10] Moreover, the distinction between industrial and craft training is etched too sharply since, after all, many tools and operations were much the same both in small artisanal shops and in factories.[11] Finally, Blankertz overlooks the considerable transformation that these schools underwent at the turn of the century, and her position makes it difficult to interpret the often vociferous opposition voiced by much of the artisanate against the direction these schools took after 1900, opposition that we will subsequently explore.

By contrast, Wolf-Dietrich Greinert, who acknowledges such widespread artisanal opposition, has advanced a more subtle position.[12] He claims that after the Handicraft Law of 1897, the schools became compromise formations embodying two counterposed conceptions of stabilizing the social order by preserving the artisanate. The first was an anticapitalist social protectionist one favored by artisans and supported by the Conservative and Center parties. Through their support for legally recognized mandatory guilds and chambers of handicrafts, proponents of this view sought to restore the preindustrial corporate order. The second position was a liberal one, held by Kerschensteiner or the Magdeburg city councillor Sombart. Spokespersons for this position asserted that improved education was the key to artisanal preservation. Better technical and business training would enable craftsmen to survive in a competitive economy. Within this compromise formation, however, Greinert considers the first conception dominant and the second subordinate, an evaluation that brings his analysis close to Blankertz's. The notion of the continuation schools as compromise formations is certainly a valuable one, but Greinert's overall interpretation can be challenged on two grounds. First, although the major justification for the expansion of the continuation

Table 4.1. *Expansion of industrial continuation schools and enrollments in the leading German states, 1885–1910*

State	1885		1910	
	Schools	Enrollments	Schools	Enrollments
Prussia	664	58,400	2,162	352,000
Bavaria[a]	256	24,031	356	60,093
Saxony[a]	n/a	n/a	208	30,384
Württemberg[a]	158	10,152	208	21,608
Baden[a]	n/a	n/a	194	18,721
Hesse[a]	n/a	n/a	156	9,521

[a]These states, in contrast to Prussia, retained general continuation schools in smaller communities. Enrollments of males at general schools in 1910 were 124,742 in Bavaria, 91,931 in Saxony, 27,133 in Württemberg, 21,857 in Baden, and 26,431 in Hesse. *Source:* Compiled from Alfred Kühne, "Die Fortbildungsschule," in *Die jugendliche Arbeiter in Deutschland,* 6, *Schriften der Gesellschaft für Soziale Reform* (Jena, 1912), pp. 11–12, 52–4.

schools was unquestionably preservation of the artisanate, the schools soon acquired functions that went well beyond their original purpose. Second, as will be shown, Greinert overestimates the weight of the antimodernist coalition in influencing the direction of the continuation schools. It would be the liberal educators, not the artisans and their supporters, who would largely shape the continuation schools.

What is indisputable, however, is the enormous expansion of the number of continuation schools and enrollments throughout Germany between 1885 and 1910 (see Table 4.1). Requirements for attendance soon extended from craft apprentices to all young workers, whether skilled or unskilled. (Even commercial employees with only an elementary education were generally legally bound to enroll in special commercial continuation schools.) In Prussia by 1900 Rhenish cities were in the process of erecting the scaffolding for mandatory industrial continuation schools. Berlin legislated compulsory continuation schools in 1905, and by 1910 all Prussian cities with populations over one hundred thousand, with the exception of Essen, had passed such statutes. Nor were continuation schools confined to large cities. By 1910 most towns with populations of over ten thousand and even many rural communities had followed suit.[13]

In order to gain a sense of the nature of urban continuation schools as they took shape at the turn of the century – their organization, financing, facilities, teachers, disciplinary regimes, curricula, and extracurricular activities – it will be best to examine them on a local basis. Two systems that elicited substantial interest from government officials, educators, and foreign visitors and can be taken as representative were those of Munich, where the schools were refashioned by Kerschensteiner in 1900, and those of Düsseldorf, which first began operation in 1902.[14] There is a further reason for scrutinizing these two systems. The case for the artisanally oriented character of these schools can be argued most forcefully for Munich, where small-scale craft shops continued to predominate throughout the Imperial era, whereas in Düsseldorf, with its burgeoning metallurgical and machine industries, the continuation school presented a somewhat different and slightly more industrial face.

In Munich general continuation schools had existed since 1875, but as the name implied, the curriculum consisted exclusively of general education courses like arithmetic and German supplemented by mechanical drawing, detached from any specific trade.[15] Moreover, classes were held either in the late evening or on Sunday afternoons so as not to interfere with working hours, which meant that students arrived either exhausted or resentful. Hence the accomplishments of the schools were meager at best. Almost immediately upon becoming the director of Munich's schools in 1895, Kerschensteiner embarked on a major program of educational reform. His most novel innovation lay in his emphasis on the principle that the students' particular trades should constitute the core of the curriculum, which he thought would both have practical advantages and immeasurably heighten student interest.[16]

To realize this principle, he sought to enlist the aid of the guilds, to persuade them that a broader education of their apprentices was vital for the future well-being of the trades and to encourage the active participation of guild members in the affairs of the schools. Despite considerable resistance from many of the guilds, by 1900 he had secured the cooperation of the butchers, bakers, shoemakers, hairdressers, and chimney sweeps, all rather low-reputation trades that probably hoped to enhance their status through education. The city set up special craft workshops where their apprentices could be instructed, and guild officials were involved in planning curriculum, teaching, inspecting, and supplying materials. Other crafts were gradually if grudgingly converted to the new system, such that by 1912 workshop instruction was available for Munich's over six thousand apprentices in fifty-two distinct trades. Munich boasted four buildings

Table 4.2. *Curriculum and hours per week at the Munich industrial continuation schools*

Subject	Class			
	1	2	3	4
A. For mechanics				
Religion	1	1	1	—
Arithmetic and bookkeeping	1	1	1	1
Reading and business composition	1	1	1	—
Civics and hygiene	1	1	1	1
Trade drawing	3	2	3	3
General physics	2	—	—	—
Mechanics with practical work	—	3	2	4
Total	9	9	9	9
Voluntary practical work	—	4	4	4
B. General course of the unskilled				
Religion	1	1		
Composition and reading	1	1		
Arithmetic	2	2		
Civics and hygiene	1	1		
Gymnastics and swimming	1	1		
Drawing and handicrafts	2	2		
Total	8	8		

Source: Georg Kerschensteiner, *The Schools and the Nation* (London, 1914), pp. 319–21.

in various neighborhoods solely devoted to such craft instruction, although a few of the larger clusters, such as building and metalworking trades, could only be housed in special workshops and classrooms attached to elementary schools throughout the city. After 1907, young workers who were employed in trades with fewer than twenty apprentices, unskilled laborers, and even unemployed youths were also compelled to attend continuation schools, but they were assigned to general classes. The period of required attendance for the general students was limited to only two years, in contrast to four for the skilled. Kerschensteiner was also successful in placing instruction during daytime hours and on weekdays, with each apprentice usually attending classes for four hours on two afternoons. But school officials attempted to accommodate shopfloor schedules of various trades by canceling classes in peak seasons, such as before Christmas or during Carnival (see Table 4.2).

In Düsseldorf the organization of the continuation schools was in most respects similar to that in Munich. There, too, concerns over artisanal survival loomed large, since the stimulus for reorganizing the continuation school, which had been in existence as a Sunday and evening drawing school since the 1830s, came from the Prussian Handicraft Law of 1897. Soon after its passage, several local newspapers launched a campaign to regenerate the school. The *Düsseldorfer Volksblatt,* allied with the Catholic Center party, called for closer integration between the work of the school and the shopfloor and for adding craft representatives to the board of directors to facilitate this. The politically colorless *General Anzeiger* expressed the fear that the crafts in Düsseldorf were falling behind those in Cologne and other regional cities and held that a mandatory continuation school might halt this slide by bettering artisanal skills.[17] This press campaign combined with pressure from the Trade Ministry prompted the city council to reconsider whether to make the school mandatory, a policy it had previously voted down.[18] In late 1898 the city council selected a committee to investigate continuation schools in other cities and to draw up proposals for the local school. After two years of assiduously collecting information and visiting schools in Saxony and Hannover, where continuation schools were already mandatory, the committee issued its report in 1901.[19]

This report embodied the moral and intellectual perspectives and shared much the same outlook and vision as Kerschensteiner's almost concurrent essay, "Civic Education." Since only 15 percent of the city's economically active males under eighteen years of age were enrolled in a continuation or technical school, and since even these were often tardy or absent, henceforth the school would be mandatory. The revamped school was charged with the threefold task of imparting intellectual, vocational, and moral education. Although the continuation school was not conceived as a mere prolongation of primary school, it was to offer some measure of general education, especially for young workers who had been unable to complete primary school or who had been educated in inferior rural schools before migrating to the city. All students, however, needed civic education as a requirement for contemporary public life. On this issue, the report avowed, "Universal manhood suffrage and the self-administration of modern social and economic institutions also demand of the worker a certain level of civic knowledge and an understanding of a citizen's rights and duties that cannot be taught in the primary schools." Nonetheless, since the foremost task of the school was to rescue the handicrafts and counteract the one-sided training and stultification resulting from an excessive division of labor, the main emphasis of instruction would be on teaching principles that underlay practical shopfloor experience. The report also asserted the necessity for the school to assume the role of moral preceptor since urban youths were becoming irreligious, unpatriotic, materialistic, and amoral, qualities usually attributed to Socialists, but it incorporated no specific course in moral instruction and rejected mandatory religious instruction, a controversial subject throughout Prussia, ostensibly because of lack of time.

Several sections of the report handled organizational questions. Attendance was to be mandatory for all regularly employed male youth under seventeen years of age. The unskilled were also encompassed since many subsequently switched to skilled employment; the boundaries between skilled, semiskilled, and unskilled were fluid, and if the unskilled were exempted, many young workers might flock to unskilled jobs to avoid schooling, thus undercutting the purpose of the schools. As was the case in all continuation schools, however, the school's program both confirmed and solidified the fundamental division between apprentices and the unskilled, and in fact cemented the lines separating the various crafts. Students were to be placed in classes according to their occupations, although when necessary, certain closely related crafts, such as shoe- and saddlemaking, might be combined. Students were to attend classes two hours a day, three times weekly, preferably in the mornings when they would be more alert, although the report recognized that it might be necessary to schedule evening classes to placate various trades. To ensure that the needs and interests of the trades were taken into consideration in designing the school, the committee regularly consulted the Chamber of Handicrafts, and both master artisans and factory owners were heavily represented on the school's board of directors after its inception.[20]

On March 19, 1901, the committee submitted its report to the city council, which unanimously endorsed it after a brief discussion.[21] As a concession to the objections of businessmen, the council pared the number of years of mandatory instruction from three to two, a position it reversed two years later. The objection of several council members to charging employers fees for each of their young employees was also symptomatic of the tension between the costs of reproducing qualified labor and immediate profitability that would be expressed periodically in debates over continuation school finances. But Lord Mayor Marx pointed out that since employers would directly benefit from this education, imposing a modest annual fee of six marks per student was reasonable.

Neither fees from employers nor supplemental city funds were adequate, however, to meet the starting costs of the mandatory continuation school.[22] Hence its inauguration was delayed until spring of 1902 so that a special grant of twenty thousand marks could be obtained from the Prussian Trade Ministry. Financial difficulties and disputes over funding would plague these schools throughout the late Imperial era. Operating expenses soared from seventy-five thousand marks the first year to almost four hundred thousand marks in 1913/ 14, 85 percent of which went for salaries. (By 1902 the budget in Munich, where costs per pupil would invariably be triple those in Düsseldorf because of superior workshop facilities, was already more than two hundred thousand marks, which, as Kerschensteiner understatedly noted, was "by no means light.") In 1914 employer contributions would account for less than one-eighth of the total costs since artisans were effective in blocking any increase in the fee adopted in 1902. The city paid most of the expenses from its regular education budget, but an annual subvention from the Trade Ministry was also needed to keep the schools functioning. Out of a total of almost 9.7 million marks budgeted for industrial continuation schools in Prussia in 1912, the Trade Ministry spent 3.3 million marks, 34 percent of the total, while the communities themselves expended over 5.0 million marks (52 percent) and employers contributed 1.1 million (11 percent).[23] In addition to funding ongoing operating costs, cities had to advance the original outlay for equipping schools with workshops.

One of the initial handicaps that hobbled the Düsseldorf school was the absence of specialized facilities for craft instruction. Orginally classes met in ordinary primary school rooms that were not outfitted for vocational education. Moreover, the desks were often too low and small for growing adolescents. Only in 1910 was a central building constructed comparable to the four in Munich, with well-designed and properly accoutered workshops for instructing typesetters, printers, bookbinders, shoemakers, tailors, painters, upholsterers, paper hangers, decorators, barbers, bakers, and confectioners.[24] The Trade Ministry helped to finance the purchase of equipment for the central building, such as printing presses and heating ovens for the irons of tailor apprentices.[25]

Just as classes met in primary schools, so too the classroom instruction was originally entirely in the hands of 114 primary school teachers and rectors hired on a part-time basis, a common practice throughout Germany.[26] Over the years, however, the composition of the teaching corps incrementally altered in favor of the technically qualified. By

1912, of the forty-seven full-time continuation school instructors in Düsseldorf, twenty-six had technical backgrounds, as did fourteen of the one hundred part-time teachers. But even the primary school teachers who taught in continuation schools were obliged to familiarize themselves with the world of industry and the workshop. In 1903/4 the Düsseldorf Commercial Art School began training regular drawing instructors to master techniques for machine and construction blueprints.[27] The Ministry of Trade developed a series of formalized seminars in Berlin to prepare primary teachers for continuation school instruction.[28] For example, a month-long seminar on industrial affairs covered bookkeeping, cost accounting, credit, cooperatives, the Industrial Code, industrial health, housing hygiene, civics, and an introduction to basic economic concepts. By 1913 continuation school teaching had become professionalized and distinctive enough that a year-long seminar could be offered.[29]

Still, the initial reliance on primary school teachers brought numerous problems in its wake. Teachers who had often taught the same youths a year or two earlier in primary school apparently had difficulty treating their sometimes touchy adolescent charges as more mature and economically active young men. As a result, continuation school teachers and administrators frequently debated the degree of authority the teacher should exercise and related issues, such as whether students should be addressed with the familiar *du,* as were children in primary school, or the formal *Sie* reserved for adults.[30]

Although the numerous photographs taken of continuation school classes after the turn of the century invariably show neatly attired, well-groomed young apprentices listening attentively to the instructor or working sedulously on some project, problems of authority and order bulked large in the early years.[31] Classes were often less than orderly and indeed were beset by student resistance, indiscipline, and absenteeism. A Munich school official in 1901 spoke of the active and passive resistance of the butchers' apprentices.[32] The first annual report in Düsseldorf admitted that students had exhibited little joy in their work and that resistance, both overt and latent, was noticeable.[33] Teachers sometimes complained of having to contend with general silence.[34] The unskilled were especially refractory, with absentee rates often exceeding 10 percent. Teachers divided the absentees into two types: the incorrigible loafers and those who were the sole supports of their families and hence were already weighted down by the burdens of life. "Most of these students live in sad circumstances, lack fatherly discipline or have escaped parental supervision, are often

work shy or live without regular work," asserted one report.[35] Those
forced to attend classes against their will sometimes responded by
"making instruction entirely impossible, with loud laughing, talking,
scraping their feet and roaring."[36] Some students sat crosswise on the
benches and urged their classmates to do likewise, perhaps in protest
of the diminutive size of the benches. A teacher who whipped students
to restore order, a form of discipline generally discouraged in continuation schools, was greeted by deafening *Katzenmusik* when he entered the darkened school courtyard after classes. The Prussian Trade
Ministry had suggested that rather than introducing schools for all
males from fourteen to seventeen at once, cities should expand the
schools gradually, starting with students who had just finished primary
school in order to avoid confrontations.[37] Most cities heeded this sug-
gestion, but even so, apparently, older unskilled workers, who regarded the idea of mandatory schooling for those already working as
an affront to their dignity, incited younger students to defy the authorities by skipping or disrupting classes.[38]

To maintain order and discipline, in every city continuation school
administrators issued standardized and elaborate codes to regulate
the behavior and deportment of students, codes that in Foucauldian
terms could be called mechanisms of normalization.[39] Students were
supposed to arrive at classes at the bell, scrubbed, wearing clean
clothes, and fully prepared, with all learning materials at hand. They
were to rise when the teacher entered and left the room and to obey
all orders and instructions promptly and willingly. They were forbidden to make loud noises or to engage in horseplay between classes or
in going to or from school. If absent, they were supposed to bring a
written excuse signed by their employer. The school even attempted
to control the leisure hours of students by prohibiting them from
going to taverns unless in the company of a parent or other responsible
adult and from frequenting public dances or smoking. In short, by
being deprived of the major public pleasures of working-class male
adulthood, students were to be reminded of their subaltern status.
But many of these provisions were either unenforceable or at best
partially observed.

Nonetheless, school authorities disposed over a broad battery of
sanctions to enforce these disciplinary codes. Students who failed to
reach the prescribed standards of the school could be compelled to
repeat a year.[40] Unskilled young workers, for example, were tested
on their comprehension of a narrative text of intermediate difficulty,
their ability to solve arithmetic problems, and their knowledge of

urban and national institutions. School authorities granted teachers discretion to weigh moral maturity and conduct in determining whether or not a student would pass. In addition to inscribing grades for course work, student report cards also bore assessments of diligence, attentiveness, and attendance that the student had to present for signature to his employer. Students repeatedly absent without excuse were forced to make up the lost hours on Sunday afternoons. If they refused to appear, the police could fetch them, or a civil court could summon and fine them.[41] Although corporal punishment was certainly legal, in most continuation schools it was rarely if ever used. The director of the Düsseldorf continuation school, Karl Gotter, believed that effective learning depended on trust between teachers and students. Hence, he frowned on corporal punishment except in extreme cases and fired "whipping pedagogues" who were unable to win the respect of their students by other means.[42] The Prussian Trade Ministry also recommended softer methods of pedagogy and as early as 1897 had warned teachers against resorting to disciplinary methods common in primary schools since the students were older and already working.[43]

With the passage of time, students became accustomed to the schools in both Munich and Düsseldorf, and although disciplinary problems certainly never disappeared, they nonetheless diminished. This process of accustomization was also aided by the greater practical orientation of the instruction and the regularization of the curriculum. A Munich school official claimed that when butcher apprentice classes began holding their sessions in the city's slaughterhouses, students demonstrated greater enthusiasm.[44] When the Düsseldorf school opened in 1902, apart from a preparatory class for youths who had only finished five years of primary school and eight general classes for the unskilled, all were at least nominally vocational, with courses for metalworkers, construction workers, commercial artists, butchers, bakers, barbers, gardeners, and leather workers.[45] Until 1908, when the city built a separate commercial continuation school, young clerical workers also had their own classes. But despite this division by trade, because of the lack of trained vocational teachers and proper facilities, the occupational emphasis was played down and subordinated to general education. Even by 1914, when school enrollments had increased fivefold to over 7,000 students partitioned into 289 classes, this deficiency had not been fully remedied. That year only 9 percent of class hours were given over to purely practical vocational training, whereas 60 percent were spent on civics, bookkeeping, or arithmetic, and 31 percent on drawing.[46] On the basis of such evidence, one might well conclude, not without considerable justification, that Kerschensteiner's concept of a continuation school unified around the student's trade remained something of an ideological fiction.[47]

In terms of vocational training, even in Düsseldorf, the crafts fared best. As mentioned, the central building was fitted with numerous craft workshops. Moreover, several of the guilds worked closely with the school authorities to guarantee that instruction was attuned to the demands of the shopfloor.[48] The bakers' guild, for example, whose apprentices were known for their ability and uprightness, took a warm interest in the progress of the school. The shoemakers, tailors, decorators, and typesetters all agreed to eight hours of weekly instruction for their apprentices, rather than the standard six. Although in the prewar years Gotter repeatedly proposed more specialized courses for young metalworkers, apart from a laboratory for electricians, there were no courses planned solely for industrial apprentices. Gotter considered this the gravest shortcoming of the school and thought that rectifying it was crucial if German industry was to stay abreast of its English and U.S. competitors. As a model, he pointed to the apprentice workshops of major industrial firms, such as Krupp or the Nürnberg Machine Factory.[49]

Nonetheless, some of the general courses, especially drawing, contained a strong industrial component. Apparently the efforts of the commercial art school to train teachers for industrial drawing were crowned with success. When Arthur Shadwell, a leading English proponent of national efficiency, visited the Düsseldorf continuation school, he was highly impressed by the drawing instruction "which is taught in the most methodical manner and on a carefully devised system. The principle is, while training the hand and eye, to make the exercise bear specifically upon the trade in which the pupil is engaged, and great ingenuity is expended on adapting the lessons accordingly."[50] The *General Anzeiger* waxed enthusiastic over an exhibition of student drawings in 1905, an exhibition that attracted many employers, remarking that the school was evidently surmounting its early growing pains and that "a diligent effort to accommodate the instruction to the real needs of industry is making itself felt."[51] The reporter singled out the drawings of the class of machine builders for special praise in this respect. Thus, despite the absence of workshops exclusively for industrial apprentices, it is clear that industrial interests were far from completely neglected.

The other courses offered in Düsseldorf were business and civics

instruction, both of which were supposed to raise the youth's awareness of his role, obligations, and rights in the workplace and the state.
Since apprentices might eventually own a shop or at least could aspire
to proprietorship, bookkeeping and business courses, which usually
took up an hour weekly, were intended to acquaint the students with
a few elementary principles of cost accounting and to impress on them
the importance of routine business procedures.[52] By contrast, the
bookkeeping course for the unskilled emphasized family finances and
consumerism. Each student was required to keep a personal and family account book that was used to teach him "the healthy percentages"
of income that should be allocated for rent, food, and recreation.[53]
The major goals of this course were to disabuse the young unskilled
worker of the notion that he was no longer economically dependent
on his parents and to habituate him to thrift. Far from presenting
some systematic analysis of the modern economy, instruction remained within the old middle-class moral framework that encouraged
laborers to be industrious, sober, and provident. Apart from bookkeeping, the business course for apprentices treated the historical
development of their trades, economic concepts like competition,
credit, and the division of labor; craft institutions like the guilds and
guild courts; and finally social legislation. Both skilled and unskilled
students learned the main features of Bismarckian social insurance
legislation and the youth protection provisions of the Industrial
Code.[54] In introducing these last topics, business courses intersected
with civics instruction, to which they were often closely linked.

According to the Berlin official and prominent youth reformer
Alfred Kühne, the task of civics instruction in the continuation school
was to make the young conscious of their relation to the workshop,
community, and Reich. It would "explain the development and operation of important institutions of public life, cultivate respect for
the law and constitution, foster love of locality [*Heimat*], fatherland,
and ruling house, and prepare the student to participate joyfully in
the life of the state."[55] Although he was skeptical that sixteen-year-
olds could be expected to grasp fully the complexity of public life,
like Kerschensteiner he maintained that the best prospect for success
was to proceed from the youth's trade and horizon of experience.

This was what teachers in Düsseldorf attempted to achieve. Instruction coursed outward from the city to the Reich and from the Reich
to the world. The point of departure was the history, municipal institutions, industry, and arts of Düsseldorf. Urban history was closely
associated with familiar landmarks, statues, and buildings. This type

of instruction stemmed from the movement for urban *Heimatschutz*, or urban preservation, that arose among teachers and other sectors of the urban middle classes after the turn of the century out of a combination of civic pride and nostalgia for the preindustrial city, and it was designed to overcome the supposed lack of historical sense and the uprootedness of urban students.[56] Teachers observed that young workers seldom made use of the city's resources and facilities, and they hoped that through such an approach their students' horizons would be broadened.[57] (Only 32 percent of the school's unskilled young workers, for example, had visited the mammoth industrial exposition of 1903; in contrast, however, 63 percent of the apprentices had seen it.) Students also studied those welfare institutions they would be likely to encounter, such as health insurance, and learned to apply for benefits. From municipal institutions, teachers moved on to the relation of Düsseldorf to Prussia and briefly discussed the constitutions of Prussia and the Reich, the rights and duties of citizens, administration, and military service.[58] The final terminal was Germany's position in the world, its foreign trade, tariffs, and colonies. Certainly the course extolled colonialism and ascribed the welfare system to the generosity of Wilhelm I; nonetheless, the image of the worker was that of a citizen endowed with rights and entitlements, rather than an obedient and depoliticized subject (*Untertan*), evidence of the essentially liberal spirit embodied in the curriculum.

Although upper-level civics instruction was similarly patterned in Munich, there, hygiene was included as well since the course aimed at "giving the boy an insight into a sensible way of living."[59] A muted anti-Socialist vision of social harmony was also highlighted in the instruction since it was to teach the student "to understand that the interests of all classes and all trades are necessarily interdependent." In the first year the focus was on manners and health:

Behaviour: manners in the house, in the school, in the street and in company, to superiors, to teachers and to employers. Hygiene: the physiology of the human body in general; nourishment, and the uses and disadvantages of various foods; breathing and the circulation of the blood, care of the skin, mouth and teeth; housing and clothing; work and recreation; improvement of the senses and care of the nerves. First aid in accidents. The chief source of disease; the cultivation of cleanliness.

Many doctors and medical officials hoped that such regular attention to hygiene could help combat venereal disease, alcohol abuse, urban degeneracy, and the deleterious effects of the work environment and keep the young fit for military service.[60] To these ends, the

Munich schools also mandated an hour weekly of gymnastics, swimming, or other sports – a course that was optional in Düsseldorf.

Optional, too, were a variety of voluntary associations and extracurricular activities appended to the continuation school that Kerschensteiner had argued were important vehicles for cultivating behavior and qualities conducive to good citizenship, such as self-restraint, altruism, and a sense of responsibility. Fostering these virtues and reinforcing patriotic sentiment numbered among the tasks set for the continuation schools' extracurricular program, both in Munich and Düsseldorf. Even before the mandatory continuation school had opened in Düsseldorf, the director had attended a seminar sponsored by the Prussian Trade Ministry on organizing recreational activities.[61] From the school's inception he worked assiduously to build an extensive extracurricular program, effort that was clearly successful because over the next decade government officials repeatedly commended the Düsseldorf school for being exemplary in this area.[62] Private associations were immediately drawn into the life of the school.[63] Volunteers from the German Gymnasts, Germany's largest and most patriotic sports association, led the optional evening gymnastic classes and used these as an opportunity to widen their largely middle-class membership by reaching out to young workers who would otherwise have been likely to gravitate to the Socialist-affiliated Worker Gymnasts. Apparently, however, their ability to retain continuation school students on a long-term basis proved limited. Spokesmen for nationalist associations like retired Admiral Westphal of the Naval League delivered lectures and presented slides of the German fleet to celebrate the kaiser's birthday and other patriotic festivals. A local choir dedicated to preserving and promoting German folk music participated in the school's annual graduation ceremony.

Some free-time activities were devised to enable students to acquire useful skills like stenography or first aid, others to introduce students to acceptably middle-class forms of edifying recreation.[64] Through the school, students could obtain inexpensive tickets to city-sponsored cultural events, such as the industrial exposition of 1903, a production of Schiller's *Maid of Orleans* to mark the centenary of the poet's death, and a lecture by the famous polar explorer, Ritter von Payer. At a more mundane level, the school's central building housed a reading room and a game room open on weekday evenings and Sundays. Some students joined the reading club or the school's small orchestra; others simply played chess, dominoes, or fleet maneuvers.[65] In the reading room, students leafed through illustrated magazines or read short stories, although the director regretted the unwillingness of students to check out technical literature from the school's 2,400-volume library and doubted that the collection served as an adequate dike against the flood of lurid penny dreadfuls widely consumed by the students. (In 1909 the Prussian government had charged the continuation schools with more actively combatting penny dreadfuls by building up their libraries, among other measures.) Attendance was high for special events like the kaiser's birthday celebration, sometimes reaching seven hundred students, and as many as one hundred students crowded into the game and reading rooms on ordinary weekday evenings. These figures certainly indicate a pressing need for public space where youths could foregather and socialize, as well as for entertainment, and they far surpassed attendance at comparable events held under the auspices of the Socialist or religious youth organizations.

Through their curriculum and recreational activities, continuation schools clearly attained a degree of legitimacy among young workers, but their programs continued to provoke controversy in the wider community, especially among the artisanate. Despite the heavy representation of master artisans on school boards of directors and the constant attempts of school authorities to secure the cooperation of artisanal corporations, many craftsmen were never reconciled to the continuation schools. Artisanal objections were of four kinds.[66] First, many preferred traditional practical craft instruction to the theoretical rational instruction purveyed by the continuation schools, which they thought eroded the master's authority. Second, they objected to such courses as civic education, which, they held, overemphasized rights and protective legislation. Third, they resented paying school fees for their apprentices, and fourth, they complained that the scheduled hours disrupted shop routine. In both Munich and Düsseldorf, however, after an initial storm of protest from artisans during the period when the continuation schools were becoming mandatory, such complaints subsided. By 1902 Kerschensteiner could write: "Many, if not all, of those who had first opposed the scheme were won over; many who at first derided or even abused it were converted by their own apprentices, who returned from the school with interest, with pleasure, and with useful practical knowledge of every description."[67] Two years later in Düsseldorf the Chamber of Handicrafts reported that fewer craftsmen spoke out against the school in meetings and that many thought that it "was absolutely necessary for the artisanal estate," and in 1908 Director Gotter of the Düsseldorf school stated sanguinely that artisans "no longer regard the school as a burdensome institution, but rather as a means for raising and advancing their estate, which naturally imposes sacrifices on them."[68] Such optimistic assessments, however, proved to be premature.

Two nationally publicized court challenges in 1909 awakened slumbering artisanal resentment.[69] The first of these cases challenged the legality of financing the schools from employers' fees in Prussia. The courts ultimately decided that such fees were legal but set an upper limit of ten marks annually. In the second and successful challenge, a judge ruled that a simple public notice of continuation school hours was insufficient. Instead, the hours had to be established legally as a local statute each semester. As these cases became known in Düsseldorf, artisans began withholding their apprentices. Absenteeism in craft classes rose to 10 percent, the same as for the unskilled and three times higher than the absentee rate for industrial apprentices.[70] In the hope that the guilds could apply pressure to recalcitrant craftsmen, the city began sending them lists of habitual absentees, but to little avail. Some artisans contrived heart-rending excuses about the hardships the hours entailed; others simply ignored requests to release their apprentices. In the case of some locksmiths who adamantly refused to release their students, Gotter pressed for revocation of their licenses to train apprentices.

While numerous artisans quietly boycotted the school, the more articulate executive committee of the United Guilds of Düsseldorf and the Semper Bund, a league of Catholic craftsmen, launched a frontal assault. When the Prussian Diet began deliberation on a new continuation school bill in 1911, the Semper Bund revived old grievances that had apparently been rankling for years. Spokesmen for the Bund testily criticized what they regarded as minimal artisanal input in the original planning of the school and claimed that the causes of conflict between the school authorities and the artisanate had remained constant for a decade: the hours of instruction, payment of fees, and the nature of the curriculum. At an artisans' assembly, B. Förster, the owner of a small foundry, developed these criticisms more systematically. Although he avowed that the Bund had no objection in principle to continuation schools, he insisted that these schools restrict themselves to very circumscribed tasks; namely, imparting German, arithmetic, and technical drawing. German instruction was to focus exclusively on raw materials, work processes, products, and tools, rather than on the duties of masters, health insurance, and the legal limits of work hours.

It is as if one regarded the school as a center of enlightenment against the dangers that threaten the apprentice. One can hardly expect us to regard such instruction as helpful in any respect. The Industrial Code, civic education, and explanations of the rights of apprentices have nothing to do with vocational education. On the contrary, they make craft training more difficult since they arouse the resistance, if only passive, of apprentices.[71]

In short, for many masters, the entire project of civic education constituted an attack on their authority. Förster also denounced what he considered the false humanism of youth welfare measures that sheltered the young from the raw wind of real life. "In this manner we are creeping toward state socialism," he thundered. If the government really wished to assist the artisanate, it would eliminate the fees. Since the schools were intended to supplement the primary schools, the government should bear the costs. That Förster's narrow-interest politics resonated widely among the artisanate is suggested by the fact that these points were also taken up by the United Guilds of Düsseldorf, which further demanded that the school return to its original two-year program, rather than remain at the three-year one.

Gotter, who had difficulty containing his enlightened burgher's contempt for these uneducated and clamorous craftsmen, summarily dismissed most of the charges. He maintained that the school authorities had always consulted with official craft bodies before reaching important decisions and that the sound apprentice training provided by the school was vitally important to a healthy *Mittelstand* and to the ability of Germany to conquer international markets.[72] Obviously, what was at stake were two divergent conceptions of *Mittelstand* policy. Gotter conceived the problem of preserving the artisanate largely in educational terms, a perspective common in liberal educational establishments. By contrast, the artisans themselves were more concerned with maintaining authoritarian preindustrial relations. But these divergent views and acerbic exchanges merely resulted in a stalemate. Many artisans persisted with their protests and whenever possible kept their apprentices from classes. The school continued to operate as before and to have the police enforce the local attendance ordinances. This persistent opposition certainly casts doubt on the evaluation of educational historians who have argued that continuation schools were purely craft institutions molded by backward-looking preindustrial forces and breathing a "spirit of clerical feudal reaction."[73] If they were so, then their supposed beneficiaries failed to appreciate this and indeed believed that these schools were economically disadvantageous and undermined authority within the workshop, whether intentionally or inadvertently.

During his exchanges with artisanal groups, Gotter pointed out that because of the nature of the workshop training offered in continuation school, the crafts had far fewer grounds for complaint than had large-scale industry.[74] Yet as early as 1902, a government factory inspector recounted that "wide circles of industry increasingly acknowledge the utility of well-conceived continuation school instruction, not only for the advancement of of participating young workers, but also for industry itself. . . . "[75] A Düsseldorf engineer, factory manager, and director of a machine manufacturers' interest association, writing in a leading technical journal, cautioned against overestimating the importance of the school for vocational training. "Beside the daily activity in the workshop under the continual factory discipline and instruction in practical work during the approximately 2,400 hours of yearly labor, the effect of the at most 240 hours of instruction at the continuation school is only ancillary."[76] Nonetheless, he considered it a worthwhile institution even for the unskilled. An aniline dye manufacturer who took an active interest in Düsseldorf's continuation schools held that although in general they accomplished little, they were quite helpful for able youths whose formal education would have otherwise terminated with graduation from primary school.[77] To be sure, during debates over a Prussian continuation school bill in 1911 the Central Association of German Industry petitioned against legally placing continuation school instruction during workday hours, but otherwise it raised no major objections to the schools.[78] Thus, although industrialists were not particularly enthusiastic about continuation schools, neither did they mount an active opposition, undoubtedly in part because they could more easily identify with business-oriented city councils than could the artisanate.[79] Rather than being purely passive on questions of vocational education, as has often been charged, in contrast to artisans or Socialist workers they could rest assured that their interests in educational programs would be expressed and defended within municipal government.

The positions of the political parties on continuation schools varied according to their constituencies, ideological commitments, and cultural presuppositions. Although in principle all of the parties supported continuation schools and regarded them as valuable institutions that helped to ensure the quality of German crafts and industrial wares, the debates in March 1911 over the Prussian Trade

Ministry's proposed bill regulating continuation schools on a statewide basis revealed significant differences.[80] These debates pitted conservative proponents of religious and moral instruction against liberal secularists, spokespersons for large-scale industry against defenders of a preindustrial corporate order, liberal nationalists against Socialists, who held that the schools should be purely vocational institutions. This proposed bill would have required all cities with populations of over ten thousand to institute mandatory continuation schools, extended continuing education to previously uncovered young workers, including those in insurance firms and government employees, standardized the curriculum of all Prussian schools, and given the Prussian government the right to confirm elected members to school boards. The most consistent support issued from the ranks of the liberal parties, to which most of the youth reformers and the urban educational establishment belonged. National Liberal spokespersons argued, however, that the industrialists should have greater input and were worried about expense. The Free Conservatives, closely associated with heavy industry in the Ruhr, backed the stance of the Central Association of German Industry by arguing that industry would be disrupted if instruction were placed during daytime hours, especially in industries with continuous production processes or in those, like textiles, in which youth made up a large percentage of the labor force. The Progressives fretted over the potentially tendentious nature of civics instruction and the possible abuse by the government of its veto power over school board members, matters also of concern to the Social Democrats, who accused the schools of being politically stupefying. Only the Progressives and Socialists favored extending continuation schools to young females. The Catholic Center party, although not formally opposed to the schools, sometimes lent its backing to the complaints of the conservative artisanate. In addition, it often protested vigorously against the purely secular nature of the schools.[81] The Conservatives, who, like the Center, saw the primary tasks of the schools as preserving the artisanate and deepening patriotism and moral values, also strongly endorsed the inclusion of religion as a mandatory subject. Several Conservative spokespersons adamantly opposed mandating continuation school for the unskilled. The Catholic Center party and Conservative party, which were securely bound in a political alliance in the Prussian Diet, were successful in amending the bill in committee to include articles that mandated religious instruction in Prussian continuation schools, placed clerics on the school board, and gave the education minister more power in shaping the law.[82] Recognizing that the amended bill was doomed to defeat, the trade minister withdrew it. (In Bavaria and other south German states, an hour of religious instruction weekly, taught by clergymen, was generally required. This instruction would have been problematic, however, in confessionally mixed regions, unless classes were reorganized on a confessional basis, which, as Prussian Trade Minister von Sydow pointed out, would only have sharpened religious distinctions.[83])

Perhaps more surprising than the support of the schools by industry was the generally favorable view of the continuation schools evident in the press of the Social Democratic party and Free Trade Unions.[84] One reason for this was the Socialist celebration of popular education, especially education with an industrial, scientific, and utilitarian bent. Another reason, however, was that although the schools were inspirited by a fundamentally anti-Socialist mission, as Kerschensteiner had clarified in his essay on civic education, in classroom instruction, anti-Socialism was generally far from being blatant or direct. Most continuation school directors thought that positive patriotic education and enlightenment on protective codes and welfare served more effectively to counter the Socialists than would openly dragging party politics into the schools.[85] Direct attacks would only generate unfruitful conflicts with labor and would also divide the souls of those students whose parents were Socialists. Because of this highly muted anti-Socialism, Socialists could regard the schools as useful institutions. Recruitment leaflets directed at young workers encouraged them to learn as much as possible there. However, Socialist educators like Heinrich Schulz or Julius Bruhns did distinguish sharply between the vocational and political tasks of the continuation schools. They wholeheartedly applauded the vocational training, since Socialists shared a common interest with industrialists in seeing that laborers acquired skills, according to Bruhns, although they strongly objected to so-called civic education. In fact, Schulz denounced Kerschensteiner's civic education as a hypocritical fraud. Kerschensteiner upheld existing class distinctions and was only willing to allow the dominated "acquisition of sufficient political insight so that they will place themselves *willingly* in the service of the dominant. Rather than being dumb and blind, they should be good humored, reasonable, and industrious objects of exploitation."[86] Although some Socialist journalists criticized the overemphasis on craft education to the ostensible detriment of general education, an issue also debated among middle-class educators, the Socialist press did approve of the schools' dissemination of information about labor protection laws. The *Metallarbeiterzeitung,* the journal of the Metalworkers Union, largest of the Free Unions, thought that craft instruction should remain at the center of instruction, although it held that all students should receive a common core of knowledge about tools and machines, thus bridging the separation between the skilled and unskilled and among the diverse crafts. The paper also lauded Kerschensteiner for his pedagogical principle of learning by doing. *Arbeiter-jugend,* the most widely read Socialist youth journal, actually proposed adding two hours of classes weekly and extending continuation schools to young women workers, although its columns also noted cases in which continuation school teachers abused their positions and directly attacked the Socialists in the classroom. In general, however, the Socialist press doubted that the party had much to fear from civics instruction, or even from the overt anti-Socialist propaganda of some teachers, since supposedly life, not school, was the foremost educator. Only the government's concerted campaign to deploy the schools against the Socialist youth movement after 1911 would spark a reevaluation of this complacent and comforting view.[87]

Nor was appreciation of the continuation schools based on a Kerschensteinerian program restricted to Germany. In the United States Kerschensteiner found enthusiastic supporters among Progressives, and several New England states experimented with day continuation schools, while in England advocates of national efficiency, including Viscount Haldane, Michael Sadler, Arthur Shadwell, and the Webbs, alarmed by many of the social changes that exercised their German counterparts and worried by the rise of German industrial and military power, urged their compatriots to adopt the German system of mandatory day or evening continuation schools.[88] In England, however, the major bone of contention was the coercive character of the schools, since opponents believed that mandatory instruction violated the liberty of the employed. In March 1914 the *Morning Post* wrote:

England always drops voluntaryism slowly and regretfully. This year the Education Committee of the County Council has made one more effort to reorganise its evening schools on a voluntary basis. Such efforts deserve support and success, but many people are beginning to think that, like Germany, we shall find it hopeless to rely on simple freewill and goodwill of children and employers, and that in the end we shall have to lay the benign compulsion of the State equally and impartially on all.

Contrary to the predictions of the newspaper, however, in the end employers and local educational boards were able to thwart all measures for a national system of day continuation schools, an indication of the much stronger roots and ethos of individualist liberalism and the more jealous guardianship of exclusively local control over educational policy in England than in Germany.

What finally can we conclude about the prewar German continuation school? How effective was it in achieving the aims of Kerschensteiner's two-pronged strategy for guiding the young worker from narrow egoism to communal and national allegiance? How able were they to fulfill their functions of improving labor qualifications, legitimating the political system, and reinforcing the social order? Part of the answer will have to wait until we consider the youth cultivation campaign of 1911–14, but most youth reformers regarded the schools as modest but solid successes with beneficial effects on youthful behavior.[89] The school improved the vocational skills of young apprentices and workers, disciplined the disorderly, mediated between the young and official urban and welfare institutions, controlled their leisure time to some degree, and gave teachers and voluntary associations opportunities to buttress patriotism. Despite a few concessions to the artisanate, rather than perpetuating preindustrial forms or sentiments, the continuation schools were thoroughly modern educational establishments under liberal middle-class hegemony designed to integrate young workers into the Wilhelmine polity, urban life, and the industrial order.

5

Beleaguered churches: Protestant and Catholic youth work

Although most clerical youth savers favored establishing continuation schools and continued to support them after their establishment, many criticized the absence of religion in the Prussian schools.[1] Others questioned whether these schools served as an adequate bulwark against secularization or the ostensible moral dangers facing young urban males, even in states like Bavaria, where religious education was mandatory. All agreed that however useful, continuation schools failed to provide sufficient moral fortification and could under no circumstances supplant pastoral care for the young. Hence as the youth campaign quickened at the turn of the century, both major churches undertook much more strenuous and systematic drives to recruit young employed males to religious youth associations. Despite certain differences in accent, such as the far more straightforward championing of youth welfare legislation by Catholic officials, the purposes, organizational forms, and activities of both Catholic and Protestant youth associations were broadly similar. Yet the results of these drives diverged considerably. Except in a few anomalous cases like Essen, Protestant efforts to woo young workers were minimally effective, whereas the Catholic Church was generally able to build, if not retain, a significant base of young workers. In order to explain these divergent results, we will examine the youth work of the Protestant Church before turning to that of the Catholics.

By 1900 the Evangelical Church could already rely on a lengthy experience of working with youth. The first youth associations were organized in northern Germany during the Protestant revival of the 1830s, and the Inner Mission could look back with pride on a long history of charitable endeavor on behalf of orphans, the poor, and other endangered youths.[2] At the end of the nineteenth century, however, as the youth salvation campaign accelerated, there was a pronounced broadening and intensification of church activity. New organizations oriented toward urban youth in general and young laborers in particular were called into life. One example of this was the CVJM, the German YMCA, inspired by the German-American minister Friedrich von Schlümbach and founded in early 1883 in Berlin.[3] Relations between the CVJM and the Evangelical Church were often strained, however, because more conservative ministers regarded the CVJM as a dubious American innovation and criticized its laical practices and its appeal to all young Christian males, without regard to denominational affiliation. Although most CVJM members appear to have been clerks and students, from the outset the association also held special assemblies for young workers and artisans, including bakers, barbers, and butchers, out of which developed several independent Christian occupational associations. Another new organization was the Society for the Welfare of Immigrating Male Youth (Die Gesellschaft zur Fürsorge für zuziehende männliche Jugend), founded in 1897, which sought to dissuade youths from moving to large cities like Berlin and to persuade those who nonetheless did move to join Protestant youth groups. In Berlin and a number of south German cities the Protestant churches erected new apprentice homes to ensure that the apprentice or wandering journeyman could find room and board in impeccably Christian surroundings, rather than renting a notorious *Schlafstelle*. For the first time, local youth associations, such as those in Saxony and Hannover, which had limited their membership to males over seventeen, set up special sections for youths between fourteen and seventeen.[4]

Although Protestant youth associations were loosely federated on a regional basis, youth work was basically decentralized, and the local club attached to a parish continued to be the predominant form and fulcrum of this work.[5] The primary function of these associations was religious edification. Wrote the Evangelical pastor Krummacher of Elberfeld, "As Christian associations they rest on the foundation of the godly word; i.e., they proceed from the thought that God's word is the only sufficient and also completely satisfactory means of healing the injuries of popular life. Therefore, their foremost task is to plant God's word in the hearts of youth and to bring it near their life experience."[6] To achieve this, weekly meetings of youth associations held on Sunday afternoons invariably began with twenty minutes of prayer, hymns, and an elucidation of a biblical text. Many youth associations also sponsored weekly voluntary Bible study hours. This predominantly religious orientation was further reflected in the pages of *Der Leuchtturm* (*The Lighthouse*), the Evangelical youth paper with the largest number of subscribers, filled with turgid biblical exegeses, extensive reports on missionaries in the South Pacific, and stereotyped articles on Christian character formation, although it also carried coverage of the activities of the conservative Agrarian League and consistently honored the kaiser with a kind of cultic devotion.[7]

Protestant ministers recognized that a purely religious program would have had a circumscribed appeal to the young; hence, they supplemented religion with diverse educational and recreational activities and offered opportunities for sociability. Ministers in charge of youth associations usually delivered short lectures during the Sunday afternoon meetings.[8] The kaleidoscopic array of topics ranged from biographical sketches of leading German industrial and cultural figures, such as the cannon king Alfred Krupp, the locomotive manufacturer August Borsig, or the patriotic writer Ernst Moritz Arndt, through historical and cultural subjects, such as German handicrafts before the Reformation or Egyptian mummies, to scientific and geographical themes, such as Röntgen rays or Nansen's journey to the North Pole. Despite their diversity, these lectures certainly expressed the confidence of educated Protestants in industry, science, and technology and were imbued with the unquestioning patriotism and geographical consciousness of the age of imperialism. Collections of such standard lectures were readily available from Protestant publishing houses. Although Protestant youth associations purported to eschew politics, the lectures sometimes treated politically controversial events like the Paris Commune. Moreover, out of fear that young Christians would be unarmed against well-prepared and experienced Socialist orators, Pastor Fritsch of Berlin recommended staging debates on issues like materialism, socialism, and Darwinism or the church's position on revolution. Youth associations also gathered for patriotic or religious family evenings commemorating Kaiser Wilhelm I or the anniversary of the Inner Mission with elaborate programs consisting of declamations, hymns, and nationalist anthems.[9]

The typical youth association provided facilities and occasions for strictly recreational activities as well, for brass bands and choirs, hikes and gymnastics.[10] Most churches made available rooms for reading and game playing. Some activities, however, thoroughly divided the ministry. Although organized gymnastics was generally acceptable and regarded as valuable exercise for health and discipline, many pastors were concerned that competitive sports like soccer would divert youth from matters of the spirit.[11] Even performing plays in youth groups was ambiguous morally. Secular plays had no place in Christian youth associations, and religious plays risked profaning the sacred.[12] Such criticisms indicated a sharp split within the church over how far youth associations should go to accommodate modern conditions and to what degree they should imitate their secular rivals like the Workers' Youth Movement or even the continuation schools.

Despite these divisions, between 1900 and 1912 membership in the National Association of Protestant Youth Groups grew from 88,000 to almost 143,000.[13] This growth, however, was both regionally and socially uneven, and pastors felt that in regard to the Workers' Youth Movement, other secular groups, and the Catholics, they lagged far behind. Some had predicted failure from the outset. At the opening session of the Protestant Social Congress in 1900 Otto Baumgarten of Kiel avowed that it was psychologically impossible for Protestant youth work to draw in the broad masses.[14] Indeed, Protestant youth associations were more likely to attract the effeminate and prematurely old than robust youths, who were likely to be hypercritical and rebellious during adolescence. Moreover, if they did attract normal adolescents, at best they could hope to channel the drives of such youths toward temperance, since repression contravened Protestant principles. Other speakers put forward less psychological, Calvinist explanations for the relative failure of Protestant youth work. According to Rector Christmann at a synod on youth affairs in Saarbrücken in 1912, small numbers were preordained since the de-Christianized masses would wallow in pleasure seeking and only the tiny elect minority would unswervingly cleave to the true church.[15]

The case of Düsseldorf suggests that such predictions were self-fulfilling, but whether or not they were so, the city was certainly a glaring example of complacent Protestant inertia, demonstrating the degree to which youth work depended on local initiative. In this city of almost 360,000 people of whom a third were Protestant, in 1911 membership in Düsseldorf's fourteen Protestant youth associations numbered 647.[16] Moreover, lower-middle-class youths comprised the majority and set the tone of these groups. Of these 647 members, 282 were craft apprentices or journeymen, 194 white-collar workers, thirty-four students or unaccounted for, and only 137 young blue-collar workers. In the three preceding years, the church had spent a mere ten thousand marks on youth work and, as one minister noted, had virtually abstained in this area.[17] Only the kaiser's Youth Cultivation Edict of January 1911, which codified the practices of the youth salvation campaign and which a pastor implausibly acclaimed as the most meaningful call for youth education since the days of Luther, roused the local church from its lethargy. Participants at a special synod on youth work grudgingly admitted that they had much to learn from the more developed and articulated youth work of the Catholic Church, and they also resolved to appoint a full-time youth pastor. They finally named Pastor Rose to this post; however, he distinguished himself more as a pugnacious Socialist baiter than as a charismatic youth leader.[18] But as a result of this new resolve, by 1913 membership in local Protestant youth associations had doubled to 1,300. Although heartened by this growth, one minister resignedly assured his fellows, "[W]e can undoubtedly never expect to recruit large numbers, since in our work, external growth and internal deepening stand in natural contradiction to one another."[19]

A more credible explanation for the general inability of the Protestants to attract working-class youth was the sociological thesis advanced by Günther Dehn, pastor to a Berlin working-class parish and a seasoned youth saver. According to Dehn, the difficulty was neither a technical organizational problem nor a question of the dedication of local ministers, but rather a deeply social one.[20] The church largely garnered its support from the urban petit bourgeoisie: small masters, officials, salesmen, commercial clerks. It was their sons who naturally joined the youth associations. Although honorable, upright, diligent and conscientious, such youths partook of their parents' narrowness, their satisfaction with contemporary life, their lack of concern with social issues, their sense of being people who mattered in a small circle. "The young worker feels, if not with clear insight, at least instinctively, that the air of the youth association is different from that in my own life sphere...." Young workers, even if not Socialists, were discontented with the present but entertained great expectations for the future; they already shared the future orientation, sense of social striving, and spirit of struggle common to labor. This class sentiment distanced them from the ordinary association member:

If one attempts to characterize church youth associations as a whole, one must surely say they are petit bourgeois associations. In these associations the sons of orderly families may be raised to diligent men, which undoubtedly occurs, but it remains painful, of course, that even in the center of a working-class neighborhood, the church is not capable of creating associations of working class youth, but rather can only bring together petit bourgeois groups in which the young worker does not feel comfortable.

But even though this disquieted sociological view of Protestant inability to recruit young laborers undoubtedly comes closer to the heart of the problem than either the psychological or religious explanations, the few cases of significant working-class recruitment raise questions about its complete adequacy and about whether Protestant youth work in this area was doomed to failure from the outset.

In 1908 a number of urban pastors and Protestant laypersons who were critical of Protestant failures in this area formed the League of German Youth Associations to press for a Christian social, but less narrowly religious, organizing among young urban laborers. Walther Classen was elected honorary chairman, and Clemens Schulz was selected for the executive committee. Both of these charismatic ministers were highly critical of what they regarded as the outmoded approaches of the Inner Mission to attracting young workers, and both had long experience working with youth in St. Pauli, Hamburg's rough waterfront district, where they started clubs. Over a thousand young workers, mostly apprentices, joined these clubs, perhaps, as their opponents suspected, because they offered sports, recreation, and secular educational activities and played down religion.[21] Although supervised by adult middle-class assistants, most of whom were clerics, these associations also adopted the "American principle," that is, members elected their own club leaders and administered their own affairs, probably a necessity in Hamburg, with its strongly Social Democratic labor tradition. Notably, too, given Hamburg's close English connection, Classen, who formed an interconfessional youth group, anathema to the Evangelical Church, was influenced by the Toynbee Hall experiment in London and its offshoot, the settlement house movement. He also strongly favored the professionalization of youth welfare work.

The case of Protestant effectiveness most commonly touted, however, was the rather differently oriented achievement of Wilhelm Weigle in Essen. In this city of 294,000, where 42 percent of the population was Protestant, Weigle was able to build a mass youth movement of almost 2,000 members.[22] Close to half of all boys who were confirmed immediately joined a Protestant youth association. Moreover, the composition of this movement corresponded far more closely to the social structure of the entire city than did the composition of such groups in Düsseldorf. Of the 1,967 members in 1911, 945 were young factory workers, 618 artisanal apprentices or journeymen, 318 white-collar workers, 60 students, and 26 unaccounted for. It is doubtful that without the enterprise of Weigle, the organization would have attained this level of mass membership.

Weigle, born in 1862, son of a Swabian minister, studied theology in Bonn, Basel, Berlin, and Utrecht.[23] After ordination, he served as a pastor in a number of towns in the Berg district near Solingen, where he acquired a reputation for gaining the confidence of youth by unorthodox means, such as participating in pastimes like ice skating. On the basis of this reputation he was called to Essen in 1891, where after six years of ministering in a workers' district and nurturing a parish youth group he founded, he was appointed Essen's full-time youth pastor. His abundant energy, fiery spirit, and dynamic unadorned speech enabled him to transform his initially small youth group into a tightly organized citywide brigade. Before the war, the kaiser decorated him with the Red Eagle Order, third and fourth class, and with the Crown Order for his service to the church and monarchy.

In most respects Weigle's conception of appropriate activities for the young was extremely conservative and strongly colored by authoritarianism.[24] Like Krummacher, he believed that only God's word should be used to win over and hold the young. Play was strictly subordinate activity necessary to fill free time and strengthen bonds of trust between the minister and his charges. He entirely banned those sports that he considered overly exciting, physically dangerous, and competitive, such as soccer, claiming that they destroyed receptivity to Christianity, as did gymnastic competitions for prizes. Literature could also be dangerous and needed to be selected with care and censored. The adventure stories of Karl May ruined the young, and love themes, even when firmly placed in a Christian context, were to be shunned because a premature interest in love deadened inner life. Anything that might contribute to youthful hubris was to be eliminated stringently. This included all acting and much music since youths soon fancied themselves budding artists. Experiments in self-administration like those in Hamburg were thoroughly ill advised. These, too, fostered proud, critically inclined youth. "In one's youth, one must learn to obey," Weigle proclaimed, because only obedience produced "modest and moral young people" and also prepared young males for the rigors of military life. Associations were to shield members fully from the debilitating temptations of urban life, whether penny dreadfuls, smoking, alcohol, or precocious sex.

In practice, the activities of the Protestant youth associations in Essen were far less restrictive than these authoritarian precepts might imply.[25] Although Weigle feared that music would swell youthful heads, each neighborhood shook to the blare of a big brass band. Anti-Christian soccer was strictly forbidden, but during the summer members bashed one another with padded bamboo poles in presumably Christian war games, games that ritualized the territorial fights between rival gangs common to both urban and rural Germany. Five playgrounds were open to the associations for gymnastics, and members could swim for free in the municipal pool. Certainly Sunday afternoon meetings opened with a prayer, hymn, and biblical passage and closed with a prayer, but in between came two free hours for chatting, playing games, and reading illustrated magazines. It undoubtedly mattered considerably to many adults that these activities took place under religious rather than Socialist auspices, but for the young, having access to well-equipped facilities where they could conveniently meet their friends was probably a more important consideration.

Apart from Weigle's much vaunted charisma, one major reason for success in Essen was an almost pedantic attention to organizational detail, reminiscent of Hugo Blitz. Weigle divided his youth groups into twenty-four neighborhood-based associations, each with its own band, recreational program, and regular bulletin. These sections were in turn grouped into six districts, each of which functioned as a unified entity for war games, hikes, and excursions. Weigle painstakingly culled one hundred older youths to supervise and monitor group activities. These hand-picked assistants were supposed to serve as models of piety and virtue, attending church services weekly and visiting the homes of every section member every Sunday to examine the members' religious commitment and to counter any antireligious sentiments picked up from parents swayed by the Socialists. Assistants were further responsible for handing out the more than 150,000 flyers printed annually. Each Sunday from 4:00 to 6:00 P.M., Weigle presided over a citywide assembly, usually attended by more than four hundred young males. After 1911 these meetings took place in a centrally located youth center built at the cost of a half million marks, containing a gym hall, woodwork shop, and large auditorium. Besides contributing money for construction expenses, the Krupps also donated superfluous furniture from Villa Hügel, and two Krupp managers, Gillhausen and the right-wing nationalist, Alfred Hugenberg, represented the firm at the dedication ceremony.

This material aid from the Krupps points to some of the other contributory reasons for local success in Essen. In many respects,

Essen remained a company town dominated by the Krupps, and their heavy-handed paternalistic labor practices molded the social relations of the city.[26] Given the rapid demographic growth of Essen at the turn of the century, many of the recruits may also have been recent migrants from small Westphalian towns with deeply anchored Protestant traditions. Furthermore, as mentioned in the previous chapter, until 1912 Essen alone of major Prussian cities lacked a mandatory continuation school that would have made available alternative recreational opportunities to young Protestant workers. It is, of course, within the realm of possibility that success in Essen was solely attributable to such a unique coincidence of factors, that is, Weigle, the Krupps, the absence of a continuation school, and local demography. But the mass recruitment at least casts some doubt on the standard explanations put forward to account for the inability of Protestant youth associations to capture a mass following. Although unprovable, it does hint that vigorous intervention by local pastors, centralized bureaucratic organization, a close supervisory regime, extensive recreational programs, and outside financial support, as opposed to a kind of passive and pietistic elitism, might have been effective in creating a youthful working-class constituency in industrializing cities.

Although considerably more effective, the youth work of the Catholic Church was also plagued by perennial problems, both internal and external in origin. In many cities the building of churches and the extension of pastoral care were unable to keep pace with the massive influx of urban newcomers, and consequently the relations between priests and their parishioners tended to weaken.[27] The repressive *Kulturkampf* of the 1870s had certainly heightened Catholic unity, helping to create and reinforce an integrated Catholic subculture almost as comprehensive and well organized as that of the Socialists.[28] But the socially heterogeneous character of the Catholic subculture would make it difficult to reconcile the aspirations of its multiple components. Moreover, Catholics continued to suffer from a kind of discriminatory and latent *Kulturkampf*, especially in municipalities administered by liberal Protestant oligarchies.[29] Such liberal establishments often smoothed the road for the youth work of secular and nationalist organizations like the German Gymnasts, who were invited into the continuation schools while liberal officials placed impediments in the paths of priests who sought to initiate religious instruction.

This official discrimination exacerbated intrachurch conflicts, which compounded the difficulty of formulating and implementing policies.

In late Imperial Germany the church was split between a modernist wing exemplified by the People's League for Catholic Germany, a mass Catholic organization centered in the Rhineland founded in 1890 to enlighten Catholics on political and social issues and to combat socialism, and a staunchly conservative wing supported by aristocratic notables and solidly ensconced in the upper echelons of the hierarchy.[30] This split affected every sphere of church activity, including youth work. Although the modernist wing favored imitating and adapting forms of popular persuasion and action pioneered by the Socialists, the conservative wing viewed such imitation with suspicion, fearing that it would inevitably result in a capitulation to secular values. Despite their differences, both wings agonized over the dilemma of balancing secular efficacy with preservation of the church's religious soul.

For Catholics too, church organizations for the young stretched back to the mid-nineteenth century. In response to the plight of young artisans, which had played such an important role in sparking and radicalizing the Revolutions of 1848, Adolf Kolping, an ex-cobbler turned pastor in Cologne, had started a society of journeymen in 1849.[31] It soon spread throughout Germany, with hostels for wandering journeymen and programs of religious uplift, ongoing education, and sociability. The Kolping societies later became the models for Catholic associations of specific occupational groups: craft apprentices, factory workers, commercial employees. Beginning in the 1850s but advancing more rapidly and steadily in the 1880s and 1890s after the official termination of the *Kulturkampf,* parish priests formed youth sodalities comparable to the Protestant parish associations. Catholic youth work would be characterized by the coexistence of these dual organizational forms, general parish youth groups and occupational youth groups, although the former continued to be far more significant. Until the mid-1890s, however, each parish was largely left to its own devices, and there was little systematic or coordinated youth activity.

This began to change at the annual Catholic Assembly of 1895, when Joseph Drammer, one of the founders of the People's League and chairman of the Cologne Association of Young Workers, proposed establishing a central committee for youth activity in every diocese in order to exchange information and facilitate youth work.[32] This proposal was approved by the assembly and ratified by the bishops' conference. Soon these committees were operating in most dioceses, stimulating the organization of new youth groups, maintaining contact both with prelates and with government officials, lobbying for new protective legislation for youth. In 1908 these committees took a further step toward centralization, with the creation of a youth secretariat in Düsseldorf headed by Chaplain Karl Mosterts, previously the youth pastor at Düsseldorf's St. Maximilian's Church. This unquestionably gave a fillip to Catholic work. In 1899, 745 Catholic youth groups existed in Germany (115 for apprentices, 25 for young workers, and 605 sodalities), with an average membership of 140,000 males and females between the ages of fourteen and eighteen. By 1908 there were 1,200 groups with 195,000 members, and during the following eight years the number of associations more than tripled to 3,800, and membership almost doubled to 365,000. Most of this growth and strength were concentrated in the Rhineland and Westphalia, the bastion of the middle-class and populist wings and the region where competition with the Socialists reached its maximum intensity. Apart from spurring impressive organizational growth, centralization also made a more uniform approach possible. The Catholic youth paper *Die Wacht* (*The Watch*) could be distributed to virtually every member of the sodalities. Publicists like August Pieper, the indefatigable and prolific chairman of the People's League, wrote handbooks proffering detailed advice on every aspect of youth work, from psychology to youth legislation.[33]

Centralization also aided the parish sodalities, which were the living cells of the Catholic organism. In Düsseldorf by 1912 every parish, except two small suburban ones, had organized youth groups. Two years later membership had reached 5,000, two-thirds of which was male, membership comparable to that of the voluntary associations that were part of the municipal continuation school.[34] The social composition of these sodalities tended to reflect the largely working-class character of Catholic Düsseldorf. Whereas St. Rochus, which sustained the most extensive youth program in the city, primarily appealed to young white-collar workers in the central city, and St. Andreas was almost equally divided between young blue- and white-collar workers, the 260 members of St. Elizabeth included a few craft and commercial apprentices, but the overwhelming majority was made up of young factory laborers. According to the local priest's appeal for government funds, the 113 members of Herz Jesu's youth group were so desperately poor that some were supposedly unable to pay the monthly dues of a pfennig. Youth groups in the new industrial suburbs were almost exclusively working class. In Unterrath almost all of the 150 male members were employed by Mannesmann or other large steel mills, and in Rath more than 70 of the 105 young women who belonged to the maiden sodality were factory employees. There was, however, no equalization of resources among these youth associations. St. Rochus, a well-endowed and largely middle-class parish, assigned a chaplain exclusively to youth affairs, set aside a room for youth meetings and events, and could afford a well-stocked library and gymnastics equipment, whereas an impoverished parish like Herz Jesu was led by an overworked priest who had to make do with improvised facilities and materials.[35]

Despite enormous discrepancies in resources, all the youth sodalities had remarkably similar goals, programs, and activities, a direct result of centralization. As with the Protestants, the foremost task was religious education that was aimed at fortifying faith, forging Christian character, and shepherding the young to partake regularly of church sacraments: communion and confession.[36] Priests generally lectured on religious subjects once monthly, treating topics like the life of Christ, church history, or Catholic doctrine. Although church pedagogues advocated positive teaching that emphasized the reasonableness of Catholic positions, rather than ridiculing opponents, they acknowledged that in the large cities, which were denominationally mixed and had large Socialist movements, apologetics and polemics could not be excluded.[37] Priests had to avoid an amorphous interdenominational Christianity by differentiating between Catholic and Evangelical beliefs and explaining the Reformation from a Catholic perspective. Young Catholic workers had to be prepared to refute the slogans and criticisms they were likely to hear from Protestant and Socialist co-workers, including assertions that popes had been corrupt and debauched, that the church unfailingly sided with the rich and powerful, and that Catholicism accompanied economic and social backwardness. But even polemical rebuttals were to accentuate the positive by featuring pious popes, Catholic social reformers, or Renaissance Italy's contributions to trade and discovery.

The second task of intensive work in youth sodalities was civic education. August Pieper cited Kerschensteiner on the need for consistent mass political education if Germans were to use their rights more constructively. Pieper and other Catholic educators regarded civic education in Catholic youth groups as a supplement to that in the continuation schools and as a means of laying the basis for future Center party membership.[38] Since the Imperial Association Law prohibited discussion of political issues in youth groups, the monthly Catholic lectures in this area purported to be purely informative.[39]

Some really were, such as those examining the constitution or institutions like the Reichstag, but others compared the political parties
and, in the guise of factual description, judged them on the basis of
their stances on religious issues and social policy.[40]

The Conservative party, which in 1909 was allied with the Catholic
Center party against Chancellor Bülow's ostensiblly antiagrarian fiscal
policy, was considered closer to the Catholics because of its support
for agriculture and the crafts and its defense of religious orthodoxy.
Lectures condemned the liberal parties for their vacillations on social
policy and their allegiance to unrestrained individualism and secularization. Supposedly liberals had also catalyzed the development of
socialism by their advocacy of laissez-faire capitalism during early
industrialization and their unwillingness to underwrite the timely welfare schemes striven for by the pathbreaking Catholic social reformer,
Bishop Ketteler, in the 1860s and 1870s.

The most blistering criticisms were directed against the Socialists,
the Center's most dangerous rival. As even the Socialist revisionists
acknowledged, much of the party's *Erfurt* program was demonstrably
false, avowed Catholic lecturers. Predictions of the demise of small
farms and shops under capitalism were unwarranted; the conditions
of labor were manifestly improving, not declining, and in any event,
the Socialist vision of the future was nebulous. Although many Socialist planks transgressed the God-given natural order, such as abolition of social distinctions or equal rights for women, others were
simply naive, such as the call for replacing the standing army with an
amateur militia. Young Catholics were urged to shun Socialist co-
workers and warned to be wary of all that Socialists said, since otherwise they might be ensnared by promises of "mountains of joy and
paradise on earth," an attempt to quarantine young Catholics that
testified to the serious threat that church officials believed Socialist
youth work posed for their own efforts.

In contrast to the other parties, the Center party was presented as
the indispensable center of balance, preventing centrifugal political
and social forces from tearing apart the Reich. Instead of advancing
particular interests, the Center was said to work untiringly for the
general interest and to defend steadfastly the rights of all classes.

Youth group members could also look for political guidance in the
pages of *Die Wacht*, although because of their more public and official
character, articles had to be more purely informational and circumspect than youth group lectures, especially since the Church castigated
the Socialists for politicizing youth work and violating the association

laws.[41] *Die Wacht* lavishly praised the Hohenzollern dynasty and the kaiser, not least for their work on behalf of peace and social welfare. Frequent articles provided accounts of Germany's political institutions, welfare legislation, and civil rights and discussed the duty of military service. The journal was unwaveringly patriotic and never openly criticized the government; however, it commended policies like participation in the Hague peace conference and domestic social legislation agreeable to Catholic moderates.

The third area of Catholic youth work after religion and civic education was the cultivation of sociability and leisure activities. These activities, which differed little from the comparable Protestant ones, included visiting museums, industrial sites, and municipal institutions, attending plays deemed suitable for the young, or taking part in gymnastics and hikes. Priests conscientiously strove to make certain that these activities were stamped with a religious and moral imprint. Thus, for example, the general assembly of youth associations in Cologne recommended that youths visit the theater at most once or twice yearly and that the play should not only be "ethically and religiously unobjectionable, but also of educational value."[42] Before the play, the priest was to analyze its content and form so that "the youth learns that a rational man never sees a production without having previously assured himself of its value." In contrast to the stance of the Protestant Church, there was no opposition among Catholic clergy to the young themselves performing in plays, as long as they depicted outstandingly heroic and moral deeds like those of Charlemagne or the anti-Napoleonic statesmen of the War of Liberation. The 1910 meeting of the general assembly passed a resolution in favor of introducing gymnastics in Catholic sodalities.[43] Speakers argued that such exercise was especially beneficial in large cities and industrial districts, where working conditions and unhealthy pastimes were conducive to disease. In addition, gymnastics would help the church compete with both the German Gymnasts and the Worker Gymnasts, and it was needed for military preparation. Like the Protestants, however, Catholic clergymen recoiled at the prospect of permitting increasingly popular mass competitive sports like soccer, which they were certain brutalized the young. Asserted *Die Wacht*, "When a youth has no higher ideal than to win a soccer match or other sports contest, he can only become brutal."[44] Thus, in regard to sports, the church's accommodation was belated and hesitant and largely came as a result of competitive pressures from other organizations.

This was also partially true of the fourth major area of Catholic youth work, defending the social and economic interests of young workers. All youth groups promoted some social and economic education.[45] Catholic youth workers persistently accused Socialists of undermining personal responsibility and individual morality through their calls for a revolutionary transformation of the social and economic system and their scornful attacks on self-help measures like family saving. By blaming all human misery on the social order, Socialists made it more difficult to educate the young to frugality and moderation in pleasure, whether of alcohol or sex. For this reason, many youth sodalities set up savings chests, often used to assist members drafted into military service. (In addition, of course, such chests kept alive the ties between soldiers and their old Catholic youth groups.) Priests stressed self-control and discipline in lectures on the need for savings, insurance, careful household budgeting, and a hygienic mode of life. But Catholic social thinkers recognized that individual self-help alone was insufficient to ameliorate the conditions of the laboring classes and consequently placed considerable weight on social legislation and the collective self-help and solidarity fostered by "estate" organizations. Priests made members aware of labor protection laws, the role of the factory inspectorate, and legislation regulating apprenticeship. Youths were encouraged to bring violations of labor legislation to the attention of their priest. Young laborers and artisans were also called upon to join occupational associations, although the Church was badly divided over the legitimacy of Christian trade unions, both because they were interdenominational and because they seemed to presuppose conflict between employers and employees, which ran counter to the Catholic notion of the harmonious interests of the different estates.[46]

A pervasive clerical bias against industrial labor and discord over the legitimacy of trade unions, however, partially handicapped the Church's work with young laborers. Although even the modernist wing of the church continued to use the vocabulary of estates, with its connotation of a rigidly stratified hierarchy, the People's League repudiated any association with medieval or romantic notions of social order.[47] In modern society all occupational groups resulted from a functional division of labor, deserved equal political rights and social recognition, and were entitled to pursue their economic interests. If well performed, any occupation was honorable and respectable. Nonetheless, much Catholic literature for youth belied this official position by revealing a strong prejudice in favor of craft and white-collar employment.

Although most Catholic youth associations left job placement to municipal employment agencies, with which they developed close ties, they did counsel members on occupational choices.[48] Occupational leaflets distributed to parents and young job seekers listed every conceivable handicraft from *Anstreicher* to *Zimmermann* (painter to carpenter) and hammered home the message that only craft apprenticeship laid the foundation for a happy and industrious life, a sense of order, joy in creation, a prosperous family. Best were trades like decorative painting that, rather than merely providing a livelihood, demanded some degree of artistic expression.[49] Church officials denied any ideal value to industrial labor since, at most, machine tending merely required care and diligence. Such work was honorable, but it would be impossible to arouse the youth's joy in such monotonous and routine labor. The fact that priests shared this common bias against industrial labor had practical consequences. In socially mixed sodalities, they tended to ignore the social and economic interests of young laborers and allowed young white-collar workers to control the proceedings. Sodalities generally ceded vocational training to the continuation schools, but when they did offer instruction, it was usually courses in stenography and foreign languages, which could advance the prospects for promotion of commercial employees.[50] Moreover, young workers who had finished continuation school often chafed at close clerical supervision and therefore quit the sodalities.[51] In 1910 only one-sixth of Catholic male factory workers between the ages of seventeen and twenty in the archdiocese of Cologne still adhered to a Catholic youth group. Thus, although the Catholic sodalities, in contrast to the Protestant associations, could initially attract young workers, they had great difficulty retaining their members.

One way of attempting to avoid this difficulty was to construct youth groups much like the Kolping Associations, along occupational lines, with separate organizations for young factory workers, artisans, and commercial employees, groups where members could feel comfortable.[52] These had programs similar to those of the sodalities, except for a somewhat more explicit job-related emphasis. Apart from well-established occupational groups like the Kolping Associations and a few experiments in larger cities, however, such forms never really took root, whether because priests were overburdened, lacked suitable experience and training, or simply preferred overseeing general organizations. But as the Socialist-affiliated Free Trade Unions intensified their efforts to recruit young workers in 1908, a number of Catholic youth savers reviewed their previous half-hearted labor policies. At a special convocation of south German Catholic youth workers in 1910, August Pieper and Chaplain Karl Mosterts suggested adding youth sections to the Christian trade unions.[53] Catholic union officials were skeptical about this solution, doubting that young workers could be induced to join; nonetheless, the assembly enthusiastically endorsed this proposal. A minority favored setting up youth sections instead in Catholic workers' associations, which rather than defending workers against their employers, served as mutual aid, friendly, and educational societies. The convocation agreed, however, that Catholic youth workers should press more vigorously for more rigorous enforcement of protective legislation.

This more vigorous approach was soon noticeable in *Die Wacht*, which henceforth regularly reported cases of employers' violations of the youth provisions of the Industrial Code and insistently informed young readers of their legal rights. *Die Wacht* and other Catholic papers ran articles clarifying the purely economic functions of Christian trade unions and castigating the Free Trade Unions both for taking political positions and for supposedly forcing young workers to join, employing intimidating tactics, such as breaking their tools and using physical coercion, or seducing them with cigarettes and beer. The paper also assailed company-sponsored yellow unions, like those of Krupp, for depriving workers of their self-reliance.[54]

But the youth recruitment drive of the Christian trade unions was at best moderately successful. In 1911 the Catholic trade union leader Adam Stegerwald complained of the lack of cooperation between youth associations and the Christian trade unions and called for more systematic and professional Catholic youth work.[55] Other Christian union leaders regretted that members expected priests to recruit young workers; at any rate, during 1911–12 the priests were too heavily involved in the Center party's electoral campaign to devote much attention to union affairs. Thus in Düsseldorf, for example, by 1912 only 250 of the Christian trade unions' 5,300 members were younger than twenty. Nor, apparently, were the health and burial benefits of the Catholic workers' associations any more attractive, since only 150 of their more than 9,000 members were youths.[56]

Even these limited attempts to challenge the Free Trade Unions by recruiting young workers provoked a sharp reaction from ultraconservative prelates. Cardinal Kopp of Breslau charged Chaplain Mosterts with ignoring two principal church rules when advocating trade union sections for young workers.[57] First, although the church now recognized unions as acceptable labor organizations, it did not grant them privileges over other forms of association. Second, the church had decreed that youth be organized on a strictly denominational basis, but since Protestant laborers also belonged to them, the Christian trade unions were inappropriate for young Catholics. High church officials also strenuously objected to *Die Wacht*'s attack on yellow or company unions, which they viewed as an assault on the authority of employers. The editor had to plead with the archbishop of Cologne not to issue a public reprimand, which would simply provide ammunition for opponents of Catholic youth work. He justified the sharp tone of the paper's attack, claiming that Catholics often underestimated the dangers company unions posed for Catholic youth programs, and he categorically denied that the piece was calculated to discredit the authority of employers.[58]

In Düsseldorf the director of the continuation school likewise roundly condemned the article on company unions. Although praising Catholic youth groups for their past contributions to social harmony, he warned that such assaults not only sharpened relations between young laborers and their employers, but also jeopardized cooperation between Catholic youth workers and the continuation school.[59] One of the rare occasions when the latent antagonism between Catholic youth savers and the city's liberal educational establishment flared into the open, this rift was a constant source of worry for Catholic officials. In 1913 Mosterts wrote to Cardinal Hartmann of Cologne lamenting that the promotion of interconfessional clubs at the continuation schools was harming Catholic activities.[60] Nor were the continuation schools the only major competitor. The Socialists disposed over several well-accoutered rooms for youth in their People's House, and even the Protestant associations, despite their few members, could boast of five youth centers.[61] Undoubtedly Mosterts drew an overly bleak and gloomy portrait in this appeal for financial assistance, but it is equally clear that in the years immediately before the war the Catholic Church was facing stiff competition and had to expend ever-increasing amounts of money and energy simply to maintain its influence over young Catholic workers.

Thus between 1900 and 1914, both major churches tackled youth activity considerably more systematically than before, and both confronted a series of hurdles. Probably most young workers, entering the labor force and eager to explore this new world of work and semiautonomy, would have been difficult to recruit and retain on a voluntary basis under any circumstances, as clergy often lamented. Many youths clearly regarded confirmation as a kind of rite of passage, finally releasing them from the constraints of religious supervision, which they associated with childhood and primary school.[62] Many probably were as rebellious and questioning as Baumgarten asserted. When viewed from the perspective of the clergy, complaints of youthful levity and irresponsibility were unquestionably partially well founded, since most young workers were unencumbered by family responsibilities and in their free time sought relaxation, recreation, diversion, and relief from the exhausting labor and discipline of the workshop.[63] Consequently, the long-term considerations stressed by Catholic youth groups, like saving for the military or an accident, must have seemed considerably less urgent for the youths than for many adults, since the different generations had very different time horizons. Almost all religious youth savers did realize that if they were to succeed at all, their religious porridge would have to be made more palatable by the sweetener of secular education, sports, and the cultivation of sociability. Both churches continued to underscore the primacy of religious indoctrination while in fact substantially diminishing the religious element, but their endorsement of recreational activities was often uncertain and hedged round with qualifications. Moreover, if they secularized too much, their activities would become indistinguishable from the clubs of the continuation school or the Workers' Youth Movement, a conundrum in an increasingly competitive environment.

Another problem for both churches was that they harbored biases against young laborers, whether overt or unconscious. Although there were differences in the social origins of Protestant and Catholic clergy, in general ministers and priests had middle-class origins, often came from rural or small-town settings, were invariably recipients of university or seminary educations, and often unreflectively shared the scale of values and ethos of the *Bildungsbürgertum:* a preference for craft or white-collar occupations, a deep-rooted antagonism to the Socialists, and at least in the case of Protestant ministers, a total and uncritical identification with the monarchy and the nation.[64] Dehn was assuredly right in defining most church youth groups as essentially petit bourgeois, both in their membership and in their social tone. The Catholics were somewhat more sensitive on these issues and tended to be closer to the "people." Moreover, since they divided religious and secular spheres less sharply, they had longer experience with occupational organizations and in general a firmer commitment to the welfare of young laborers. In any event, the repression of the *Kulturkampf* had strengthened Catholic unity, a unity reinforced by continued discrimination at the municipal level, and had thus slowed class fracturing within the Catholic community. But having vied politically with the Socialists for the loyalties of Catholic workers since the 1890s, the Catholic Church was also in better position to battle for the souls of young Catholic workers than was the Evangelical Church for the hearts of young Protestants. From the outset most Protestant ministers were largely pessimistic about their prospects for exercising any influence over young workers, whom they believed had already been forfeited to the Socialists. It was significant that in many cities, like Düsseldorf, they waited for government direction on youth affairs before mobilizing. Accustomed to a close relation to the Prussian government and to a kind of cozy rentier existence, the Evangelical Church was less prepared to enter the fray against the Socialists or other secular youth groups. Thus the Catholic Church was better armed for the struggle for German youth after the turn of the century. Nonetheless, both churches booked considerable increases in youth membership after 1900, although perhaps not commensurate with effort expended, but both churches also clearly felt beleagured and embattled. Though much more pronounced in the case of the Protestants, an undercurrent of *Kulturpessimismus* ran through all their statements and writings. The titles of their newspapers (*The Watch, The Lighthouse*), with their sense of lonely and isolated vigilance, their censorious attitudes toward young workers, the refrain that urban youth were beset by threatening hosts of temptations and evils, and the obsessive introspective examination of reasons for failure – all bear expressive witness to this. As much as anything, the Socialist youth movement, which they used as a standard of comparison, became a sign that the tide of the world was rapidly eroding the foundations of their fortresses.

6

The Socialist youth movement

The origins and development of systematic German youth policy were direct results of the fears and anxieties shared by government officials, teachers, clergy, and other social reformers about the growing strength and widening influence of the Social Democratic party. At one level, youth savers regarded socialism as a clear and serious menace to the unity of the nation and to the stability of the social and political order. At another level, they viewed socialism as a manifest symptom of a host of debilitating and pernicious diseases associated with an advancing modern economy and polity: materialism, hedonism, urbanization, mass popular culture, democracy, and secularization. Thus, as we have seen, major youth savers charged the Socialists with fostering pleasure seeking, demanding arrogance, and irreligiosity among the young. In whatever avatar the Socialists appeared, whether as actual social revolutionaries or as symbols of disorder, youth savers found them deplorable. The Socialists challenged both their authority and their most cherished beliefs and values, whether their intense loyalty to the Imperial State, their idealism, their religiosity, their notions of social and political harmony or their commitments to personal responsibility, individualism, and social inequality. Hence anti-Socialism became the keystone, holding together the disparate building blocks that constituted the youth salvation campaign.

Almost all youth programs contained a strong dose of anti-Socialism prescribed to weaken the viselike grip in which the Socialists ostensibly held young workers. Civic education in the continuation schools was to teach young workers that their future welfare depended on Germany's strength, which in turn hinged on class cooperation rather than conflict. Recreational programs not only offered alternatives to enfeebling urban vices and promoted the fitness vital for future military service, but were also supposed to keep young males from joining the Socialist-affiliated Worker Gymnasts. To achieve this, the German Gymnasts, well known for their virulent anti-Socialism and "hurrah patriotism," were invited to lead the gymnastics instruction in continuation schools. The lectures and recreational activities of both official Christian churches not only emphasized religion but also introduced overtly anti-Socialist themes. In Catholic youth groups even savings chests served as a means of countering Socialist disparagement of individual responsibility. Such positive measures could, if necessary, be supplemented with repressive ones as well, especially in Prussia, where since the 1848 Revolution, apprentices and students under eighteen years of age had been legally prohibited from attending political meetings or belonging to political associations.[1]

Although playing down the importance of the working-class household as a center of political socialization, youth savers were especially worried about two areas where the Socialists supposedly exercised uncontested influence over youth: in social organizations like the Worker Gymnasts and after 1904 increasingly in the formally organized Socialist youth movement. Although it is impossible to gauge the politicization of working-class households with any certainty, youth savers were probably right to discount the importance of familial political training. Given the rapid growth of the SPD after the turn of the century, it is clear that the socialist beliefs of even many SPD members were fairly superficial and that these doctrines often jostled promiscuously with conservative and patriotic ones.[2] Moreover, the overwhelming majority of SPD members and trade unionists were, after all, adult males, who played a relatively small role in child-rearing since they worked long and exhausting hours and often spent evenings engaging in party-related activities or relaxing and recuperating in the *Kneipen*. Socialist educators frequently complained of the indifference shown by even devotedly Socialist parents to the political education of their children. As a result, available evidence suggests that the schools and youth salvation campaign had considerable impact on the political orientation of working-class children and youth. For example, in his reminiscences, Karl Ottinger, a member of the Socialist youth movement in Frankfurt am Main during and after World War I, recollected that from early childhood he came into contact with the ideas and struggles of the labor movement since his father was a Socialist, trade unionist, member of a consumer co-operative, and reader of the local Socialist press.[3] Moreover, his parents and their friends frequently discussed political issues in his presence. Nonetheless, he remembered that, as a child, he and his friends had mindlessly shouted the slogans of a liberal candidate about bread prices, that he and his sister had met with incomprehension their father's refusal to permit them to participate in the festivities surrounding a visit by the kaiser in 1913, and that he had greeted the outbreak of the war with jubilation and had intensely desired to join the Pfadfinderbewegung (Boy Scouts) during the war, which his father also forbade. Thus, even the household of an organized Socialist was far from being fully insulated against the pressures of monarchical and nationalist propaganda disseminated by the schools and youth salvation campaign or simply picked up on the streets.

The first area that worried youth savers, the social, sports, and cultural affiliates of the SPD, had also been a cause of concern for state authorities since the 1890s. The association most successful at recruiting young male workers was the Free, or Worker, Gymnasts. Although officially constituted in 1893, the Free Gymnasts had been preceded by numerous local secessions by pro-Socialist workers from the hyperpatriotic and largely middle-class German Gymnasts.[4] These breakaway gymnastic clubs called for a return to the democratic, equalitarian, and radical ideals and practices that had prevailed in gymnastic societies during *Vormärz*. From the outset the Worker Gymnasts drew young laborers, not only because they made available facilities and instruction in gymnastics, but also because personal relations were closer than in the party and unions and when political issues arose they were debated in an atmosphere of informal camaraderie.[5] Partially because of this ability to recruit youth, the Worker Gymnasts also had to contend from their inception with government repression and police harassment.

In 1895 the Prussian interior minister issued a circular claiming that the Social Democratic party was using gymnastics to broaden its influence, especially among youths just completing primary school.[6] To impede this, the minister proposed banning participation of all students in activities of the Worker Gymnasts, denying their members access to schools and other public facilities, and stopping them from taking part in government-sponsored training courses for gym instructors. Many mayors and police officials doubted the utility of these proposals since most young workers weren't students, the Worker Gymnasts could afford to rent other facilities, and they had enough trained instructors to survive without participating in government courses. But after the turn of the century as major cities established mandatory continuation schools, prohibiting student membership became a more plausible measure for inhibiting recruitment.

Following the 1905 conference of the Worker Gymnasts, which resolved to pursue youth work more vigorously and consciously, the government's crackdown greatly intensified. All major cities now rescinded the right of the Free Gymnasts to use public facilities and subjected their local branches to close surveillance for signs that they were conducting political activity with youth present, in violation of Prussia's 1850 association law.[7] Such surveillance was necessary according to the mayor of Remscheid, since although the gymnastics associations appeared to be completely harmless and carefully excluded overtly political statements, even at major festivities, agitation among youth was patiently carried out on a one-to-one basis.[8] Through such gradual persuasion the Worker Gymnasts operated as a prep school for socialism. Many local authorities, undeterred by their lack of legally credible evidence, declared branches political associations, compelled them to hand over their membership lists, and fined or even jailed their executive committees for transgressing against the youth provisions of the association laws or for defying police orders.[9] In several instances, evidence as threadbare as a notice in the Socialist press for a gymnastics festival or the passing out of the gymnasts' ten commandments, which included a commandment to promote social equality, was deemed sufficient to label a Worker Gymnasts branch political, though such police and administrative chicanery was often rejected by the courts. Because of the formidable difficulties involved in obtaining credible legal evidence of political activity, police officials disinterred long-mothballed antiliberal laws from the 1830s that required private educators to obtain official certification attesting to their untarnished political loyalty and unblemished moral character, dusted off these anachronisms, and used them to prosecute Worker Gymnast instructors. The same measures were also deployed against Socialist-affiliated bicycle and singing clubs, which also recruited youth, albeit on a much smaller scale. But although this persistent harassment certainly hampered local branches and raising funds for legal defense often entailed considerable sacrifice, nonetheless, the Worker Gymnasts seem to have been able not only to hold their own, but to thrive in the face of repression during the prewar years. Thus in 1913, for example, the director of the industrial continuation school in Düsseldorf surmised that more than two hundred fifty students belonged to the Free Gymnasts, a considerably larger membership than was enrolled either by the Evangelical gymnastic groups or the school's own secular gymnastic club.[10] It has been estimated that in 1913 perhaps half of the membership of the Worker Gymnasts nationwide, or approximately one hundred thousand of its adherents, were under twenty-one years of age.

Increasingly, however, after 1904, when Socialist youth movements first organized, youth savers directed their attention to this new and, to their minds, highly dangerous development.[11] Apart from a few lackadaisical discussions on providing suitably Socialist books for the children of party members, the SPD had completely ignored work with youth until 1904, when the labor youth movement arose from two almost simultaneous initiatives, one in Berlin, the other in Mannheim.[12] The precipitant for the formation of a young workers' organization in Berlin was the grisly suicide of a mechanic apprentice who had been brutally beaten by his master. This suicide starkly dramatized the unconstrained power of masters and the lack of legal protection and deplorable conditions suffered by craft apprentices, conditions that, as we have seen, probably deteriorated after the turn of the century as many small craft shops fought for survival in a more competitive economy and many craftsmen responded by mercilessly exploiting their apprentices. Outraged over this suicide, much publicized and analyzed in the Berlin Socialist press, twenty-five journeymen, apprentices, and young workers led by Helmut Lehmann, a twenty-one-year-old trade union functionary, met on 10 October 1904, to organize for the defense of their social and economic interests. This meeting resulted in the formation of the Association of Apprentices and Young Workers of Berlin (Verein der Lehrlinge und jugendlichen Arbeiter Berlins).

In less than a year membership had skyrocketed to over five hundred as branches sprouted in most of Berlin's working-class districts. One of the most important ways of building attendance for meetings, leafleting the city's newly obligatory industrial continuation schools, gives evidence of these schools' part in facilitating the organizability of young manual workers by gathering them in a few locales. By 1906 the organization had spread to other Prussian cities with large concentrations of craft apprentices, such as Königsberg. That year the various local branches held a conference, founding the Federation of Free Youth Organizations of Germany. Although loosely tied to the SPD, which aided with the publication of its newspaper *Die Arbeitende-Jugend* and offered legal advice, the Free Youth Organization largely administered its own affairs and could certainly put forward as good a claim for being an association of, by, and for youth themselves as the much more well-researched and lovingly documented middle-class *Wandervogel.*

The aim of the organization was to advance the economic interests, legal rights, and intellectual understanding of young manual workers. To attain these ends, it sponsored talks, discussion evenings, educational courses, and common visits to museums. In addition, it campaigned against alcohol abuse and penny dreadfuls.[13] In order to comply with the Prussian association law and thus avoid dissolution by the police, branches restricted lectures and discussions to nonpolitical topics, although as Karl Korn, the worker youth movement's first and most reliable historian, noted, a Socialist world view could be furthered through historical sketches of personalities like Thomas More, Charles Fourier, Marx, and Engels or by presenting heterodox accounts of Germany's War of Liberation against Napoleon that ascribed national resistance to popular discontent rather than the steely determination of the Hohenzollern monarch. But formal compliance with the law often failed to avert police intervention. The police halted the first public meeting in Königsberg, where a lecture was scheduled on the problems of apprentices, and ruthlessly persecuted Franz Krüger, a mainstay of the labor teetotaler society, for his involvement with the local youth movement. Many members in Berlin had to participate in branch life clandestinely, since the city's master artisans were bent on extirpating the organization root and branch. Thus during its initial phase, this north German association was essentially a necessarily apolitical organization of craft apprentices and journeymen reacting to the intensification of labor and physical abuse in artisanal shops by combining defense, education, and fraternity. In many respects, it hearkened back to the semiunderground brotherhoods of journeymen that had survived during the reactionary 1850s and served as an important link between the democratic movement of 1848 and the early Socialist movement.[14]

The second initiative that laid the groundwork for a working-class youth movement in 1904 was undertaken by Ludwig Frank, a thirty-year-old lawyer who had already acquired a reputation as one of the ablest intellectuals and orators of the revisionist wing of the Social Democratic party. A reformist with a difference, Frank was an advocate of militant action in favor of democratic reform and in opposition to militarism. Upon returning from the International Socialist Congress in Amsterdam in August 1904, where he became apprised of the antimilitarist agitation of the Belgian Young Guards, he was determined to launch a similar organization in southern Germany.

The first branch, composed largely of young workers who belonged to the Worker Gymnasts, was soon functioning in Mannheim. Within a year further branches had taken root in most of the major cities and towns of Baden and Württemberg, where, in contrast to Prussia, no laws barred young laborers from political engagement. Thus, from the start the southern German youth groups could openly espouse socialism. Moreover, their newspaper, *Die Junge Garde*, regularly brought to public attention cases of manhandling and maltreatment of enlisted men in the German army. Antimilitarism, which also included draft resistance, was also the dominant theme at the 1906 conference of these south German Socialist youth groups, where the branches united to form the League of Young Workers of Germany. This conference was addressed by the radical Karl Liebknecht, who subsequently expanded this address into his famous pamphlet *Militarism and Antimilitarism.*

It was only at the Socialist Party Conference in Jena in 1905, held at the crest of the wave of radicalism that swept through Europe at the time of the first Russian Revolution, that the Social Democratic party first officially took note of the burgeoning Socialist youth movement and resolved to assist it.[15] The following year at Mannheim, the SPD tepidly endorsed the organization of the south German branches, largely at the instigation of Liebknecht. Already, however, the party's increasingly bureaucratic and stodgy leadership and the reformist trade union officials were clearly discomfited by this semiautonomous youth activity that, because of its antimilitarist thrust, threatened to provoke a head-on confrontation with the Imperial state. But in the still radical climate of 1906 they hesitated to bridle the youth movement.

In the wake of the Mannheim conference, local conferences in regions where no Socialist youth movement existed began considering ways of initiating youth activity. Thus on 6 August at a meeting in Solingen, one speaker avowed that a youth organization was absolutely indispensable.[16] "The youth must be made acquainted with the idea of human rights. Furthermore, they must be educated as autonomous free thinking men," he proclaimed, although cautiously adding that political speeches would not be possible because of the law. The first actual attempts to organize youth sections in the Rhine and Ruhr took place in mid-1907. On 7 July in Solingen-Höhscheid, the editor of the local Socialist paper attempted to answer the question, "What Do the Free Youth Organizations Want?" for a group of forty-one youths.[17] He condemned a number of firms in the Solingen area with

large bodies of apprentices and journeymen for neglecting their training and concluded that legislation was necessary to ensure that apprentices were not exploited. Apart from pressing for such legislation,
the Free Youth would foster sports, sociability, and youthful independence. A week later at an assembly in Essen, the union functionary
Limbertz lectured on "The Right of Youth to Education and the
Pleasures of Life" to a group of about fifty-five male workers and five
female workers between the ages of fourteen and eighteen.[18] In his
talk he argued for the extension of protective legislation to apprentices
and servant girls, stressed the importance of organization, warned
that the religious youth associations, so prominent in Essen, were not
earnestly concerned about the welfare of the young, and urged the
young workers to read both Socialist youth papers. According to the
police, a flyer of the Labor Teetotalers' League was also distributed
and "the known SPD leader Zenz called on those present to
join . . . 'because capitalism and alcohol are the two greatest enemies
of the workers.' "

A major stimulus for a coherent and comprehensive Socialist youth
policy came the following year, however, when the Reichstag passed
the Imperial Association Law.[19] Originally Interior Minister Bethmann Hollweg had omitted any provisions covering youth since he
believed they would be unenforceable. But in order to slow the ac-
celeration of the Socialists, both Liberal and Conservative parties insisted on amending his proposal with a section prohibiting political
activity by persons under eighteen years of age. Socialist deputies
decried the amendment, fearing that it would open the sluice gates
for arbitrary repression and would ultimately destroy any possibility
of working with youth, but to no avail.[20] The amended Imperial Association Law basically generalized the youth provisions of the Prussian law of 1850 to the entire Reich. Thus, although the political
situation in Prussia was unaltered for youth (although not for women),
in states like Baden the new law abrogated rights previously taken for
granted.

Although SPD and union officials publicly denounced the new law,
within the counsels of the party many of them were inclined to countenance it with good grace. In the major programmatic speech on
youth work at the Congress of the Free Trade Unions in Hamburg
in 1908 Robert Schmidt, a Berlin union functionary, stated that although it would have been better if the unions had controlled the
youth movement from the outset, the new law made supervision a
necessity.[21] His speech, remarkable both for its circumspect legalism

and its image of young laborers, which corresponded in every particular with the one common among middle-class youth savers, asserted that supervision was all the more urgent because of the spiraling crime rate among the young and other accumulating evidence of moral degeneration. He commended such liberal legal experiments as youth courts, pointed to the recent successes enjoyed by religious youth groups as an example, and enjoined the unions to defend apprentices and sponsor educational and recreational programs. Schmidt and other speakers, clearly anxious about the emergence of a left-wing youth movement and its potential effects on relations with the government, also attacked the appropriateness of antimilitarism for a youth group, both because it would intensify repression and because it would prove ineffectual. They also opposed any organizational autonomy for youth. In a notorious statement, bitterly resented by young militants, the bluff and paternalistic Schmidt advised apprentices that it would be healthier to buy a piece of sausage than to pay dues to a Socialist youth group.

At its annual congress held in Nürnberg the SPD acquiesced to the partial depoliticization of the movement and brought its resolution on youth affairs in line with the trade union one, testimony to the increasingly decisive sway of the trade union leaders over key party decisions.[22] It encouraged branches to sponsor educational events that would imbue young workers with "a proletarian world view." Committees composed of party, trade union, and youth representatives were to preside over local youth affairs and to remind the party and unions constantly of their obligations to further the interests of young employees. The congress also created a national commission with the same tripartite representation, and to underline the commitment to youth work, such party and union luminaries as Friedrich Ebert, Carl Legien, and Luise Zietz, all notable figures on the party's center and right, agreed to serve on it. A national youth paper, *Arbeiter-Jugend*, was approved and was soon rolling off the presses. Thus within six months of the passage of the Imperial Association Law, not only had the movement apparently been largely depoliticized, deradicalized, and centralized, but effective control had also devolved into adult hands.

Although party centrists had nominally wrested control over the youth movement at the national level, in the localities the handful of members really dedicated to youth work tended to be well-known but somewhat marginal figures often associated with the party left-wing or cultural affiliates. Many were women, since work with children and youth was regarded as an appropriate sphere of female activity.[23] Equally common were party journalists and other intellectuals, as well as zealous single-issue reformers of proletarian manners and morals, such as members of the German Abstinent Workers' League and free thinkers.[24] In addition to serving on local youth committees, such members also sat on regional educational committees that selected suitable lecture themes and reading lists for youth, disbursed funds for educational projects, and maintained contact with their national counterparts, such as Heinrich Schulz, a former primary school teacher and reformist publicist who authored much of the party's literature both for and about the young and directed national recruitment activity.[25]

This new and concerted emphasis on youth work certainly unleashed a wave of organizational growth.[26] Youth groups sprang into life in cities where they had previously been absent, such as Düsseldorf. There, Emil Müller, editor of the Socialist newspaper *Die Volkszeitung,* and Ewald Ochel, a sculptor, began holding weekly meetings where they discussed alcohol abuse and natural science.[27] The police suspected that they openly treated socialist themes as well, since meetings broke up whenever policemen arrived. In addition, the local youth committee repeatedly leafleted the continuation school and had won two hundred subscribers for *Arbeiter-Jugend.* Nationwide, subscriptions to *Arbeiter-Jugend* climbed from almost 40,000 to over 65,000 between 1908 and 1910. In that year local committees held a combined total of 1,804 single lectures, 82 lecture series, 69 educational courses, 326 artistic presentations, and 282 museum visits. Attendance at lectures topped 62,000, although many of those counted were undoubtedly repeaters.

Who were these youths who subscribed to *Arbeiter-Jugend* and attended lectures of the labor youth movement? Statistics kept of 640 young visitors to the Socialist youth center in Elberfeld, of whom 548 already read *Arbeiter-Jugend* at the time of their initial visit, indicate that almost 80 percent (499) were males between the ages of fourteen and twenty and that the majority were either apprentices or journeymen, rather than unskilled laborers.[28] Over 25 percent (136) worked in the textile industry, Elberfeld's largest branch of employment, and about 20 percent (111) in the metal trades, with trade and transport workers coming in third with almost 15 percent (73). Traditional crafts were also represented, with twenty-two bookbinders, fourteen printers, eleven leather workers, and eight young tailors, among others. A mere seventeen male visitors to the youth center, however, were white-collar employees. Among the 141 young female visitors, almost 45 percent (63) were textile workers, although these female workers were much less likely to be skilled than their male counterparts. A survey of 5,134 *Arbeiter-Jugend* readers in Berlin compiled in 1914 showed that the gender gap in the capital was equally pronounced, with a male readership of 4,258 (almost 83 percent), in contrast to 876 (slightly more than 17 percent) female subscribers.[29] But the occupational profile of young Socialists in the Imperial capital was significantly different from that in Elberfeld. Not surprisingly, given the industrial structure and union organization of Berlin, almost 30 percent of the young males (1,254) were skilled metalworkers, and an almost equal number held jobs as unskilled factory laborers (1,249), but the third-largest category of male readers in this commercial and administrative, as well as industrial, center was young white-collar workers (331, or almost 8 percent), followed by wood workers (291), printers (282), and tailors (170). Here, too, those training in the traditional crafts subscribed: upholsterers (52), leather workers (47), and bookbinders (23), as well as apprentices and journeymen learning a host of other trades. Glaring in both cities, however, was the virtual absence of young construction workers, perhaps because such jobs tended to be taken by recent rural migrants to the city who were less likely to have contacts with the SPD. There were also few young workers in food-related trades with strong guilds, for example, among butchers and bakers. Most common among young women who subscribed in Berlin were unskilled factory laborers (328), followed by seamstresses (111). But female subscribers also found employment in a variety of pink-collar occupations, as commercial clerks (87), shop assistants (68), and salesgirls (64), a sign of the changing structure of opportunity for young working-class females.

The strong presence of young metal workers in the youth movements of both cities can certainly be attributed in part to the fact that the Metalworkers' Union was the major Free Trade Union agitating actively among young workers and regularly staging programs for youth.[30] Some spokespersons for the SPD left grumbled that trade union work simply duplicated party efforts and hence dissipated valuable energy, although this was probably simply an organizational pretext for excluding the reformist trade union leaders from this arena.[31] But although the unions may have occasionally recruited a young worker directly from the shopfloor, both the literature of the youth committees and Socialist autobiographies leave little doubt that the overwhelming majority of youth movement members were children of party and union stalwarts.[32] If growth lagged, Socialist parents were blamed. Although in contrast to other youth groups, the Free Youth was sexually integrated, the paucity of female members was imputed to the moral conservatism of working-class mothers, who were chided for raising their daughters to be "hermits and frightened mice."[33] The SPD also admonished parents for allowing their children to join patriotic or religious youth groups.[34] This coaxing and cajoling of Socialist parents points to an unresolved ambiguity about parental authority. On the one hand, the young were promised the fullest possible freedom to follow their own inclinations and to assume responsibility for their own conduct. On the other hand, when party elders disapproved of their choices, Socialist parents were scolded for abnegating their parental duties.

Recruitment literature was generally produced at the national level and divided almost equally between material aimed at Socialist parents and at young workers. Material for the former attempted to counter parental objections to membership in the Socialist youth movement by reminding them that since they were harnessing their entire strength to forge a better world, they were duty bound to raise class-conscious children who could conquer the future.[35] Moreover, they owed their children an opportunity for education, sociability, enjoyment of art, and protection from employers. Leaflets for young workers certainly mentioned education, but primarily they celebrated youthful freedom and joy in life, the cultivation of feeling as much as knowledge. Thus the national leaflet "To Those Completing Elementary School" criticized the schools as drill institutions "where the masterworks of our poets are ground into rubbish heaps of words and sentences instead of bringing to life their sense and beauty."[36] After school came the treadmill routines of the factory or housework. Older workers who vented their frustrations and fatigue on the young often worsened matters. But the flyer assured young workers that their situation was not hopeless, especially if they banded together with others confronting the same predicament. In contrast to the religious youth associations, with their Sunday preaching and pious incantations, or the patriotic ones, which would reduce youth to "will-less slaves," in the labor youth movement knowledge would advance their freedom. Through education, festivities, and sociability they would develop their strength and prepare for the struggle against exploitation and repression.

Although such flyers might initially pique the curiosity of young workers, the biweekly *Arbeiter-Jugend* was a more effective vehicle for explaining the viewpoint of the Socialist movement. Even middle-class youth savers praised it for its well-designed layout and vivid writing, and one Protestant minister in Düsseldorf confessed that Protestants had nothing to equal it.[37] Although characterizing its attacks on religion as satanic, he grudgingly conceded that it was well written, campaigned effectively against alcohol and penny dreadfuls, and "preached socialism like a new gospel." Usually the topics of articles closely corresponded to the most common lecture themes in Free Youth branches: German authors, natural science, history, and travel and foreign culture. But newspaper articles could be more openly Socialist since youths under eighteen could buy political literature unmolested by the police. Thus the first issue in 1909 contained an article on the meaning of socialism and another by the literary critic and Marx biographer Franz Mehring on the importance of Ferdinand Lassalle for the early German labor movement. Ludwig Frank, writing on the Imperial Constitution, excoriated Germany's inequitable suffrage system for giving preponderance to rural interests and unfavorably contrasted the German monarchy and ministerial rule with England's parliamentary government. Articles even assailed other political parties for serving the wealthy and powerful and attacked the Center party for elevating the supposedly private matter of religion into a political issue. In addition to the polemics, *Arbeiter-Jugend* carried purely informational pieces on issues like protective legislation, pieces that differed little from those appearing in the Catholic youth paper, *Die Wacht*.[38] The ongoing importance of *Arbeiter-Jugend* as an organizing tool and for defining and unifying the movement can be inferred from the fact that when local branches were dissolved by the police for overstepping the Association Law, they almost invariably and immediately reconstituted themselves as clubs of *Arbeiter-Jugend* readers.[39]

Apart from leaflets and the newspaper, another way of drawing in and retaining young workers was by setting up well-equipped public rooms where they could socialize. The 1910 conference of Socialist youth committees suggested that local SPD branches and the trade unions should jointly fund youth centers with game and reading rooms and a library.[40] Such centers would serve as alternatives to the bars, where amidst the smoky, alcohol-suffused atmosphere, youths would ruin their health. These centers could be assured of broad support within the party since those on the left, such as Klara Zetkin, were as worried as those on the right or as middle-class reformers about the exposure of young workers to smoking, drinking, cabarets, and pornography.[41] The guidelines also closely paralleled typical plans for continuation school recreational facilities and were undoubtedly conceived as a means for competing with these well-financed official institutions. In most large cities, the party and unions accepted these recommendations. Thus, in Düsseldorf in 1912 the Free Youth moved from cramped quarters in the People's House to four capacious rooms rented at a cost of one thousand marks annually.[42] The new center included a lecture hall and a library stocked with approved books and a wide array of Socialist, union, sports, popular scientific, and humor periodicals. It was open every evening after continuation school and on Sunday afternoons to welcome any youth who was willing to abide by minimal rules, such as refraining from smoking. In the course of an ordinary evening between twenty and sixty young people would drop by to converse, read, or play board games. Police observers noted that when adult supervision was lacking, as was frequently the case, there was much horseplay and rowdiness, but they considered these evening activities "sociable and quite harmless." This assessment is confirmed by biographical accounts written by former members of the Socialist youth movement. Thus Karl Retzlaw, a member in Berlin and son of a devoutly Baptist mother, wrote that the Labor Youth Movement

... was a really innocent affair. Tobacco and the enjoyment of alcohol were not permitted at the gatherings in the youth center. In lectures we were taught how harmful these habits are for youth. With these principles it was hardly possible to get together in other places. Saloon keepers rent no rooms to nonsmokers and nondrinkers. There were mostly sons and daughters of fathers organized by the Socialists or trade unions. More than thirty youths almost never appeared on one evening, and among these were at most four or five girls. It was just as "well behaved" as earlier in Baptist Sunday school. All believed in a better future, and they knew this would not come of itself but had to be fought for. Their idealism was muted by tiredness; all had long workdays behind them.[43]

This respectability, however, may have distanced some young Socialists from their fellow workers. Retzlaw, who tried to persuade his workmates to drink wholesome milk rather than unhealthy beer, was probably considered hopelessly eccentric.

Less harmless than the sociable evenings, maintained the police, were the organized lectures and cultural events of the Free Youth. Although one policeman surprisingly granted that "it cannot be denied that in literary and artistic matters, the young people are offered much that is good and unobjectionable," he nonetheless deduced that the lectures proved that "now, as before, the goal of the association is to initiate the young into the world of socialist ideas and thoroughly eradicate any patriotic sentiment that might be retained from school with social democratic history and partially overt, partially covert, antimilitary propaganda."[44] Given that few workers, young or old, read heavily, and that the Socialist subculture remained a predominantly oral one, the police were probably justified in focusing on lectures and informal discussions as the paramount way of influencing young workers, even though the content of lectures diverged little from articles in *Arbeiter-Jugend*.[45] In oral presentations, however, Socialist educators relied on repeated slogans, parables, and tropes that, like the refrains of poems and songs, delighted by their complete familiarity and that often barely concealed political criticism behind an Aesopian cloak.[46]

As in the Protestant youth associations, lectures covered an extraordinary mélange of topics: the youth and labor movements, literature, educational issues, biography, cultural history, natural science, and alcohol abuse, among others.[47] Many of these were at most marginally political, although Socialist speakers tried to infuse even travelogues with didactic commentary on the living and working conditions of exotic peoples. The Socialist youth movement took religion as seriously as the religious youth groups took the gospel of socialism. Natural science, which in the SPD milieu exclusively meant popular Darwinism, was used to debunk the teachings of the churches and primary schools, which because of their literalism were vulnerable on this score. Fossil evidence and comparative anatomy were arrayed to demonstrate the factual inaccuracy of *Genesis*. Although debunking was the most common way of grappling with residual religion among the young, other approaches were tried as well. On Easter and Pentecost, both major festivals for the labor youth movement, speakers often represented socialism as the legatee and realization of original Christianity. A more sophisticated approach conjoined Feuerbachian anthropology with a materialist evolutionary scheme by treating religion as a necessary projection of human needs and an attempt to comprehend natural forces at a specific stage of a people's social development.

Even poetry assumed a political function and contributed to shaping a radical counterculture. Schiller, Heine, and Freilgrath were the most popular poets, and freedom and social injustice the most popular themes.[48] Visions of rebel heroes and popular revolt embodied in memorable rhymes and refrains could certainly inspire young workers more after a day on the shopfloor than could an introduction to political economy. Such poems could also put to flight the paeans to German military glory memorized in the primary schools. Recognizing this, the police regularly interrupted recitations of Heine's "The Silesian Weavers" or "Germany: A Winter's Tale" as violations of the Association Law.[49] Even under the expansive definition of the "political," which encompassed any discussion of the constitution or governmental bodies and institutions, such police intervention was questionably legal. But even in a more restrictive sense, many Socialist lectures would have fallen under the rubric. Biographic lectures on Marx, Lassalle, and Bebel not only held up their lives as models, but also provided simplified accounts of their doctrines.[50] Other lectures took up central problems of the materialist conception of history, including the origins of social classes. Thus the lectures were undeniably designed to imbue young workers with "a proletarian world view" or, in police terminology, to "initiate the young into the world of Socialist ideas."

The administration and police feared the effects of other Socialist activities as well. They certainly knew that at the festive evenings for departing army inductees, on prudential grounds Socialist elders exhorted the draftees against insubordination or political activity while in service, but they believed that the young men were secretly armed with antimilitary instructions.[51] Whereas the police viewed excursions and hikes as golden opportunities for Socialists to proselytize and indoctrinate youth, the youth committees expressed concern that such activities were purely recreational and contributed nothing to the political education of youth.[52] Originally the trips to the countryside were more excursions than hikes. Young participants wore their finest Sunday clothes, marched to some picturesque vista, and stopped for refreshment in a tavern. To be sure, the marchers carried a red flag and tussled with any religious youth groups they encountered along the way, but the regenerative powers and unsurpassable beauty of nature rather than class or political struggle gave purpose to these outings.[53] By 1912, admittedly influenced by the style of the middle-class *Wandervogel*, Socialist educators were encouraging the young to dress informally for real hiking, to eat in the open air, and to hike in small groups, but such informality, of course, neither politicized excursions nor distinguished them from those of other youth groups.[54] To steer them in a more educational direction, regional committees attempted to transform these outings into "social hikes" that would "sharpen the eyes for social relations in various regions" and teach young laborers about "fundamental processes in nature and society," apparently with some success, judging by accounts of former members of the Socialist youth movement in Frankfurt, who wandered through the countryside, observing the poverty and bad health of rural laborers. But to the disappointment of youth committees in the Rhineland, young workers showed little interest in visits to industrial sites or to municipal plants like the gas and water works.

In addition to such regular local events, the Socialist youth calendar culminated in massive Easter celebrations and three-day regional rallies and hikes ending on Pentecost, which imitated and substituted for religious observance. On Easter Sunday the Düsseldorf SPD, for example, rented a large theater and brought in a nationally prominent speaker on youth affairs like Wilhelm Sollmann, the editor of the Cologne Socialist newspaper, or Jürgen Brand, a former school teacher from Bremen and author of countless children's books.[55] Before a mixed audience of some fifteen hundred adults and youth, the speaker preached on the deficiencies of Germany's primary schools, the stultification induced by non-Socialist youth groups, and the degenerative consequences of alcohol and penny dreadfuls for the young. The most important annual youth event was the Pentecost hike that, like a Catholic pilgrimage, wound along some scenic route in the Lower Rhine.[56] On Pentecost Luise Zietz, one of the most prominent SPD women's leaders, or some other SPD notable, would address a mammoth outdoor rally of three to five thousand listeners, a rally that, with its audience responses and semireligious overtones, resembled a Protestant revival. Since the speakers castigated government-sponsored youth cultivation, these rallies were declared political assemblies by the police, who only allowed them to reconvene when all youth under eighteen had been cleared from the area.

Of course, both the movement's political caution and organizational forms were conditioned by the omnipresent threat and reality of repression, although repression seems to have engendered somewhat contradictory results. It certainly nudged adults toward greater restraint and was probably a major reason why so few Socialist parents pressured their children into joining. Socialist educators who bore the brunt of arrests and fines were generally angered by the arbitrariness of the police but nonetheless gradually became more moderate and measured in their public statements.[57] For the young, however, defying the authorities by mocking, baiting, taunting, and outwitting the police, those supposedly slow-footed and slower-witted pillars of

Imperial Germany's system of class justice, added an aura of excitement and danger to Socialist youth activities.[58]

In the Rhine–Ruhr region two waves of repression descended on the Socialist youth movement, the first in early 1911, the second in 1913. With considerable plausibility, SPD members concluded that the motive behind the first wave was to injure the party's electoral chances by goading it into illegal actions during a closely contested Reichstag campaign. The second wave coincided with a period of demoralization, self-doubt, and disarray within the SPD, as members discovered the hollowness of their stunning nationwide victory in the elections of 1912. This centrally orchestrated onslaught against the Socialist youth movement confirmed the oft-repeated Socialist epigram about the Prussian government, "When they whistle in Berlin, they dance in the provinces."[59] But many local police officials, responsible to elected liberal city councils, more or less committed to *Rechtsstaat* principles, not only questioned the wisdom of this second repressive drive, but also frequently respected legal procedures much more than did the juridically educated officials of the administrative bureaucracy, who were answerable only to the interior minister.

Taking Düsseldorf as an example, 1911 was a year of especially severe repression from the beginning. In January, six undercover agents and ten uniformed policemen stormed into the People's House, took the thirty youths present into custody, and forced them to divulge their names and empty their pockets before releasing them.[60] Two months later the police dissolved the local youth organization because of its "repeatedly ascertained political activity and close association with the Social Democratic Party."[61] Reconstituting the group as a loose club of *Arbeiter-Jugend* readers brought no relief from constant surveillance and relentless harassment. A police escort accompanied every hike and excursion, and occasionally a policeman would try to seize the company's red flag.[62] At the summer festival of *Arbeiter-Jugend* readers, police commissioner Gauer halted the proceedings as soon as a girl began to read the opening poem. Numerous agents provocateurs attempted to precipitate violent resistance; hence, a few minutes after Gauer's dissolution order, a squad of policemen rushed into the hall with sabers drawn. But aware that any tumult would detract from the party's chances in the upcoming election, those present were already calmly and peaceably departing. A few days later the SPD held a large public rally at which Socialist editor and youth worker Müller protested this provocation. Whether because of the size of the rally or the SPD's electoral triumph, this was the last major police action against the Socialist youth movement for two years.

In the aftermath of the SPD's electoral success in 1912, Prussia's administrative bureaucracy began applying pressure to local police departments to crack down on the youth movement. In April 1913 the district governor reprimanded the Düsseldorf police commissioner for failing to stop the annual Easter assembly.[63] Although Gauer acknowledged that the featured speaker's lecture had warranted dissolving the meeting, he argued tactically that this would have only strengthened the radicals in the SPD. Two months later he refused to follow the recommendation that the police close the local youth center and forbid all lectures. There were no legal grounds for doing so, according to Gauer, since the center was largely used for sociable purposes, and moreover, such measures were superfluous since the local labor youth movement had no special significance.[64] But the district governor did not tolerate such local imperturbability for long.

During the fall of 1913 Socialist youth were confronted with a coordinated campaign of repression. In September and October the police in Solingen prosecuted several young workers for engaging in political activity.[65] The city's continuation school hammered home this lesson by warning students against joining political associations. At a meeting attended by educators, city officials, and police, the commissioner of the rural county adjacent to Solingen cynically declared his intention of prohibiting the local SPD's youth committee by stretching the law. "To be sure," he regretted, "article II of the Imperial Association Law is a *lex imperfecta,* but the proclamation of dissolution may still have a moral effect and ease the way for more forceful police measures later." In Elberfeld, police confiscated leaflets proffering advice to military draftees.

Repression continued unabated through the winter and following spring. To loud calls of "Pfui" and protests against shoving, the Düsseldorf police hustled all youths under eighteen at the Easter assembly from the hall.[66] A week later they broke up a meeting of a hundred youths at the People's House, despite the complaint of a Socialist lawyer that since the meeting was private, they had no business there. But the police were adamant, so the youth sang "The Young Guard" and dispersed. A similar fate awaited the regional Pentecost rally in Krefeld that year, where Luise Zietz was slated to speak on the ironic theme "Happy Youth."[67] The attendance at the 1914 rally, approximately two thousand youths, was considerably diminished from previous years, evidence that repression and Socialist demoralization were beginning to take their toll. In that instance the local authorities publicly revealed that the district governor had ordered and planned the dissolution, a revelation that infuriated the governor, who chastised the Krefeld police for leaking intraadministrative orders. But without the steady pressure from above, it is doubtful if this wave of repression would have occurred at all. Whether in Düsseldorf, Solingen, or Essen, the police were agreed that the expansion of the government's positive youth cultivation campaign was by far the most effective means of undermining the Socialist youth movement and that this program had already demonstrated remarkable efficacy.[68]

The Lower Rhine conference of the SPD held in late 1913 concurred. The conference recognized that no progress had been made in youth work during the previous year because of the rigor of official repression, the millions of marks expended on state youth cultivation, and "not least the criminal equanimity of many proletarian parents."[69] Speakers also remarked that the sons of SPD members were joining bourgeois youth groups. Earlier at the SPD's annual conference of 1913 in Jena, Sollmann of Cologne and other Socialist educators had already reached a similar conclusion.[70] Sollmann pointed out that in a number of localities the Socialist youth movement had retreated. "I have the impression," he stated, "that in broad party circles the significant danger of the bourgeois youth movement is underestimated." He also accused the party of writing leaflets incomprehensible to youth and completely ignoring work with young women. Some of these points were seconded by the trade union journalist Adolf Braun, who forthrightly told the delegates, "Let us not deceive ourselves with the official report; we're not going forward, but the bourgeois youth movement is. The young people in the bourgeois youth movement have the feeling of far greater freedom and independence, of much less supervision than ours have. Perhaps they're more pushed around and supervised than ours, but they don't notice it as much. With us they perceive that they're to be watered down and disciplined."[71] Certainly such laments cannot be taken entirely at face value. The points about discipline and political dilution were rhetorical moves in the intense internal faction fight between left and right, with the left championing youth as a radical and potentially regenerating force;

nonetheless, such remarks attest to the Socialist youth movement's lost momentum in the face of repression, Socialist moderation, and the massive campaign of youth cultivation by the Prussian state. It is to the extraordinary expansion of governmental youth programs and its consequences that we shall now turn.

7

Youth cultivation: the centralization and militarization of youth salvation

The year 1911 marked a major inflection point in the trajectory of the youth salvation campaign. That year both the tendencies and developments characteristic of the campaign to save working-class youth since 1900 reached a culmination, and at the same time there was a sharp break from the campaign's previous direction and activities. In the first place, the Prussian state assumed a considerably expanded role as the motor force, steering mechanism, and coordinating center of youth activity. The drive for centralization undertaken by the administrative bureaucracy led to the subsumption of much local initiative under central state direction and resulted in far greater uniformity in youth policy. Because of the secular character of state policy, it also diminished the role of the Catholic Church in shaping youth welfare measures. Second, in response to prodding from the army, youth work underwent a pronounced militarization, with emphasis placed on building paramilitary formations like the Jungdeutschlandbund (Young Germany League). Third, as we have already seen in part in the previous chapter, these shifts were accompanied by a far more aggressive attack on the Socialist youth movement.

The major source of impetus for the new course was the proclamation of the Youth Cultivation Edict by the Prussian Ministry of Religious, Educational, and Medical Affairs on 18 January 1911.[1] Even the date of the proclamation underscored its importance, since it coincided with the fortieth anniversary of the founding of the Empire. Another clue to its importance was indicated by the neologism *Jugendpflege* (youth cultivation) coined to replace the previously standard *Jugendfürsorge* (youth welfare). Whereas *Fürsorge* was freighted with connotations of welfare work with orphaned, endangered, or delinquent youth; *Pflege,* usually applied to cultivating plants, stressed a need for protection and nurture to foster development, and although paternalistic, could cover all youth without pejorative overtones. Apart from such symbolic accents, however, the most important feature of the edict was its promise of a considerably enlarged part for the Prussian state. Certainly, as noted in Chapter 3, the central Prussian government had played an inspirational and facilitating role in the youth salvation campaign from the outset. After the conferences of 1900, the Education, Trade, and Interior Ministries had called upon teachers and clergy to become involved in recreational programs for urban working-class males and had stamped the efforts of several religious youth organizations with their official imprimatur. Through training courses and financial aid the Trade Ministry had also assisted the recreational activities of continuation schools. But the central government became much more interventionist only as the Socialist youth movement began to acquire a significant following and the Worker Gymnasts focused on recruiting young workers. To allay largely justified conservative criticisms that his draft of the Imperial Association Law abandoned the last legal barrier against open recruitment of youth by the SPD, in 1907 Interior Minister Bethmann Hollweg proposed broadening the patriotic and recreational tasks of the continuation schools.[2] Although Chancellor Bülow threw his authority behind this proposal, it was delayed for over three years by interministerial squabbling, especially between the Trade Ministry, which regulated the continuation schools, and the Education Ministry, which oversaw other areas of youth activity. Moreover, the finance minister was adamantly opposed to allocating funds for major new projects at a time when the government was mired in an acute fiscal crisis. Thus, when the Youth Cultivation Edict was finally written in January 1911, essentially along the lines originally envisaged by Bethmann Hollweg, it ended a decade of somewhat haphazard and disjointed intervention by the Prussian government and had been hammered out after protracted intragovernmental wrangling and negotiating to frame a more comprehensive policy.

Given this lengthy incubation period and the fanfare that surrounded the promulgation of the edict, its content was remarkably anemic. A brief preamble reiterated the standard litany of concerns common to youth savers about the ways in which economic transformation had undermined family life and eroded the morals of youth.[3] These dangers required a national policy that depended on the assistance of all "who have a heart for youth and who are prepared and able to further their patriotic education," although teachers and clergy were specifically designated appropriate youth cultivators. The preamble was followed by a series of guidelines that basically codified existing practices and proposals. Among the means to be used in raising a "joyful, physically capable, ethically proficient youth filled with a sense of community, fear of God, love of locality and the Fatherland" were gymnastics and swimming, handicrafts, visits to museums and monuments, libraries with prescribed books, and youth centers. The edict recognized that youth cultivation would have to take account of such characteristics of hitherto unorganized youth as their alienation from the churches and their desire to determine their own leisure activities after their daily rounds of strenuous labor. Although denouncing bureaucratic measures and stating that the free play of all forces was needed, the edict's major innovation lay in setting up a formal organizational apparatus at the district and county (*Kreis*) level under the aegis of the Education Ministry. Two weeks later Kaiser Wilhelm, in an address to the Prussian Diet, outlined the goals and tasks of youth cultivation and recommended that the legislators budget a million marks to these ends.[4] Both the edict and the kaiser's address were greeted enthusiastically by both major Christian denominations and by the political parties, with the exception of the Socialists, who disparaged the entire youth cultivation campaign as an anti-Socialist swindle designed to imbue laboring youth with the Prussian spirit of servility and sanctimonious religious bigotry.

Despite royal patronage and the welcome lubricant of finance, the wheels of the bureaucracy revolved slowly. It was early summer before Francis Kruse, the governor of the Düsseldorf district, spurred the localities to set up youth cultivation committees.[5] Some towns had taken the initiative earlier, without waiting for direction from the center. For example, in late February the welfare committee of Solingen-Ohligs added youth cultivation to its duties and debated the most effective ways of pursuing it.[6] Committee Chairman Mohrenstecher, director of the local continuation school, favored close cooperation with local factory owners and master artisans to win over the 40 percent of young males not enrolled in sports clubs or other associations. Although wishing to avoid competition with religious groups, the county commissioner rejected relying on them exclusively since many youths were either religiously indifferent or hostile. One speaker suggested that the religious groups should confine themselves solely to spiritual matters, whereas sports clubs would be interdenominational and purely secular. He also felt that heavy-handed patriotism

would be counterproductive and that political discretion was necessary, "since many youths are already inclined to a political party,"
testimony to the importance of the Socialists in the Solingen area. In
Düsseldorf, by contrast, a youth committee was never formed. According to Lord Mayor Oehler, it would have been entirely superfluous since all patriotic youth groups had demonstrated their ability to
cooperate for important events and projects on an ad hoc basis.[7] But
the ensuing debate in the city council, in which Center party representatives repeatedly urged the mayor to appoint a committee, leaves
little doubt that enmity between the council's liberal majority and
Center minority, rather than amity, accounted for the mayor's decision. But Düsseldorf was an exception. By 1914, 230 local youth cultivation committees were operating in the Düsseldorf governmental
district alone.[8]

The districtwide committee was not called into life until April 1912,
at a regional conference initiated by Kruse.[9] To this conference Kruse
assigned the objective of evaluating progress made in the previous
year and charting a course for the coming one. In his opening speech,
District Court Judge Adelmann summarized recent advances. Although applauding the rapid growth of youth groups, which now
enlisted half of the two hundred thousand young male workers in the
district, he nevertheless feared that those in greatest need of youth
cultivation had eluded the widening network of religious, sport, and
patriotic associations. Nor, he thought, had the campaign been able
to reduce significantly the moral dangers assailing youth, whether
arising from dissolution of the family and patriarchal master–apprentice relations or from irreligion, reading penny dreadfuls, abus-
ing alcohol, and ethical confusion. A district committee, he avowed,
would provide an organizing center for a more concerted and coordinated campaign. The contingent from Düsseldorf serving on the
district committee was typical of the membership selected for these
regional bodies throughout Prussia. Most were knowledgeable and
seasoned youth workers, for example, Karl Gotter of the industrial
continuation school, Theodor Herold of the commercial art school,
Karl Mosterts, director of the Catholic Youth Associations, Chaplain
Esser, youth pastor of St. Rochus, and Hans Schubart, a merchant
active in the Poseidon Swimming Association and chairman of the
Düsseldorf Federation of Physical Exercise Clubs.[10] Several women
from Düsseldorf were also named to the committee, including Maria
Russell, a middle school teacher, and Marie Baum, a former factory
inspector in Baden and the director of the Association for Infant

Welfare in Düsseldorf.[11] The full committee, with more than seventy members, was far too bloated and immobile a body to function efficiently, however, and so it selected a working subcommittee of twenty-two that was to meet quarterly in order to recommend good books for youth, publicize regional activities, and promote youth centers and sports.

Apart from publicity and coordination, one of the major responsibilities of the district committee was advising the district governor on disbursing the specially earmarked government youth funds. Available funds averaged a rather meager one hundred thousand marks annually in the densely populated, heavily industrial Düsseldorf district.[12] The governor distributed much of this money as grants to sports and religious youth groups.[13] Applicants for such grants had to supply detailed information on membership, past programs, and expenditures, as well as projected budgets and future plans. Awards, which generally ranged between fifty and one thousand marks, were usually dispensed for permanent facilities and equipment, such as vaulting horses or library books, rather than for operating expenses. The largest grants often went to associations with long-established and comprehensive youth programs, a policy that advantaged the haves and therefore often ran counter to the ostensible purpose of the funding. Thus, for example, four or five times more government money flowed into the coffers of the middle-class Catholic parish St. Rochus in Düsseldorf than into those of the struggling parish youth group in Eller, a working-class suburb. Similarly, the almost entirely middle-class and highly nationalist German Gymnasts in Düsseldorf was granted three hundred marks, whereas the politically and denominationally neutral neighborhood gymnastic clubs, where many young workers exercised and socialized, could only procure fifty or one hundred marks. It also appears that Catholic youth groups were subject to discrimination. To be sure, since the majority of youth groups in the Düsseldorf district were associated with the Catholic Church, they brought in the lion's share of the funds, but secular sports clubs and Protestant groups almost invariably received larger individual grants.

Funds were also spent on the further training of teachers and other youth workers. Already in 1911 training expenses reached six thousand marks, and this expenditure skyrocketed as conferences, seminars, and special programs proliferated.[14] Such training was calculated to enhance the skills of teachers, clergy, and interested laypersons by introducing them to the rudiments of youth social work.

Some well-known youth reformers, however, among them the Hamburg minister Walther Classen, had long criticized such hasty and superficial preparation as inadequate and instead advocated transforming youth work from a part-time occupation of overburdened teachers and clergy into a fully independent profession.[15] Many middle-class women also hoped that the edict of 1911 presaged a new profession open to them, but voluntary part-time work would remain the norm until the Weimar Republic.

Typical of these training courses was the "Düsseldorf Week for the Further Education of Male and Female Youth Cultivators" held in the municipal concert hall in October 1913, with 2,060 in attendance.[16] Sessions featured nationally prominent figures as drawing cards, including Pastor Classen, who elaborated on Kerschensteiner's theme of civic education, and Field Marshal Freiherr von der Goltz, founder of the paramilitary Jungdeutschlandbund, who expatiated on the value of war games for developing strength of character and physical fitness. Speakers from Düsseldorf or the region delivered organizational reports or detailed more specialized aspects of youth work. Chaplain Mosterts reported on the growth of Catholic youth associations while Pastors Weigle of Essen and Rose of Düsseldorf recounted Protestant efforts. Gotter praised woodwork for instilling self-discipline in youth, and Rector Grund described the recreational program of Düsseldorf's industrial continuation school. Two clerics railed against the contribution of films to youthful moral degeneracy, while Josef Wilden, an official of the Düsseldorf Chamber of Commerce, lectured on the intimate link between youth cultivation and the preservation of public monuments. Marie Baum drew on her experience as a factory inspector in Baden and a welfare worker with infants in the Düsseldorf region to limn the plight of young women factory workers. Her speech signaled the arrival of youth cultivation for young female laborers (a subject that will be taken up separately in the next chapter). Thus participants were bombarded by a bewildering array of themes and issues in this variegated educational bazaar, where each speaker touted his or her favorite nostrum as the thaumaturgic potion for the recovery of laboring youth. Through such programs, however, over twenty-two thousand new youth workers were trained in Germany during 1912, and over twenty-eight thousand the following year.[17]

The availability of government funds and the influx of new youth workers often rejuvenated existing youth groups or precipitated the founding of new ones. Fueled by government monies, Catholic and Protestant youth groups were able to beef up their gymnastic programs and start libraries or add on to existing ones. In a rare display of ecumenicism, clergy of both denominations, infused with the crusading spirit of the edict, organized an interdenominational sports club in Oberkassel, a suburb of Düsseldorf, which soon boasted 165 members.[18] Purely secular sports associations, whether the German Gymnasts or exclusively neighborhood clubs, also prospered in the feverish atmosphere of youth cultivation. Large industrial firms with traditions of paternalism and company unions either boosted or inaugurated employer-sponsored youth programs.

The Krupp firm, highly paternalistic and closely linked to the government because of its centrality for armaments manufacture, created the most elaborate industrial youth program. This program originated in 1902 as an offshoot of the Krupp Educational Society, a company-subsidized association of employees founded in order to advance general education and practice common recreation.[19] The youth section, composed of members' children, messengers, and apprentices, met on Sundays under the supervision of a teacher or other adult for lectures in winter and hikes in summer. In 1909 this section counted a membership of 120 youths between the ages of fourteen and seventeen and twenty-five members in a separate section for clerical employees younger than twenty-one. Nonetheless, in reply to a questionnaire from the city of Essen in April 1911 a Krupp official admitted, "Krupp youth cultivation is still in its formative period."[20] Already, however, a large company youth cultivation committee with over one hundred nominal members had constituted itself, and the handful of really active participants had prepared themselves by attending periodic lectures on subjects like youth work in Hamburg or the meaning of civic education.[21] Inspired by the pretentious medieval revivalism of the *Wandervögeln,* the romantic cult of the medieval wanderer and chivalry, Krupp's youth cultivation committee severed the bond between the youth groups and the Educational Society and recast the groups, dubbing the clerks' section with the romantically inspired Roland and sections for younger workers Young Roland and Eckhart. Three age-stratified youth groups of female clerks and laborers were forged as well and christened with the equally medieval names Barbara, Freia, and Treuhilde. In reporting on these developments, the engineer Bänser confessed, however, that the *Wandervogel* could not be fully imitated since the members of the Krupp youth groups weren't students and most would not be willing or able to pay the cost of *Wandervogel* equipage. Clearly the cost of studied naturalness and unadorned simplicity ran high.

By 1912 Jungroland had three sections, one of which was based in the apprentice workshop, with a total of three hundred members, although an attempt to start a section at a Krupp coal mine foundered when exactly six youths appeared for the initial meeting. The groups for young women had recruited almost two hundred members. These youth clubs festively celebrated patriotic and religious holidays like Christmas, Sedan Day, and the kaiser's birthday, which as the report noted, kept their members off the street. Jungroland held regular Friday meetings, with lectures by Krupp managers or public officials usually handling patriotic themes like "German Sea Heroes," "Colonial Policy," "The German Constitution," and "Army and Navy," although they occasionally treated moral and health issues like "Alcohol and Its Dangers." The annual report regretted that provoking discussion on some lectures, especially on statistical ones on Germany's population, had proved to be virtually impossible, whereas it had been easiest to raise interest in constitutional questions. Recreational meetings with opportunities for playing board games or reading periodicals occurred on Sunday afternoons, and instruction in woodworking was also available. During the summer the associations arranged excursions to other cities or scenic spots in the Rhine–Ruhr region or hiked on wooded terrain placed at their disposal on company property. These hikes and excursions usually climaxed with competitive sports or war games. After the formation of the Jungdeutschlandbund, members of Roland and Jungroland partook in its activities, whereas the gymnastics section of Roland affiliated with the German Gymnasts. A savings chest was also set up to supplement members' income during their terms of military service. Thus the Krupp firm's youth cultivation committee built associations that could serve as models of the sort of activities favorably regarded by the Prussian government after 1911. The program was highly nationalist, maintained close ties with other patriotic associations, and emphasized physical fitness, with overtones of military preparedness. Certainly it attracted only a small minority of young Krupp employees, even among the skilled and white-collar employees, but many others already belonged to acceptable denominational youth groups, and the Krupp committee assiduously avoided competing with the Protestant youth group of Pastor Weigle, which, as previously stated, enjoyed the regular beneficence of the Krupp family.

Because of the expense, the lack of suitably trained personnel and facilities, or even the sheer indifference of most business people to their young employees, such industrial youth cultivation programs were relatively rare and generally limited to large firms with paternalistic traditions like Krupp or Bayer.[22] In most instances it was still the municipalities, whose officials had accumulated considerable expertise on youth affairs during the decade since 1900, that under pressure from the Prussian government embarked on new large-scale youth salvation projects. Thus in order to close the final gap between continuation school and the army along the lines proposed by Pastor Hugo Blitz in his Erfurt contest essay of 1900, the Düsseldorf city council voted to allocate a half million marks from a special Kaiser Wilhelm Jubilee Fund in 1913 for a massive recreational center for youth that was to be constructed as an annex to the new central building of the commercial continuation school.[23] When completed, it was to house a mammoth auditorium, a library, a bowling alley, bathing facilities, and rooms for lectures, reading, and refreshments. Center party councillors argued plausibly that smaller neighborhood centers would be more heavily used than a large central one, and they also objected to the neglect of provision for religion; but the council's liberal majority overrode their objections on the grounds that neighborhood centers, although probably abstractly preferable, would be too costly and that provision for religion would drive away precisely those youths whom they were trying to reach. The SPD interpreted this latter claim as meaning that the recreational center was intended to undermine its work, an interpretation given greater credibility by the original council memo on the center, which assigned a high priority to channeling young people to patriotic organizations. Work on the new center soon commenced, but construction was halted almost immediately after the outbreak of the war, never to be resumed. Thus like many other youth cultivation projects, recreational complexes would fall victim to the war.

But even without the recreational complex, after two years of official youth cultivation, voluntary organizations for youth were thriving as never before. Over half of Düsseldorf's 6,500 industrial continuation school students belonged to such groups in 1913: 1,740 to Catholic sodalities, 232 to Protestant youth groups, 413 to nationalist gymnastic clubs, 158 to swimming clubs, and 544 to various other organizations.[24] Another thousand had joined school-affiliated clubs and associations. Although the unorganized continued to perplex and worry youth savers, who appear to have believed that all problems would be solved when every young worker was slotted in an approved club, only a third of the student body had held out as resolute nonjoiners in the face of this relentless organizing mania.

As these club membership figures suggest, the industrial continuation schools functioned as the major focus of the postedict youth cultivation campaign. Because they encompassed all young male workers who had completed primary school, continuation schools were obviously the ideal site of attack for the campaign. Indeed, in the wake of the edict, these institutions became central for transmitting and translating policies defined by the Prussian bureaucracy into programs designed to control the leisure time of young laborers. Soon after the promulgation of the edict, Lord Mayor Oehler decreed that in Düsseldorf youth cultivation would be coupled directly to the continuation school.[25] Activities and events were to be planned and classified in accordance with a tripartite scheme: those furthering the economic interests of the students, those providing recreation and learning, and those raising the level of physical fitness. An extra fifteen thousand marks was budgeted to youth cultivation at the continuation school, most of it slated to pay teachers for supervising recreational activities.

The first area of youth cultivation at the continuation school, defending the economic interests of young workers, was least developed. Clearly it was conceived partially as a means of outflanking the SPD and partially as a means of placating artisanal discontent by funneling students into craft apprenticeships. Although extending legal protection for the young was a proclaimed goal, in fact little was accomplished. The director, Gotter, did make some half-hearted attempts to persuade employers to grant vacations to their young blue-collar employees as they did to their white-collar workers, but he weakened his own case by expressing doubts that this would be possible in industries with continuous production processes and fears about the wisdom of allowing young workers to spend such vacations idly roaming the metropolis.[26] With considerably greater determination and resourcefulness, the industrial continuation school sought to canalize students to the traditional crafts, a major issue for the Prussian government in the prewar years as it attempted to placate the artisanate.[27] The school newspaper and teachers regularly notified students of openings for apprentices, and the school held frequent evening assemblies where teachers and representatives of the artisanate extolled the advantages of learning a skilled trade. An income supplement of as much as twelve marks monthly, sustained in part by contributions from *Mittelstand* associations, was available to impoverished students who entered craft apprenticeships rather than taking unskilled jobs with higher initial earnings. But given large wage differentials and the occupational structure of the city, the continuation school could do relatively little to impede the flow into unskilled occupations.

Nor, despite much reflection, could school authorities discover any promising method of instilling the unskilled with love for their work, diligence, and reliability. Gotter, like many other Wilhelmine educators, believed that woodwork or other handicrafts might prove especially beneficial for the unskilled since they demanded patience, perseverance, and self-discipline.[28] In addition, if instruction were geared toward the creation of useful household items, it would nourish a sense of providing for one's family. But despite Gotter's encomium to the virtues of woodworking for the unskilled, the voluntary course apparently drew young apprentices. Moreover, in keeping with their fascination with the latest technological marvels, those enrolled preferred building model airplanes rather than utilitarian household items. The school's newly founded interest-bearing savings account also apparently appealed most to the skilled, with classes of machine builders saving their pfennig for excursions to Munich and Holland.[29]

Recreation and Learning, the second major classification of youth cultivation activities in the continuation school, covered the heterogeneous bundle of indoor pastimes sponsored by the school since its inception: uplifting lectures, celebrating patriotic holidays, playing board games, reading journals. After the edict, however, this area of work grew prodigiously.[30] By 1913 the library contained almost three thousand volumes, mostly history, general fiction, and vocational manuals, but students checked out a mere five hundred books monthly, predominantly entertaining light fiction. In contrast to the library, the school's game room was heavily trafficked, with between sixty and eighty students using it nightly. Clubs catering to a variety of vocational and avocational interests mushroomed. There were clubs for chessplayers, photographers, and technicians. Members of this last club, mostly electricians, constructed simple electrical devices or persuaded technical teachers to lecture on recent advances in aeronautical engineering. For the musically inclined, an orchestra and fife and drum corps were available. Some apprentices, including young butchers and building trade workers, organized in guildlike occupational associations. Altogether, however, only about two hundred continuation school students joined such clubs, which clearly met the needs of a narrow stratum of skilled, sober, serious, and self-improving

young workers, very much the same type that gravitated to the Socialist youth movement. Thus such activities could compete with those
of the SPD for youth but were unlikely to appeal to the undisciplined
and unskilled.

More special lectures were also given, most of which complemented
the vocational and patriotic goals of the continuation school.[31] Vo-
cationally oriented lectures either offered somewhat sententious advice on making the best use of apprenticeship or else described
industrial materials and processes, for example, the manufacture of
steel. A few such lectures lauded Krupp and other industrial magnates
as model employers and reveled in German industrial might, thus
blurring the distinction between vocational and patriotic lectures.
More explicitly nationalist lectures sought to enlist the students' support for colonialism by praising the economies and administration of
Germany's overseas possessions or to prepare students for the military
by examining past Prussian military victories or portraying life in the
army and navy. Whenever possible, these lectures were given in conjunction with the kaiser's birthday or other patriotic commemorations.
The year 1913 was especially rich in possibilities for anniversary celebrations and brought forth a somewhat artificially induced wave of
nationalist fervor from teachers at the continuation school. One lecture counted the blessings that the quarter-century of Kaiser Wilhelm's reign had bestowed on his devoted subjects, and no less than
three marked the centenary of Prussia's emancipation from the des-
potic Napoleonic yoke. To make lectures on both historical and contemporary themes more vivid, slides usually illustrated the oratory.
Rarer were evening assemblies given over purely to entertainment,
but even in travelogues or lectures on and readings from German
authors, the subdominant motif was the incomparable beauty of the
German landscape and the unsurpassable achievements of German
culture.

Lectures were reinforced by articles appearing in the *Monthly Bulletin for Laboring Youth,* a modest school paper that announced upcoming events and contained an amusing short story, often in dialect,
a serious piece on a patriotic or scientific subject, and humorous poetry, as well as ads for apprenticeships, printed without charge.[32] Like
school lectures, the bulletin attempted to prepare students for military
service. Typical in this respect was the story, "The Soldier Celebrates
the Kaiser's Birthday." "Then they sew, mend, and polish," its author
informs us, "since on this day of honor every soldier takes pride when
everything is in irreproachable order." After a dazzling military pa-

rade, the soldiers attend a fest where their captain leads them in a *hoch* for the kaiser: "Oh, the enthusiasm for the soldier's calling, which holds such riches! Oh, what joy to be a soldier!" We have no way of knowing, of course, how students responded to such stories, but despite the celebratory prose and cultic worship of the kaiser, attentive readers could have surmised that they were destined to occupy subaltern positions and that even on fest days, much of soldiering consisted of drudgery like sewing and polishing.

By the paper's third year, articles dovetailed tightly with the rest of the school's youth cultivation program. For example, issues ran abridged versions of the lectures on the anti–Napoleonic War of Liberation and articles pointing out the advantages of saving or making a wise choice of one's trade. Although school administrators conceded that the quality of the paper was consistently poor, according to Director Gotter, students read it with interest and enjoyed the articles because they were less critically minded than adults and hence "readier to notice the good in a modest gift."[33] The Trade Ministry and the Ministry of Education also pushed a number of inexpensive, professionally produced youth journals, among them *Feierabend,* to which seven hundred students at the Düsseldorf school subscribed, and *Werden,* which found few readers because of its somewhat higher price and belated entry into an already crowded market. Such secular youth papers, with articles on German history, science, literature, and travel, were an implicit tribute to the impact of the Socialists' *Arbeiter-Jugend,* which clearly served as the prototype.

Occasionally lectures or articles in the *Bulletin* warned of the risks of alcohol abuse, narrated the life of the rabidly nationalist prophet of German gymnastics, Father Jahn, or took up other topics closely allied to the third area of youth cultivation, the improvement of physical fitness. In this area too, already existing programs were much strengthened.[34] By contrast with some of the other programs, however, sports elicited the spontaneous enthusiasm of the students. A general sports club combined hiking, volleyball, and soccer. On summer Sundays a number of teachers led their students on hikes in the hilly Berg region in order to awaken the appreciation in these urban dwellers, supposedly alienated from nature, for the beauty of the countryside. But it was a fervid soccer craze, rather than natural beauty, that gripped sports club members. Students regarded this sport as uniquely their own and played religiously, not only on Sunday, but also after evening classes, when they formed their own teams, selected their own captains and referees, and proceeded vigorously with the game until overcome by nightfall or exhaustion. Gymnastics continued to be extremely popular as well, as shown by the fact that almost a thousand of the industrial continuation school's students belonged to a gym club. School gymnastic clubs divided along craft lines, with each trade organizing its own, with names like *Hammerschlag* for the smiths and *Kraft* for the young butchers. In keeping with the school administration's desire to encourage self-administration as part of Kerschensteinerian civic education, these clubs elected their own executive committees, but gymnastic exercises were supervised by instructors from the German Gymnasts, and educators valued gymnastics as a means of teaching discipline and physical control. It would also be the vaulting horse that doubled as the Trojan horse through which the paramilitary Jungdeutchlandbund, with its emphasis on steeling youth for the rigors of military service, entered the portals of the school.

The notion of paramilitary training for young workers had a long history before 1911. Since the 1890s E. von Schenckendorff, a Conservative Reichstag representative and founder of the Central Committee for Fostering Popular and Youth Sports, had been tirelessly propagandizing for sports and physical fitness on the grounds that they would create a well-developed and hardy youth ready for military service.[35] As previously mentioned, in his essay on civic education Kerschensteiner had proposed that religiously oriented youth militias modeled on the British Boys' Brigades might be a good vehicle for disciplining the unskilled. A number of Protestant clerics also looked with favor on military formations for youth, albeit for somewhat different reasons. In 1906 both Pastor Weigle of Essen and the retired pastor Friedrich von Bodelschwingh, mainstay of the Protestant Church's Inner Mission, Conservative delegate to the Prussian Diet, and sometime royal adviser petitioned the kaiser to mandate military training for youth, apparently in order to rouse martial spirit, to lighten the army's training tasks, and to combat the Socialists.[36] The Prussian ministers of education and war, however, both rejected these proposals. In part, they were apprehensive that the military training of youth would be used as an argument, especially by the Socialists, for shortening the term of military service or even for replacing the standing army with a defensive militia. Instead, they agreed with Field Marshal Count Haesler that "playing at soldiers is to be forbidden; it doesn't benefit the army. A systematically led training of the body through gymnastic exercises, swimming, and other exercises of a physical nature, however, does benefit the army." The cabinet ministers justified these claims by arguing that in order to keep physically fit, growing youths working at monotonous tasks needed a variety of recreations and exercises to counteract the uniform motions of their employments, rather than equally monotonous military training. To combat the Socialists, establish trust in governmental institutions, and keep alive enthusiasm for the military among the young, the officials recommended that military officers become more engaged in the gymnastics, competitions, and other activities of the various youth associations. Eventually this recommendation resulted in an edict by Prussian War Minister von Heeringen in November 1909, in which he emphasized that in order to maintain and promote a lively interest in things military among youth, continuation school classes should be permitted to observe military parades and maneuvers, that gym halls, swimming pools, and other exercise places should be made available to students free, and that both commissioned and noncommissioned officers should attend gymnastic competitions, patriotic festivals, and so forth.[37]

This edict, immediately replicated and signed by the Bavarian war minister, prompted forty young Bavarian officers to launch the Munich Military Association in the city's continuation school, to provide an antidote to "the increasingly dominant fantasies of 'eternal peace.'"[38] Both the war minister and Kerschensteiner became honorary members of its board of directors. Denied public funds by the majority Center party because of its secularism, the organization was financed from an endowment set up by the Bavarian prince regent and contributions from members of the nationalist middle class, including the president of Munich's Chamber of Commerce. Membership in the Military Association rose from two hundred fifty Munich continuation school students in early 1910 to over ten thousand Bavarian youths by 1914, although the number of members at higher schools soon surpassed membership at continuation schools. As the historian Klaus Saul has written of the company's activities:

On Sundays in groups of between forty and eighty the youth were led by officers on hikes in the Munich region. On these hikes...patrol and war games were held, and exercises appropriate for the field, such as observation of terrain, map reading, designating goals, estimation of distance and bivouacking were practiced. Library, reading, lecture, and singing evenings, a monthly pioneer exercise, and, originally and in small measure, shooting instruction completed the program. To "educate future leadership material" higher-school students were recruited and trained in special sections. Careful attention was paid to preserving the "romantic, even leatherstockinglike" characteristics of the war games.

This Bavarian initiative quickly aroused the interest of staff officers in Berlin, who took the Bavarian companies as a potential template for youth organization.[39] Immediately after the Youth Cultivation Edict, General von Jacobi prevailed upon his friend the military inspector Field Marshal Freiherr Colmar von der Goltz to found a similar troop in Prussia. A favorite of the kaiser, von der Goltz was exceedingly well placed to undertake this venture. The archconservative von der Goltz was a leading proponent of the idea that Germany, surrounded by envious and hostile neighbors, would inevitably have to fight a large-scale preemptive war in the near future. Moreover, he welcomed such a war since it would force the nation to repudiate the overrefinement and degeneration that he believed had set in with its transformation from an agrarian to an industrial state. In June 1911 the field marshal outlined his plans for this new endeavor to the kaiser.

Although this youth formation, the Young Germany League, would rigorously exclude all party politics, it would aspire to "make our youth able bodied and truthful, strengthen them physically and mentally, train them in orderliness and obedience, inspire them with devotion, dedication and ésprit de corps, so that they will recognize that service to the fatherland is the highest honor for the German man."[40] These classically Prussian virtues were to be attained through hikes, marches, war games, camping, gymnastics, and swimming. Officers would have the opportunity to teach youth about Prussia's heroes, civics, and first aid and, in doing so, learn to lead men without the disciplinary sanctions available in the military. Much like Kerschensteiner, von der Goltz further hoped that as officers of upper-class origins became more immersed in youth cultivation activities, young laborers would come to trust them, and thereby class antagonism would be blunted.

Von der Goltz obtained royal approval for his plans in August 1911, and he could certainly count on financial aid from a number of Berlin's wealthiest bankers, merchants, and industrialists and rely on strong backing from the military establishment. Some leading generals, however, wanted the Young Germany League to "inscribe on its banner" its struggle against Social Democracy.[41] In reply to military critics and spokespersons for the mass middle-class anti-Socialist propaganda association, the Imperial League Against Social Democracy, which also called for openly confronting the Socialists, von der Goltz countered by arguing that blatantly anti-Socialist propaganda would preclude reaching youth most subject to Socialist influence and therefore would exclusively attract middle-class students who had no real need for youth cultivation. He faced other opposition as well. Religious youth groups were suspicious of the new organization from the outset because of its purely secular character and one-sided emphasis on physical activity. The German Gymnasts and other organizations active in youth cultivation worried that the league would be an unfair competitor, a worry shared by the educational minister, who spoke against "new general experiments" and secured the field marshal's promise that the league would restrict its activities to assisting with physical fitness.

With this promise in hand, in November 1911 the Educational Ministry began soliciting directors of continuation schools for their evaluations of the league's local prospects for success. In Düsseldorf Gotter confidently predicted that many students would be willing to join a military formation and he was equally convinced that many of the school's teachers, with experience as noncommissioned or reserve officers, would gladly assume responsibility for leading a company of students.[42] He foresaw, moreover, that the league would be more likely to enhance, rather than interfere with or destroy, existing programs, and he was delighted by the promise that army equipment and facilities would be made available free of charge for hikes. Heartened by the optimistic assessment, the league's staff began laying the groundwork for a Düsseldorf brigade.

Local notables were lined up for the twenty-member local executive committee, among them Major Cederholm, commander of the infantry unit stationed in the city, von Beckenrath, county commissioner of Düsseldorf's rural hinterland, and such youth cultivation perennials as Gotter, Chaplain Esser, and Herold.[43] At its founding meeting, the committee agreed that its energy should be concentrated at the continuation school, where officers would take over gymnastics instruction. The committee also resolved that members of the league would be required to wear uniforms for summer outings, both to prevent them from ruining their best suits and to obliterate all external signs of social distinction. Since they doubted that young factory workers could afford uniforms, they voted for a subsidy that was ultimately financed by an exclusive charity ball staged by the wife of the district governor and attended by the city's industrial and governmental elite. On 1 May 1912, the committee placed large advertisements in Düsseldorf's three major non-Socialist newspapers, publicly announcing the formation of the local Young Germany League. The text accented the nondiscriminatory inclusiveness of this new military youth group, which recognized "no distinction on the basis of religion or political party as long as they stand on the basis of love of the fatherland and faithfulness to the kaiser and the Reich." But by publishing these advertisements on a major Socialist holiday and boycotting the *Volkszeitung,* the committee made clear the anti-Socialist animus behind the league.

The way in which Young Germany became implanted in the local industrial continuation school and the difficulties accompanying its initial phase were recounted at length in the school's annual report for 1912–13:

The continuation school also adhered to the Young Germany League movement and immediately after the formation of the Düsseldorf area troop provided the overwhelming majority of participants in its war games. Altogether about 1,250 students took part in the five war games, which were led by local officers, both active and reserve. The leaders rapidly concluded that it wasn't sufficient to be active intermittently in war games at which a different group of students appeared every time depending on chance and inclination, but rather that steady and systematic work with the same group of students was necessary. Consequently in October 1912, the so-called quadruple alliance [*Vierbund*] was formed, consisting of four reserve officers who wished to dedicate themselves to youth cultivation in the continuation school. These were joined by a further fifteen reserve officers and about forty-four members of veterans' associations (officials, teachers, businessmen, etc.) who had already declared their intention of being active in youth cultivation at least once a week. After thorough deliberation, they decided that basic training would be imparted in gym halls, and then during the summer war games, hikes, etc., would be held. These gentlemen took over sections formed by continuation school classes, each with thirty students. Gymnastics exercises took place...every evening except Sunday in halls located in various parts of the city. In order to achieve uniformity in training, as well as diversity in the work, the leaders received a plan every week giving the order of drills.[44]

Thus by winter of 1913 a network of army officers and veterans had constructed a comprehensive and regularized program for physical fitness and patriotic education with a military cast directed at young laborers enrolled in continuation school. Both the program itself and the role of officers and veterans exemplifies the militarism that the historian Hans-Ulrich Wehler has viewed as a distinguishing characteristic of Imperial Germany.[45] It should be noted, however, that as Wehler's critics have argued, this militarism was not a constant, but rather a response to the particular "prewar" conjuncture.

Especially popular during the summer were the war games. Although youth cultivators liked to trace their genealogy back to Friedrich Ludwig (Turnvater) Jahn and the era of Prussia's War of Liberation against Napoleon, in a less chauvinist vein, they admitted,

"[M]odern German war games for youth derive above all historically from the English Boy Scout movement," which had been organized as the Pfadfinder by two German army officers with experiences of genocidal colonial war in southern Africa similar to those of Baden Powell and began to take root in Germany after 1909 among middle-class boys.[46] German advocates of war games, however, prided themselves on the fact that in contrast to the English movement, they left real military tasks to the army and instead devoted themselves purely to training "physically and mentally healthy, strong, well-rounded, lively youths" in the spirit of Turnvater Jahn. For the actual games, the uniformed continuation school students were divided into two hostile armies. After several hours of marching and maneuvering, the troops arrayed in opposing lines. The school's fife and drum corps and brass band played martial airs that contributed to the military ambience of the maneuvers and roused the troops for the impending battle. The victory was determined by a short, bloodless, but decisive battle fought with padded bamboo poles. The afternoon was given over to instruction on first aid, singing patriotic songs, and postmortems of the morning's maneuvers by the commanding officers.

Less than a year after its inception such activities had helped the league to establish itself firmly as the largest single organization among continuation school students, with 450 regularly attending its events and another 600 mustering somewhat less consistently. By early 1914 the league claimed a nationwide membership of almost 750,000 youths, a grossly inflated figure arrived at by incorporating religious and regional youth groups that had nominally affiliated with the Young Germany League but preserved complete autonomy and otherwise had no substantive connection to its activities.[47] A more realistic estimate would place membership at approximately 67,000, the number registered in the 761 local military companies like the one at the Düsseldorf continuation school. Even this lower figure indicates phenomenally rapid growth, given the recent origins of the League. It is clear that the combination of war games, gymnastics and camaraderie practiced in the Young Germany League appealed to many young workers, and there is no evidence that they were repelled by the nationalist propaganda that, of course, differed little from that standardly purveyed in the primary and continuation schools. Hence the self-congratulatory tone of the league's propaganda would seem to have been fully vindicated.

It is doubtful, however, that the league's rapid headway can be explained completely by its internal institutional dynamics. Moral and material backing from the Prussian government and wealthy patrons certainly catalyzed this rapid expansion, while privileged access to the continuation schools smoothed the road. Catholic and Socialist critics of the league marshaled evidence that teachers and administrators applied considerable pressure to dragoon students into joining.[48] Such formidable competitive advantages soon galled other patriotic and religious youth associations that became disillusioned as they discovered that the league's repeated promises of ongoing consultation and joint work were hollow and that instead the league's all-embracing recruitment drive was strangling their own work. Nevertheless, because of the league's powerful patrons and unimpeachable nationalist credentials, such groups muted their opposition in order to avoid being perceived as having succumbed to sour grapes because of their own failures at youth cultivation.

First to protest in Düsseldorf was the German Gymnasts, which expressed astonishment that after years of dedicated service its members had been summarily dismissed as gym instructors at the industrial continuation school and replaced by army officers.[49] Gotter brusquely brushed aside these protests by charging that in all their years at the continuation school they had been unable to kindle the faintest spark of enthusiasm among the students, evidenced by the high absentee and turnover rates in gym classes. Even feebler and more easily stilled was the criticism of the Protestant clergy, who grumbled that too much brawn coarsened the spirit, that the interconfessional nature of the Jungdeutschlandbund undermined religion, and that Sunday field maneuvers kept the young from church. In exchange for the prospect of preaching field sermons on Sunday outings, however, they readily reconciled themselves both to muscles and the decline of Sabbatarian observance.[50]

More sustained and resolute by far was the criticism articulated by the Catholic Youth Association. The initial Catholic reaction to the Young Germany League was cool and distant but formally cooperative.[51] Like their Protestant counterparts, many priests disdained the movement's raw physicality. While the secretariat of the Catholic Youth Association tepidly endorsed the goals of the league, it was concerned that the new organization might compete with Catholic youth groups. The secretariat's report also voiced the fear that the Prussian government, working through the continuation schools, was intent on completely eliminating religion from youth cultivation. To minimize competition and avoid interdenominational mixing, the report concluded that it might be wisest for the church to start its own paramilitary youth units. After taking this report into consideration, the federated Catholic youth associations of Düsseldorf sought affiliation with the league, but only on condition that the league in turn respect the autonomy of the Catholic associations and place Sunday field exercises in the late afternoon.

In March 1913 representatives of the church and the league met to discuss these points and resolve differences.[52] The resulting accord guaranteed that those already members of Catholic youth groups would join the league through these church associations, that any Catholic sodality that set up its own paramilitary unit could participate in league activities on equal terms, and that the league would only recruit unorganized Catholic students at the continuation school. Finally, the league agreed to direct its Catholic members to church sodalities and to hold its maneuvers on late Sunday afternoons. On paper this amounted to a complete victory for the church, but in fact the league systematically violated every term of these agreements. Consequently, the church periodically protested the league's privileged position in the continuation school and the pressure tactics it ostensibly employed to recruit members. Moreover, the Catholic youth paper, *Die Wacht,* became increasingly alarmed at the league's contribution to a bellicose atmosphere, and in an article entitled "Youth Cultivation and War," in October 1913, it denounced the league's apparent goal of transforming "all of Germany into a giant barracks."[53] Certainly, the article avowed, Catholics staunchly believed in military preparedness and thought that, within reason, hikes and gymnastics were suitable means for achieving it. But the devotion of every spare moment to military drill, the wearing of uniforms on hikes, and the bombast of the hurrah patriots were excessive. Worse still, at a time when tensions between Britain and the Reich seemed to be easing somewhat, such behavior was endangering the forty years of peace. But however incisive and prophetic such criticisms were, the league, intoxicated with its success, could and did ignore them. Then, too, the church often complied with official requests that it dampen its public criticisms of the league since negative publicity would simply play into the hands of the "enemies of government youth cultivation."[54]

"Enemies of government youth cultivation" was, of course, a thinly veiled circumlocution for the Socialists. Given that officials of the Young Germany League made no secret of their desire to extirpate the Socialist youth movement, the deep hostility reciprocated by the Socialists is hardly surprising. Despite the league's claim of apoliticism, its annual report for 1913 declared that "the more important Social Democrats find it to sow divisiveness and class hatred even in the hearts of the young, the more we must strive to implant a sense of the unity of our people, bound by love for their common fatherland in the hearts of the young."[55] Whether in the press or at party conferences, the SPD responded in kind. In Düsseldorf the *Volkszeitung* invariably treated Prussia's youth cultivation as an insidious scheme to bludgeon the Socialist youth movement and remarked with contemptuous irony that young workers who had hitherto been despised or ignored were now being converted into objects of concern for everyone "from orthodox pastors, to dashing lieutenants, from field marshals to the last simple school teacher."[56] It scathingly denounced the Prussian Diet as the "world's most reactionary parliament" for voting a million marks extracted from the taxes of workers for antilabor youth activity. But despite the unprecedented mobilization of resources and personnel, originally the SPD foresaw few prospects for long-term success by the government's youth cultivation campaign. The party's faith in the inevitable victory of socialism remained unshaken.

This belief lay behind the deprecating humor with which the Socialist press originally greeted the Young Germany League. After the league appealed for funds in the press, the *Volkszeitung* quipped that "feudal-sounding signatories" (i.e., officials with *von* before their family names) and Catholic or liberal editors had been reduced to begging for alms.[57] The *Arbeiter-Jugend* declared that the league appealed "to better young people. One gives them something resembling a uniform jacket or at least sews some colorful buttons on and lets them play soldier." By late 1912, however, this tone of supercilious hilarity had yielded to anxiety tinged with panic.[58] "Worker parents," importuned the *Volkszeitung*, "keep your children away from Young Germany. Don't hand them over to Prussian 'youth cultivation.' As the animal defends its child against enemy attacks, so should every worker mother, every worker father defend their children from the attack of Prusso-German 'youth cultivation.' " Clearly the Socialists were dismayed by the success of the league in recruiting young workers at the continuation schools. The Düsseldorf police administration informed the district governor that "the efforts directed against the Socialist youth movement by middle-class circles and parties (Young Germany League, militias, etc.) are being fought in the Socialist press as well as by the Free Youth itself in the most untruthful and hateful manner, such that one feels instinctively that these efforts are highly suitable for containing Socialist growth."[59] The SPD also began taking countermeasures. When Field Marshal von der Goltz spoke as a roving emissary for the league, a cohort of Socialists would appear to heckle or to intimidate the speaker and middle-class audience by sitting through the field marshal's speech in stony silence, although Socialists were generally disappointed to find von der Goltz's oratory was that of a smooth-tongued courtier rather than a firebreathing rabble rouser.[60]

Despite such tactics, the Socialists could neither impede recruitment in the Young Germany League nor galvanize the Socialist youth movement. As mentioned at the end of the last chapter, by 1913 many party members, especially those on the left, were castigating the party leadership for its blinkered underestimation of the bourgeois youth movement. But such criticisms were vitiated by the opposition's tendency to reduce all problems to technical pedagogical ones and to offer no concrete alternatives. If the Socialist youth movement was stagnating, it was because the SPD lacked a sufficient number of trained pedagogues, was overly paternalistic, or published overly difficult youth literature. To have admitted that, in contrast to the excitement of war games and field maneuvers, its own rational and sober educational approach was uninspiring and dull or that the SPD was still simply too weak to compete effectively with state agencies, which could mobilize and deploy vast resources, thousands of trained youth workers, and coercive power, would have challenged some of the SPD's most cherished assumptions.

However unequipped or simply unwilling the Socialists were to examine the reasons for the Young Germany League's relative success among young workers, they nonetheless viewed it as a symptom of a sea change both in the character of middle-class youth work and in the general political climate. This shift had caught them unprepared and had forced them into a defensive posture. The Socialists correctly depicted the League's endeavors as an attempt to weld all patriotic youth groups into a common anti-Socialist front.[61] This effort was politicizing activities, such as sports, that had previously been largely sociable and was thereby further heightening tensions between labor and middle-class-sponsored youth groups. The SPD regarded this new course as a direct consequence of imperialism, by which it meant the intensified rivalry among nations supposedly resulting from competition between industries to secure new markets. The ideological reflex of this rivalry was the replacement of traditionally pacific liberalism by the "evangelium of power." With its disparagement of intellect and its cult of crude force, paramilitary youth cultivation clearly demonstrated "the way in which the new imperialist ideas of the modern bourgeoisie are externally forceful and barbaric, internally empty and hollow...." Despite the considerable divergence in rhetoric between the Catholic and Socialist press, both perceived the mindless celebration of force and military might as a salient characteristic of the new youth cultivation, and both converged in attributing responsibility to their traditional enemies, the middle-class liberals, with whom they were locked in political struggles over education and municipal governance.

This attribution is certainly open to question. As we have seen, initiative for military-style organization originated among army officers and in the administrative bureaucracy. It arose from apprehensions about Germany's internal situation, especially the continued growth of the SPD and its youth movement, and was probably given a further fillip by concern about Germany's evident international isolation, strikingly revealed in the second Moroccan crisis in 1911. From that year talk of an inevitable war against France and Russia became commonplace in the military and official circles to which Field Marshal von der Goltz belonged and of which he was representative.[62] Preparation for war demanded a larger army, but many generals were afraid that a major expansion would inundate the army with enfeebled urbanites and infect it with Socialist ideas. To obviate these dangers, military youth cultivation was intended to turn out robust, stalwart, and patriotic youth. Despite these conservative and military origins, without widespread support and cooperation from urban liberals, paramilitary youth cultivation would have fizzled rapidly. As the social profile of youth cultivation conference participants confirms, liberal constituencies, including urban officials, teachers, and business people, were the indispensable pillars of the government's program. To this degree they bore responsibility for its direction. More dubious, however, was the Socialist claim that liberal support for paramilitary youth cultivation entailed the abandonment of classical liberalism for the worship of naked power and brute force.

From the turn of the century, when they had first defined post-school-age laboring youth as a social problem, liberal educators like Kerschensteiner had considered the possibility of introducing military training as a means of instilling discipline in the unskilled. The mere existence of the unskilled posed troubling questions about the validity and viability of the liberals' model of the citizen in an advanced industrial society. Youth savers recognized that the numerous unskilled jobs necessary for industrial production neither bred a commitment to labor nor contributed to forming autonomous, self-motivated citizens. They were therefore confronted with the task of devising institutions where these qualities could be forged. Given the liberal doctrine of the value of education for character formation, the continuation school with a program that conjoined vocational and political instruction was a logical contender to fulfill these tasks. Of course, it was mandatory, but by being allowed room to improve their skills, express themselves, and participate in a variety of voluntary clubs and activities, young laborers would gradually develop a broader sense of the importance of their work and acquire the qualities necessary for citizenship. Paramilitary units, with their hierarchical structure and chain of command, were less obvious nurseries for incubating self-determining citizens, although this could sometimes be papered over with dialectical wordplay like "Through Force, to Freedom."[63] But generally apologists for the Young Germany League like Gotter bristled at the charge that students were being compelled to join and pointed instead to its purely voluntary nature and its contribution to physical fitness, while playing down its military aspects.[64] Liberal educators transfigured the league into a kind of model society with classes but no class conflict, where external badges of social inequality were eliminated, where working-class youth willingly accepted the leadership of middle-class officers, where the ideal of national unity overcame the secondary attributes of social distinction. Thus, liberal educators certainly sanctioned the increasing importance assigned to military youth cultivation and indeed accepted the paramount role of the central government in defining the aims and shaping the direction of youth work after 1911. However, despite the criticisms of Catholics and Socialists, this didn't necessarily mean that they endorsed an unqualified evangelium of power.

Their acquiescence was partially motivated by the modest success of their previous programs. In 1911 the Socialist youth movement was obviously still growing, supposed signs of moral degeneration that had prompted the youth salvation campaign in the first place, like delinquency or reading penny dreadfuls, were still evident, and the ranks of the unskilled continued to swell. Moreover, the massive intervention by the government opened new opportunities for youth workers. The government increasingly acknowledged the vital importance of primary and continuation school teachers as preceptors of the nation. Educators were invited to seminars and conferences, appointed to public committees, rewarded with praise and honors, including such coveted badges of middle-class distinction as the Order of the Red Eagle fourth class, awarded to prominent youth cultivators.[65] Moreover, in exchange for the support of urban liberal constituencies, the government pumped money into venerable liberal associations like the German Gymnasts and aided in financing municipal projects like the youth center that could be used to counter both the Socialists and Catholics, while presenting a well-tended facade of high-minded patriotism. Well might the Socialists sneer, "When they whistle in Berlin, they dance in the provinces" and the Catholics protest the physical rawness, secularism, and discriminatory character of the new direction in youth cultivation, but the close symbiosis between urban youth workers and the Prussian government appeared to strengthen both measurably. Within two years of the promulgation of the Youth Cultivation Edict the Young Germany League had cast the Socialist youth movement into the shadows, and the multifarious recreational activities of the continuation schools were flourishing. For the first time since 1900 youth savers could realistically believe that they were winning the struggle for German youth.

8

Preparing for motherhood: the inclusion of young working women in youth cultivation

On 30 April 1913, slightly more than two years after the promulgation of the Prussian Youth Cultivation Edict, the minister for religious and educational affairs, Trott zu Solz, issued a new edict that extended government financial support to youth cultivation activities for post-school-age females. The reason for this inclusion, according to the new edict, was that

...whoever wishes to raise a physically and morally strong, God-fearing, monarchical, and patriotic generation must also help ensure that young females are healthy in body and soul, of firm character, and armed with the knowledge and ability that are indispensable for their future profession as helpmate of the man, educator of children, nurturer of family happiness, bearer and protector of good morals.[1]

Although the edict declared that, in general, youth cultivation for post-school-age females should be pursued in the same manner as that for young males, nonetheless some means would necessarily be gender specific:

Essentially different are only such means that in part serve to protect against those dangers to which the female sex is specifically vulnerable and that lead in part to a higher evaluation of the profession of housewife and mother and should help teach and develop the necessary qualities and skills to this end.

Among the measures recommended by the new edict were the promotion of physical culture through gymnastics, hikes, and gardening and the establishment of simple, homey rooms or recreational centers for economically active young women, where standard youth cultivation activities like lectures, religious instruction, singing, and sociable gatherings could take place. In addition to talks treating economic themes appropriate for young women of various occupations, centers were also supposed to hold lectures on caring for children and the sick. Whenever possible, such centers were also to provide opportunities for practicing housewifely skills like sewing, knitting, mending, and ironing under the supervision of a knowledgeable instructor. Moreover, the youthful members themselves were to take care of the cleaning and upkeep of the rooms as a practical lesson in homemaking.

All patriotically inclined associations dedicated to working with young females were to be represented on youth cultivation boards set up in response to the Prussian edict of January 1911, and women engaged in such activities were to be appointed to local, county, and regional youth cultivation committees. The minister made funds available to pay the salaries of part-time female youth workers at the local and regional level and to defray the costs of training female youth workers. Thus, youth cultivation for employed females was to be incorporated fully into the bureaucratic apparatus already erected to deal with post-school-age males and was to benefit equally from increased government funding.

This edict of 1913 can be viewed as a signal victory for organizations like the Association of Catholic Women Teachers and the State Association of Prussian Women Teachers, which had long been active in fostering youth work but whose members had been sorely disappointed by the Prussian government's explicit exclusion of young women from the edict of 1911.[2] As a teacher from Charlottenburg, Alwine Reinald remarked bitterly of the original edict, "[Y]oung women weren't somehow forgotten, but rather care for them was consciously rejected."[3] The edict of 1913 crowned a successful effort by many groups, including teachers' associations and the semiofficial Central Agency for Popular Welfare to broaden coverage of youth cultivation to post-school-age females. Yet just as the Youth Cultivation Edict for young males had its roots in the public campaign originating in the late 1890s and at the same time marked a new and more energetic phase in that crusade, the 1913 edict could also be seen both as a culmination of welfare work with young female laborers undertaken by the churches, employers, and private associations since the turn of the century and as the inception of a new era of official recognition, coordination, and centralization of this work by the Prussian government. Nonetheless, the designation of young women workers as a social problem passed rapidly from the natural history phases of awareness to those of policy determination and reform.

However, although many of the same moral concerns associated with rapid industrialization and urbanization that had prompted the definition of post-school-age males as an officially recognized social problem would also figure prominently in the constitution of post-school-age females as objects of social policy, the definition of the problem and the solutions advanced would be quite distinct. Whereas youth cultivation for young males was intended to diminish the dangers that threatened their future roles as stalwart soldiers, patriotic citizens, and competitive producers, as indicated by the language of the 1913 edict, young laboring women would be defined almost exclusively in terms of their future roles as dutiful wives, nurturing mothers, and assiduous homemakers. It would be the imperiled contribution of young women to Germany's demographic vitality and domestic happiness as a result of conditions of employment, rather than their limited occupational prospects, that would call forth the greatest concern. As Elizabeth Gnauck-Kühne, an eminent Christian social reformer who had long championed working women, proclaimed, "The female sex, the sex of the mother, sees itself in contradiction with the thousand-year tradition that the house is the world of the woman. No sector of the female sex, however, is more affected by this break with tradition than post-school-age youth and especially the economically active youth."[4] Ironically, however, it would often be female teachers and doctors and other successful middle-class career women like Gnauck-Kühne who would consistently emphasize the domestic destinies of young working-class females.

As mentioned, the campaign to organize and safeguard young female workers could be traced back to the 1890s. During that decade both major Christian churches had launched new initiatives related to employed post-school-age girls, especially to recent migrants to large cities. Thus, beginning in 1898 with the encouragement of Munich's bishop, Princess Sophie zu Oettingen-Spielberg formed protective associations (*Patronagen*) in the Bavarian capital that were to pursue the aim of "gathering economically active post-school-age girls on Sunday afternoons, widening their religious knowledge, fortifying their ethical life, and enabling them to participate in innocent recreation."[5] The *Patronagen* were also supposed to provide them with charitable support in times of trouble and to immunize them against the Social Democrats.[6] By 1902 there were five such associations in Munich under the direction of fifty upper-class patronesses. This type of association soon flourished in south German cities from Bavaria to Alsace. Gnauck-Kühne even spoke of these groups as being *the* appropriate form of organization for young women workers. Critics, however, attacked these organizations for their Lady Bountiful maternalism and their failure to foster the autonomy of their young "wards." Partially in response to such critiques, over the next fifteen years these associations underwent a series of reorganizations and developed more elaborate programs. Older former members of the *Patronagen* founded a Catholic Women Workers Association. Sunday afternoon meetings appended instruction in home economics and civics. By the war these associations claimed fifteen thousand young women as members.

Most common in northern Germany and the Rhineland were maiden sodalities attached to parishes that carried out much the same sort of religious and recreational activities as those standard in parish groups for young males, although there was special emphasis on Marian piety for young women.[7] Although such organizations originated in midcentury, they grew rapidly after 1890. In the important Cologne archdiocese, for example, whereas ten Marian sodalities had been founded in the 1880s, eighty were started in the 1890s, and another 184 between 1900 and 1910.[8] Before the war at least thirty-one thousand working women between the ages of fourteen and twenty belonged to Marian sodalities or specific Catholic organizations for young working women in the archdiocese. Sometimes in a relatively socially homogeneous industrial district a priest might introduce activities specifically oriented to meet what he perceived to be the needs of factory girls. For example, a Pastor Kruchen in Hochneukirch near the Rhenish textile center Mönchen-Gladbach, assisted by several women teachers, started a voluntary continuation school in association with the local maiden sodality.[9] Evening classes available for factory girls included hygiene, cooking, sewing, and household management, which were to prepare them for their future roles as homemakers. Since he believed it was necessary to ennoble and stimulate the mental lives of factory girls whose intellects and imaginations were supposedly stifled and deadened by the daily routines of mind-numbing labor, Pastor Kruchen determined to "open their hearts to higher pleasures" through excursions to regional art museums, monuments, and churches. Thus sodality activities were sometimes consciously designed to offset or remedy deficiencies ostensibly resulting from industrial life.

Apart from such general Catholic groups for young women, a number of more clearly labor-oriented associations sprang up, such as the Association of Catholic Servants and the youth organization of the Federation of Catholic Associations of Economically Active Women and Girls of Germany.[10] Both of these "estate" societies, as Catholic social thinkers referred to occupational organizations in order to evoke tradition and avoid the conflictual connotations of "class," complemented religious uplift and home economics instruction with social self-help measures like savings chests and supplementary health insurance. They also offered placement services and held lectures and discussions addressing specific occupational problems facing young women. The church touted organizations that stressed social harmony as preferable alternatives to trade unions, which generally manifested proclivities toward class struggle.

The female youth organizations of the Evangelical Church closely resembled their Catholic counterparts in most respects; however, they were less effective. Protestant attempts to reach out to servant girls and other post-school-age employees began in the 1850s, but the few associations that existed owed whatever vitality they possessed entirely to the local initiative of individual Protestant women or pastors. This period of intermittent interest in the welfare of young females ended in the early 1890s, however, when Pastor Johannes Burckhardt, a Berlin minister and indefatigable organizer on behalf of the Inner Mission who was dismayed by the lack of groups for young Protestant women in the capital, called several conferences to systematize Evangelical work in this area.[11] In part this may have also been a response by the Evangelical Church to the social consciousness and solicitude for labor expressed in the middle class during the early 1890s as a pendant to the kaiser's efforts to portray himself as a populist monarch. At an 1890 conference in Berlin's Tonhalle directed at Protestant women and girls, the well-known Pastor von Bodelschwingh charted the church's course for future work. There, the pastor urged participants to found associations of young maidens, to provide care for girls migrating to the large city, to offer good literature, and to build centers for young women.

Such conferences set a wave of organizational growth in motion. In 1893 Protestants active in organizing girls institutionalized their efforts in the Executive Federation of Evangelical Maidens' Associations and in conjunction with the Inner Mission soon began formally training women for welfare work with girls. The local church associations that assembled young women on Sunday afternoons for religious instruction and recreation inscribed over two hundred thousand members before the war.[12] Most of these members came from lower-middle-class families, however, rather than being factory girls or daughters of the educated classes, and membership was geographically concentrated in Prussia east of the Elbe. Worried by the social narrowness of its recruitment base, the federation delegated a commission to consider ways of attracting factory girls, but little came of its deliberations.

Similar to the Catholic Church in its approach, from the late 1890s the Protestant Church sponsored Railroad Missions which attempted to dissuade rural girls from seeking their fortunes in the large cities.[13] When efforts to deter migrants failed, however, the missions, located in urban railway stations, made available information and assistance for new arrivals on safe, inexpensive lodgings and employment opportunities. These missions, which arose from worries about the white slave trade, sought to save naive rural girls from moral ruin. A related specialty of the Evangelical Church was building dormitories for factory girls, where religious spirit could be cultivated. Several such Marian homes were opened in Berlin. The Association for the Welfare of Female Youth in Berlin, a Protestant charitable society patronized by the empress, constructed a well-accoutered dormitory that housed over a hundred factory workers in the city.[14] Only young female factory workers could reside there, and costs of rooms, meals, baths, and educational or recreational activities were kept at a level well within the range of their wages. With its tidy, individualized rooms, its well-appointed recreational and reading areas, and its educational programs in home economics, it served as a model for such dormitories. So attractive was this facility supposedly, young women departing to get married bid farewell with great reluctance and sadness.

Nor was the Evangelical Church alone in constructing dormitories for single young women workers. Socially concerned Catholic textile manufacturers in towns like Mönchen-Gladbach and Viersen often cooperated closely with local priests to build such housing for young women recruited from small towns and rural settings. These pioneer efforts were later followed by some of the major industrial firms of the Lower Rhine and Ruhr, among them Bayer of Leverkusen.[15] These economical domiciles allowed manufacturers to assure parents and the girls themselves that the firm would guarantee their safety and security. At the same time, they enabled paternalistic employers to oversee and regulate the nonwork time of their youthful charges through curfews and other regulations enforced by house mothers and sanctioned by fines or even expulsion from living quarters for repeated or serious violations. By means of organized group activities, employers could also control residents' leisure time. The provision of supervised housing, however, didn't exhaust the forms of corporate youth cultivation for females. Many large employers hired home economics teachers to give courses in domestic skills like cooking and sewing, both for the company's young female workers and for the daughters of male employees. Moreover, as we have seen, a few corporations, the foremost being Krupp, actually created secular educational and recreational clubs for their youthful female clerical and industrial workers.

In comparison with the churches and even employers, German municipalities were somewhat laggard in initiating youth services for employed post-school-age females. As the public health physician Ignaz Kaup wrote in 1911, "Extraordinarily little, namely in the cities, has hitherto occurred in youth cultivation for the benefit of employed female youth. Regular physical education for young women is virtually nonexistent."[16] A year later the report of the Central Agency for Popular Welfare confirmed the existence of this glaring deficiency by noting: "In general little is still being done in the cities to foster or centralize the existing welfare institutions for female youth. Only Charlottenburg and Frankfurt am Main are praiseworthy exceptions in this respect."[17] Some cities, for example, Charlottenburg, had made continuation schools obligatory for young female commercial clerks, a possibility in Prussia only after 1900, when the Industrial Code was amended so that municipalities could require young women clerks to attend.[18] Many cities also funded voluntary technical schools and classes in home economics instruction.[19] Voluntary classes, however, generally enrolled a handful of atypically ambitious students. Probably the best-known voluntary continuation school was the Victoria Technical and Continuation School in Berlin, founded in 1878 by the Lette Society, a middle-class association for fostering vocational education for women. This school was patronized by Crown Princess Victoria and directed by the early feminist Ulrike Henschke, who developed a comprehensive educational program that combined general education with special emphasis on German and vocational instruction.[20] But in general amid the burgeoning system of continuing education for males, the provision of comparable education for young females was largely ignored or repudiated, especially for female industrial employees, since officials believed they would only work a few years before getting married.

A few women's associations pioneered career counseling for post-school-age girls, although these agencies were often conceived as vehicles for channeling working-class girls into domestic service. Nor was the provision of facilities and opportunities for leisure activities of young females as widespread or well established as that for males. In Berlin and Charlottenburg women school teachers tried with some success to start up recreational and social clubs composed of recent graduates of neighborhood elementary schools, but such experiments were limited to the capital and were rare even there.[21] A few gymnastic associations periodically made halfhearted efforts to recruit post-school-age girls, but all such approaches were haphazard. Consequently, the degree of organization of urban female youth was extremely low in comparison to rates for young males. In 1912 the municipal statistical bureau in Frankfurt am Main estimated that somewhere between 15 and 20 percent of young women between the ages of fourteen and twenty had joined a youth organization, whether religious, sport, labor related, or other.[22] The estimate for Cologne sank to 9 percent, whereas Neukölln, an industrial district of Greater Berlin, reported that of sixteen thousand girls between the ages of fourteen and eighteen, only two hundred belonged to religiously affiliated youth groups and perhaps another hundred adhered to associations for sports, hiking, or music. Thus, the vast majority of employed post-school-age females were strangers to any youth organization.

Despite the relative backwardness of welfare work with employed female youth and the paucity of organizations appealing to these young workers, in pressing for their inclusion as an integral part of the Prussian government's youth cultivation campaign, women teachers and other youth savers could draw on the extensive experience acquired in this area since the 1890s. They could also hold up existing associations as viable prototypes for the organization of these girls. To persuade officials that inclusion and the resulting expenses were necessary, however, they were compelled to articulate carefully their reasons for believing that the conditions of young working women posed a dangerous social problem demanding public attention and action. Further, they had to formulate implementable reform measures designed to alleviate or overcome this ostensible crisis.

Youth savers arguing for inclusion would point to the dual role of post-school-age girls as current employees and future mothers and highlight the ways in which conditions of employment were undermining the fertility of German women. Thus, they would treat young working women largely as an issue of public health and social hygiene. Of course, issues of health linked to military fitness had played an important role in precipitating discussion of post-school-age males as a social problem, and the declining fitness of young males had been invoked to elicit public support for sports and recreational programs.

But, asserted Alice Profé, although physical exercise might enhance the fitness of young males for military life in the short run, "welfare for our girls is of the greatest importance from the point of view of permanently securing our military capacity, since the health and life force of women conditions in every respect the health and efficiency of future generations."[23] Hence, youth savers set out to demonstrate that the health of young working women left much to be desired, both in comparison with that of young males in Germany and with that of young females in England and other leading industrial states. Moreover, this health deficit was gradually depleting Germany's demographic strength.

Physicians like the public health specialist Kaup and the gynecologist and well-known antialcohol campaigner Agnes Bluhm called attention to the fact that working girls entered the labor force just at the onset of puberty, when their physical development began to accelerate rapidly.[24] During this developmental phase their bodies were especially sensitive. "Unfavorable living conditions, especially overexertion, cannot only inhibit their development, but can also cause diseases that are correlated to this special sensitivity, that is, so-called constitutional disorders, diseases of the nervous system, etc."[25] Such statements were underpinned with statistics collected by the states, local health insurance offices, and industrial enterprises on the mortality and disease frequency of female employees between the ages of fifteen and twenty. Particularly worrisome was the fact that, whereas the mortality rates of English and German females between the ages of fifteen and twenty had fallen in tandem between the 1870s and late 1890s, during the first decade of the twentieth century, although the English mortality rate for this age group continued to drop, reaching a historical low of about 2.7 per thousand in 1908, in Prussia the mortality rate for young females in this age group had remained almost constant at about 3.4 per thousand.[26] This recent divergence was also apparent in the twenty- to twenty-five-year-old age group. After distinguishing urban from rural mortality rates in Prussia, Kaup deduced:

One can conclude from the mortality statistics for the cities and especially for the large Prussian cities that the origin of the unfavorable development of these numbers vis-à-vis England lies chiefly in the cities and that these unfavorable effects also hold for the age group from twenty to twenty-five years of age, in part even sharpen. Thus, this phenomenon speaks for the relation of mortality and the degree of employment of girls and women in the cities.[27]

The chief reason for this failure of mortality rates to fall was the continued virulence of the "white plague." Tuberculosis was the single most lethal disease contracted by young women, accounting for 44 percent of all female deaths in the fifteen- to twenty-year-old age range. By contrast, only 33.3 percent of male deaths in this age group resulted from TB.[28] Young women workers in commercial enterprises and the clothing industry were especially susceptible to this debilitating and potentially fatal disease. Bluhm attributed this susceptibility to the young women workers' lack of exposure to light and air and their vulnerability to anemia, another disease common among working girls during the development years and one that weakened resistance to infectious ailments. In her study of the working conditions and health of young seamstresses in Munich, Elizabeth Hell had posited similar causes for tuberculosis.[29]

In general young women workers were consistently sicklier than their male counterparts. Although young males were much more likely to be injured on the job, when injuries were subtracted, statistics from the Leipzig health insurance office revealed that out of each hundred youths mandatorily registered for insurance, 32.3 of the young women fell ill annually, compared to 25.7 of the young males. Moreover, days missed by these young females on account of illness averaged 477, whereas young males were absent only 358 days. This differential again came almost exclusively from the frequency of anemia among young females. Of each one hundred, 7.9 were forced to miss work because of incapacity due to anemia, compared to 0.5 of every hundred males.[30]

The etiology of anemia clearly lay in the notoriously poor eating habits and diets prevailing among working girls, which were probably worse than those among young male workers. According to Kaup, "[A]ll too great haste in the morning, lack of appetite because of the work and bad air in the workshops, lack of information on the importance of sufficient nutrition often lead to anemia and a poor nutritional state."[31] A number of studies of the diets of young female commercial and factory employees sustained these remarks. One study disclosed that female office clerks in Leipzig spent less than 30 percent of their income on food. They often completely omitted breakfast or else merely poured down a cup of coffee, for lunch they consumed sausage and potato salad at best, and for supper they ate bread and sausage, rarely supplemented with milk or fruit. Young female factory workers in Munich, who bought their meals out, usually lunched on soup, vegetables, and bread washed down with a glass of beer. They seldom ate meat. From such evidence, youth savers concluded that the schools should enlighten children, youth, and their parents on the importance of nutrition and that cheap, wholesome restaurants were needed in the vicinity of firms employing large numbers of female workers.

High mortality rates and the prevalence of tuberculosis, anemia, and poor nutrition among working girls certainly added up to a palpable public health problem, but how were these health deficits impinging on Germany's demographic future? Although they readily acknowledged that because of the inadequacy of the available statistical material, it was impossible to put forward ironclad proof, medical youth savers nonetheless deployed fragmentary statistics on premature births and miscarriages to suggest that the deficient health of young women was having serious repercussions for German infants.[32] In Hamburg the percentage of premature births had risen steadily since the late 1880s, from 3.74 to 5.98 percent of all newborns, an upward spiral also apparent in Baden. Over the same period the percentage of miscarriages had also increased in Baden, where termination of pregnancies by miscarriage had risen from 2.23 to 3.00 percent since the mid-1880s. Health officials recognized that such statistics were suspect for making inferences about female health, however, because of the likelihood that deliberately induced miscarriages had become more commonplace. Nonetheless, the frequency of premature births and miscarriages, as well as especially long lying-in periods, was considerably higher than average for young women between the ages of twenty and twenty-four employed in the chemical, leather, hides, and metal preparation industries, evidence that specific occupations demonstrably reduced the capacity for giving birth. Moreover, despite improved medical care for newborn infants in Germany, the number of feeble babies dying in the first month after birth had inched slowly upward since the early 1890s, from 31.4 per thousand live births to 31.5 in the early years of the new century, almost double the death rate in Norway and a rate clearly conditioned by the health and economic circumstances of the mother. Even the overall drop in the birthrate could be interpreted as a sign of incipient if not irreversible national degeneration. Although far from conclusive, a plausible circumstantial case could be adduced from these statistics for making health care for economically active female youth a matter of national demographic policy.

While underlining such public health issues in their brief for including girls in official youth cultivation, youth savers also emphasized other alarming aspects of the situation of economically active post-school-age females to buttress their argument, most notably the moral dangers that beset these youths, both on the job and in the broader urban setting. To be sure, in contrast to the criminality of males, that of young women appeared minimally problematic.[33] The crime frequency of female youth was less than 20 percent of the male rate. Only for a few types of crime, among them petty larceny and arson, did the rate even approach half of that for males. Moreover, the crime rate of young women had in general been falling since the 1880s. In 1909 it was 12.7 percent lower than it had been in 1882. But the figures for endangered youth assigned to welfare education were less heartening. Not only had the numbers of young females generally risen after 1901, from 1,114 in that year to 1,767 in 1910, but over 40 percent of all welfare charges were female. Almost all cases brought before magistrates under the welfare education law concerned sexual delicts of various sorts, for example, promiscuity, prostitution, unwed pregnancies. Although such cases were still relatively rare, youth savers interpreted them as symptoms of the more widespread sexual dangers facing young working women.

Youth savers regarded certain occupations as being singularly dangerous from a moral perspective. Sales clerks stood under constant male supervision and had to make themselves attractive to male customers, often of higher social status, through their movements, hairdos, and clothing.[34] Not only did such sales jobs wrench young working girls away from their own class, since placing them in constant contact with those of higher social status aroused aspirations incommensurate with their incomes and social position, but constant accommodation to masculine wishes made girls vulnerable to seduction. A similar dynamic was often at work in posts as household servants as well. In terms of potential sexual dangers, factory work was viewed as safest, a moral view vindicated by statistics on occupations of unwed mothers.

Vulnerability to seduction was ostensibly heightened by the labile psychological state and household situations of pubescent girls. Although some male youth savers mentioned the touchiness of adolescent males, supposedly unstable psyches were much more commonly discussed in connection with young female workers, whether because female youth savers accepted traditional stereotypes or because they were more attuned to the emotional states of their charges – or because there were real differences. Moody, tempestuous, and hypersensitive, these sexually awakening girls purportedly swung rapidly from pride and vanity to extreme dejection punctuated by streams of tears.[35] Lacking inner security and confidence, they were highly dependent on the judgments of others. Moreover, monotonous work regimens followed by onerous family chores in drab, cheerless two-room flats drove these youths to long for color, pleasure, and escape. Some found this escape by reading "backstairs" romances, which according to the Berlin teacher Alwine Reinald, "are dedicated to erotic problems, full of ambiguity and calculated to awaken desires in these often love-starved adolescents, which given their still weak moral grasp, they are incapable of resisting."[36] Others escaped to the streets, where they paraded in tawdry finery and entered into flirtations that, however, were usually harmless. Youth savers consistently decried the addiction of young working women to cheap but flashy clothing and their "distorted hairdos," aspects of working girls' subculture that middle-class reformers imputed to the superficiality of these youths.[37] Worse still in the eyes of youth savers, young working girls often sought pleasure in the crowded and smoky dance halls, where after a night of reeling in this disorienting ambience, "many maidens in overheated sensual states fall victim to passion."[38] But even the household was far from being a secure haven since young females were sometimes subjected to the attentions of young male subtenants with whom they shared cramped living quarters.[39] Reinald claimed that these conditions and leisure-time activities of working girls helped to account for the one hundred eighty thousand out-of-wedlock babies born annually in Germany.

Not only was the working-class family often failing to provide shelter from moral perils, but working mothers were also remiss in transmitting to their daughters domestic skills that were crucial for their future performance as mothers and housewives, supposedly further evidence of the advanced disintegration of working-class family life. Previously the skill and assiduity of the German housewife had enabled German workers to enjoy living standards comparable to those of English laborers despite lower wages.[40] The breakdown in the transmission of domestic skills was eliminating this compensatory advantage. Consequently youth savers agreed that instruction in housework had become a necessity for young female factory workers. As Kaup stated, "The relations in the parental household, the employment of the mother, the activity of the girl in an easily learned unskilled job, the marriage of over 90 percent of young women after six or eight years of employment makes it necessary to guarantee that these girls receive a solid training in domestic skills after primary school."[41]

Such claims were not new. Already in 1887 O. Kamp, a teacher and welfare worker in Frankfurt am Main, had made similar claims and called for continuation schools to offset the decline in domestic skills.[42] As a result of his agitation, which was backed by several women's groups, the Reichstag considered amending the Industrial Code in 1890/1 so that municipalities could make continuation schools teaching household arts mandatory for young women. The liberals supported this measure, as had the Socialists. The Socialist leader August Bebel, author of a widely read book on women's emancipation and socialism, asserted that such schools were necessary in view of the little time that women factory workers had to pass on their domestic skills to their daughters. But at that time, conservatives attacked Bebel's assertion as slanderous to diligent German mothers and were able to defeat the amendment.

Nonetheless, a number of German states had taken action on this issue, among them Baden, where the grand duchess had promoted housework continuation schools from the late 1880s, and Saxony-Meiningen. In these states factory girls were required to take part-time continuing education courses in home economics. This was also true in Munich, where Georg Kerschensteiner, cooperating closely with Helene Sumper, a talented teacher and author of textbooks, was instrumental in securing the introduction of a three-year mandatory continuation school for young working women with household arts as its instructional core.[43] During the first year, nutrition was emphasized; during the second, household and clothing; and the family during the third year. In addition to their practical work in this area, both Kerschensteiner and Sumper indefatigably publicized the Munich continuation schools for girls in journals and in various associations of educators. Itinerant sewing and cooking courses for post-school-age girls were also becoming familiar institutions in rural districts. Such instruction was geared toward bridging the divide between wage labor and preparation for motherhood.

These educational measures, however, formed only a small part of the broad battery of reform initiatives proposed by the youth savers at conferences like those of the Central Agency for Popular Welfare in Danzig in 1912. These proposals were conceived as means not only to prepare working girls for family life and motherhood, but also supposedly to "maintain their youthful spirit, to increase their physical strength, to awaken their sense of community, and to educate their sense of responsibility and their joy in work."[44] One way of achieving these desirable goals was by extending continuing education schools to females, although such schooling for young women would combine occupational instruction with home economics.[45] To avoid overbur-

dening young women and to ameliorate their health, classes would
be held during regular daytime work hours and opportunities for
recreational activities like gymnastics and gardening would also be
made available. A few female youth reformers, aware that working
women increasingly tended to remain in the labor force even after
marriage and that lack of skills often consigned these women to the
poorest-paying and least desirable positions in the labor force, protested mildly that vocational education was being slighted,[46] but since
more emphasis on labor force skills dampened the heavy accent on
homemaking and maternity, these protests were to little avail. Nonetheless, some proposed reforms did touch on the prospects of young
women in the work force. Suggestions were generally well received
for strengthening occupational counseling to ensure that school leavers found jobs corresponding to their capacities and inclinations.[47] To
fortify girls' health during the crucial phase of development, some
reformers urged that the working day of fourteen- to sixteen-year-
old girls be restricted to half shifts, that the work week end at 1:00
P.M. on Saturdays, and that these youths be legally guaranteed two
weeks of paid vacation annually that could be devoted to recreation
and physical renewal through energizing activities like hikes and excursions.[48] Imposing these restrictions on the work time, however,
would have necessitated substantial amendments to several provisions
of the Industrial Code. If all young working women were to be gathered for recreation, innocent sociability, and edification, it would be
necessary for women's groups like the patriotic women's leagues to
inaugurate new youth groups and for already existing associations to
enlarge their activities considerably. Finally, reformers were unanimously committed to extending the Prussian Youth Cultivation Edict
of 1911 to encompass young women.

Even during the discussion of the original Youth Cultivation Edict
in the Prussian House of Representatives, a number of conservatives
had introduced a motion calling for this extension. Moreover, Dr.
von Vogel, a physician serving on the army general staff, sadly regretted in an article entitled "The Army, Post-School-Age Youth, and
the State" that "[T]raining girls through physical education to be
healthy and strong mothers still isn't being taken seriously enough."[49]
Such expressions of conservative apprehension, as well as conferences
by female teachers and the Central Agency for Popular Welfare, soon
spurred the Ministry for Religious and Educational Affairs to reevalu-
ate its position. Already during the summer of 1912, the ministry

requested reports from district governors on existing local welfare provisions for young working women and the means and materials necessary to foster them.[50]

Clearly sensing that a policy shift was in the offing, mayors and county commissioners responded with considerable enthusiasm to the prospect that the government would underwrite programs for the welfare of young women. The commissioner of Solingen county sounded the tocsin of political alarm by claiming that the Socialists had recently multiplied their social functions and meetings aimed at influencing and recruiting young women.[51] In order to undermine these efforts and contribute to the welfare of the more than four thousand post-school-age girls in the district, most of whom were industrial workers, he favored funding already existing patriotic and religious groups and setting up new ones in association with the itinerant home economics courses. The mayor of the nearby textile center Elberfeld sent a detailed account of the city's tangled financial arrangement with the private Association for the Common Welfare for providing weekly instruction in sewing, household arts, and hygiene to eight hundred young women, most of whom worked in factories.[52] He also noted that the further initiatives by the local Association for Physical Culture, which had recently added hiking and gymnastics sections for girls, depended on the receipt of subsidies. The commissioner of a county near the Ruhr coal-mining city of Essen stated that money was desperately needed to cover the costs of an itinerant home economics school scheduled to open the following April, since student fees would prove inadequate.[53] Thus, local officials consistently designated numerous areas where central government financing could be put to good use.

When the Prussian government finally reversed its policy in April 1913 and extended youth cultivation to young women, not only female youth cultivators but most local Prussian officials eagerly embraced this departure and immediately began implementing the recommendations contained in the new edict. Only in a few rural districts, where young women were constantly busy with farm chores, did county commissioners voice some misgivings.[54] But for the most part, during the spring and summer of 1913 officials were able to report a host of planned projects and actual undertakings to reach young employed females. According to the commissioner from Solingen county, the local patriotic women's league had made youth cultivation for females the central topic of its most recent meeting and was pledged to building throughout the county youth clubs that mixed recreation with sewing instruction.[55] Although he had hitherto been unable to find suitable women to serve on the county youth welfare board, the commissioner expected to be able to appoint several members of the patriotic women's league in the near future.

Large cities in Prussia like Düsseldorf were able to broach far grander visions of youth cultivation for girls. Since the 1890s Düsseldorf had operated a voluntary continuation school for young women, with courses like household bookkeeping, home economics, sewing, German, and arithmetic. Beginning in 1909, almost one thousand young female clerical employees had been obliged to attend the city's commercial continuation school.[56] In May 1913 the city council entertained a proposal to require eight hours weekly of continuing education for all employed females between the ages of fourteen and seventeen.[57] This proposal would have brought education for industrially employed female youth in line with that for males, although, of course, domestic arts were to take precedence over industrial skills. Although Lord Mayor Oehler defended the proposal by citing the complaints of employers about the educational deficiencies of their female employees and by appealing to urban pride, since even smaller cities had already instituted mandatory continuing education for young females, liberal opponents killed the bill. One liberal councillor denounced what he saw as the cancerous growth of educational institutions. These institutions were producing a "half-educated proletariat" that readily succumbed to Socialist demagogery. But most liberal councillors simply considered such schooling inimical to the interests of business. The Düsseldorf Chamber of Commerce had already objected in 1901 to what it called the "mechanical extension" of industrial continuation schools to female workers under the age of eighteen, on the grounds that it would injure the competitiveness of German industry.[58] Liberal spokesmen on the council showed that the objections of business people to continuation schools for young women had not changed in twelve years. Some objected that since instruction was to occur during daytime hours, it would disrupt production, an old point standardly trotted out against continuing education for males. Moreover, if business people were going to have to foot the costs of instruction, practical occupational instruction rather than household arts ought to occupy central place in the school. However, declared one councillor, such vocational instruction was superfluous for young women since they merely worked until they married. Only spokespersons for the minority Catholic Center party, which defended the family over industry, warmly endorsed the proposal as a positive piece of social legislation and added that since employers derived substantial benefits from employing young females, a small sacrifice could be demanded in return. But recognizing that the bill was doomed to fail, the mayor referred it back to the educational committee for review. This procedure effectively suspended the city's consideration of broadening continuing education for females in the prewar era. Nor was Düsseldorf alone in this respect. The Lübeck city council twice rejected petitions for setting up an industrial continuation school for young women in 1913, although Berlin did finally mandate such schools the same year.[59]

Other recommendations for female youth cultivation fared somewhat better, however, or at least encountered a more generous reception. The lord mayor soon named four women to the regional youth cultivation committee on the basis of their considerable experience in working with young females.[60] Those appointed included the chairwoman of the Association of Women Commercial Employees, two leading members of the local Association for Youth Welfare, and a middle school teacher. In August 1913 Theodor Herold, the city's educational councillor, drafted a comprehensive plan for municipal youth cultivation for young women.[61] In this draft Herold stressed the need for a female youth club with provisions for physical culture, a library, reading rooms, and a theater, a proposal that closely followed the guidelines embodied in the ministry edict. Presumably, this club for young women was to be housed in the mammoth central youth center already approved by the city council. Rejecting the one-sided emphasis on preparation for domestic life, Herold considered occupational counseling a crucial component of a successful youth policy for post-school-age females. "It seems to me," he opined, "that occupational counseling is of fundamental importance because only those humans who find callings that correspond to their abilities and inclinations become useful members of their estate. . . . " The upshot of this proposal was the creation of the municipally supported Information Center for Female Occupations.[62] This center collected questionnaires on the occupational choices of girls completing primary school, sent speakers to higher schools to discuss career prospects, and advised the undecided on available options. In 1914 the center was able to place 211 of the 511 girls seeking apprenticeships, most of them in positions as seamstresses, domestic servants, and salesclerks.

The full arrival of youth cultivation for young women was manifest at the Düsseldorf Week for the Further Education of Youth Cultivators in October.[63] Not only did Baum movingly depict in her speech, mentioned in the last chapter, the hard, joyless lives endured by young female factory workers, but several other speakers addressed themes like prostitution and unwed mothers, the emotional strains suffered by adolescent girls, and the need to train young women for a rapidly changing labor market. Several speakers discussed the domestic and economic benefits that could be expected from extending continuing education to young female employees. Moreover, over half of the 2,060 conference participants were women, evidence of their interest in this exponentially growing area of social welfare with its promise of opening up a new female profession.

Between 1912 and 1914 the question of the professionalization of youth welfare work with young females was frequently debated and surrounded by controversy. Many women teachers strongly believed that by virtue of their educational background and their understanding of girls, they were inherently best suited to take on the additional tasks entailed by extending this new area of youth cultivation. Thus, at the conference of the Central Agency for Popular Welfare in 1912 one of the major speakers, Elise Deutsch, a teacher from Charlottenburg, argued for the primacy of women teachers, asserting that "the direction of youth cultivation in public and private institutions must lie in their hands, that they must be paramount during the girl's development years."[64] Youth cultivation for young women, avowed Deutsch, would offer female teachers, who were legally required to remain celibate as a condition of employment, the opportunity to display their natural motherliness. Such arguments dovetailed with the pronounced tendency in late Wilhelmine Germany to justify female employment in caring professions by claiming that such work constituted public projections of natural feminine maternity.[65] The claims for women primary school teachers were also patently intended to raise the public status of a profession whose members had long felt undervalued. Other professional women, like the statistician Hertha Siemering, however, doubted that youth cultivation could be effectively performed on a voluntary and part-time basis, especially by teachers who were already heavily overcommitted.[66] Youth cultivation was complex and demanding. Tasks like leading clubs, teaching domestic skills, or counseling on occupational choice were full-time duties requiring specialized preparation. Anna von Gierke, director of a home for endangered working-class girls in Charlottenburg, advocated the creation of special seminaries to educate women youth savers, similar to those for other areas of social work like the one

instituted by the Inner Mission of the Evangelical Church.[67] Students
would become thoroughly grounded in civics and pedagogy, although
they would also have to be familiar enough with hygiene, physical
education, cooking instruction, and sewing courses to be able to hire
qualified personnel for female youth centers or clubs. Teachers, ministers, and others who had previously taken the lead in youth cultivation would still be warmly welcomed and prized as valuable
assistants, but administration would become the exclusive domain of
professionals. Nonetheless, during the prewar era, voluntary work
would continue to predominate, although educational conferences
like the one held in Düsseldorf in October 1913 in part mediated
between the counterposed perspectives. Such conferences presupposed that special knowledge of youth psychology, already extant
youth organizations, and the variegated recreational and educational
activities of these groups was a necessary prerequisite for the aspiring
youth cultivator. Ironically, however, a new middle-class female
profession was already beginning to emerge whose practitioners were
trained to alleviate a crisis ostensibly caused by the breakdown in
working-class domesticity resulting from the massive growth of female
employment outside the home.

Certainly in the slightly less than a year and a half between the
Prussian government's extension of youth cultivation to young women
and the outbreak of the war, issues like the professionalization of
female youth work, continuing education for young female employees, occupational counseling, and establishing youth centers became
matters of public discussion aired in city councils, churches, professional associations, the press, and training conferences like the one
held in Düsseldorf. Actual accomplishments, however, lagged considerably behind the proposed projects. A few municipally supported
institutions, such as the Center for Female Occupations in Düsseldorf,
were able to get underway; women active in female youth cultivation
took their places on local and regional youth cultivation committees.
Probably the major beneficiaries of the Educational Ministry's largesse
were already functioning Catholic and Evangelical associations for
young women, which were eligible for government funding to expand
and upgrade their programs by purchasing gymnastic equipment,
library books, and materials for household instruction.[68] But most
projects, like the female youth center in Düsseldorf, never left the
drawing board. Initially the war would totally disrupt both the planning and execution of comprehensive female youth cultivation. However, as we shall see, after this initial reversal, youth cultivation for

females was able to recover far more rapidly than would that for males. Indeed, despite its long neglect and belated start before the war, after August 1914 youth cultivation for young female employees would prove more resilient than the far more institutionally anchored provisions for young male workers.

9

Youth cultivation and young workers in war

Despite considerable apprehension on the part of government officials and army commanders, the response of young laborers to the outbreak of the war and their behavior during its first year and a half could be perceived as a confirmation of the considerable effectiveness attained by the prewar youth salvation campaign in instilling patriotic sentiment. Initially industrial continuation school students volunteered in large numbers for premilitary training, and generally they celebrated nationalist commemorations like the kaiser's birthday with enthusiasm.[1] As the Social Democratic party acceded to the *Burgfrieden*, the peace of the fortress, suspending class struggle for the duration of the war, and as older members and advisers to the Socialist youth movement were drafted, the Free Youth faded into a shadow existence.[2] The spirit of patriotic harmony also extended to youth cultivation activities. Swayed by the general nationalist euphoria, the Catholic Church, which had been disenchanted by the increasingly military direction taken by prewar government youth activity, a direction exemplified by the Young Germany League, at first stopped criticizing government youth policy. Even some sectors of the Socialist party and affiliated subcultural associations like the Worker Gymnasts moderated their criticisms and expressed some interest in incorporating their programs into the broader youth cultivation campaign. As one well-known Rhenish Protestant teacher, active in youth cultivation, proclaimed, echoing the kaiser, "The storm wind of war has swept away all the party haggling of the German people."[3]

But what could be swept away by the stormwind of war, could also be blown back. The collapse of the civic side of youth cultivation for males and its replacement with an almost exclusive emphasis on premilitary training would soon reawaken both Catholic and Socialist opposition to government policy. Moreover, by 1916, after two years of strained exertion and constant sacrifice, a new restiveness and smoldering discontent were becoming noticeable among laboring youth. Depending on conditions and opportunities, expressions of this discontent were polymorphous. The forms it assumed ranged from the apolitical and individual, including absenteeism from work, frequent job changes, and petty theft, to the collective and political: looting food stores, joining youth strikes, and even joining the reconstituted youth movement of the antiwar Socialist left. In light of this sea change in popular reactions, many administrative officials and military commanders revised their previously optimistic assessments of young laborers. Whereas a few more discerning officials cautioned against premature generalizations about youthful bad conduct, many who in 1914 had viewed young workers as fervent converts to the national cause now examined them through the jaundiced eyes of the disillusioned and found them to be morally derailed, wild and disrespectful hooligans or potential revolutionaries. They generally attributed these manifestations of deviance to the absence of forceful masculine presence in home and school, the high wages earned during wartime, which gave young males greater independence, and the ease with which highly suggestible youth were influenced by films, penny dreadfuls, or Socialist propaganda. Despite the overstatements and shrill moralism of many conservative officials, their perceptions were not completely distorted. By 1916 many young workers clearly were becoming fed up with the war and wartime conditions, and many would subsequently participate in the strikes, demonstrations, and riots that shook the Reich in the last war year and in the revolutionary upheavals of the immediate postwar period.

What accounted for this gradual volte-face, this shift from war enthusiasm to grudging acquiescence or even open revolt? Apart from the pervasive war weariness and exhaustion, three major causes can be adduced for this transformation. First, as all other activities were subsumed by the war, youth cultivation for males (but not that for females) approached collapse. Although church groups attempted to maintain their activities, the continuation schools, with their clubs and extracurricular programs, virtually ceased functioning. Only premilitary preparation along the lines charted by the Young Germany League remained of the once-luxuriant variety of government-sponsored youth cultivation. This collapse released young laborers from much of the previous institutional surveillance and constraint. Second, after years of rising expectations, the working conditions and living standards of young workers deteriorated markedly. Having been taught to appreciate the welfare and protective measures accorded the German worker, the young laborer instead confronted longer hours for shrinking real wages in workshops where all safety measures and protective legislation had been suspended. Third, the army and its civilian allies used the war as an opportunity to impose the stringent moral policing and repression long advocated by conservatives. Instead of granting young workers greater freedom commensurate with their greater responsibilities as family providers and mainstays of the war effort, the army instituted hidebound authoritarian measures that young workers found galling and openly defied. Thus as liberals like Wilhelm Troeltsch had warned at the turn of the century, anachronistic paternalism proved counterproductive and simply alienated youth. Participation by youth in the radical actions of 1917–20 was catalyzed by a desire to throw off this unwelcome and onerous yoke. Young workers would aspire to greater personal freedom and autonomy, parity of treatment with adult workers, and a voice in those institutions that affected them. Thus they would sometimes play a distinctive role in the antiauthoritarian revolt of the late war and immediate postwar era.

Symptomatic of the dissolution of prewar youth cultivation was the fate of the continuation schools. Soon after the outbreak of the war, the Trade Ministry urged continuation school directors to keep their institutions in operation while accommodating the needs of industry for exemptions whenever possible.[4] During the first months of the war, when business was unsettled and industry depressed, students continued to come to class, but with the conversion to a war economy during autumn of 1914, this short-lived phase of normalcy speedily ended.[5] The recommendations of the Trade Ministry quickly proved to be incompatible. Because masters and journeymen were often drafted, the survival of many artisanal shops became completely dependent on the full-time labor of apprentices. Heavy industry began to suffer from chronic labor shortages. Hence in Düsseldorf the industrial continuation school permanently released almost a third of its students and partially exempted many more.[6] This was true elsewhere as well. In 1914 the industrial continuation school in Magdeburg had enrolled 5,113 students in 185 classes, but by 1918 only 200 students in 44 classes remained. Knowing that policing was largely ineffectual in enforcing attendance, unmotivated students simply ceased coming. In some regions where policing did persist, students increasingly disregarded attendance requirements. Thus, in Schleswig in 1914, 150 students had been punished for skipping continuation school, whereas by 1918 the number would rise eightfold to 1,200. Hence only a handful of students appeared for classes; moreover, different students attended from week to week. Many regular teachers were called to the colors, and finding adequate replacements proved difficult. Faced with these insuperable obstacles to routine operation, in Düsseldorf the school's director Gotter followed the Trade Ministry's advice and dropped all practical instruction, leaving only two hours of theoretical instruction weekly.[7] Even this vestige of instruction was seldom crowned with success, since upper-level students not only worked all day, but were also compelled to perform the newly introduced military exercises before classes and hence arrived in a state of utter exhaustion. Nor could the school's recreational activities be maintained.[8] Initially the continuation school kept its reading and game rooms open in the evenings, but attendance declined precipitously from prewar levels, and the previously vital club life dissolved. Thus, except for serving a few younger laborers in nonstrategic industries, industrial continuation schools were essentially converted into centers for preparatory military training.

Since October 1913 the Prussian War Ministry had been discussing and drafting legislation requiring all males between the ages of fifteen and twenty to undergo premilitary training. This training, conceived in response to post-1912 alarm about military preparedness, was designed not only to improve the physical stamina of new recruits but also to strengthen patriotic sentiment and to reach those youth growing up under "antimilitary influence, in an antistate, unpatriotic, and antimilitary spirit" – in short, Socialist youth.[9] But discussions of this universal premilitary training quickly revealed a considerable number of practical difficulties if such a comprehensive project was to be carried through. Young males were already burdened with excessive demands for their time from industry, continuation schools, and youth associations. Moreover, a vast increase in militarily and pedagogically trained instructors willing to work with youth, as well as a massive augmentation of funds, would be necessary if such military training was to succeed.

In light of these practical problems and because Socialist deputies unanimously voted for war credits in August 1914, within weeks of the outbreak of the war the War Ministry in conjunction with the Educational and Interior Ministries instead introduced a much modified program for premilitary training. In contrast to earlier proposals, this training was to be voluntary, although officials were expected to make every possible effort to recruit the unemployed, since otherwise these urban youth were likely to idle away their time and make mischief. Also in contrast to previous premilitary training like that of the Young Germany League, more emphasis was to be placed on directly war-related exercises, such as using maps and digging trenches, rather than concentrating exclusively on indirect but militarily beneficial tasks, such as building endurance or sharpening observational skills. However, the War Ministry explicitly precluded practice with weapons. The ministry charged the regional deputy army commanders with overseeing and administering premilitary preparation of youth, and in turn deputy commanders appointed an officer, usually retired and often previously involved with the Young Germany League, as regional supervisor.

In the wake of the call by the War Ministry to launch premilitary preparation for males over sixteen, regional deputy commanders and lord mayors issued proclamations informing young males that "the defense of our dear German fatherland demands that all possible means be expended to steel the forces of our youth for military service and to instruct them in all the skills necessary for the struggle against the enemies of our people in order to secure permanently the success achieved by the blood of our brave soldiers."[10] Initially both Catholic bishops and Protestant synods conferred their blessings on this project. Given the experience of continuation schools in fostering the Young Germany League, which was to serve as a model for premilitary training, these schools were obvious candidates for implementing these tasks. In Düsseldorf over two thousand students at the industrial continuation school responded to this call, many of these volunteers under sixteen years of age.[11] Within a month of the war's outbreak the school had formed thirteen companies and scheduled four hours of weekly drill. The only sanctions applied to those over sixteen were those normally used by the school for nonattendance: fines, notification of employers, and in repeated cases arrest hours (compulsory hours of sitting in a classroom as punishment). At first, however, students exercised willingly, and absenteeism posed no problem. In addition to continuation schools, some large industrial firms like Krupp in Essen and both German General Electric and the Ludwig Loewe Armaments Factory in Berlin created their own youth companies, which their apprentices were compelled to join.[12] Government employers like the railroads and the Imperial Naval Docks in Wilhemshaven, as well as some municipal enterprises, followed suit. Participation rates in the "voluntary" youth companies varied considerably, however, depending on local traditions of militarism or antimilitarism. In Pfalz (Palatinate) by early 1915 supposedly 88 percent of young males had enrolled in premilitary training, and in the Posen district 69 percent had joined by October 1914. In Hamburg, in contrast, with over nine hundred thousand residents, slightly more than four thousand young males were participating during fall. Nonetheless, in 1914 the army could only be heartened by the largely voluntary turnout, since by the end of the year approximately six hundred thousand youths over the age of sixteen were practicing militarily useful skills.

Apart from the few exceptions already noted, organizational structure, physical training, and patriotic indoctrination during premilitary training sessions were closely patterned on those pioneered by the Young Germany League.[13] Reserve officers, who regularly pursued middle-class careers as professionals, businessmen, and teachers, took command of the companies. In principle companies were supposed to be representative of the social and religious composition of the community in the expectation that wartime nationalism would transcend Germany's deep political, social, and religious schisms. In practice, however, such mixing seldom took place. Continuation school companies were usually religiously integrated, but because they were completely insulated from higher schools, cross-class mixing of age peers was negligible. Regular evening drills were supposed to increase strength and stamina by alternating brief periods of marching, gymnastics, and calisthenics with races and other competitions. Hikes with maneuvers and war games were held on Sundays. On both weekday evenings and Sundays the officers spent a few minutes recounting episodes from national history or delivering patriotic pep talks. Pedagogues with experience in youth cultivation advised them to try to sound natural, as though their words sprang from the heart, rather than being carefully rehearsed, but the deficient pedagogical qualities of reserve officers clearly bulked large as a problem. Nonetheless, as Germany's military situation worsened and as the "peace of the fortress" began to break down, such propagandistic interventions acquired greater urgency. Late in the war officers began appropriating socialist themes and reshaping them for nationalist ends, when they delivered addresses like "The War of English Big Capital Against German Labor" or "The Rights of Workers in the So-called Democracies of France, England, and America." This rhetoric testified to the class homogeneity of most of the companies and the notion entertained by the military authorities that the youthful ranks were highly susceptible to the antiwar campaign of the left-wing Socialists. Even early in the war the military authorities tended to blame the Socialists for any problem associated with premilitary exercises, whether declining participation rates or waning enthusiasm. By 1915 the decline of participation not only made many officers regret the principle of voluntary enrollment but also spurred them to begin weighing a move to mandatory premilitary training.[14]

In fact, the initial reaction of the Socialists to premilitary training was far from being consistent or unified.[15] Some Socialists saw universal military instruction as a down payment toward the militia-type defensive army they had long endorsed and considered participation a golden opportunity for ending repression of their organizations. The Socialist left, however, regarded any form of cooperation as an egregious betrayal of the party's time-honored antiwar tradition. In Schleswig-Holstein the Socialists cooperated eagerly with the government, while in Württemberg the Socialist youth commission summarily rejected any truck with "genocidal militarism." However, even in Württemberg representatives of the Metalworkers' Union and the Worker Gymnasts did join the executive committee of the government-sponsored youth guard. When the youth commission of the Berlin SPD sent out a nationwide circular in September 1914 denouncing the youth companies as the Young Germany League writ large, regional military commanders pressed mayors to investigate the SPD's impact on military preparation.[16] They felt that such an investigation was all the more necessary, given that the circular appealed to Socialists to strive actively to prevent youth from joining and to resist coercion by the continuation schools. Essen's lord mayor immediately set up a commission of inquiry composed of several city council members, educational officials, and a Krupp manager.[17] When it reported in early 1915, however, the committee categorically denied that the SPD had impeded military preparation and concluded that the causes of declining participation lay elsewhere. Young coal miners likely to be influenced by the SPD had consistently demonstrated considerable enthusiasm for military exercises. Their enthusiasm contrasted markedly with the attitude of many gymnasia students who showed a remarkable lack of interest. It was long hours and shift work, rather than SPD propaganda, that interfered with regular attendance. The report also noted the manifest pedagogical inadequacy of many of the officers, who were utterly incapable of exciting and holding the interest of youth. But most detrimental, indeed, far more serious than ostensible SPD opposition, according to the Essen committee, was the uncooperative and even hostile stance adopted by the Catholic clergy.

The objections of the Catholic clergy to premilitary preparation were essentially the same as those they had raised against the Young Germany League. In short, they advanced no objections to military exercises per se; rather, they opposed those features of the program that struck them as insidious intrusions of secularism. Again, the placement of maneuvers and war games on Sundays was an especially contentious issue.[18] When held in the morning, maneuvers kept young Catholic males away from mass. When held in the afternoons, they robbed families of their sole weekly opportunity for common activity. Priests regarded this latter point as especially important, since Sunday maneuvers were further undermining the foundations of a viable family life at a time when family survival was already being threatened by the absence of many fathers and the demands of the war economy. Consequently some religious instructors at higher schools were even willing to risk being fired by surreptitiously telling their Catholic students to skip Sunday exercises.[19] Catholic priests also rejected the interconfessional character and interdenominational religious services of youth companies and were worried that the mandatory companies under consideration would severely damage Catholic associations. Purely military training neglected spiritual values. Moreover, forcing students to join confessionally and socially mixed companies eliminated the rights of parents to control the education and social contacts of their children. On behalf of the executive committee of the Catholic Youth Associations of Germany, Chaplain Mosterts broached these issues with the Interior Ministry in August 1915.[20] Catholic youth associations also sought the right to organize their own autonomous youth companies, which would then coordinate their activities with those of their secular counterparts. To mollify the Catholic clergy and youth associations, the ministries and army commanders were willing to compromise on these issues. Increasingly they attempted to hold exercises late on Sunday mornings and to guarantee that at least one sabbath monthly was left free.[21] In addition, commanders conceded the right of Catholic youth associations to set up their own voluntary militias. In Düsseldorf alone over four hundred males between the ages of fifteen and twenty joined such church-sponsored units.[22] But the army's intermittent transgressions against Sunday observance would rekindle clerical protest throughout the war.[23]

The willingness of the ministries and regional military commanders to reach an accord with the Catholic Church was conditioned by their recognition that the church was fundamentally loyal to the Wilhelmine state. When their autonomy was accepted, Catholic youth associations arrayed themselves in a solid phalanx behind the war effort. To mark the kaiser's birthday, Düsseldorf's youth sodalities jointly rented the municipal concert hall and staged a youth festival spotlighting mass choral singing of standard patriotic anthems like "Die Wacht am Rhein" and "Heil dir im Siegerkranz."[24] The firm antistrike pledge adopted by both the youth sodalities and the Christian trade unions won them the praise and gratitude of the military command late in the war.[25] Priests were also favorably disposed to the army's campaign to control youthful leisure activities through compulsory saving schemes, bans on smoking and drinking, and censorship of books and films, a campaign that will be treated below.[26] Catholic youth sodalities steadily carried on in the spirit of prewar youth cultivation, shepherding the young in their religious, educational, and athletic programs.[27] Sodalities also continued to receive financial assistance from the Prussian state throughout the war as they had since the Youth Cultivation Edict of 1911. Thus, despite periods of high tension between the Prussian state and the Catholic Church over Sunday observance and interconfessional mingling, both parties benefited sufficiently from this somewhat strained relationship, such that neither seriously contemplated a real rupture.

In August 1915 the Evangelical Church also protested against devoting every Sunday to military exercises, which imperiled church youth work.[28] Its solution to this problem, however, was the further statification of military preparation so that obligatory exercises could be placed on weekdays, leaving Sundays free. In most respects the Evangelical Church had greater cause for alarm than did the Catholics. Whereas the Catholic Church, with its long experience in youth affairs, its pedagogically trained personnel, and its well-institutionalized youth sodalities, was able to retain its influence with the majority of post-school-age Catholic laborers, the programs of the Evangelical Church, largely belated hothouse plants of the government's 1911 youth cultivation initiative, soon withered. Protestant clerics shared the grave concerns of their Catholic counterparts over the supposed moral consequences of the war: the further disintegration of family life, youthful misconduct, and disregard for religious values.[29] They admired Catholic efforts to dam this tide of amoralism, but they were utterly incapable of translating their admiration into effective imitation. At the Evangelical synod of the Düsseldorf region in 1917, Pastor Euler's report on Evangelical youth work presented a dismal record of past failure coupled with pious but abstract hopes for future remedy.[30] Five local youth clubs had disbanded entirely since the beginning of the war, and although the thirteen still in existence in Düsseldorf could claim a thousand members, their athletic and music programs had lapsed into serious disarray. A mere 15 percent of Evangelical boys confirmed in Düsseldorf ever joined a Protestant youth association. Admitting sadly that young males were "ever more alienated from the Church," Euler feared for its future. To reverse this trend, he admonished the gathered clergy to celebrate the four-hundredth anniversary of the Reformation with worthy deeds rather than mere commemoration, but he offered no guidelines specifying the nature of such deeds. Judged by its public declarations, the Protestant Church was even more committed than the Catholic Church to furthering the war effort and to winning youth to the national cause.[31] To maintain the morale of troops in the field, the church established numerous well-stocked reading rooms and centers for young soldiers and inundated combatants with uplifting tracts. Evangelical youth papers regularly featured articles vividly portraying Russian atrocities and deriding anyone who dared criticize German militarism. But the church's eager and willing spirit was no substitute for years of painstaking organizational work; hence, much energy was expended and dissipated without achieving the desired results.

Deprived of the continuation school as a focus for experimentation and intervention, the youth cultivation committees founded after the Youth Cultivation Edict proved to be almost as ineffectual as the Evangelical Church. Not only had the associational life of continuation schools disintegrated, but prewar projects, such as constructing youth centers for post–continuation school youth, ground to a halt. Despite the loss of institutional locus, which deprived youth committees of much of their raison d'être, the rounds of regional conferences, frequent meetings of youth advisory committees, and flow of newsletters, published reports, and bulletins continued unabated throughout the war. Officials and teachers tracked and deplored the economic and moral impact of the war on youth, consulted on ways of cooperating with the army in promoting moral regeneration, and laid plans for reviving civil youth cultivation after the war.[32]

As mentioned in Chapter 8, however, the sole area of youth cultivation that not only was able to survive but actually made some headway during the war was that for post-school-age girls. This advance occurred largely because women teachers and others experienced in working with young females were not drafted. To be sure, in some towns, such as Rheydt in the Rhineland, all plans to provide occupational counseling and recreational opportunities for girls completing primary school were abandoned in August 1914.[33] But this was not true everywhere. Many of the clubs for working girls, newly founded or rejuvenated after the extension of the Prussian government's youth cultivation to females in April 1913, rapidly reoriented their activities to meet the challenges of the war. As a woman youth cultivator in the heavily Catholic Trier district reported, both religious and secular associations for young women

> ... distinguished themselves by the cultivation of patriotic concerns. Lectures were held on the ... maintenance of Germanness and a sense of homeland [*Heimatsinn*]. Gifts of every sort were prepared for the troops. When the sewing, ironing, and dressmaking courses that had been set up in many localities had to be closed because of lack of materials, courses on mending and repairing clothes and even shoes were held. Although the officially established traveling cooking courses, which sometimes were conducted in co-operation with the patriotic women's associations, could not continue through the entire war, even in the countryside, because of lack of foodstuffs, with demobilization an attempt was made to revive them. . . . [34]

In 1916 as large numbers of young women entered heavy war industries for the first time, chiefly as a result of the Hindenburg Plan, and as support for the war eroded dramatically, the Prussian government made a concerted effort to breathe new life into youth cultivation for young female workers. The district governor of the Düsseldorf region, Dr. Kruse, sent out a circular reminding youth organizations of their duties in preparing post-school-age girls for their dual roles as workers and future mothers through occupational counseling, "by improvement of health through gymnastics, swimming, sports, and hikes, by instruction in home economics and introduction to the educational and nurturative duties of motherhood, and education to communal spirit."[35] Kruse also recommended that every county appoint a part-time female youth cultivator, for which the Prussian government made available a three-hundred-mark subsidy, a recommendation soon realized in most counties within the district.[36] In September he opened a regional counseling center for welfare work with young females in Düsseldorf, headed by a full-time director. That same month the city of Düsseldorf held a conference to train female youth cultivators.[37] At this conference, attended by twenty-eight hundred women, speakers took up topics like the psychology and health of adolescent females, physical education, and home economics, all of which, of course, had been standard fare before the war. However, women teachers, who played a prominent role in this conference, sounded some new nationalist notes. The rhetoric of sacrifice, selflessness, and moral purity was more pronounced than before the war, as were calls to extirpate foreign influence and to restore hallowed German folkways and customs, including colorful local costumes and dance. Absent from this celebration of populist patriotism and German womanhood, however, was any concrete discussion of or program for the young women in the war industries, who were often working long hours under deplorable conditions.

The government soon recognized the glaring need to take wartime circumstances into account in its welfare work for young females. In December 1916 Kruse sent forth a new circular regarding youth cultivation activities for factory girls.[38] Avowed the circular:

> The increasing recruitment of young female workers in heavy industry and in assembling munitions requires that local and county committees for youth cultivation assume the duty of zealously undertaking activities for these young female war workers in conjunction with factory management. It remains to be seen if these female workers, who are heavily taxed physically, can be persuaded to take part in cooking and sewing courses on workdays. In any event, they would gratefully welcome it if they were given opportunities on Sundays for noble and cheering recreations.

It appears, however, that despite such government encouragement, the appointment of female county youth cultivators, and the conferences with their bombastic rhetoric of self-sacrifice (because of the insatiable demands for the labor time of young women), few new educational or recreational initiatives actually took flight during the later phases of the war.

As the failure of such initiatives suggests, apart from the war minister's decision to institute premilitary training for young males, the other major reason for the atrophy of youth cultivation was the heavy burden placed on youth by the war economy. Although the war had initially led to a deep recession accompanied by high youth unemployment, soon the total mobilization of industry for victory transformed the entire structure of the labor force – and with it, the employment opportunities, wages, and working conditions of young laborers.[39] Although the Imperial Statistical Office changed its age categories during the war, making meaningful comparisons with prewar data more difficult, according to its occupational census of 1916 1,009,899 males between the ages of fourteen and seventeen were industrially employed, as were 356,094 females in the same age group (see Table 9.1). Thus, males and females in this age range constituted

Table 9.1. *Occupational census of Germany, 1916*

	Males		Females	
Branch of industry	14–60 yr	Youth 14–17 yr	14–47 yr	Youth 14–17 yr
Mining and foundry	652,967	117,822	73,112	16,568
Metal processing	610,373	209,778	136,273	31,879
Machine and instruments	642,426	175,323	189,005	21,733
Chemicals	261,323	52,160	256,280	43,271
Lighting, oils, resin, soap	34,748	4,173	11,221	2,569
Wood	215,216	57,705	43,329	10,460
Printing	65,922	22,033	28,683	6,116
Paper	54,961	15,612	62,247	16,839
Leather	61,978	18,131	22,606	5,036
Stone and earth	124,805	27,988	44,089	9,613
Food processing	291,430	122,932	235,916	58,253
Clothing	132,954	52,760	285,151	72,152
Textiles	96,142	18,834	247,507	43,725
Construction	410,057	78,718	25,693	4,341
Cleaning	32,744	16,651	41,599	5,565
Artistic	6,106	2,117	1,000	216
Miscellaneous	48,397	17,156	37,292	7,758
Total	3,742,549	1,009,899	1,341,007	356,094

Source: From Waldemar Zimmermann, "Die Veränderungen der Einkommens- und Lebensverhältnisse der deutschen Arbeiter durch den Krieg," in Rudolf Meerwarth et al. (eds), *Die Einwirkung des Krieges auf Bevölkerungsbewegung, Einkommen und Lebenshaltung in Deutschland: Wirtschafts- und Sozialgeschichte des Weltkrieges* (Stuttgart, 1932), p. 372.

over 25 percent of the entire work force during the war, and in some branches, such as metal processing, males below military age made up over one-third of those employed. Despite the limitations of the data collected by the Factory Inspectorate, which confined itself to shops with at least ten employees, its figures do enable one to compare both the level and structure of prewar and wartime youth employment. These figures offer an approximate measure of the dramatic sectoral shifts in labor allocation during the war (see Table 9.2). Not only did the total employment of young males in medium and large shops increase almost 10 percent, but young laborers clearly poured into war-related heavy industry and left consumer-oriented light industry, construction-related trades, and craft apprenticeships. In some regions there was a "wild flight of apprentices" into war indus-

Table 9.2. *Employment of young workers (under 16 years old) in Germany, 1913 and 1918*[a]

Branch of industry	Males <16		Females <16	
	1913	1918	1913	1918
Mining and foundry	46,246	64,266	870	6,250
Metal processing	65,114	71,392	12,180	25,154
Machine and instruments	86,095	136,967	4,991	23,865
Chemicals	4,894	12,904	2,981	9,565
Lighting, oils, resin, soap	1,453	2,292	1,411	1,579
Wood	29,893	31,842	4,859	11,345
Printing	15,376	5,187	13,349	6,952
Paper	8,413	8,637	10,773	12,561
Leather	5,110	4,321	2,726	3,423
Stone	29,480	16,195	8,449	6,464
Food processing	32,296	32,405	22,052	16,819
Clothing	10,396	6,917	48,395	26,237
Textiles	35,032	10,668	59,162	27,380
Construction	13,287	7,308	16	348
Cleaning	675	872	2,248	2,442
Miscellaneous	719	1,059	217	450
Total	384,489	421,293	186,517	180,764

[a] Includes firms with at least ten workers.

Source: Based on the *Jahresberichten der Gewerbeaufsichtsbeamten* reprinted in Waldemar Zimmermann, "Die Veränderungen der Einkommens- und Lebensverhältnisse der deutschen Arbeiter durch den Krieg," in Rudolf Meerwarth et al. (eds), *Die Einwirkung des Krieges auf Bevölkerungsbewegung, Einkommen und Lebenshaltung in Deutschland: Wirtschafts- und Sozialgeschichte des Weltkrieges* (Stuttgart, 1932), pp. 350–1.

tries.[40] Thus, youth employment in mining rose almost 40 percent, in the machine and instrument branch almost 60 percent, and in chemicals a staggering 264 percent, whereas employment in textiles declined to 30 percent of its prewar level and in stone and quarry work to 55 percent, and the level in food processing remained virtually stationary. In terms of total employment, slightly fewer post-school-age females worked for wages during the war than in 1913, probably because older women who entered the labor force could expect higher earnings than girls; hence, in order to maximize family income, they left their fourteen- or fifteen-year-old daughters home to tend infants. Nonetheless, the seismic shift in the types of employment available for young females was as pronounced as that for young males. Employment in metalworking firms more than doubled, in the machine industry it more than quadrupled, and in chemicals it increased more than sevenfold, whereas employment in the clothing and textile industries, the largest prewar industrial employers of young females, halved. Thus, not only were young laborers a more significant component of the labor force, but they occupied key roles in vital and strategic industries necessary for German war production.[41]

The sectoral shift can be confirmed and refined by using local statistics, which also provide some insight into changes in the skill composition of the youthful labor force, at least for males. Whereas youth employment in Düsseldorf's previously exponentially growing commercial sector stagnated during the war, the growth of industrial employment soon quickened. This growth accelerated the shift from traditional craft apprenticeships to skilled factory trades and even more rapidly hastened the move to unskilled positions.[42] In 1913, 3,666 (54 percent) of the students enrolled in the city's industrial continuation school performed skilled labor. Of these, 1,672 (24 percent) were working in craft shops and 1,994 (30 percent) had found employment as factory apprentices. Five years later, in contrast, only 921 traditional craft apprentices were enrolled, 14 percent of the school's 6,708 nominal students. There were 2,084 (31 percent) employed as factory apprentices, and the remaining 3,703 (55 percent) were holding unskilled factory jobs. There were also considerable shifts within the major sectors of employment. Traditional crafts like the building, clothing, and artistic trades uniformly halved the number of their apprentices, whereas the food trades only reduced theirs by a third. Because of the more central importance of bread for sustenance, Düsseldorf's bakers actually added twenty-seven apprentices during the war, raising the number to 154. Moreover, because butchers and bakers were among the few crafts still providing board, as food shortages worsened, these notoriously hardworking trades, which before the war had often experienced difficulty attracting apprentices, were swamped with applicants.[43] The structure of skilled trades within industry also changed substantially. Openings for technicians' apprentices rose 35 percent during the war years, whereas those for machine builder apprentices grew a moderate 6.6 percent, and the number of apprentice electricians, a highly desired position, fell from 191 to 133. The decline of apprenticeships cannot be entirely explained by simple labor demand, however, since positions in trades like carpentry, housepainting, and bookbinding, all considered unappealing before the war, still went begging.

In part, supply was determined by immediate earning prospects.

As a postwar report on the continuation school lamented, "The high earnings that war work in the factory offered and the hard necessity of having to rely on their sons' earnings in many cases caused parents to have their sons enter free labor relations, rather than placing them in apprenticeships. . . . Other youths who had originally registered for an apprenticeship took unskilled factory work since in the meantime their fathers had been drafted or their parents' economic situation had worsened in some way."[44] As this report indicates, questions of pay loomed large in directing the occupational choices of young labor force entrants, since in many cases their incomes mattered more to their families than ever before. Although many observers, like the author of the report cited above, believed that young workers were paid extremely high wages during the war, this impression could only have been based on a failure to distinguish nominal, relative, and real wages.

Some apprentices, such as those in construction in Berlin, who were locked into long-range contracts, took home the same wages in 1916 that they had two years earlier.[45] But such cases of contractually frozen wages were rare. In general, nominal wages for young workers did rise quite significantly between 1914 and 1918. In early 1914 a worker under sixteen years of age employed at the Krupp plant in Essen was earning an average wage per shift of 1.08 marks, while workers between sixteen and twenty-one years of age received 4.00 marks.[46] By 1918 average shift wages for these two categories had risen to 2.97 and 9.20 marks, respectively. In the chemical industry in Leverkusen the average weekly wage of young males climbed from twenty marks in October 1914 to thirty-nine marks in October 1917, before finally peaking at forty-nine marks in October 1918, while the average wages of females under sixteen rose in tandem, spiraling up from twenty-one marks in 1914 to forty marks in 1917, before reaching fifty-one marks at the end of the war.[47] A large-scale survey of wages in unionized Düsseldorf metal-processing firms, first carried out by the Metalworkers Union in 1913 and then repeated in 1917, showed that the average daily wages of young workers had inched up from an average ranging between three and four marks in the former year to one between four and six in the latter.[48] Thus the nominal wages of youth often advanced as much as 150 or even 250 percent during the war.

But in comparison with other categories of workers or with the rapidly inflating price index, young workers tended to fare quite poorly. In the Berlin metal industry in 1916 the average hourly pay for youthful workers was 72.0 pfennig, compared to 107.7 for adults.[49]

Thus a new labor force entrant could count on being paid at about 67 percent of the adult rate. Two years later, however, young metalworkers were receiving 92.1 pfennig an hour, whereas adults were averaging 200.7. Thus in 1918 youth were being paid less than 46 percent of an adult wage. In fact, this tremendous relative decline resulted from a deliberate army policy to introduce a forced savings scheme and to depress the wages of youth, a policy ostensibly justified on the grounds that young workers squandered their wages on frivolous amusements. Elsewhere declines were less sharp. In 1914 young workers in nineteen chemical firms in the Cologne region were being paid 2.5 marks daily, compared to 5.5 marks for a skilled adult male worker, 45 percent of an average skilled wage.[50] By 1918 the daily average for a youth was up to 6.5 marks, but during these same years, the daily wage of a skilled male worker had risen to 16.0 marks; hence, average youth wages had dropped to slightly over 40 percent of the adult skilled rate. Such instances could be endlessly multiplied. Although one can also find a few industries and regions where the wages of youth almost kept pace with those of adults, in general the relative wages of youth fell, and it was a fall that was in some instances fast and steep.

More important than such relative setbacks, however, was the substantial loss of real earning power, a loss obscured by the apparently greater nominal wages. As the Düsseldorf Metalworkers Union survey pointed out, the cost of living for young workers far outstripped the rise in nominal wages between 1913 and 1917.[51] The cost of room and board for single young workers living away from their families had gone up 225 percent, whereas price increases for clothes ranged from 1000 percent for blue work shirts or 700 percent for overalls to a mere 333 percent for boots or a hat. With his entire average daily wage, a youth employed in a Düsseldorf metal firm could afford 1.5 pounds of sausage late in the war.[52] Not surprisingly, as we shall see below, young workers would fight vigorously against the attempts by regional army commanders to curb their wages.

Plummeting real wages and living standards were accompanied by an equally rapid deterioration of working conditions. In August 1914 Imperial Chancellor Bethmann Hollweg hastily drafted emergency legislation suspending all protective measures covering youth and women and pushed it through the Reichstag.[53] War producers, who by autumn of 1914 were beginning to feel the pinch of labor scarcity, seized the opportunity to lengthen and intensify the working day.[54] In Düsseldorf, with its concentration of metal factories using continuous production processes, night work, swing shifts, Sunday labor, and overtime soon became common. By 1918, eleven out of every one hundred employed youths in the city were regularly working night shifts, an assignment legally prohibited before the war.[55] The frequency of nocturnal employment was even more common in Oppeln and Arnsberg, where thirty-two and eighteen youths per hundred, respectively, worked this shift. In Berlin, however, it was a rare exception for youths to work nights (0.06 percent), probably evidence of the considerable power wielded by the Metalworkers Union and shop stewards, who tried to preserve prewar standards. As mentioned, overtime also became common. A sample of twenty-one firms in Düsseldorf showed that workers under sixteen averaged almost seventy-seven hours of overtime for each one hundred days worked in 1918. In Arnsberg young workers worked eighty-five hours of overtime every one hundred workdays. To obtain much-needed rest, young workers changed jobs frequently and waited several days after quitting before taking a new position, this being one of the few ways they could turn the tight labor market to their advantage.[56]

Not only were hours longer, but work also became more dangerous. The factory inspectorate reported numerous instances of youth operating steam hammers and performing foundry work previously regarded as too unsafe.[57] As a result, the injury rate for youth increased considerably, almost doubling in munitions plants in Spandau. Local health insurance office records also indicate higher youthful mortality. In Aachen the number of deaths of fifteen- to twenty-year-olds more than doubled between 1915 and 1917, from thirty-six to seventy-six.

In 1916 the Socialist party and Free Trade Unions once again began attempting to alleviate the exploitation of young workers. The SPD women's committee petitioned the Reichstag for the reinstatement of protective legislation, arguing that suspension had been premised on a short war.[58] After two years any further failure to curtail working hours would not only injure the health of the young but would also jeopardize their long-term intellectual and moral development. The Free Trade Unions deplored the haphazard training that apprentices received, training further reduced after the Auxiliary Service Law of December 1916, conceived by the army to implement the Hindenburg Plan, which called for doubling the output of armaments and munitions. The unions feared that poorly trained youth would either be unemployable or exert downward pressure on wages in the postwar economy, a major concern for unions that had always drawn their members from among the skilled. In return for supporting the government and over objections from employers, in 1916 the unions had been able to secure the passage of an amendment to the Imperial Association Law that enabled them to recruit and represent young workers over eighteen years of age.[59] But despite their newly won right to represent youth openly, the unions were unable to persuade the government to reintroduce protective legislation.

Nor were the Socialists and unions alone in decrying the working conditions of young laborers or in foreseeing negative long-term consequences. In August 1917 the new chancellor, Georg Michaelis, expressed concern that the long hours worked by young laborers, sometimes approaching fifteen hours daily, could both undermine their health and lead to a permanent decline in productivity.[60] In early 1918 the Federal Council issued guidelines to limit exceptions to protective legislation for youths and women. But the interests of war producers in maximizing profits, of army commanders in optimizing output, and of parents in ensuring the largest possible family income meant that protective legislation remained in suspension for the duration of the war.

Given their grim and constrained lives during the war (the long and exhausting work week, the monotonous premilitary drills, the material deprivation), not surprisingly, whenever possible, young laborers attempted to spend their little free time escaping the oppressive grayness of everyday life and restoring their resiliency with cheap but exciting diversions.[61] When money jingled in their pockets, they frequented the movies and bars or sought recreation in the music and dance halls. In private they voraciously read vast numbers of lurid and violent penny dreadfuls, which after 1914 were filled with episodic war adventures in which heroic German soldiers outwitted perfidious French spies.[62] When penniless, young workers wandered about aimlessly or congregated on street corners to smoke, chat, idle, and relax. Although many urban officials grudgingly conceded that under wartime circumstances such behavior was unexceptionable, conservative military commanders, teachers, and clergy regarded such activities as clear evidence of decaying authority and morality.[63] Freed from parental discipline; the young had acquired too much independence. Moreover, their supposedly war-swollen incomes now enabled them to indulge in dissolute pastimes. But if the war revealed this extent of wanton pleasure seeking and hedonism, conservatives hoped that it would also offer a golden opportunity for national purgation, moral cleansing, and popular regeneration. Under the aegis of the army command, measures could be enacted and enforced that would create a highly disciplined, upright, and respectable youth, willingly obedient to the authorities. Moreover, conservatives intended that such measures would outlast the war.[64]

Already in late 1915 deputy commanders of regional army districts initiated a regime of stringent moral policing. On December 13, for example, General von Geyl, deputy commander of the Seventh Army Corps in Münster and the military administrator responsible for the Ruhr and Lower Rhine regions, issued a decree circumscribing the leisure activities of youths under sixteen.[65] Citing the precedent of measures taken after the Revolution of 1848, he prohibited these youths from smoking in public, from visiting bars, cinemas, or music halls, and from aimlessly wandering about or loitering. Shopkeepers were forbidden to sell tobacco or alcohol to youths or to assist them in any way in bypassing these regulations. The general also both empowered and encouraged police commissioners to impose curfews and to declare certain streets and areas off limits during evening hours. This army initiative signaled to civil officials that they were to exercise more vigilant surveillance and to proceed less cautiously in repressing young laborers. Two months after this decree, Kruse, district governor of the Düsseldorf district, sent out a circular proposing that school boards and youth cultivation committees undertake joint action against any serious public misconduct of youth.[66] He attributed such misconduct to the "lack of forceful male presence in the home, school and workplace" and to high wartime wages that permitted youthful wantonness (*Uebermut*) and pleasure seeking (*Genusssucht*). He urged clergy, teachers, and other youth workers to enlighten mothers on the moral dangers facing their children; meanwhile employers could aid in bridling youth by restricting wages or else delivering pay packets directly to parents. Kruse also called the army's recent decree to the attention of youth cultivators and recommended setting up committees to assist local police in enforcing its provisions. To meet the clearly pressing need of the young for wholesome recreational activities, he suggested reviving prewar youth cultivation insofar as possible. This circular inspired some teachers and youth committee members to find ways of becoming active in moral policing.

Those new forms of mass culture and entertainment that youth cultivators had opposed before 1914 were now indicted for a frivolity that ill corresponded with the deadly seriousness of the war. A school rector named Koch in Essen organized a network of teachers' committees throughout the Rhineland and Ruhr that sought to suppress

penny dreadfuls by inspecting stores, vetting writings for children
and youth, and working to transform the supposedly noxious reading
habits of the young.[67] Koch secured the active support of both the
district governor and the regional army command, which printed his
committee's list of recommended and proscribed readings.[68] Koch's
fanaticism and zealotry, however, ultimately wearied some public officials, who used his inclusion of war adventures as a reason to coun-
terattack. One government counselor assailed the imprecision of
Koch's criteria for banning books and claimed that " 'a patriotic penny
dreadful' is a contradictio in adjecto."[69] Even without excluding "patriotic penny dreadfuls," the army was kept busy with efforts at censorship. In March 1916 the army published a central list from Berlin
banning 135 individual titles or series of penny dreadfuls.[70] Films
were also scrutinized for sensationalism and lack of moral seriousness,
rather than being judged on the basis of their aesthetic or entertainment value.[71] Along with its other ventures in moral policing, the
Seventh Army Corps command started a regional film censorship
board in cooperation with the Düsseldorf police in late 1915, a board
staffed by clergy, educators, city officials, and representatives of the
military and police.[72] By January 1916 this assiduous body had already
determined that ninety-six films were unfit for public screening. The
regional youth committee hoped that this board would further extend
its charge to include censoring suggestive or lurid film titles like *The
Suicide* and regulating the colorful advertising placards that cinema
proprietors displayed.[73] Among films deemed intolerable were those
that, while purporting to warn against the evils of urban life, graphically depicted bar and cabaret scenes. Equally reprehensible were
films that explicitly treated sexual themes, celebrated adultery and
lower passions, injured religious institutions or sentiment, engaged in
political agitation, or merely promoted senseless vulgarity. Participants in this film censorship campaign clearly recognized the blatant
class control inherent in this project; as the Central Committee of
Catholic Youth Organizations matter-of-factly remarked, "[I]n large
cities . . . cinema viewers come almost exclusively from the lower stratum of the population, mostly pubescent youth."[74]

Despite the institution of this widespread system of restrictions and
moral policing, regional deputy army commanders remained thoroughly dissatisfied with the deportment and attitudes of young laborers. As the "peace of the fortress" began crumbling and the
Independent Socialists began protesting the prolongation of the war,
the fear of the generals intensified. They began to interpret every

sign of weariness or discontent as latent or active political opposition. In each case of indifference to premilitary exercises they detected the specter of potential disloyalty and revolt. According to General von Haugwitz, the deputy commander responsible for the upper Rhine region, by August 1916 the existing system of premilitary preparation had become untenable.[75] It could only be saved by introducing legislation making such training mandatory and enforcing attendance with sanctions. The general declared:

> ...although at the outset of the movement it could be hoped that the youth of the laboring people might be won, it soon became evident that little progress could be made on a voluntary basis. Now this plan must be considered a complete miscarriage, since the active struggle of the left wing of the socialists, with their unparalleled hate-filled leaflets and flyers, is now added to the previous passive resistance of wide circles.

He also found deplorable the pronounced inclination to indiscipline shown by many youths, indiscipline that necessitated the army's resorting to disciplinary countermeasures. Colonel Herrlich, the retired officer entrusted with supervising the premilitary training of youth in Düsseldorf, had previously curtly rejected every call for coercive measures to induce young workers to muster for drills.[76] But he now joined the chorus of those demanding the passage of a military preparation bill with draconian punishments for noncompliance. Herrlich complained that since even students at higher schools manifested little understanding of the strenuous tasks posed by the war, "it should therefore cause no wonder when similar phenomena come to light at the continuation school and when the great national spirit threatens to become stale and flat." Despite such demands, however, the government never brought such a bill before the Reichstag since a coalition of Catholic Centrists and Socialists would almost certainly have defeated it.[77]

Few mayors and urban administrators shared the fears and anxieties articulated by regional deputy army commanders in 1916. When queried by the district governor in December of that year on whether they had witnessed a noticeable increase in youthful unruliness and criminality, most mayors of industrial cities in the lower Rhine and Ruhr unreservedly gave a denial.[78] The lord mayor of Essen replied that the rate of youth criminality had remained unchanged. The most common crime was pilfering food, hardly evidence of an epidemic of youthful misconduct. In the predominantly Catholic textile city of Mönchen-Gladbach, the mayor commended the city's continuation school students for their exemplary behavior and morals. Although the mayor of nearby Rheydt did mention the absence of fathers and thought it might be contributing to a certain rebelliousness, he completely discounted youthful unrest as a general problem. In the bleak mining city of Hamborn, apparently young workers regularly disobeyed the army's prohibitions against smoking, drinking, and visiting bars, but the mayor still doubted that this added up to evidence for "general or manifest unruliness among adolescents." The tight labor market and the effective work of local youth organizations prevented general rebelliousness, he believed. One of the most detailed reports was submitted by the mayor of the adjacent steel and coal city Duisberg, who checked with city school officials before replying. He, too, lauded young workers, stating that "the number of youths who give cause for serious concern is far surpassed by the great number who distinguish themselves by industriousness and good behavior." This positive note was somewhat modulated, however, by concerns over ostensibly high wages. The city's continuation school director thought that high wages and lack of parental oversight were making the job of educators more difficult. Moreover, he regretted the high turnover rate of young workers, especially when they transferred from skilled to unskilled positions, transfers common between artisanal crafts in the consumer sector and the war industries, and spent the interim between jobs, loafing, enjoying themselves, and prodigally dissipating their savings. Among those responding, however, he alone castigated employers for exploiting and exhausting young workers by long workdays and consecutive shifts. He also related the desire of youth to stimulate their nervous systems with nicotine and exciting films to the tremendous strain and tiredness resulting from work. Lord Mayor Oehler's office in Düsseldorf declared that little had changed since the previous year. The army's regulations had cut down on immoderate smoking and had reduced visits to bars and movies. The crusade to wipe out the penny dreadful trade was in full swing. Thus, despite the tendentious phrasing of the district governor's inquiry, not a single mayor's office reported widespread delinquency or rebelliousness. Rather, most considered the conduct of young workers to be generally praiseworthy.

To the degree that specific problems of youthful misconduct did emerge, they can be attributed to a combination of the repressive course initiated by the army and to material deprivation. To be sure, the number of youths convicted of crimes almost doubled during the war years, from 54,155 in 1913 to 99,493 five years later (see Table 9.3).[79] Much of this increase, however, fell within two categories of

Table 9.3. *Youths sentenced for crimes, 1913–19*

Year	Total	Males	Females
1913	54,155	46,034	8,121
1914	46,940	39,734	7,206
1915	63,126	54,108	9,018
1916	80,399	69,463	10,936
1917	95,651	82,047	13,604
1918	99,493	84,840	14,653
1919	64,619	55,447	9,172

Source: Based on Moritz Liepmann, *Krieg und Kriminalität in Deutschland* (Stuttgart, 1930), p. 98.

offenses: those against public order and those against property. Thus, between 1913 and 1917 crimes by juveniles against public order rose from 1,981 to 2,625 (33 percent), and crimes against property sky-rocketed from 26,572 to 41,833 (57.4 percent). But most of the re-corded violations of public order involved precisely those activities criminalized at the army's behest, such as loitering on street corners or wandering the streets during curfew, and most of the crimes against property were incidents of pilfering food, as indicated by Essen's lord mayor.

Food stealing surged to epidemic proportions during the bitterly cold winter of 1916/17.[80] The following spring the long-overstrained supply, transport, and distribution networks were on the verge of buckling, and major industrial cities like Düsseldorf lacked staples like potatoes for as long as nine consecutive weeks. Fanned by the agitation of the left Socialists, many laborers came to believe that municipal governments bore full responsibility for the shortages. Food riots frequently broke out. Despite attempts of the lord mayor to placate labor by cooperating with the unions in distributing food, on June 26 a major food riot took place in Düsseldorf, where a crowd of "half-grown lads, children, and women gathered in various parts of the city and then looted stores and damaged wares."[81] The enraged crowd of rioters, in which youth figured prominently, especially targeted bak-eries and food shops, which they probably suspected of hoarding and price gouging.[82] In response, the army immediately tightened its con-trols. A new decree prohibited youth under seventeen from setting foot on the streets after 7:00 P.M. unless directly going to or coming from work. It further forbade all public meetings, loitering, or idle wandering about. To try the rioters, the army set up special tribunals. One tribunal sentenced a young worker who had led an assault on a bread factory and had insulted the military to six years' imprisonment. Women and youth convicted of lesser offenses were condemned to serve jail terms ranging from three weeks to nine months. Although the district president hoped that the summary punishments meted out had clamped the lid on unruly elements, he feared that their harshness, especially for women and youth, had embittered labor.[83]

Young laborers were certainly embittered in those districts where the army cooperated with employers in inaugurating schemes for forced savings of the type favored by conservatives since the turn of the century. Such a scheme was introduced in Berlin in mid-March 1916. The regional deputy commander limited the weekly take-home pay of workers younger than eighteen to eighteen marks and ordered that the remainder of their earnings be sequestered in savings accounts until they reached their majority.[84] Until then, young workers could only gain access to their savings after obtaining special permission from communal authorities. The general commission of the Free Trade Unions roundly denounced this measure. Its spokespersons doubted that forced savings would have much effect on youth who already showed proclivities to frivolity. For most youth the measure might well serve as a disincentive to hard work and would probably bring hardship to their families, who heavily depended on their income. A year after its introduction, the director of the Berlin Guardianship Agency, which had been assigned responsibility for determining whether young workers were to be granted access to their savings, asserted, however, that the negative effects of the measure had been far fewer than predicted. Although young workers had greeted forced savings with an initial storm of outrage, only a handful had actually left Berlin for districts where no such regulations were in effect. Despite fifty thousand requests for release of funds during the first year, the agency had not been overwhelmed. Without such a measure there would have been little incentive to save. Moreover the money accumulated was often later disbursed for beneficial purposes, such as purchasing household items or supporting the further education of siblings. One official even lauded the army's forced savings scheme as an innovative form of social insurance.

It is highly doubtful, however, that most young workers regarded forced savings in this benign and flattering light. When a scheme virtually identical to the one launched in Berlin was introduced in Braunschweig in late April, it sparked an open revolt.[85] On May Day youths at several factories struck, and over the next several days virtually every young laborer in Braunschweig joined this protest. Their cause was given a further boost by demonstrations of housewives, in their traditional role as guardians of family consumption, against potato shortages in the city market. Hoping to contain and quiet the mounting unrest, the army agreed to raise the maximum weekly take-home pay of young laborers to twenty-four marks. But an illegal mass assembly of youthful strikers steadfastly rejected this concession. In the face of youthful intransigence, the army occupied the city on May 4, but when the local trade union cartel came to the support of the young workers and threatened a general strike in response (one of the few instances in which the Free Trade Unions actually took action to defend young workers) the army backed down and rescinded all wage limits for youth. This stunning victory, much publicized by the Socialist left, apparently impressed other regional deputy commanders with the need to proceed with caution. In Berlin the maximum allowable weekly take-home was upped to thirty marks and in the Rhine–Ruhr region, instead of issuing decrees, deputy commanders confined their efforts to importuning employers to place limits on the take-home pay of their youthful employees.

Certain general conclusions can be drawn about the predisposing conditions for different forms of action on the basis of such cases of youthful protest, crime, and other types of resistant behavior. Although every form of resistance presupposed widely shared grievances and discontents, when grievances were purely economic, the forms of resistance tended to be individual, that is, theft, absenteeism, high turnover, whereas when political and economic issues interpenetrated, resistance usually assumed collective forms. In such cases, like the Düsseldorf food riots or the Braunschweig strike, young laborers were also able to coordinate their actions with the trade unions and housewives. Whether individual or collective in form, however, until late in the war acts of resistance to the authorities were invariably informal and spontaneous. Only as the military dictatorship of Ludendorff and Hindenburg tightened its grip on the economy and public life did a significant number of young workers begin gravitating toward the antiwar Independent Socialists.

This shift to the left can be shown by following the development of a left Socialist youth movement in Düsseldorf and the Lower Rhine after mid-1916. As previously mentioned, at the outset of the war all activities of Düsseldorf's Free Youth halted. Once the initial chaos died down, the editor of the *Volkszeitung,* Paul Gerlach, assisted by the mechanic Emil Müller and the editorial secretary Kretzen, resumed evening readings and sponsorship of educational and social events for the forty to fifty youths who remained interested.[86] This revival was short-lived, however, because all three adults were drafted in early 1915. After that, organizational life almost disappeared. An indication of this disappearance was the rapid fall in the number of subscriptions to *Arbeiter-Jugend*. In Düsseldorf subscriptions plummeted from eleven hundred to four hundred, and in the entire lower Rhine they dropped from seventy-four hundred to twenty-three hundred.[87] Given its tepid criticisms of premilitary training and general government policy, the Socialist party also had considerable difficulty persuading young workers that they should join.[88] Moreover, as party income dwindled and the intraparty factional conflict over support for the war absorbed more time and energy, the interest of party and union leaders in youth affairs steadily declined.[89] When the lease for the Socialist youth center expired in March 1916, the party reverted to making a room in the People's House available for youth, as it had before 1911. From this, the police concluded that the Free Youth movement was practically moribund. In view of the sharpening factional competition within the SPD, however, they predicted that this phase of quiescence would be brief and that a new, more radical youth movement would probably emerge – a prescient prognosis.

Within two months Lore Agnes, one of the Düsseldorf party's most outspoken and energetic radicals, began reconstructing the youth movement.[90] This resuscitated movement would not only offer youth the opportunity for activity, but would also be inspirited by Karl Liebknecht's uncompromising opposition to the war. To this end, Agnes corresponded with other radicals who were attempting to reconstitute youth work in other urban centers. During this initial phase of reconstruction, adults far outnumbered the band of young militants. Thus, for example, at a hike in early May called for young supporters of Liebknecht, only six of twenty participants were youths.[91] The radicals were also a small but growing minority among SPD members with experience in youth affairs. At the annual meeting of the SPD's regional youth committee held in Elberfeld in June, the regional youth secretary Wilhelm Enz, a staunch defender of the party's prowar stance, commanded a decisive majority.[92] His two-hour-long organizational report painted a depressingly detailed portrait of the many hurdles impeding effective youth work. The labor youth movement was hobbled and fettered by the drafting of members, the dearth of funds, the pervasive official censorship, and continued and blatant government discrimination. Enz did foresee some prospects for successful lobbying to restore protective legislation for youth, but his address basically explained the reasons for the youth movement's decline and made excuses for continued inertia. In contrast, the radical Mathilde Wurm of Berlin delivered a ringing denunciation of premilitary exercises for youth and proposed embarking on a struggle for their abolition. This proposal was defeated by a solid two-thirds margin, however, since most delegates believed that such a struggle would constitute a breach of the "peace of the fortress."

This serious defeat, however, neither dismayed nor discouraged the oppositionists. A week earlier they had been gladdened by the surprisingly large turnout and radical tone of the lower Rhine Pentecost rally for youth in Hagen, the first such rally since 1914.[93] Crowd responses there clearly indicated strong agreement with Liebknecht's vote against war credits in the Reichstag. Again, despite the fact that the Pentecost rally was ostensibly a youth affair, the number of adults surpassed the number of young workers. Only ninety young laborers were present from Düsseldorf, under a third of the prewar average. Nonetheless, for the radicals those youth attending formed a kernel around which an antiwar Socialist youth movement could crystallize.

Inspired by this relative success, the radical activists began organizing more diligently. To elude police surveillance, they conducted most of their agitation clandestinely, inviting groups of reliable young workers to ostensible social gatherings in private apartments; such meetings, and even hikes, were devoted to discussing articles published in the opposition youth paper *Jugend Internationale*.[94] Occasionally the Socialist left tried to reach a broader audience by distributing leaflets and pamphlets. During the summer of 1916 the police were alarmed by the extensive circulation of two leaflets. The first chronicled the successful youth strike in Braunschweig; the second excoriated both the government for its mandatory premilitary training for youth and the "bourgeois" youth groups.[95]

Over time this balanced combination of small secret meetings and mass propaganda began to show results, results that became apparent at the Independent Socialists' Pentecost rally in Velbert in 1917.[96] This rally, their first major youth assembly in the Lower Rhine since the consummation of the formal split from the Majority Socialists, enabled the two parties to gauge their relative strength among the young. Despite constant police harassment, the Independents were able to turn out more than twice as many young followers at their rally than could the Majority Socialists in Duisberg. With larger than expected contingents arriving from every industrial town in the lower Rhine and Ruhr, the auditorium in Velbert, with an audience capacity of eight hundred, was badly overfilled. The ebullient optimism of the newly founded Independents rang forth in their keynote address, a paean to freedom and the ideals of youth. The Majority Pentecost rally was both a far smaller and far more somber affair. There, Karl Haberland, Düsseldorf's Socialist Reichstag deputy, enumerated the impediments crippling the Socialist youth movement and castigated the Independents for being destructive splitters.

Three factors gave the Independents a decisive edge in this bitter and acrimonious rivalry. First, the Independents possessed a cadre of dedicated and indefatigable youth workers. Energized by their deep moral aversion to the war, they were willing to harness all their efforts to persuading and recruiting young workers, in whom they reposited their hopes for a rejuvenated labor movement. Second, the Independents fostered forms of organization that allowed youth extensive scope for "self-activity" (relative autonomy). Third, the Independents framed a youth program that embodied the antiauthoritarian sentiments of young laborers. The Majority, by comparison, with its half-hearted support of the war and its stolid, sober, prosaic, and paternalistic counsel for youth, had little to offer. To be sure, neither socialist party exercised deep or lasting influence among young workers, but late in the war, the Independents at least faithfully reflected the grievances and aspirations of laboring youth.

Even before the split, the Independents had formulated a fourteen-demand program for young workers that covered three major areas affecting them.[97] The first area concerned industrial labor. This program included demands for a shorter work day and improved shop-floor conditions, abolition of night shifts, a six-hour work day for youths under sixteen years of age, an annual vacation, and more rigorous factory inspection. The second area concerned education and called for its extension both at the elementary level and in continuation schools. Moreover, according to the Independents, students were entitled to participate in school governance. The third area touched some central features of the apprenticeship relation. The document demanded the abolition of such humiliating features of the contract as the right of masters to inflict corporal punishment and to force their apprentices to perform housework and other duties unrelated to skills being learned. Other demands pressed for a shortening of apprenticeship and for easing the conditions under which an apprentice could break his contract. This was certainly an advanced reform program, but it in no way transcended the existing institutional framework. Most of the points about wages, hours, and working conditions had been favorably discussed by both liberal and Catholic social reformers before the war, as had plans to reform the abuses of the apprenticeship relation. The educational demands in no respect challenged the class hierarchy of the German educational system. The Independents' program testified to the hegemony achieved by prewar youth reformers, since it was their agenda and programs that established the boundaries of legitimate discourse about youth affairs. That young workers accepted these boundaries can only be inferred from the little evidence that exists on their actions during the revolutionary upheavals of 1918–19.

During these upheavals young workers seldom acted on their own account; rather, they merged and blended with the broader movement of social protest in favor of democratization, higher wages, and shorter hours. Observers of all political tendencies, however, agreed that young workers were consistently overrepresented in crowds of demonstrators. Being little inclined to sustained organizational work, they often aligned themselves with proponents of direct action, whether Independents, Spartacists, or anarchosyndicalists.[98] Apparently, young workers also flocked to the Free Trade Unions in record numbers. Young workers quickly joined the demonstrations of demobilized soldiers on 8 November in most major cities, thus reasserting their presence on the central squares and thoroughfares from which they had been excluded by the regional army commands and municipal administrations.[99] During the following months, their discontent and willingness to take part in demonstrations were undoubtedly heightened by the fact that many young workers forfeited their jobs in the transition to a peacetime economy. Youthful unemployment followed both from the inevitable industrial dislocation accompanying this transition and from the SPD's policy of preferential hiring for returning veterans as a means of easing a return to normalcy.[100] Tired of the forced sacrifices of the war period and the puritanical suppression of high spirits, young workers celebrated the end of the army command's moral measures in an often rowdy carnivalesque spirit. Once again, young laborers turned to cheap amusements, smoking in public, filling the bars, drinking prodigiously, and packing the dance halls, where a dance craze raged.[101] Soon, traumatized mayors and hidebound county commissioners who retained office were denouncing the loosening moral fiber resulting from the revolution. They began nostalgically looking back to the era of military moral policing and longing for its restoration.

Attempts to bring continuation schools back to full operation met with only partial success in the revolutionary atmosphere of the immediate postwar period. In Düsseldorf in 1919 unexcused absences fluctuated between 30 and 60 percent. According to the annual report, unskilled students had "completely lost their feeling for propriety, respect for others, and moral behavior. In countless cases they revealed such brutality in their association with fellow students and teachers and so little sense of uprightness that one must recoil in fright at such inner savagery."[102] Skilled apprentices, by contrast, certainly accepted the reestablishment of classes. Indeed, already in the last war years there was a tremendous increase in demand for technical education among young skilled workers who sought to master new industrial proceses and who desired to share in shaping the future of German industry.[103] But just as clearly, they expected to be treated as adult citizens with recognized and respected rights. In order to gain this recognition, young skilled metalworkers from the Krupp firm struck at the Essen continuation school in 1919. Since this was one of the few instances during the revolutionary period when young laborers fought expressly in their own interests and for their own demands, this strike deserves closer attention as an expression of their aspirations.

A leaflet distributed by several students close to the recently founded German Communist party (Spartacists) in early October 1919 precipitated this strike.[104] The leaflet, directed to the "entire youth of the working class," reminded students of the misery endured during the war, "when we had to work night and day under the greatest privation." It then contrasted their lives with the carefree youth enjoyed by children of the rich, "who at higher schools appropriate knowledge denied us." According to the leaflet, only a proletarian victory could eliminate such injustice, but in the meantime students could press for an education at the continuation school conducted in "a spirit of brotherly solidarity of all mental and manual laborers." More concretely they demanded that all instruction be placed during the regular working day and that students be fully compensated for this time. Moreover, all materials were to be supplied without cost; all punitive sanctions, including corporal punishment, fines, and arrest hours, were to be abolished; and a student council with codetermination in all school affairs was to be elected.

Although this leaflet may well have been the work of outside agitators as school officials predictably asserted, nonetheless, several of the demands resonated strongly in the school body.[105] Most students, however, seem to have been less inspired by visions of major social transformation or resentment against the supposedly carefree lives experienced by children of the rich than by the prospect of achieving parity with white-collar apprentices and adult workers. The question of the hours of instruction was an especially neuralgic point. This issue had been taken up previously by both the Ministry of Labor and the Demobilization Committee, which had issued contradictory preliminary rulings. Consequently, pending a national resolution, each community was free to determine the hours of continuation school instruction. In cities in which the labor movement was powerful, like Frankfurt and Berlin, all instruction was placed during working hours, and employers were required to pay their young workers for school time. At the Krupp firm in Essen, however, only young white-collar and drafting apprentices had daytime classes and were paid for continuing education, a discriminatory practice that blue-collar apprentices naturally resented.[106] Evening classes also meant that blue-collar apprentices had less leisure time at their disposal than adult workers. In protest, on 16 October several hundred students struck the continuation school to win parity, a strike joined by almost the entire student body of seven hundred within four days.

Initially the school's administrative board refused to discuss these issues or negotiate with the student strikers. Instead, they claimed that these matters should be settled by the students and the Krupp firm.[107] But when the strike persisted, the administration began examining alternative class schedules and brought in representatives of the Krupp firm and the Metalworkers Union to negotiate. Krupp spokespersons, however, rejected the students' demands out of hand. Krupp had agreed with the union to reduce the period of apprenticeship from four to three years only on condition that continuation school instruction occur during evening hours after work.[108] Even so, the union backed the students, pointing out that Krupp directly benefited from the schooling.[109] Union officials, however, were unwilling to support student demands for codetermination, although they did criticize the director, Kayser, for his often maladroit handling of student grievances. After the strike, they suggested that frank periodic discussions among the director and student representatives might improve the atmosphere at the school.[110] Beyond haggling in conferences, however, the Metalworkers Union was prepared to do little on behalf of the students. Consequently, after two weeks of striking, students returned to classes after reaching an agreement with the administration that no disciplinary action would be initiated against strike participants.[111] Agitation continued, however, and over the next several years, the same issues of hours of instruction, discipline, and democratic representation resurfaced several times and resulted in several protests.[112]

In the revolutionary context of 1919 school administrators were predisposed to interpret student demands as unreasonable and alarming manifestations of a pervasive spirit of rebelliousness. But apart from the rhetorical flourishes decorating the original leaflet, the demands raised and expectations harbored by the students were far from immoderate. They took the conditions and educational opportunities of white-collar apprentices as their reference points, rather than the carefree lives of *jeunesse doré*. Although prewar youth cultivators and indeed the Trade Ministry had agreed that corporal punishment in continuation schools was needlessly humiliating and counterproductive, the strikers' demands to abolish other forms of coercion unquestionably went beyond what most educational administrators would have found acceptable if attendance and classroom discipline were to be maintained. Kerschensteiner and others had advocated student governance of extracurricular activities and club life when possible, so if skilled students sought to elect delegates to exercise codetermination, it could certainly be seen as a logical extension of some of the aims of civic education, which, after all, had been conceived as a means of developing responsible, self-determining citizens. Thus if the demands of the students can be taken as representative of the aspirations of young skilled workers, these youths fought for the elimination of outmoded forms of authoritarian control, for an end to overt discrimination against blue-collar workers, and for the extension of democratic control within institutions that directly impinged on their lives, demands that went only slightly beyond the original project of civic education.

Epilogue and conclusion

Although some significant modifications in official youth policy were introduced during the Weimar Republic and several major ones under the Nazi regime, nonetheless, in large measure the youth salvation campaign during the late Empire had established the discourse, the range of policy options, and the bureaucratic and institutional framework available to public officials through World War II and beyond. Certainly various aspects of youth cultivation were given more solid legal underpinnings during the Weimar Republic. Indeed, legislators passed a raft of legislation concerning youth, and various ministries issued a battery of decrees. Thus, for example, Article 118 of the Weimar Constitution made possible legislation protecting youth against questionable public presentations and penny dreadfuls, and Article 122 stated that youth was to be protected "against exploitation, as well as ethical, spiritual and physical neglect."[1] The Youth Welfare Law of 1922 guaranteed youth the right to education and systematized some of the prewar experiments with welfare education for delinquent and wayward youths. The juvenile justice system and its procedures were regularized and generalized in the Youth Court Law of 1923. On the basis of Article 118 of the Constitution, a cinema law went into effect in 1920 admitting youths under eighteen only to films approved by special boards in Berlin and Munich. A similar law controlling youthful access to "trashy and dirty" literature went into effect in 1926.[2] Blocked on financial grounds by the federal states was a law proposed by the interior minister and supported by educational reformers to mandate vocational school instruction for all post–primary school youths, including females, until their eighteenth birthdays.[3] Moreover, a vigorous campaign by the Imperial Committee of German Youth Associations, an offshoot of the Central Agency for Popular Welfare that served as an umbrella group for national youth associations during the Weimar Republic, was unable to effect passage of legislation designed to improve the health and labor conditions of young workers.[4] The committee's program called for extension of all protective legislation measures to young workers until the age of eighteen, the reduction of the work week to a maximum of forty-eight hours, elimination of all night work for youth, and three weeks' paid vacation for all young workers. But such demands encountered stiff resistance from both industry and the artisanate. What is notable, however, about all of these laws and legislative proposals, whether they passed or were defeated, whether they dealt with conditions of employment, moral policing, or delinquent and wayward youth, is that both their content and their justification derived from the prewar youth salvation campaign, and their pedigrees were traceable to the turn of the century.

The bureaucratic youth cultivation apparatus created after the decree of 1911 also survived the war and would be further expanded during the Weimar Republic. By 1920 at latest, the Prussian government had organized regional conferences in every district to assess the impact of the war, resuscitate comatose organizations, and chart a course for the future.[5] The composition of regional and local youth committees with their school rectors and teachers, gymnastic instructors, clergy, interested businessmen, and urban officials remained largely the same as before the war, although as a concession to the greater power of organized labor, a trade union official or two was usually coopted as well.[6] As before, the Prussian government paid the salaries of two part-time youth officers, one of each sex, in every county, charged with coordinating and overseeing local youth work. The number of county and district youth officers in Prussia increased from 392 to 1,069 between 1919 and 1929.[7] Because of the new republic's fiscal chaos, assistance to youth organizations from the Prussian government was initially quite limited. Even at the height of the hyperinflation of 1923, however, the government still channeled some funds to youth organizations, including those in the French-occupied Ruhr, evidence of how firmly the line for youth cultivation was anchored in the budget.[8] With the return of stability after 1923, Prussia budgeted at least three million marks annually for aid to youth organizations.

Although the fiscal crisis of the state and municipalities severely constrained new initiatives, prewar institutions like the continuation schools were still funded. Increasingly, however, continuation schools were renamed vocational schools (*Berufsschulen*), a name change that pointed to a slight shift in the mission of these establishments. As Kerschensteiner had advocated, the young worker's occupation now stood in the forefront of classroom instruction, while the roles of general education and even civic education diminished. There were several reasons for this. Socialists, who now entered urban governments, had always favored schools devoted solely to upgrading industrial skills, free of political indoctrination. Employers, worried about looming scarcities of skilled labor, took a more active interest in the schools and preferred that they be reduced to purely economic functions. There was considerable discussion about civic education in the continuation schools, but no specific program in support of the democratic republic was ever made an integral part of the curriculum, largely out of fear of drawing youth into party conflicts. In 1923 Paul Ziertmann, a councillor in the Trade Ministry, argued – somewhat disingenuously – that there was no need to alter the character of civic education. Even before the war, civic education had placed little emphasis on celebrating the monarchical form of government since the constituency of the schools was largely made up of youths reared in laboring households, which were inclined toward a democratic republic.[9] Although right about the schools' constituency, his claims were only partially true. After all, school festivities had certainly glorified the kaiser, and although the schools had informed students about their rights and entitlements, civic education had always purveyed a muted anti-Socialism by representing society as a conflict-free organism to which all occupational groups and classes contributed. During the republic, civic education continued to present a normative image of society as a harmonious community and to stress the duties of the young worker to the people and nation, duties performed by cultivating secondary virtues like honesty, modesty, industriousness, and uprightness. Thus the curriculum avoided grappling with any of the substantive problems or issues plaguing the republic.

The fiscal crisis also hampered the full-scale introduction of vocational or household schools for young working women, despite a widespread consensus among youth savers that instruction in household arts had become even more crucial since it had been neglected during the war.[10] During demobilization, the program for returning young women to their supposedly proper roles as housewives and mothers acquired even greater resonance. Nonetheless, only a handful of Prussian cities could afford to establish household schools for young working women or those former workers laid off or displaced by returning veterans. Despite opposition on fiscal grounds, the number of continuation schools for young female workers, with some combination of job-related instruction, household arts, and general education, inched slowly upward during the 1920s, though even by the end of the decade less than a quarter of all young working women under eighteen were enrolled in such institutions in Prussia. Young working women fared better in some of the other states. Hamburg made continuation schools obligatory for all young working women until the age of eighteen, and although not going as far as Hamburg, some of the southern and central German states developed more extensive systems than Prussia's.

Apart from the government apparatus and the continuation schools, the other key institution of the prewar youth salvation campaign, the adult-sponsored youth association, soon revived as well. With the demise of the Jungdeutschlandbund and premilitary training, both secular and religious youth groups could flourish once again. By 1927, 3.6 million youths, over half of all young males and over a fourth of all young females, belonged to organizations affiliated with the Imperial Committee of German Youth Associations.[11] About 1.5 million were members of athletic associations, and an almost equal number of youths belonged to Catholic or Protestant youth groups. By contrast only fifty-six thousand joined the Socialist youth movement and about twenty-nine thousand were grouped in the small bands, or *Bünde,* that modeled themselves after the prewar *Wandervögeln.* Despite the demise of the paramilitary organizations, much of their raison d'être was preserved. As the enormous membership of sports associations suggests, in the aftermath of the war and throughout the Weimar Republic, physical fitness and steeling the body took on considerably heightened significance. Moreover, such physical fitness was viewed as a preliminary commitment to Germany's future military resurgence.[12] Frequently invoked was the tradition of Father Jahn, the founder of German gymnastics, and his attempts to regenerate German youth at the time of the Napoleonic conquest. Middle-class youth savers soon regarded assiduous bodybuilding as a national duty. They equated the well-toned muscles of young males with armor and deemed robust health a vital necessity for young females, who would bear children to replace the war dead. Bodily strength symbolized Germany's will to regain its rightful place as a leading nation. This mania for physical culture clearly benefited sports clubs, although it certainly cannot be assumed that youths who joined necessarily embraced the nationalist agenda or shared the symbolic meanings that youth savers attached to physical fitness. Nevertheless, gymnastics instructors arrogantly claimed to be the driving force behind youth cultivation and national rebirth, claims that not surprisingly irritated other youth savers, who criticized the exalted status assigned to bodily strength as a further devaluation of the spirit. Although greatly magnified after the war, both the emphasis on steeling the body and its linkage to military preparedness, demographic vitality, and national will were already deeply rooted before the war.

Despite this revival and expansion of youth cultivation during the 1920s, conservative officials persisted in voicing most of the moral criticisms of young workers that had been bruited in the prewar era and had risen to a hysterical crescendo during the late war years. Throughout the early 1920s conservative mayors and county commissioners who remained in office constantly denounced the wildness of youth and alleged signs of moral degeneration like cinema visits, cigarette smoking, following dance crazes, and reading penny dreadfuls.[13] They abhorred the frivolity of many youths in the face of the seriousness of Germany's domestic crises and international isolation. Many called for a restoration of wartime moral policing and for once again setting up compulsory savings accounts from young workers' wages, legislated on a national scale this time, however, to make such schemes inescapable. As mentioned at the outset of this chapter, some legislation, such as the Cinema Law, allowed elements of wartime moral policing to be retained. To enforce the cinema laws, urban police made occasional raids to check the papers of movie patrons.[14] But for conservatives, who longed for a full restoration of the moral climate of the early war years, such attempts to restrict the amusements of young workers were considered insufficient.

Not only supposed youthful wildness aroused considerable alarm among officials, but also a wave of juvenile delinquency and vagabondism arising from the dislocations, upheavals, and economic crises of the postwar period.[15] In accordance with the Imperial Youth Welfare Law of 1922, municipalities instituted youth offices to handle the cases of delinquents and wayward youths and to align the responses of the police, courts, welfare services, schools, and youth organizations. Thus the cities erected a more formal bureaucratic structure to carry out surveillance and control of youthful "deviants," the foundations of which, however, had been laid during the Empire.

Certainly continuity between the Empire and the Weimar Republic was far from complete. There were a number of changes and modifications in youth cultivation during the Weimar Republic, some of

which have already been mentioned, such as the monomaniacal devotion to physical culture and the implementation of some aspects of
youth cultivation for young working women that had merely been
adumbrated before the war. Youth cultivation during the Republic
was far more comprehensive than during the Empire. By governmental decree, the Socialists were included in official youth functions.
The Socialist youth movement became eligible to apply for government funds, and its adult representatives could sit on local and regional youth committees. In reality, this inclusion was only partially
realized because of the mutual suspicions and antagonisms dividing
Socialists from their middle-class opponents, whether clerical or secular.[16] Although the overt antisocialism of prewar youth cultivation
would be considerably dampened, middle-class youth cultivators reg-   ·
ularly deplored what they considered the dragging of party politics
into youth work, a coded expression of distaste for the Socialist presence. Far from eschewing politics entirely, middle-class youth savers
touted an integral nationalism that supposedly transcended party politics.[17] Indeed, such views had been incorporated in the new youth
cultivation edict of 1919, which had excluded party politics while
explicitly stating that youth work should promote unity among all
German youth, regardless of social origins, and foster loyalty to the
fatherland in its period of misfortune. Because of the pervasive integral nationalism of middle-class youth savers, the Socialists and their
youth movement were far from being positively integrated even during the Republic. Moreover, the Communist youth movement was
completely excluded, ostensibly on the grounds that all of its activities
furthered party politics among the young and that it completely disdained the fatherland.[18] Thus the Communists assumed the position
of negative reference group partially vacated by the SPD's youth
movement.

Also encompassed by youth cultivation during the Weimar Republic
were the small *Bünde* composed of middle-class gymnasia students
dedicated to hiking and fostering folk traditions along the lines pioneered by the *Wandervögeln*. One consequence of including these
groups was that local youth committees tended to sponsor more events
in keeping with middle-class cultural norms, such as special orchestral
concerts for youth.[19] Another result was the dissemination of *Wandervogel* style and forms, forms that superficially allowed limited autonomy while rendering it politically harmless. The partial absorption
of both the Socialist and middle-class youth movements raised questions about the authority of adults and the relation of youth move-

ments and youth cultivation. For example, should youth be permitted to conduct their own hikes? Did excursions without adult supervision harbor significant moral dangers? The anxious tone of such debates in the 1920s probably resulted from the antiauthoritarian youth revolt at the end of the war and the crumbling of the Wilhelmine order, which had shaken adult confidence. Throughout the years of the Republic, even hikes tended to be bureaucratically normalized, with preselected routes and nightly stops in designated youth hostels. A governmental decree of 1923 provided guidelines for hikes that received financial support from the government. Not only were these hikes to "strengthen love of the fatherland, foster health, and awaken sensitivity to nature," but they had to be carefully planned beforehand to ensure that their didactic functions would be maximized.[20] Moreover, after the conclusion of the hike, a full report had to be submitted.

Despite such mutations and accent shifts, however, continuities in youth policy between the Empire and Republic were far more noteworthy than breaks. The years 1900, 1911, 1913, and 1914 were considerably more decisive moments in the construction of young workers as an official social problem than were 1919, 1922, or 1923. This essential continuity and lack of major innovations during the Republic are the most cogent and compelling reasons for concluding this study soon after the war. The continuation school revolt of 1919 in Essen, discussed at the end of Chapter 9, in many respects demonstrated the effectiveness of the Wilhelmine youth salvation campaign in fixing the boundaries of acceptable discourses and institutional practices affecting young workers, while simultaneously marking some of the limits of hegemony by indicating the ways in which those affected could reinterpret features of youth cultivation to their own advantage. Thus this is an appropriate point to conclude by reflecting on the achievements and failures, the scope and limits of the youth salvation campaign in Imperial Germany and by discussing the campaign's significance for and bearing on some of the recent historiographical controversies about Imperial Germany.

Although postulating major lines of continuity linking the Empire and the Weimar Republic, this study has certainly not argued for continuity of youth policy during the last decades of Imperial Germany. As in much of the recent literature on Wilhelmine Germany by English historians, the 1890s have been treated as a major inflection point in German history.[21] During that decade it became clear that facing up to the accumulating tensions arising from industrialization, urbanization, and the emergence of mass politics could no longer be postponed. Nor could action be delayed on those problems associated with the obverse side of these processes, namely, the decline of rural and artisanal Germany. It was at the turn of the century that clergy, doctors, educators, and other urban officials crystallized a host of disparate and amorphous concerns and misgivings into a somewhat more unified problem of post-school-age male youth. Indeed, one could assert without exaggeration that the youth savers invented young urban workers as a social category and problem. Ranking high among their concerns were the decay of craft apprenticeship and the imperiled survival of the artisanate, the flight of young workers from the land, the rapid growth of unskilled industrial labor, the attainment of earlier independence from the household by young workers, the spread of supposedly deleterious products of the mass culture industry, such as penny dreadfuls, and last but not least, the expansion of the Social Democratic party's influence after the lapse of the exceptional laws in 1890. Thus the constitution of young workers as a social problem was an integral part of the shift from an "agrarian to an industrial state" and the concomitant emergence of mass politics, consumer culture, and a full-fledged factory system. Although the structural transformation of German society certainly formed an objective substrate underlying the perception of young workers as a social problem, from the outset saving young workers assumed the character of a symbolic crusade. Youth savers' denunciations of an epidemic of youthful wildness, delinquency, and moral degeneration appear to have been only weakly supported by documentable social fact. Rather, they were expressions of anxieties shared by urban professionals about the direction of embryonic mass society and of fears about loss of authority, status, and control, fears condensed in their emotionally charged portrayals of the *Halbstarken*.

The early phases of the youth salvation campaign show the limits of German history viewed from the vantage point of the ministries in Berlin. The Prussian government certainly supported the campaign to save young workers, but it was Wilhelmine reform associations, urban officials, clergy, and educators, rather than the ministries, that gave the campaign its original impetus and generated its ongoing energy. Among the more prominent and representative figures of the early years of the campaign were Georg Kerschensteiner, Andreas Voigt, August Pieper, and Clemens Schultz. It was at the municipal level that such urban officials and clerics shaped the campaign, determined policy, and constructed a new network of institutions. Despite the strong anti-Socialist animus of the campaign and the inclination of its spokespersons to idealize pre–industrial age relations in family and workshop, the leading figures recognized that this world was being irreversibly destroyed. Despite certain elements of cultural pessimism and antimodernism, youth savers generally accepted the new urban and industrial order and acknowledged that it would necessarily entail significant changes in age and social relations. They were confident that they could curb youthful wildness, not by restoring an anachronistic patriarchal order, but rather by creating institutional substitutes for the old supervisory regime that corresponded to the needs of a modern industrial society. A minority among the youth savers, typified by Pastor Weigle in Essen, did advocate repressive and even draconian measures to assure youthful subordination and obedience, but apart from local exceptions, until the war this wing, with its reactionary disciplinary utopia, had little to show for its efforts. Certainly a new disciplinary regime was installed in the industrial continuation schools and youth associations, as well as in factory apprentice workshops and reformatories. But the chief characteristics distinguishing this new disciplinary order from the old patriarchal one were its far greater emphasis on persuasive pedagogy and rewards, its softer techniques, and its partial and certainly halfhearted accommodation to youthful autonomy, rather than its new array of punitive sanctions. The liberal elements in the programs of Kerschensteiner and the other youth savers should not be overlooked. Civic education and youth associations were supposed to wrest young workers away from the grip of the Socialists, and simultaneously they were to prepare young workers to play responsible roles in the administration of public institutions in a constitutional state. Unless one reduces the political options in Wilhelmine Germany to either socialism or reaction, such a program cannot be dismissed as a retrograde defense of the status quo.

In the decade from 1900 to 1910, the more liberal youth savers achieved some remarkable successes in implementing their program. Most remarkable was the triumphal march of the mandatory part-time continuation school endowed with a Kerschensteinerian mission combining vocational and civic education. During this decade the industrial continuation schools became the paramount public institutions for socializing young male artisans and workers "between primary school and barracks." Although many young workers initially resisted these institutions, the schools were soon able to surmount their growing pains and gain acceptance. Nor can they be regarded solely as institutions exercising social control over young workers and improving labor skills in industry and artisanal workshops in order to promote national efficiency, though they were unquestionably designed to fulfill both these tasks. The schools' curriculum clearly benefited some young workers by broadening their horizons and enhancing their labor qualifications. School recreational facilities clearly provided a needed public space for leisure time activities. Industrial continuation schools enjoyed a modest but solid success in improving industrial skills, organizing the leisure of young workers, and integrating them into urban life.

Consequently these schools could rely on broad community support, not only from many industrialists, but, insofar as they taught vocational skills, from the Socialist labor movement as well. Ironically, although several historians of education have represented these schools as backward-looking institutions serving the declining artisanate, it was only the artisanate that would openly assail the mission of these schools. Conservative master artisans not only resented having to pay school fees but strongly believed that the emphasis on rational theoretical instruction and the dissemination of information on apprentices' rights were misbegotten and undermined their own authority. To be sure, industrial continuation schools were supposed to preserve the artisanate. But Kerschensteiner's program for preserving the artisanate assumed that the only way to accomplish this was by raising the level of skills and education among young craftsmen. Both Kerschensteiner in Munich and Gotter in Düsseldorf accepted a competitive capitalist system. German crafts had to be in a position to compete both with domestic firms and with rivals abroad. Thus a liberal program for artisanal survival counterposed education to social protectionism, a position rejected by much of the artisanate.

The other major institutional success achieved by the youth reformers was the proliferation of adult-sponsored but voluntary youth associations, whether under religious or secular auspices, associations that probably encompassed half of all young male workers in the prewar era. These associations ranged from soccer and technology clubs at continuation schools to local gymnastic associations and Catholic sodalities. Some were organized around a single activity like gymnastics, whereas others developed far more comprehensive and ambitious educational, recreational, and religious programs. Most were apolitical, although both Catholic and Protestant youth groups undertook some form of civic education. Catholic youth sodalities certainly propagandized on behalf of Catholic social policy and the Center party, but they also informed young workers about their legal rights and explored central issues of party politics. Such associations were organized and supervised by adults, but all except the most authoritarian, for example, those built by Weigle in Essen, offered some leeway for youthful members to determine their own activities, and some, like those founded by Pastors Schultz and Classen in Hamburg, even adopted the so-called American principle of allowing members to elect their own leaders and largely administer their own affairs. To the degree that these associations promoted self-administration, they probably did contribute to fostering civic spirit and laying the foundations for an order of liberty, as Kerschensteiner had hoped.

Thus from the perspective of most youth savers, the first decade of the century was marked by largely successful reform efforts that promised to alleviate the post-school-age youth problem. Nonetheless, their success was far from complete, and dark clouds continued to lower on the horizon. First, youth savers were disturbed by the increasing number of unskilled young workers, just as their British counterparts were worried about "boy labour."[22] Unskilled youths challenged the youth savers' central assumptions, since these youths demonstrated little interest in their work, attained independence early, and were not particularly enthusiastic about the sober educational and recreational associations favored by the youth savers. Instead, they preferred the earthier and more sensual pleasures of the streets, bars, bordellos, and cinemas. These youths revealed a streak of the untamed plebeian anarchism and resorted to the regular contravention of bourgeois norms that Richard Evans has made central to his call for a reexamination of working-class life in Imperial Germany.[23] To discipline such refractory youths, even liberal youth savers like Kerschensteiner conceded that more authoritarian forms of organization might be necessary. Among those considered were paramilitary groups along the lines of the British Boys' Brigades. Second, as previously noted, liberal youth savers faced ongoing and sometimes vociferous opposition to their programs from sectors of the artisanate, as well as from Catholic clergy, who objected to their secularism. Third, the new Imperial Association Law of 1908, which extended restrictions on the political organization of youth to the entire Reich, spurred the rapid growth of a Socialist youth movement.

This paradox emerged when the law impelled the centrist and reformist party and trade union leadership to harness the preexisting semiautonomous labor youth groups in order to avoid a confrontation with the state. The leadership succeeded in replacing the antimilitarist south German group and the Berlin-based association for the defense of young workers and artisans with a unified but less political, more educationally and recreationally oriented labor youth movement. But at the same time the SPD threw its highly developed organizational muscle behind the creation of a mass youth association. Although most party leaders and members involved in organizing this movement accepted many of the positions espoused by middle-class youth savers about dangers to proletarian youth like drinking, smoking, juvenile delinquency, penny dreadfuls, and urban mass culture, in its attracting tens of thousands of new recruits and youthful subscribers to *Arbeiter-Jugend,* this organizational drive alarmed the youth savers and the Prussian government. This entire episode largely confirms the criticism leveled by Vernon Lidtke against Guenther Roth's old interpretation of the SPD as "negatively integrated" in Imperial Germany, namely, that Roth underestimated the degree of the labor movement's positive integration and at the same time overlooked the ways in which the SPD destabilized the Wilhelmine polity.[24]

In response to the rapid growth of the Workers' Youth Movement, the Ministry of Education and Religious Affairs promulgated the Youth Cultivation Decree of January 1911. This decree inaugurated a new phase in the campaign to save young workers, a phase in which the campaign flourished as never before. Continuation school activities prospered, as did religious and secular youth associations supervised by adults. Even large industrial firms like Krupp and Bayer leaped onto the youth cultivation bandwagon by launching extensive corporate recreational and educational programs. Government centralization resulted in the recruiting and training of thousands of new youth workers, albeit without the degree of professionalism advocated by some seasoned youth savers, setting up hundreds of regional and local youth committees, multiplying conferences on young workers, and making available funds for purchasing equipment and improving the facilities of youth associations.

In the face of considerable pressure from middle-class women's organizations and military concerns about declining birthrates, the Prussian government finally recognized young working women as a distinct social problem and agreed to extend the 1911 decree to cover them. This new branch of youth cultivation was to emphasize training in household arts, so that working girls would be able to perform their future duties as housewives and mothers, duties that were held to be indispensable for Germany's future industrial competitiveness and military strength. The terms in which young working women were cast as a social problem, however, were symptomatic of the more conservative turn taken by the campaign after 1911; household arts took precedence over skills needed in the labor market. Ironically, however, as a result of this emphasis, a new female profession was aborning, the task of which was to teach domesticity, since reformers, middle-class women's organizations, and the state designated birth-rates and a well-ordered and blissful proletarian home life matters of grave national concern, thus blurring the boundaries between the public and private spheres and politicizing the latter.

Even more indicative of the conservative turn was the formation by Field Marshal Freiherr von der Goltz, with the warm support of the kaiser and the blessing of the army, of the Young Germany League, an organization propelled forward by antisocialism and doubts about Germany's military readiness. The new organization, with its stress on premilitary training, Sunday maneuvers, and war games, all conducted in the spirit of hurrah patriotism, became the primary government-backed organization for young workers in the immediate postwar years. The more centralized and militarized phase of the youth campaign after 1911 was accompanied by a far more aggressive attack directed against the Socialist youth movement, al-though local police officials often discounted the importance of this movement and banked on the government's positive youth cultivation to bury it. By 1913 at latest this coupling of positive youth cultivation and repressive measures had checked the growth of the Socialist youth movement. For the first time this movement stagnated and was gripped by an uneasy sense of malaise. Despite some arm twisting to induce industrial continuation school students to join the Young Ger-many League, its exponentially expanding membership, as well as high attendance at celebrations like those for the kaiser's birthday at the continuation schools, suggested that the influence of the Socialists among young workers was decidedly weaker than had commonly been supposed, a weakness belatedly recognized, with near panic, by SPD leaders. Moreover, these phenomena further implied that patriotic organizations and festivities could tap into a considerable reservoir of nationalist enthusiasm among young workers.

In general liberal youth savers wholeheartedly welcomed this en-ergetic government initiative, since they not only were the chief bene-ficiaries of the Prussian government's largesse and conferral of ap-probation but could also foresee realistic prospects for containing the Socialist youth movement. But as even the Prussian education minister had feared, the militarization of youth work was not greeted with unanimity and uncritical enthusiasm even within the anti-Socialist bloc. The German Gymnasts disliked the competition, whereas the Protestants objected to the raw physicalism of the Young Germany League. Catholic youth savers, who had previously stood in the forefront of the youth salvation campaign, were deeply disenchanted by the monopolistic aspirations, physicality, and secularism of the league. In many respects, militarization exacerbated tensions and conflicts among anti-Socialist youth cultivators, especially those between secular urban administrators and the Catholic clergy, thereby making manifest the fragmentation within the youth salvation campaign.

Thus, if more repressive actions and a wave of militarism defined much (though certainly not all) of Prussian youth policy in the immediate prewar period, the road to militarization and statification were certainly circuitous and labyrinthine. The prewar turn was less the revelation of latent tendencies inherent in either youth cultivation or the Wilhelmine state, as historians highly critical of the Kaiserreich, such as Klaus Saul, suggest, than a controversial and cobbled-together conjunctural reaction by state officials and local youth savers to the unexpected and alarming growth of the Socialist youth movement and the deterioration of Germany's international position. Moreover, the civil side of youth cultivation continued to thrive alongside the paramilitary. In any event, the militarization and statification of youth work in the prewar era were hardly uniquely German. The Young Germany League, for example, admitted to taking much of its inspiration from the British Boys' Brigades, and a new-found eagerness for the premilitary training of youth was evident in prewar France as well.[25] As was the case for all phases of prewar youth policy, the conservative turn was inaugurated in an atmosphere of international competition, interchange, and imitation.

Although it is doubtful that Germany's decision for war can be imputed to purely domestic factors or accurately depicted as a flight forward or last desperate gamble by generals and junkers intent on preserving the old order, nonetheless, such social types and their conservative allies in the Protestant Church and government certainly made good use of the wartime situation to implement authoritarian policies.[26] Measures that had been widely rejected in the prewar era could now be imposed. Not only was the civic side of youth cultivation in continuation schools and clubs almost completely submerged in favor of mandatory premilitary exercises and a much lengthened working day, but the deputy army commanders soon issued a series of decrees introducing forced savings schemes, establishing curfews, and all but eliminating the possibility for young workers to enjoy urban pleasures. Such reactionary moral policing, when combined with the heavy demands and worsening conditions facing young workers on the shopfloors, not only bred resentment, but finally precipitated open revolt. Much as liberal youth savers had predicted since the turn of the century, draconian repressive measures proved counterproductive and provoked the very rebellious and scofflaw behavior that conservative youth savers feared and decried. Nonetheless, the early war years, with their imposing but false façade of national unity and their spirit of single-minded dedication to military victory, would remain a period fondly and nostalgically recalled by conservatives throughout the years of the Weimar Republic.

The prewar conservative turn and wartime policies would be bequeathed to the Hitlerjugend and the youth policy of the Third Reich. Much of the organizational continuity would trace back to the Young Germany League as an all-encompassing, cross-class, anti-Socialist, paramilitary youth association dedicated to service to the fatherland. Certainly there were personal ties between the Young Germany League and Hitler Youth. Thus Baldur von Schirach, the Imperial Youth Leader in the Third Reich, belonged to the Young Germany League during World War I, although there is no real evidence elucidating the meaning of this membership for his subsequent development.[27] There are clear rhetorical continuities as well. The proclaimed aims and the favored activities of the early Jungbund of the Nazi party, such as promoting "love of home and folk, joy in honorable open struggle and in healthy physical activity, respect for all ethical and spiritual goods" cultivated through "patriotic evenings, lectures, common hikes, and calisthenics of all kinds," were virtually interchangeable with those announced by the Jungdeutschlandbund in 1911, although there were also some notable differences.[28] From the outset, the Nazi youth movement was more overtly politicized and racialist than the Young Germany League had ever been. Whether the Jungdeutschlandbund served as a recognized prototype for the Hitler Youth remains an open question.

Less open to question are the clear continuities binding Nazi social policy with some proposals advanced in the course of the Wilhelmine youth salvation campaign.[29] The Nazi regime's provisions for occupational placement, vocational education, limitations on work time, vacations, and weekly half-day releases from work for youth all had their origin in late Imperial Germany, although not necessarily within the conservative wing of the youth salvation campaign. In Nazi Germany such measures were justified by the need for furthering economic and military efficiency, rather than by the goal of improving the well-being of individual young workers. Thus, when Nazi officials redefined national priorities, restrictions on the working day of youth could be readily rescinded on the grounds that the nation was in danger. Protective legislation covering youths would be abolished during the Second World War as it had been during the First. Moreover, almost exactly the same measures for the moral policing of young workers decreed by the deputy army commanders during World War I were contained in the Law for the Protection of Youth passed in March 1940. Among the limitations placed on youths were curfews, bans on smoking and drinking, and prohibitions against visiting cinemas and other places of amusement unless accompanied by adults. The systematic and universal premilitary training of young males initiated in the late 1930s also reproduced similar schemes discussed before 1914 and started in August of that year. As in so many other areas, in youth policy the Nazi regime would hearken back to the early years of World War I as a kind of concrete utopia. In power, the Nazi regime attempted to conjure up that era by suppressing all self-activity of young workers, herding all youth into obligatory associations under tight surveillance of the state and party, and restoring the military preparation and moral policing in an even more comprehensive and stringent manner than army commanders had countenanced during World War I. But as documented by recent research on the nonconformity of young workers in Nazi Germany and the open resistance of working-class youth gangs like the Edelweiss Pirates late in World War II, visions of absolute order and rigid discipline could not be realized even under the Nazi regime with its totalitarian aspirations.[30] Ultimately the Nazis would have no more lasting success than their conservative predecessors during World War I. Through coercive and draconian measures neither the youth nor the future could be secured.

Notes

Chapter 1, pp. 1–18

1 Fritz Kalle, "Das gewerbliche Fortbildungswesen," *Schriften des Vereins für Sozialpolitik*, 15 (Leipzig, 1879), p. 26.

2 Jürgen Reulecke, "Bürgerliche Sozialreformer und Arbeiterjugend im Kaiserreich," *Archiv für Sozialgeschichte*, 22 (1982), pp. 304–12.

3 Ibid., pp. 313–15.

4 For Floessel, see Detlev J. Peukert, *Grenzen der Sozialdisziplinierung: Aufstieg und Krise der deutschen Jugendfürsorge 1878 bis 1932* (Cologne, 1986), pp. 35, 109. On measures to improve the skills of apprentices in the Handicrafts Protection Law of 1897, see Herwig Blankertz, *Bildung im Zeitalter der grossen Industrie* (Hannover, 1969), pp. 125–7. For both the speech of von Gossler and the recommendations of the Prussian House of Lords, see C. Fritsch, "Die Thätigkeit der Inneren Mission auf dem Gebiete der Fürsorge für die heranwachsende männliche Jugend," *Die Fürsorge für die schulentlassene gewerbliche Jugend: Vorberichte und Verhandlungen der X Konferenz vom 6 und 7 Mai 1901: Schriften der Centralstelle für Arbeiterwohlfahrtseinrichtungen*, no. 21 (Berlin, 1901), pp. 69–70. For the Prussian Landtag proposal on restricting the migration of youth, see *Die Verhandlungen des elften Evangelisch-sozialen Kongresses abgehalten zu Karlsruhe 7–8 Juni 1900* (Göttingen, 1900), p. 38. On the *BGB* (civil law code) discussions, see J. F. Landsberg, "Die öffentliche Erziehung der gefährdeten Jugend," *Einführung in das lebende Recht*, no. 8 (Hannover, 1913), pp. v–vi.

5 Andreas Voigt, "Bericht über den zweiten Verhandlungstag 24 April, 1900," *Fürsorge für die schulentlassene Jugend: Vorberichte und Verhandlungen der IX Konferenz: Schriften der Centralstelle für Arbeiterwohlfahrtseinrichtungen*, Heft 16 (Berlin, 1900), p. 319.

6 Fritsch, op. cit., pp. 69–70.

7 See nn. 4 and 5 supra for the proceedings of the conferences of the Protestant Social Congress and the Center for Workers' Welfare Institutions. *Jahrbücher der königlichen Akademie gemeinnütziger Wissenschaft zu Erfurt*, N.F. 27 (Erfurt, 1901), pp. iv–v.

8 In his presentation for the ninth congress of the Centralstelle für Ar-

beiterwohlfahrtseinrichtungen, Voigt noted this multiplicity of criteria. Andreas Voigt, "Die schulentlassene Jugend," *Schriften der Centralstelle für Arbeiterwohlfahrtseinrichtungen,* Heft 16 (Berlin, 1900), p. 10. For the various categorizations of youth, see Edmund Friedeberg, "Die Minderjährigen im Straffrecht, Straffprozess und Straffvolzüge," pp. 116–17; Martin E. Fuchs, "Das Minderjährige im Rechte des Arbeiterverhältnisses," pp. 144–66; and T. Ziehen, "Psychologie des Entwicklungsalters," pp. 61–4, in *Handbuch für Jugendpflege* (Langensalza, 1913). On the increasing use of an age category bounded by primary school and army barracks, see Klaus Saul, "Der Kampf um die Jugend zwischen Volksschule und Kaserne: Ein Beitrag zur 'Jugenpflege' im wilhelminischen Reich 1890–1914," *Militärgeschichtliche Mitteilungen,* no. 1 (1971), p. 97.

9   For participants in the conference of the Centralstelle für Arbeiterwohlfahrtseinrichtungen, see *Schriften* no. 21, Heft 16, and *Schriften* no. 21 of the following year. For the composition of the congress of the Evangelisch-sozialen Kongress, see Harry Liebersohn, "Religion and Industrial Society: The Protestant Social Congress in Wilhelmine Germany," *Transactions of the American Philosophical Society,* 76, no. 6 (1986), p. 32. A breakdown of the occupations of the Erfurt essayists is provided in *Jahrbücher,* p. iv.

10 Apart from the Centralstelle conferences of 1900 and 1901 already cited, after being rechristened the Centralstelle für Volkswohlfahrt, the organization would hold a conference on industrially employed youth in 1909, one on young female workers in 1912, and one on youth during the war in 1916. *Schriften der Zentralstelle für Volkswohlfahrt,* N.F. Heft 3, 7 (1909), Heft 9 (1912), and Heft 13 (1916). The Gesellschaft für Sozialreform, founded in 1901, by leading members of the Reichstag belonging to the liberal parties and the Catholic Center Party, along with representatives of nonsocialist labor organizations, began an extensive survey of the conditions of young laborers in 1910 and discussed the results at the conference of the following year. *Die jugendlichen Arbeiter in Deutschland: Verhandlungen der 5. Generalversammlungen der Gesellschaft für Soziale Reform,* vol. 5 (Jena, 1912). On membership of the Society for Social Reform, see also Ursula Ratz, *Sozialreform und Arbeiterschaft* (Berlin, 1980), pp. 48–52.

11 For the concept and composition of the *Bildungsbürgertum* in Imperial Germany, see Klaus Vondung, ed., *Das wilhelminische Bildungsbürgertum* (Göttingen, 1976), pp. 5–33.

12 *Mitteilungen des Bezirksausschusses für Jugendpflege im Regierungsbezirk Düsseldorf,* 1 December 1913, for the social composition of the attendees at the "Düsseldorf Week for the Further Education of Youth Cultivators."

13 Given National Liberal and left liberal dominance of Germany's municipal governments until 1918 and the fact that most prominent youth savers were middle-class professionals employed by the municipalities, one can infer that most were backers of the liberal parties. See James J. Sheehan, *German Liberalism in the Nineteenth Century* (Chicago, 1978), pp. 226–30. Georg Kerschensteiner, the most commonly cited youth saver, was elected to the Reichstag in 1911 as a Progressive. Leading Catholic spokespersons for youth reform, such as August Pieper, were

generally active in the Volksverein für das katholische Deutschland and hence belonged to the populist (Mönchen-Gladbach) tendency of the Zentrumspartei.

14 Günther Dehn, *Grossstadtjugend* (Berlin, 1922), p. 1.

15 The *locus classicus* for the issue of the degree of national integration of labor in Imperial Germany is in Guenther Roth, *The Social Democrats in Imperial Germany: A Study in Working Class Isolation and National Integration* (Totowa, N.J., 1963), where he argues that the German situation was a complex hybrid between parliamentary England, where labor was integrated into the national polity, and repressive Russia, where labor was completely isolated. In Germany the Social Democrats and their trade union and cultural affiliates were "negatively integrated" into the Empire. Socialists had the possibility for controlled expression of opposition and could build their organizations, but they exercised little real power. This negative integration contributed, according to Roth, to the stability of the Empire. Recent critical assessments of Roth's functionalist perspective that have pointed to the destabilizing features of the SPD's presence include Richard J. Evans, "The Sociological Interpretation of German Labour History," in Richard J. Evans, ed., *The German Working Class: The Politics of Everyday Life 1888–1933* (London, 1982), pp. 18–46. Evans also calls for distinguishing between Social Democratic and working-class cultures and exploring the untamed, lawless, and anarchic character of the latter. A somewhat more judicious critique of Roth's position is to be found in Vernon L. Lidtke, *The Alternative Culture: Socialist Labor in Imperial Germany* (New York, 1985), pp. 6–20. Lidtke takes Roth to task for overestimating the coherence of Wilhelmine society and underestimating somewhat paradoxically both the positive integration of the labor movement and the SPD's role as a destabilizing force – criticisms I share.

16 Hans-Ulrich Wehler, *Das Deutsche Kaiserreich 1871–1918* (Göttingen, 1973), is a highly controversial broadside against the Empire. Nipperdey's critical response, "Wehlers 'Kaiserreich': Eine kritische Auseinandersetzung," appears in *Geschichte und Gesellschaft*, 1 (1975), pp. 539–60. More recent critiques that attack Wehler for his emphasis on the role of preindustrial elites, his notion of a bourgeois revolution, and his use of English politics and society as norms against which to measure the deficiencies of Germany can be found in David Blackbourn and Geoff Eley, *The Peculiarities of German History* (Oxford, 1984).

17 Quoted in Howard S. Becker, ed., *Social Problems: A Modern Approach* (New York, 1966), p. 11.

18 The attempt to reconstruct the experienced life worlds of workers, small farmers, youth, and other subordinate groups has been a major feature of German historiography since the late 1970s, a specifically German version of "history from below" most closely associated with historians like Jürgen Reulecke, Alf Lüdtke, Lutz Niethammer, Detlev Peukert, and Klaus Tenfelde. Examples are to be found in collections like Jürgen Reulecke and W. Weber, eds., *Fabrik, Familie, Feierabend* (Wuppertal, 1978), and Detlev J. Peukert and Jürgen Reulecke, eds., *Die Reihen fast Geschlossen* (Wuppertal, 1981). For a brief and highly unsympathetic critique of some of the conceptual and substantive shortcomings of this

school, see Hans-Ulrich Wehler, "Neoromantik und Pseudorealismus in der neuen 'Alltagsgeschichte' " reprinted in Wehler, *Preussen ist wieder chic...*, (Frankfurt am Main, 1983), pp. 96–106. For a recent critical survey of the entire school, see Geoff Eley, "Labor History, Social History, *Alltagsgeschichte*: Experience, Culture and the Politics of Everyday Life – a New Direction for German Social History?" *Journal of Modern History*, 61 (June 1989), pp. 297–343. An interesting attempt to reconstruct the life worlds of young workers in England at the turn of the century, relying on oral sources, is Stephen Humphries, *Hooligans or Rebels? An Oral History of Working Class Childhood and Youth 1889–1939* (Oxford, 1981). Peukert has also pursued a similar project, both in his book on working-class youth in the Weimar Republic, *Jugend zwischen Krieg und Krise* (Cologne, 1987), and in his work on the Third Reich, *Inside Nazi Germany* (New Haven, 1987), pp. 145–74.

19   For the following, see Karl Mannheim, "The Problem of Generations," in *Essays on the Sociology of Knowledge* (New York, 1952), esp. pp. 286–90. See also the discussion of Mannheim and the generation concept in Anthony Esler, *Generations in History: An Introduction to the Concept* (1982), pp. 41–79. For the reception of Mannheim and the "emptying" of the generational concept, see Helmut Fogt, *Politische Generationen* (Opladen, 1982), pp. 9–17.

20   For German youth in literature at the turn of the century, see Roy Pascal, *From Naturalism to Expressionism* (New York, 1973), pp. 211–28 – a literature that, as Pascal states, invariably expresses a bourgeois bias. For a recent statement of the importance of the revolt of the sons in the middle-class youth movement, see Hermann Giesecke, *Vom Wandervogel bis zur Hitlerjugend* (Munich, 1981), pp. 31–3. In all fairness to Giesecke, he believes neither that the households of *Wandervögeln* were particularly repressive nor that the downfall of the father has been unambiguously beneficial.

21   *Verhandlungen des elften Evangelisch-sozialen Kongresses,* (Göttingen, 1900), p. 31, for the comments by Troeltsch.

22   John R. Gillis, *Youth and History: Tradition and Change in European Age Relations 1770 to the Present* (New York, 1974), pp. ix, 149. See also George L. Mosse, *The Crisis of German Ideology* (New York, 1964), pp. 171–89.

23   Walter Laqueur, *Young Germany: A History of the German Youth Movement* (New York, 1962), p. xv. See also Peter Stachura, *The German Youth Movement 1900–1945* (New York, 1981), pp. 3–9, 13–37.

24   Laqueur, op. cit., pp. 10–14, 48–9, 236–7; Mosse, op. cit., p. 188; Giesecke, op. cit., pp. 30–1.

25   Gillis, op. cit., pp. 150–1.

26   Laqueur, op. cit., pp. xv–xvi.

27   Gillis, op. cit., pp. 149–50.

28   Ibid., p. 155.

29   A representative East German work is that of the Autorenkollektiv headed by Karl Heinz Jahnke, *Geschichte der deutschen Arbeiterjugendbewegung 1904–1945* (East Berlin, 1973).

30   For a survey review of recent German historical and sociological research on youth, see Heinz-Elmar Tenorth, "Jugend und Generationen im his-

torischen Prozess," *Internationales Archiv für Sozialgeschichte der deutschen Literatur*, 13 (1988), pp. 107–39. For a historical sociological overview that examines the invention of youth in the nineteenth century as part of a transformation in the modes of social control, see Trutz von Trotha, "Zur Entstehung von Jugend," *Kölner Zeitschrift für Soziologie und Sozial-psychologie*, 34, no. 2 (June 1982), pp. 254–77, esp. p. 258. Because of the close relation of the social control concept with deviance and the implicit emphasis on coercion, I prefer the notion of hegemony in a Gramscian sense. The battle for youth was an attempt by middle-class reformers to impose their values, morals, and behavioral codes on young workers through both coercion and persuasion. Some of the fate and uses of the various notions of social control are discussed in Ronald A. Farrell and Victoria Swigert, *Deviance and Social Control* (Glenview, 1982).

31   Giesecke, op. cit., pp. 38–80.
32   Klaus Tenfelde, "Grossstadtjugend in Deutschland vor 1914: Ein historisch-demographische Annäherung," *Vierteljahrschrift für Sozial- und Wirtschaftsgeschichte*, 69., no. 2 (1982), pp. 182–218. Table 1 lumps together persons under 30; Table 2 lists 0–15, 15–40, 40–60, older than 60; Table 3 divides the population into ten-year age groups, for example, 10–20, 20–30, and so on.
33   Reulecke, op. cit., pp. 299–329.
34   Klaus Saul, op. cit., pp. 97–143. An older article that stressed the physical and premilitary aspects of youth cultivation after 1911 and its role in combatting the Socialist youth movement is Heinrich Muth, "Jugendpfle-ge und Politik," *Geschichte in Wissenschaft und Unterricht*, 12, no. 10 (October 1961), pp. 597–619. Muth also emphasizes – indeed, over-emphasizes – the opposition of the churches to the increased physical orientation of youth cultivation.
35   Klaus Saul, "Jugend im Schatten des Krieges", *Militärgeschichtliche Mit-teilungen*, no. 2 (1983), pp. 145–74.
36   Klaus Harney, *Die preussische Fortbildungsschule: Eine Studie zum Problem der Hierarchisierung beruflicher Schultypen im 19. Jahrhundert* (Weinheim, 1980).
37   Wolf-Dietrich Greinert, *Schule als Instrument sozialer Kontrolle und Objekt privater Interessen: Der Beitrag der Berufsschule zur politischen Erziehung der Unterschichten* (Hannover, 1975).
38   Peukert, *Grenzen der Sozialdisziplinierung*, 17–19.
39   Giesecke does briefly mention the extension of youth cultivation to young working women in 1913 (Giesecke, op. cit., pp. 78–80), and Peukert at least justifies his exclusion in terms of the different discourse for wayward girls (Peukert, *Grenzen der Sozialdisziplinierung*, p. 29). See also my article, "Between School and Marriage, Workshop and Household: Young Working Women as a Social Problem in Late Imperial Germany," *European History Quarterly*, 18, no. 4 (October 1988), pp. 387–408.

Chapter 2, pp. 19–47

1   For a survey of some of the major economic and social transformations occurring in Germany during the late nineteenth century, see Karl Erich

Born, "Structural Changes in German Social and Economic Development
at the End of the Nineteenth Century," in James Sheehan, ed., *Imperial
Germany* (New York, 1976), pp. 16–38. For an attempt to relate demographic changes and increasingly youthful urban population directly to
the emergence of a specific working-class youth problem, see Klaus
Tenfelde, "Grossstadtjugend in Deutschland vor 1914: Ein historisch-
demographische Annäherung," *Vierteljahrschrift für Sozial- und Wirtschaftsgeschichte*, vol. 69, no. 2 (1982), pp. 182–218.

2   See the tables in G. Horhorst, et al., eds., *Sozialgeschichtliches Arbeitsbuch
II: Materialien zur Statistik des Kaiserreiches 1870–1914* (Munich, 1978),
pp. 23–4.

3   Table 3, *Statistisches Jahrbuch deutscher Städte* (Breslau, 1914), pp. 80–1.
For a discussion of migration to various types of cities and its importance
for the youthfulness of Germany's urban population in the late nineteenth century, see Tenfelde, op. cit., pp. 192–209.

4   *Statistisches Jahrbuch der Stadt Berlin* (Berlin, 1913), p. 215.

5   Karl Bittmann, "Die jugendlichen Arbeiter in Deutschland I. Arbeits-
verhältnisse der den SS135–139a der Gewerbeordnung unterstellten
minderjährigen Arbeiter," *Schriften der Gesellschaft für Sozialreform*, vol.
4, no. 1 (Jena, 1910), p. 12.

6   "Pflege der schulentlassenen weiblichen Jugend: Vorbericht und Verhandlungen der 6. Konferenz der Zentralstelle für Volkswohlfahrt,"
Schriften der Zentralstelle für Volkswohlfahrt, N.F. Heft 9 (Berlin, 1913),
pp. 8–9.

7   Ibid., pp. 9–12.

8   The question of whether there was a "Great Depression" between 1873
and 1896 has been much debated. Originally given currency by Hans
Rosenberg, *Grosse Depression und Bismarckzeit* (Berlin, 1967), as a moving
force behind trends toward social protectionism, interest group politics,
antiliberalism and anti-Semitism in Bismarckian Germany, the concept
has subsequently been challenged. Volker Hentschel, in *Wirtschaft und
Wirtschaftspolitik im wilhelminischen Deutschland* (Stuttgart, 1978), p. 209,
dismissed the notion of a Great Depression as "false and misleading."
Reinhard Spree, in his careful quantitative analysis of economic growth,
*Wachstumstrends und Konjuncturcyklen in der deutschen Wirtschaft von 1820
bis 1913* (Göttingen, 1978), pp. 171–4, points out that although fat years
outnumbered lean, during these years disturbances in growth were more
common than in the preceding or successive period. Moreover, no one
has denied that there was a major crisis of and depression in German
agriculture as new and cheaper grain-growing regions in the Americas
and Russia came under cultivation.

9   *Verwaltungsbericht der Stadt Düsseldorf 1908–9*, p. 81.

10   See, for example, the profile of the unemployed in Düsseldorf in winter
1901–2 in "Die städtische Arbeitslosen – Beschäftigung im Winter 1901–
2," *Mitteilungen der Statistik der Stadt Düsseldorf*, p. 4. Three hundred fifty
youths, 20 percent of the total, were among the unemployed.

11   Schrader, "Berufswahl und Berufswechsel," *Handbuch für Jugendpflege*
(Langensalza, 1913), pp. 214–16.

12 Wilhelm Heinz Schröder, *Arbeitergeschichte und Arbeiterbewegung* (Frankfurt am Main, 1978), pp. 70–1.

13 Andreas Voigt, "Die schulentlassene Jugend," in "Fürsorge für die schulentlassene Jugend: Vorberichte und Verhandlungen der IX Konferenz, 23–24 April 1900," *Schriften der Centralstelle für Arbeiterwohlfahrtseinrichtungen*, Heft 16 (Berlin, 1900), pp. 39–40. See also the study by the reform socialist Richard Calwer, *Das Kost- und Logiswesen im Handwerk* (Berlin, 1908). The decline of some aspects of apprenticeship, such as *Kost und Logis*, was also of concern to the Social Policy Association in its extensive investigation of the state of the handicrafts in the mid-1890s. This investigation, which was supposed to determine the ability of artisanal shops to compete with large-scale industry, played an important role in facilitating legislation, such as the Handicraft Law of 1897. Almost all the local inquiries, such as the one on mechanic firms in Nürnberg, contained critical sections on the training, morals, and technical education of apprentices. See, for example, Wilhelm Westhaus, "Das Düsseldorfer Schlachtergewerbe," in "Untersuchungen über die Lage des Handwerks in Deutschland," vol. 1, *Schriften des Vereins für Sozialpolitik*, 62 (Leipzig, 1895), pp. 244–7, or Hans Theodor Soergel, "Zwei Nürnberger Metallgewerbe," vol. 3, Süddeutschland *Schriften des Vereins für Sozialpolitik*, 64 (Leipzig, 1895), pp. 474–82. Dr. Voigt wrote a study of handicrafts in Karlsruhe for this series.

14 Voigt, op. cit., p. 37; *Jahresberichte der königlich-preussischen Regierungs- und Gewerberäthe und Bergbehörde*, 1903, p. 383.

15 Voigt, op. cit., pp. 30–7.

16 Ibid., pp. 37–8.

17 Ibid., p. 32.

18 The flavor of the debate and the rejection of the charges by industry can be experienced by reading Handelskammer zu Düsseldorf, ed., *Beiträge der Industrie zu den Kosten der Handwerksausbildung und Handwerkswohlfahrtspflege* (Düsseldorf, 1908), pp. 34–5.

19 *Jahresberichte*, 1903, pp. 382–3.

20 *Wohlfahrtseinrichtungen der Gusstahlfabrik von Fr. Krupp*, Bd. 1 (Essen, 1902), p. 148; Fritz Wegeleben, *Die Rationalisierung im deutschen Werkzeugmaschinenbau* (Berlin, 1924), pp. 113–15; Frölich, "Das Lehrlingswesen in der Industrie," in "Das Lehrlingswesen und die Berufserziehung," *Schriften der Zentralstelle für Volkswohlfahrt*, Heft 7 (Berlin, 1912), p. 384.

21 Frölich, op. cit., p. 179; *Jahresberichte der königlich-preussischen Regierungs- und Gewerberäthe*, 1906, p. 447; Otto Jeidels, *Die Methoden der Arbeiterentlöhnung in der rheinisch-westfälischen Eisenindustrie* (Berlin, 1907), pp. 72–3.

22 Jeidels, op. cit., pp. 76–7. In some plants the master received a portion of the apprentices' piece rates during the last year. HA Krupp WA VIII 85, Errinerungen von van Werden.

23 Heidrun Homburg, "Anfänge des Taylorsystems in Deutschland vor dem ersten Weltkrieg," *Geschichte und Gesellschaft*, 4, no. 2 (1978), pp. 173–4; Ernst Barth, *Entwicklungslinien der deutschen Maschinenbauindustrie von 1870 bis 1914* (East Berlin, 1973), pp. 52–7. For a case study

of the labor force of a machine factory that undertook extensive reorganization after the turn of the century, see Heilwig Schomerus, *Der Arbeiter der Maschinenfabrik Esslingen* (Stuttgart, 1977), p. 165, n. 177.

24 "Erfahrungen aus der Werksschule der Firma Ludw. Loewe & Co. A–G," *Technik und Wirtschaft*, 6, no. 12 (December 1913), p. 836; A. von Rieppel, "Lehrlingsausbildung und Fabrikschulen," *Technik und Wirtschaft*, 4, no. 3 (March 1911), p. 150, for the eighteen firms; for Düsseldorf, see Conrad Matschoss, *Ein Jahrhundert deutscher Maschinenbau, 1819–1919* (Berlin, 1922), pp. 259–60; Handelskammer zu Düsseldorf, op. cit., p. 54.

25 "Die Lehrwerkstatt der Gusstahlfabrik Essen," *Kruppsche Monatshefte* (January 1922), p. 51.

26 Ibid., p. 51; G. Lippart, "Die Ausbildung des Lehrlings in der Werkstätte," *Technik und Wirtschaft*, 5, no. 8 (August 1912), p. 515.

27 Clemens Heiss, "Auslese und Anpassung der Arbeiter in der Berliner Feinmechanik," *Schriften des Vereins für Sozialpolitik*, Bd. 134 (Leipzig, 1910), p. 193.

28 "Erfahrungen aus der Werksschule," pp. 837–8. For a defense along these lines written during the Weimar Republic, see Gertrude Tollkühn, *Die planmässige Ausbildung des gewerblichen Fabriklehrlings in der metall- und holzverarbeitende Industrie* (Jena, 1926) pp. 83–92.

29 "Erfahrungen aus der Werksschule," pp. 843–4; Lippart, op. cit., pp. 512–15. The following account of apprentice workshops relies heavily on Lippart.

30 "Erfahrungen aus der Werksschule," pp. 830–42; Matschoss, op. cit., p. 259. See also Wolf-Dietrich Greinert, *Schule als Instrument sozialer Kontrolle und Objekt privater Interessen: Der Beitrag der Berufsschule zur politischen Erziehung der Unterschichten.* (Hannover, 1975), p. 110–11. Although his observations are confined to the Weimar Republic, these claims for the superiority of vocational schools within firms, which he lists, were already well established before the war.

31 Schomerus, op. cit., pp. 163–4; Lippart, op. cit., pp. 504–5; HA Krupp WA IV 1408; Lehrlingswesen bei Fr. Krupp, 19.119.20.

32 Lippart, op. cit., p. 508; *Wohlfahrtseinrichtungen*, p. 148. For compensation, *Jahresbericht*, 1903, p. 386; *Jahresbericht*, 1906, p. 447.

33 "Pflege der schulentlassene weibliche Jugend," p. 8, Table 3. For the various cities, see pp. 12–13, esp. Table 5 on p. 13.

34 Ibid., p. 18.

35 Rosa Kempf, "Das Grossstadtmädchen der unteren Klassen," in *Handbuch für Jugendpflege* (Langensalza, 1913), pp. 26–8. For Kempf's early work, see Anthony Oberschall, *Empirical Social Research in Germany 1848–1914* (Paris, 1965), pp. 127–8. Kempf's contention about the origins of servant girls is confirmed by the excellent monograph by Dorothee Wierling, *Mädchen für alles: Arbeitsalltag und Lebensgeschichte Städtischer Dienstmädchen um die Jahrhundertwende* (Bonn, 1987), pp. 25–9.

36 Barbara Franzoi, *At the Very Least She Pays the Rent: Women and German Industrialization 1871–1914* (Westport, Conn., 1985), pp. 73–4; Franzoi, "Domestic Industry," in John C. Fout, ed., *German Women in the Nineteenth Century* (New York, 1984), p. 260.

37 "Pflege der schulentlassene weibliche Jugend," pp. 17–18.
38 Ibid., p. 16.
39 For women in clerical employment, see Carole E. Adams, *Women Clerks in Wilhelmine Germany* (New York, 1988), pp. 12–19.
40 Kempf, op. cit., p. 29.
41 Margarete Schecker, *Die Entwicklung der Mädchenberufsschule* (Weinheim, 1963), p. 79.
42 Although in 1907, 3.7 million married women between the ages of twenty-five and forty were primarily housewives with at most part-time employment for wages, almost 1.6 million married women in this age group held full-time jobs for wages. See "Pflege der schulentlassene weibliche Jugend," p. 21.
43 Voigt, op. cit., pp. 24–5.
44 Paul F. Lazarsfeld, ed., *Jugend und Beruf* (Jena, 1931), p. 7.
45 HSTAD (Kalkum) 33031, Jugendpflege 1915: #28, *Mitteilungen des Bezirksausschusses für Jugendpflege im Regierungsbezirk Düsseldorf,* 2 (1 April 1914), p. 36.
46 On age divisions within the Industrial Code, see Bittmann, op. cit., pp. 8–11. The fact that the law made youths over eighteen equivalent to adults in regard to protection of health and morals is made by Fuchs in his article, "Der Minderjährige im Rechte des Arbeitsverhältnisses," *Handbuch für Jugendpflege* (Langensalza, 1913), p. 147. I have relied heavily on these two sources in the account of youth protective legislation that follows.
47 On servants and household workers, Fuchs, op. cit., pp. 145–6, 158–60; p. 146 also lists the kinds of firms that were covered by the Industrial Code even though they employed fewer than ten workers, among them mines, brickyards, workshops involved with clothing, cleaning, or tobacco products, and ones with power-driven machinery.
48 For Wilhelm's February 1890 proclamation on reform of the Industrial Code and his position on social legislation, see Karl Erich Born, *Staat und Sozialpolitik seit Bismarcks Sturz* (Wiesbaden, 1957), pp. 10–30. For measures protecting youth discussed at the International Labor Protection Conference in Berlin in 1890, see p. 87. Among the measures adopted by conference participants were the elimination of night work and a ten-hour-day limit for youths under sixteen, although French and Belgian delegates opposed the latter.
49 Bittmann, op. cit., pp. 16–19. The quotes are taken from pp. 17 and 18.
50 Ibid., pp. 19–20. The question of paying wages directly to minors will be taken up in the context of discussions in the Evangelical Social Congress in the next chapter and in the chapter on youth policy during World War I.
51 Ibid., pp. 20–1.
52 Ibid., pp. 21–4.
53 Ibid., pp. 24–6.
54 Ibid., pp. 33–43.
55 Ibid., pp. 45–52.
56 Ibid., pp. 29–33; Fuchs, op. cit., pp. 54–6.
57 Fuchs, op. cit., p. 156.

Chapter 3, pp. 48–72

1 For the controversy surrounding Germany's transformation from an agrarian state to an industrial state, which certainly intersected with the youth question, see Kenneth P. Barkin, *The Controversy over German Industrialization 1890–1902* (Chicago, 1970). For brief accounts of these transformations as presented by leading youth savers, see *Die Verhandlungen des elften Evangelisch-sozialen Kongresses abgehalten zu Karlsruhe 7–8 Juni 1900* (Göttingen, 1900), p. 31; Paul Köhne, "Kriminalität und sittliches Verhalten der Jugendlichen," *Die jugendlichen Arbeiter in Deutschland: Schriften der Gesellschaft für Soziale Reform*, vol. 4 no. 2 (Jena, 1910), pp. 10–11; and quotes from the 1909 annual report of the Deutsche Zentrale für Jugendfürsorge in Hans Weicker, "Bildung und Erziehung ausserhalb der Schule," vol. 4, no. 4 (Jena, 1911), pp. 6–7, in the same series as the Köhne above.

2 Andreas Voigt, "Bericht über den zweiten Verhandlungstag 24 April 1900," *Fürsorge für die schulentlassene Jugend: Vorberichte und Verhandlungen der IX Konferenz: Schriften der Centralstelle für Arbeiter Wohlfahrtseinrichtungen*, Heft 16 (Berlin, 1900), pp. 318–19.

3 Alfred Kühne, "Die Fortbildungsschule," *Schriften der Gesellschaft für Soziale Reform*, vol. 4, no. 7 (Jena, 1912), p. 13.

4 For earlier critiques of the state of the working-class family and its relation to the youth problem, see Jürgen Reulecke, "Bürgerliche Sozialreformer und Arbeiterjugend im Kaiserreich," *Archiv für Sozialgeschichte*, 22 (1982), p. 315. See also Richard J. Evans, "Politics and the Family: Social Democracy and the Working-Class Family in Theory and Practice Before 1914," in Richard J. Evans and W. R. Lee, eds., *The German Family* (London, 1981), pp. 256–62. For an extensive presentation of the standard views on the working-class family held by the youth savers, see the Hamburg youth pastor, Walther Classen's, *Zucht und Freiheit: Ein Wegweiser für die deutsche Jugendpflege* (Munich, 1914), pp. 1–3; the comment below about the *Kneipen* appears on p. 2. For similar views expressed by contemporary youth savers, see Köhne, op. cit., p. 11; Weicker, op. cit., pp. 11–14. Andrew Lees, *Cities Perceived* (New York, 1985), pp. 158–60, contains a discussion of the concerns of German Protestant ministers, including Classen, about the dissolution of family life in the large city. For similar views of an English youth saver concerned about "boy labor," see Reginald Bray, "The Boy and the Family," in E. J. Urwick, ed., *Studies of Boy Life in Our Cities* (London, 1904), pp. 9–85.

5 Günther Dehn, *Grossstadtjugend*, 2nd ed. (Berlin, 1922), pp. 66–72. Dehn's book, the first edition of which was published in 1919, had been written during the war on the basis of his prewar experiences as a pastor in Berlin. It very much reflects the outlook of youth savers in late Imperial Germany. Dehn, however, lumps the scribes among the unskilled, whereas Classen, op. cit., pp. 17–19, lumps the *Schreiber* (scribes) and young *Kaufleute* (salespeople) together. Notably, both were pessimistic about the prospects for advancement of young white-collar workers from proletarian backgrounds, and both were critical of the deportment of

young white-collar workers, whom they considered to be superficial and frivolous.

6 Classen, op. cit., pp. 22–3; Dehn, op. cit., pp. 59–66; Otto Gerok, "Der Handwerkslehrling," *Die Entwicklungsjahre*, Heft 5 (Leipzig, 1913), pp. 37–41. Gerok's account, which is partially psychological, is somewhat less generous than those of the ministers. He, for example, notes the touchiness and moodiness of adolescent apprentices.

7 Classen, op. cit., pp. 23–4; Dehn, op. cit., pp. 72–83; Köhne, op. cit., pp. 10–11.

8 "Das Lehrlingswesen in der Industrie," *Das Lehrlingswesen und die Berufserziehung: Schriften der Zentralstelle für Volkswohlfahrt*, Heft 7 (Berlin, 1912), pp. 200–1.

9 Dehn, op. cit., pp. 82–92; Clemens Schultz, "Die Halbstarken," *Die Entwicklungsjahre*, Heft 2 (Leipzig, 1912), pp. 7, 12, 28–33. Schultz confessed difficulty in giving a definition to the *Halbstarken*, since he wanted to exclude vagabonds, jailbirds, and criminals. Although not quite as graphic as Dehn, he characterizes them as "sworn enemies of order" and describes them standing on street corners in torn clothes, spitting, swearing, and harassing passersby. See also the discussion of Schultz and the *Halbstarken* in Detlev Peukert, *Grenzen der Sozialdisziplinierung* (Cologne, 1986), pp. 63–6.

10 Dehn, op. cit., pp. 86–7.

11 Voigt, "Bericht," p. 320; "Eine systematische Verlotterung der Jugend," *Düsseldorfer Volksblatt*, 13 October 1899; "Fürsorge für die schulentlassene Jugend," *Düsseldorfer Volksblatt*, 31 May 1900; W. Henning, "Die Wohnungsfrage mit Bezug auf die männliche schulentlassene Jugend," *Schriften der Centralstelle für Arbeiterwohlfahrtseinrichtungen*, Heft 16 (Berlin, 1900), pp. 112–16.

12 See, for example, J. Kaup, "Schädigungen von Leben und Gesundheit der Jugendlichen," *Schriften der Gesellschaft für Soziale Reform*, vol. 4, no. 3 (Jena, 1911), pp. 8–9. For a critique of these statistics and their use, see the careful analysis by Max von Gruber, "Referat: Berufschutz der Jugendlichen," *Verhandlungen der 5. Generalversammlungen der Gesellschaft für Soziale Reform*, Heft 5, 6 (Jena, 1911), pp. 12–18. For worries about unfit one-year volunteers among gymnasia graduates after the turn of the century, see James C. Albisetti, *Secondary School Reform in Imperial Germany* (Princeton, 1983), p. 304.

13 Kaup, op. cit., pp. 10–11, for comparisons of mortality rates in England and Germany; pp. 24–40, for rates of sickness and injury in various branches of industry; pp. 7, 43, 50, for his conclusions about the dangers of industrial employments and urban streets.

14 Wilhelm Martius, "Die schulentlassene erwerbsarbeitende Jugend und der Alkohol," *Schriften der Centralstelle für Arbeiterwohlfahrtseinrichtungen*, Heft 16 (Berlin, 1900), pp. 174–5, 187–8.

15 Voigt, "Bericht," op. cit., pp. 336–7. For statistics, see the report of Max von Gruber, op. cit., pp. 37–9. In urban centers the percentage of twenty-year-old army recruits with venereal disease ranged from a high of 4.3 percent in Berlin to 1.24 percent in Essen. The average rate for the

entire Reich, however, was 0.73 percent. The average for adults was 4.54 percent in Berlin, 2.79 percent in the other seventeen cities with populations of more than 100,000, and 0.27 in the villages and countryside.

16 Andreas Voigt, "Die schulentlassene Jugend," *Schriften der Centralstelle für Arbeiterwohlfahrtseinrichtungen,* Heft 16 (Berlin, 1900), pp. 46–54; *Düsseldorfer Volksblatt,* 31 May 1900; Köhne, op. cit., pp. 4–9. The conviction rate for youth stabilized at about 7.4 per thousand after the turn of the century.

17 Eric A. Johnson and Vincent E. McHale, "Socioeconomic Aspects of the Delinquency Rate in Imperial Germany," *Journal of Social History* (Spring 1980), p. 398. The authors argue that youth crime rates were highest in areas with a high degree of interethnic tension, especially in the Polish/German areas of eastern Prussia and in areas with severely restricted social opportunities. They attribute the failings of previous analyses to the use of overly aggregated data. For another discussion and critique of the juvenile delinquency statistics in Imperial Germany, see Peukert, op. cit., pp. 82–4.

18 Schultz, op. cit., p. 14. Nonetheless, Schultz favored censoring or banning such literature, as well as obscene literature and immoral French and German dramas. For a series of crimes imputed to reading *Schundliteratur,* see "Schundliteratur und Jugend," *Düsseldorfer Tageblatt,* no. 71, 12 March 1911.

19 Köhne, op. cit., p. 15.

20 For the following discussion of youth savers and the SPD, see Fritz Kalle, "Das gewerbliche Fortbildungswesen," *Schriften des Vereins für Sozialpolitik,* 15 (Leipzig, 1879), p. 26. Martius, op. cit., p. 175; Voigt, "Bericht," p. 335; Classen, op. cit., pp. 29–33. It should be noted that Classen was writing after the formation of the Socialist youth movement. After its formation, youth savers tended to be much more pessimistic about prospects of cooperation with the SPD. Georg Kerschensteiner, "Staatsbürgerliche Erziehung der deutschen Jugend," in *Berufsbildung und Berufsschule: Ausgewählte Pädagogische Schriften,* Vol. 1 (Paderborn, 1966), pp. 11–12, 25–34. Kerschensteiner accepted the labor movement so long as it defended the particular interests of labor within capitalist society, but he opposed any attempt to transcend capitalist relations or overthrow the Wilhelmine state. For Kerschensteiner's relation to socialism in his electoral addresses for a Reichstag seat and elsewhere, see Wolf-Dietrich Greinert, *Schule als Instrument sozialer Kontrolle und Objekt privater Interessen: Der Beitrag der Berufsschule zur politischen Erziehung der Unterschichten.* (Hannover, 1975), pp. 83–4; Hugo Blitz, *Die Allgemein geistig-sittliche Fortbildung unserer Schulentlassene männlichen Volksjugend im obligatorischen Jugendvereine* (Lüneburg, 1901); Troeltsch, *Evangelisch-sozialen Kongresses,* pp. 32, 35–7, 46–50. For a discussion of distancing and partial cooperation with the Socialist labor movement in the Society for Social Reform, an organization to which many youth savers belonged, see Ursula Ratz, *Sozialreform und Arbeiterschaft* (Berlin, 1980), pp. 181–94.

21 Recent histories of education that have emphasized the social control

functions of the schools include Christa Berg, *Die Okkupation der Schule* (Heidelberg, 1973), and more explicitly Folkert Meyer, *Schule der Untertanen* (Hamburg, 1976). Other youth savers tended to emphasize the new experiences that young workers confronted after leaving primary school, rather than specific failures of the primary schools.

22 Troeltsch, *Evangelisch-sozialen Kongresses,* pp. 35–9. The Industrial Code made provision for the payment of wages directly to parents by local statute. Troeltsch pointed out, however, that most surveys showed that youths already handed over a substantial part of their wages to their parents; nor was there any guarantee that the parents would use the wages wisely.

23 Peukert, op. cit., p. 52.

24 Köhne, op. cit., p. 11; Fritz Wegleben, *Die Rationalisierung im deutschen Werkzeugmaschinenbau* (Berlin, 1924), pp. 101–2; Schrader, "Berufswahl und Berufswechsel," *Handbuch für Jugendpflege* (Langensalza, 1913), pp. 209–18.

25 For occupational counseling in Düsseldorf, see STAD III 2175, Fürsorge für die schulentlassense Jugend 1907–13; for the *Arbeitsnachweis* flyer, see #2, 11 January 1899; for the work of the Chamber of Commerce, see the letters of 16 March and 5 June 1908, #139; for the attitudes of artisans, see #302–3, 20 January and 13 February 1913. One school director characterized a job placement pamphlet produced by the Chamber of Handicrafts as being full of superficial judgments common to artisanal circles. For prewar plans supported by the Prussian government, see HSTAD (Kalkum) 33122, Berufsberatung und Lehrstellenvermittlung 1914–1919: Denkschrift of 24 July 1913, and the circular from the District Governor dated 6 August 1913. The Prussian government was attempting to crystallize the Cartel of Producing Estates.

26 William H. Dawson, *The German Workman* (New York, 1906), pp. 22–3.

27 Hellmuth Wolff, "Berufsberatung, Arbeitsnachweisse, Lehrstellenvermittlung," in *Handbuch für Jugendpflege* (Langensalza, 1913), p. 826.

28 See Kaup, op. cit., pp. 41–55, for a systematic presentation of these issues.

29 Ibid., pp. 54–5; Henning, op. cit., pp. 116–17; *Düsseldorfer Volksblatt,* 31 May 1900. For statistics on *Schlafstellen,* as well as their consequences for health and morals, see the report of City Councillor Wiedfeldt of Essen, "Versammlungsbericht," *Schlafstellenwesen und Ledigheime: Vorberichte und Verhandlungen der 13 Konferenz der Centralstelle für Arbeiterwohlfahrtseinrichtungen am 9. und 10. Mai 1904 in Leipzig* (Berlin, 1904), pp. 120–4. For young women in *Schlafstellen,* see Rosemary Orthmann, "Labor Force Participation, Life Cycle and Expenditure Patterns: The Case of Unmarried Female Factory Workers in Berlin (1902)," in Ruth Ellen Joeres and Mary Jo Maynes, eds., *German Women in the Eighteenth and Nineteenth Centuries* (Bloomington, Ind., 1986), pp. 29–33.

30 STAD III 2142, Bekämpfung des Schmutzes 1911–17: #23, letter of the District Governor of the Düsseldorf region providing guidelines for combating penny dreadfuls of 20 July 1909; #264, letter from the Essen Youth Literature Association on the role of Krupp and the lack of impact of this campaign, 1 February 1917. For the activities of teachers, see

#12, 114, 124, 184, 185, 191, and 197, including monitoring stores and setting up stalls in public markets, where they sold approved books during the Christmas shopping season.

31 "Die Bekämpfung der Schundliteratur," *Flugschriften der Zentralstelle für Volkswohlfahrt*, Heft 5 (Berlin, 1911), p. 7; the quote on censorship appears on p. 16. The pamphlet also considers some of the problems involved in defining *Schundliteratur* and some of the reasons for the appeal of penny dreadfuls (pp. 3–8).

32 On measures of the Dürerbund, see ibid., pp. 16–17. See also Gerhard Kratzsch, *Kunstwart und Dürerbund* (Göttingen, 1969), pp. 336–63, esp. pp. 343, 349.

33 For this and the following, see HSTAD (Kalkum) 9004, Kino: Letter of 24 January 1910 from the Düsseldorf police administration to the District Governor, and the censor's report on *Heisses Blut* with Asta Nielsen. HSTAD (Kalkum) 46077, Kino: Speech of 17 January 1912 by the police inspector of Duisberg at a police conference in Düsseldorf, in which he discusses the threat to respect for law and officialdom and censorship.

34 René Schwerdtfeger, "Vom Kinematographen-Zelt zum Burgtheater: Geschichte des Kinos in Kempen" (Kempen, 1967), pp. 5–7. For government circulars urging the film industry to produce commercially viable patriotic films, see STAD III 2142, Bekämpfung des Schmutzes: #28, 13 May 1911; STAD III 2178, Jugendpflege 1915–18: #395, 27 June 1917.

35 Peukert, op. cit., pp. 69–72.

36 Ibid., p. 72.

37 Ibid., pp. 72–7. The quote appears on p. 77.

38 Ibid., pp. 128–31; J. F. Landsberg, "Die öffentliche Erziehung der gefährdeten Jugend," *Einführung in das lebende Recht*, Heft 8 (Hannover, 1913), pp. v–vii, 6–7. Pp. 6–7 give the passages of the relevant laws on *Zwangserziehung* (forced education) and *Fürsorgeerziehung* (welfare education).

39 *Verhandlungen über die Wirksamkeit des Fürsorgeerziehungsgesetzes: Konferenz der Centralstelle für Jugendfürsorge in Berlin am 15. und 16. Juni 1906* (Berlin, 1906), pp. 8–9, 14, 26–30. Landesrat Gerhart and the teacher Sophie Lübke, who represented the social committee of Association of Women Primary School Teachers, cited the "hair-raising" cases of youths witnessing acts of prostitution and the like. City Councillor Münsterberg of Berlin dismissed the earlier fears of the SPD and Catholic Centrists. The jurists and Court Councillors Köhne and Kroner defended the Kammergericht's very narrow interpretation of this passage, largely on pragmatic grounds. Both Köhne and Kroner argued that if evidentiary criteria were relaxed, there would be two hundred thousand rather than thirty thousand minors in welfare education, and the entire system would be swamped.

40 Peukert, op. cit., pp. 87–96; Hagens, "Jugendgerichte," *Düsseldorfer Zeitung*, 28 May 1908. For a comprehensive examination of youth law and procedures in youth courts, including a number of case studies, see the pamphlet by the juvenile court judge in Lennep, J. F. Landsberg, "Das Jugendgericht," *Einführung in das lebende Recht*, Heft 3 (Hannover, 1912),

esp. pp. 50–4, the guidelines of the Prussian Minister of Justice in 1908. Technically, youth courts remained courts of lay assessors, with less formal procedures. For the U.S. inspiration, apart from Peukert, see Moritz Liepmann, *Die Kriminalität der Jugendlichen und ihre Bekämpfung*, (Tübingen, 1909), pp. 35–6.

41 Liepmann, op. cit., pp. 10–12; Köhne, op. cit., pp. 14–15.

42 L. Platz, "Welche Forderungen sind an die Anstaltserziehung und welche an die Familienerziehung zu stellen?" *Verhandlungen über die Wirksamkeit des Fürsorgeerziehunggesetzes*, p. 58; Liepmann, op. cit., pp. 2–3. For the Socialist position, see "Jugendgerichtstag," *Düsseldorfer Volkszeitung*, suppl. no. 242, 15 October 1912, which characterized youth courts as being based on *"die Umwertung des grundlegenden kriminalistischen Verantwortungsgedankens"* and also called for a youth court law.

43 Landsberg, "Jugendgericht," pp. 5–7, 9–12, 27.

44 Köhne, op. cit., p. 8. Of all youthful defendants in 1908, 4.2 percent were released because of lack of sufficient insight into the criminal character of their acts. But variation among regions was extremely high. In the Cologne Oberland, for example, almost 29 percent of all youth were let off for this reason. For the difficulties with the whole notion of sufficient insight, see Liepmann, op. cit., pp. 4–8.

45 Landsberg, "Jugendgericht," pp. 12–17. The legal basis for this discretion was a reform of 1895, which enabled judges to commute sentences, defer punishment, or grant a partial pardon if a convicted criminal agreed to some form of probationary supervision. Liepmann, op. cit., p. 31. For a criticism of the decline of jail sentences and the loss of a sense of individual responsibility, see the comments of Rektor Juethe in *Verhandlungen über die Wirksamkeit des Fürsorgeerziehungsgesetzes*, pp. 89–90. For the reply, in which it was argued that it was often experienced as worse punishment, see pp. 91–2. A similar point was made by Liepmann, p. 27. For a conservative attack on the new laxity see Peukert, op. cit., p. 90, for the comments by the Catholic theologian Friedrich Wilhelm Foerster.

46 Platz, op. cit., pp. 74–5. See also the comments of the Catholic priest Bartels on this question, also in *Verhandlungen über die Wirksamkeit des Fürsorgeerziehungsgesetzes*, pp. 79–83.

47 Platz, op. cit., pp. 59–74.

48 Peukert, op. cit., pp. 46–9.

49 Liepmann, op. cit., pp. 24–6; Platz, op. cit., pp. 74–5. Platz played down escapes, although according to Liepmann, the number of escapees had almost doubled between 1905 and 1906, from 5.2 to 10.1 percent.

50 Landsberg, "Die öffentliche Erziehung," pp. 3–4.

51 Platz, op. cit., pp. 64–9. For craft workshops in newly built "welfare education institutes," see *Rheinische Provincial Fürsorge-Erziehungsanstalten Rheindahlen und Solingen* (1906).

52 For a conservative critique, see the comments of Backhausen of Hannover in *Verhandlung über die Wirksamkeit des Fürsorgeerziehungsgesetzes*, p. 92. See also Dr. Osius, "Wie ist eine wirksame Aussicht über die Anstaltserziehung zu erzielen?" pp. 102–3, delivered at the same conference, for the desolate barrackslike rooms of some institutes. For a

relatively favorable sketch of a welfare education institute run by the Inner Mission of the Evangelical Church that nonetheless describes the pervasive grayness of the buildings, uniforms, and surroundings, see Landsberg, "Die öffentliche Erziehung," p. 1. See also Liepmann, op. cit., pp. 25–6, on closed institutions, with their walls and repressive regimes.

53 For the following, see Blitz, op. cit., pp. 38–56. For early proposals along these lines, see Reulecke, op. cit., pp. 316–17.
54 For a biography of Kerschensteiner that also gives an account of his other educational work and his influence, see Diane Simons, *Georg Kerschensteiner* (London, 1966).
55 Kerschensteiner, op. cit., pp. 14–20.
56 Ibid., pp. 22, 33–4, 43–8.
57 Greinert, op. cit., p. 80. For a discussion and critique of Kerschensteiner's concept of vocation, see also pp. 80–5. Klaus Harney, *Die Preussische Fortbildungsschule: Eine Studie zum Problem der Hierarchisierung beruflicher Schultypen im 19. Jahrhundert* (Weinheim, 1980), pp. 137–9, gives an analysis of Kerschensteiner's program for continuation schools.
58 Kerschensteiner, op. cit., pp. 37, 48–52, 73–9.
59 Ibid., pp. 26, 80–1.
60 *Schriften der Centralstelle*, #21, pp. 204–9, 219, 344–5.
61 STAD III 3629, Die gewerbliche Fortbildungsschule: #39 Circular of Government Councillor Post in the Ministry of Trade and Industry on the proclamation of 24 November 1901, in regard to post-school-age males. STAE Rep. 102 Abt. IX 166, Die Fortbildungsschule: Circular from the Trade Ministry of 3 August 1905. The circular of 1901 cited the work of the Center for Workers' Welfare Institutions and touted the youth work of the Protestant minister Clemens Schultz in Hamburg. STAD III 2175, Fürsorge für die schulentlassene Jugend 1907–13: #47, circular of the Education Ministry (Kultus) 24 October 1905. For the text of the 1901 circular issued jointly by the Trade, Education, and Interior ministries, see Wilhelm Weigle, "Der Einfluss der Jugendvereine auf die sittliche und religiöse Entwicklung der männliche Jugend" (Elberfeld, 1902), pp. 37–8.

Chapter 4, pp. 73–97

1 M. E. Sadler, "Compulsory Attendance at Continuation Schools in Germany," in M. E. Sadler, ed., *Continuation Schools in England and Elsewhere* (Manchester, 1907), p. 514.
2 Ibid. pp. 520–3. On the early history of the continuation school, see also Oskar Pache, *Handbuch des deutschen Fortbildungsschulwesens*, vol. 1 (Wittenberg, 1896), p. 21–4; Alfred Kühne, "Die Fortbildungsschule," in *Die jugendliche Arbeiter in Deutschland*, vol. 6, *Schriften der Gesellschaft für Soziale Reform* (Jena, 1912), pp. 5–9.
3 Kühne, op. cit., pp. 9–10, 17–21. There was already considerable debate in 1869 over whether or not the schools should be made obligatory for all young males who had completed elementary school. Similar debates

were held in Prussia in the early 1870s during the reforms of the elementary schools by the Prussian education minister, Adalbert Falk. Such universal education was generally rejected on economic grounds. For the early debates, see Klaus Harney, *Die preussische Fortbildungsschule: Eine Studie zum Problem der Hierarchisierung beruflicher Schultypen im 19. Jahrhundert* (Weinheim, 1980), pp. 66–73.

4 For the Gesellschaft für Verbreitung von Volksbildung and its work on behalf of continuation schools, see Wolf-Dietrich Greinert, *Schule als Instrument sozialer Kontrolle und Objekt privater Interessen: Die Beitrag der Berufsschule zur politischen Erziehung der Unterschichten* (Weinheim, 1975), pp. 26–32.

5 "Das gewerbliche Fortbildungsschulwesen," *Schriften des Vereins für Sozialpolitik*, vol. 15 (Leipzig, 1879), p. 26.

6 STAS J-5-1, Sonntags- und Fortbildungsschule 1836–88, May 1885. For the social protectionism of the 1880s, see Hans Rosenberg, *Grosse Depression und Bismarckzeit* (Berlin, 1967). In 1886 the Prussian government introduced a law in the Diet making continuation schools mandatory in the Posen district and parts of West Prussia with large Polish populations in order to Germanize Polish youth as well. See Greinert, op. cit., pp. 34–6.

7 Kühne, op. cit., pp. 10–11. Already, however, many master artisans in Berlin were hostile to continuation schools since they viewed them as a challenge to their educational prerogatives. See Shulamit Volkov, *The Rise of Popular Antimodernism in Germany* (Princeton, 1978), pp. 111–12.

8 STAS J-5-1, May 1885; *Verwaltungsbericht der Stadt Düsseldorf 1886–87*, p. 66. Making drawing instruction central to the continuation schools in Prussia had already been proposed to the education minister by the Standing Commission on Technical Education headed by Johannes von Miguel. This proposal was embodied in the new guidelines for continuing school education of 1884. See Harney, op. cit., pp. 83–5.

9 Herwig Blankertz, *Bildung im Zeitalter der grossen Industrie* (Hannover, 1969), pp. 127–8.

10 See, for example, "The Munich Trade Schools," in Georg Kerschensteiner, *The Schools and the Nation* (London, 1914), pp. 134–8.

11 Blankertz notes that until the 1920s, industrialists showed no interest in training their employees by methods other than those prevailing in the crafts, an indication of the lack of distinction, although because of the spread of apprentice workshops, discussed in Chapter 2, this needs to be qualified. See Blankertz, op. cit., p. 122.

12 Greinert, op. cit., pp. 63–75.

13 For the expansion and extension of the continuation schools throughout Germany, see Kühne, op. cit., pp. 11–14. Essen finally introduced an obligatory school in 1911. For the travails of the Essen school, see STAE Rep. 102 IX:178, Einführung des obligatorischen Forbildungsschule, pp. 1–4; *Essener Chronik 1911*, pp. 124–5.

14 See, for example, C. E. Stockton, "The Continuation Schools of Munich," in Sadler, op. cit., pp. 535–47; Arthur Shadwell, *Industrial Efficiency*, 2nd ed. (London, 1913), p. 613.

15 Kerschensteiner, "The Munich Trade Schools," in *The Schools and the*

Nation, p. 132. See also the comments of the Munich school inspector Schmid in "Die Fürsorge für die schulentlassene gewerbliche männliche Jugend: Vorberichte und Verhandlungen der X Konferenz vom 6. und 7. Mai 1901," *Schriften der Centralstelle für Arbeiterwohlfahrtseinrichtungen,* no. 21 (Berlin, 1901), pp. 202–6.

16 For Kerschensteiner's reorganization of the Munich continuation schools, see Kerschensteiner, "Munich Trade Schools," pp. 139–49; Stockton, op. cit., 536–47; Diane Simons, *Georg Kerschensteiner* (London, 1966), pp. 68–77.

17 "Unser Fortbildungsschulwesen," *Düsseldorfer Volksblatt,* 25 July 1898; *General Anzeiger,* 27 January, 16 February, and 23 March 1899.

18 *Verwaltungsbericht der Stadt Düsseldorf 1892–3,* p. 82; *Verwaltungsbericht der Stadt Düsseldorf 1899–1900,* p. 58. On pressure from the Trade Ministry in the Düsseldorf governmental district, see Harney, op. cit., pp. 91–2.

19 STAD III 3705, Einführung der obligatorischen Fortbildungsschule. Documents #36 to 58 are plans of continuation schools in other cities, for example, Dortmund and Dresden. Number 279: School Councillor Kessler, "Bericht über die Informations-reise nach Leipzig und Hannover," 4–10 December 1899. Number 285: School Councillor Kessler, "Die Neugestaltung der städtischen Fortbildungsschule zu Düsseldorf," pp. 1–25. The following account of the organization of the mandatory continuation school is based on the latter memorandum.

20 STAD III 3595, Die gewerbliche Fortbildungsschule 1891–1902: #161, "Vorschriften zur Regelung des Lehrlingswesens in Handwerksbetrieben," 1901. STAD III 3629, Die gewerbliche Fortbildungsschule: *Jahresbericht 1912–13,* p. 3. In 1912 the school's thirteen-man board included four master artisans, four factory owners, an engineer, an architect, the city school councillor, and the director of the continuation school. Five members also sat on the city council, among them two of the master artisans.

21 For an account of the discussion see the *Düsseldorfer Volksblatt,* 20 March 1901. For issues of hours and finance, see the *Düsseldorfer Zeitung,* 19 March 1901; *Verwaltungsbericht der Stadt Düsseldorf 1900–1,* p. 65; *Verwaltungsbericht der Stadt Düsseldorf 1903–4,* p. 80.

22 For costs and financial difficulties in Düsseldorf, see *Verwaltungsbericht der Stadt Düsseldorf 1901–2,* p. 73; *Verwaltungsbericht der Stadt Düsseldorf 1902–3,* p. 83; *Verwaltungsbericht der Stadt Düsseldorf 1913–14,* p. 73; STAD III 3629, Die gewerbliche Fortbildungsschule: *Jahresbericht 1913–14,* p. 16. For Munich, see Kerschensteiner, "The Munich Trade Schools," pp. 149–51. For general costs and problems throughout Germany, see Kühne, op. cit., pp. 26–9. Kühne estimated that the annual cost of continuation schools in Germany by 1911 was twenty-two million marks.

23 For the finances of the Prussian continuation schools, see Harney, op. cit., pp. 73–6.

24 *Verwaltungsbericht der Stadt Düsseldorf 1910–11,* p. 64. On the difficulties of holding classes in primary schools, see Oskar Pache, "Das Deutsche Fortbildungsschulwesen der Gegenwart," in *Handbuch des deutschen Fortbildungsschulwesens,* vol. 1 (Wittenberg, 1896), p. 37, and the report of

the Prussian Industrial Bureau quoted in Curt Kohlmann, *Fabrikschulen* (Berlin, 1911), p. 55. The industrial bureau considered the smallness of the benches especially detrimental for drawing instruction.

25 STAD III 3641, Lehr-und Lernmittel bei der Fortbildungsschule: #184, letters by Gotter, 2 December and 23 December 1908. Numbers 188 and 190 contain lists and costs of equipment. Despite being impressed by the Munich continuation schools, Trade Minister Rudolf Delbrück had previously been hesitant to support the sort of workshop instruction instituted in Munich because of the expense during Prussia's serious fiscal crisis of 1907–8. See Harney, op. cit., p. 139.

26 *Verwaltungsbericht der Stadt Düsseldorf 1902–3*, p. 81; *Verwaltungsbericht der Stadt Düsseldorf 1912–13*, p. 72. For teaching in Munich, see Kerschensteiner, "The Munich Trade Schools," p. 149, and for general problems of teachers, see Kühne, op. cit., pp. 41–3.

27 *Verwaltungsbericht der Stadt Düsseldorf 1903–4*, p. 80.

28 *Verwaltungsbericht der Stadt Düsseldorf 1911–12*, p. 70.

29 Greinert, op. cit., pp. 112–13.

30 Oskar Pache, "Ueber Gründung, Einrichtung und Leitung von Fortbildungsschulen," in *Handbuch des deutschen Fortbildungsschulwesens*, Vol. 5 (Wittenberg, 1900), pp. 59–61.

31 See, for example, the photographs in Kerschensteiner, *The Schools and the Nation*, after pp. 314, 316, and 318.

32 Schmid, op. cit., p. 203.

33 STAD III 3629, Die gewerbliche Fortbildungsschule 1908–11: *Jahresbericht 1902–3*, p. 74.

34 STAD III 3629, Die gewerbliche Fortbildungsschule 1908–11: #187, "Ueber die Benutzung des Adressbuches im Fortbildungsschule," p. 6.

35 For absentee rates, see STAD III 3629, Die gewerbliche Fortbildungsschule: *Jahresbericht 1907–8*, p. 22; *Jahresbericht 1909–10*, pp. 20–2, esp. p. 22 for the quote on types of absentees.

36 STAD III 3711, Die nebenamtlich beschäftigten Lehrer bei der Fortbildungsschule 1904–6: #33, letter of 4 November 1904 by Josef Weber on his first year of teaching, both for the report on disruptive behavior and for the *Katzenmusik* episode. For students sitting crosswise at their desks, see #39, the letter of Lachmann in response to a complaint by the mother of a student.

37 See the decree of the Ministry of Trade and Commerce dated 31 August 1899, translated and reprinted in Sadler, op. cit., p. 528, which also discusses other disciplinary problems and ways to deal with them.

38 STAD III 3711, Die nebenamtlich beschäftigten Lehrer bei der Fortbildungsschule 1904–6: #33, letter of 4 November 1904 by Josef Weber.

39 See, for example, the general paradigm and the Leipzig school order in Oskar Pache, "Ueber Gründung," pp. 34–7. For the Düsseldorf school order, see *Verwaltungsbericht der Stadt Düsseldorf 1901–2*, p. 74. On the mechanisms of normalization in institutions like schools, see Michel Foucault, *Discipline and Punish: The Birth of the Prison* (New York, 1979), pp. 184–94.

40 STAD III 3629, Die gewerbliche Fortbildungsschule: #24, *Jahresbericht 1904*, pp. 35–7.

41 STAD III 3629, Die gewerbliche Fortbildungsschule: *Jahresbericht 1910–11*, p. 20; STAD III 3613, Schulzucht bei der Fortbildungsschule: Order of School Councillor Kessler of 7 May 1907. See also the interview with Kerschensteiner by Stockton, op. cit., p. 545.

42 For Gotter's discussions of corporal punishment, see STAD III 3605, Die gewerbliche Fortbildungsschule 1911–14: #123, note by Gotter in response to the accusation by a garden architect against the teacher Lind that his apprentice had been whipped, 31 July 1912. For the firing of the teacher Bleylevens for excessive use of corporal punishment, see STAD III 3606, Die gewerbliche Fortbildungsschule 1914: #152–62, esp. #161–2, 22 October 1914.

43 STAD III 3705, Einführung der obligatorischen Fortbildungsschule: #180, "Vorschriften für die Ausstellung von Lehrplänen und das Lehrverfahren an dem von Staat unterstützten gewerblichen Fortbildungsschule," Berlin, 5 July 1897, p. 3.

44 Schmid, op. cit., p. 203.

45 *Verwaltungsbericht der Stadt Düsseldorf 1901–2*, p. 75; STAD III 3629, Die gewerbliche Fortbildungsschule: *Jahresbericht 1902–3*, pp. 2–6. For the new commercial continuation school, see *Verwaltungsbericht der Stadt Düsseldorf 1906–7*, p. 91.

46 *Verwaltungsbericht der Stadt Düsseldorf 1914–18*, p. 126; STAD III 3629, Die gewerbliche Fortbildungsschule: #108, *Jahresbericht 1913–14*, p. 16.

47 See Greinert, op. cit., p. 92, for this sort of conclusion.

48 *Verwaltungsbericht der Stadt Düsseldorf 1905–6*, p. 105; *Verwaltungsbericht der Stadt Düsseldorf 1914–18*, p. 92; STAD III 3606, Die gewerbliche Fortbildungsschule 1914: #154, 160.

49 STAD III 3629, Die gewerbliche Fortbildungsschule: *Jahresbericht 1913–14*, pp. 28–36. The electrical laboratory was completed in 1912. The course for electrotechnicians focused on measurements of current and resistance (Ohm's Law), circuitry, and electromagnetism.

50 Shadwell, op. cit., p. 613.

51 "Ausstellung der obligatorischen Fortbildungsschule," *Düsseldorfer General Anzeiger*, 25 March 1905.

52 STAD III 3629, Die gewerbliche Fortbildungsschule: *Jahresbericht 1911–12*, p. 20. See also Kühne, op. cit., pp. 35–6.

53 Kühne, op. cit., p. 36; STAD III 3629, Die gewerbliche Fortbildungsschule: *Jahresbericht 1907–8*, p. 13.

54 STAD III 3609, Lehrpläne: #68, "Geschäftskunde," p. 1. For an analysis of the content of textbooks oriented toward craft apprentices used in the industrial continuation schools, see Greinert, op. cit., pp. 92–100.

55 Kühne, op. cit., p. 36.

56 STAD III 3609, Lehrpläne: #68, "Geschäftskunde," p. 1. For the *Heimatschutz* movement, see Christian F. Otto, "Modern Environment and Historical Continuity: The Heimatschutz Discourse in Germany," *Art Journal*, 43, no. 2 (Summer 1983), pp. 148–54. *Heimatkunde*, by contrast, which was taught in the primary schools, focused on local flora, fauna, and geography – *natur naturans*, rather than humanized nature and historically generated human environments. For the distinction between

the teaching of *Heimatkunde* in the primary schools and that in the continuation schools, see Harney, op. cit., pp. 132–3.

57 STAD III 3629, Die gewerbliche Fortbildungsschule: *Jahresbericht 1914–15*, pp. 117–18; *Jahresbericht 1902–3*, p. 16, for attendance at the industrial exposition. See also STAD III 3604, Die gewerbliche Fortbildungsschule 1908–11: #187, "Ueber die Benutzung des Adressbuches," p. 6.

58 STAD III 3610, Lehrpläne: #95–100, the plans for the classes of butchers and machine builders.

59 See Kerschensteiner, "The Munich School System," in *The Schools and the Nation*, pp. 322–23.

60 Oskar Pache, "Die aus den Forderungen der Gegenwart sich ergebenden Aufgaben der Fortbildungsschule," in *Handbuch der Fortbildungsschulwesens*, Teil 7 (Wittenberg, 1905), pp. 3–6. Some doctors, such as Loquer of Frankfurt, believed that sex education was necessary in continuation school in order to prevent venereal disease, since most of the students were already sexually active. See also Ignaz Kaup, "Schädigungen von Leben und Gesundheit der Jugendlichen," in *Die jugendlichen Arbeiter in Deutschland*, 3, *Schriften der Gesellschaft für Soziale Reform* (Jena, 1911), pp. 43–8, in which he recommends half days of release from work for gymnastics and recreation, in part because of declining fitness for military service.

61 STAD III 3629, Die gewerbliche Fortbildungsschule: *Jahresbericht 1904–5*, p. 33.

62 STAE Rep. 102 IX 166, Fortbildungsschule: #138, Trade Ministry circular of 3 August 1905; STAE Rep. 102 IX 377, Fürsorge für die schulentlassene männliche Jugend 1910–12: #2–4, "Ratgeber für Jugendvereinigungen," August 1911, pp. 70–1.

63 STAD III 3629, Die gewerbliche Fortbildungsschule: *Jahresbericht 1904–5*, pp. 8, 25, 33–4; *Jahresbericht 1907–8*, pp. 23–25; *Jahresbericht 1908–9*, pp. 26–7. STAD III 3602, Die gewerbliche Fortbildungsschule 1905–7: letter to the board on the Worker Gymnasts by Dr. Kuypers of 8 February 1906. At the continuation school graduation ceremony, a municipal doctor delivered a lecture on the dangers of premature sexual relations, a lecture that sometimes sparked opposition from parents and employers.

64 STAD III 3629, Die gewerbliche Fortbildungsschule: *Jahresbericht 1904–5*, p. 8.

65 STAD III 3629, Die gewerbliche Fortbildungsschule: *Jahresbericht 1910–11*, pp. 22–4. For the government's desire to use continuation schools to combat *Schundliteratur*, see STAD III 2142, Bekämpfung des Schmutzes 1911–19: #23, letter of 20 July 1909 from the district governor to all county commissioners (*Landräte*), lord mayors, and mayors.

66 HSTAD (Kalkum) 8921, *Verzeichnis politische Zeit- und Flugschriften*: Editorial clipped from *Das Rheinische Handwerk* on the proposed continuation school law being considered in the Prussian Diet during 1911. The paper was characterized as politically unaffiliated but inclining to the Center party. See also "Das Lehrlingswesen in Handwerk," *Schriften der Zentralstelle für Volkswohlfahrt* (Leipzig, 1912), pp. 104–5.

67 Kerschensteiner, "The Munich Trade Schools," p. 139.

68 *Jahresbericht der Handwerkskammer zu Düsseldorf 1903–4*, p. 68; STAD
    III 3629, Die gewerbliche Fortbildungsschule: #90, *Jahresbericht 1907–
    8*, p. 10. The first assembly of the Prussian Continuation School Asso-
    ciation in December 1906 was entirely taken up, however, with arti-
    sanal opposition to these schools. See the *Düsseldorfer Zeitung*, 1
    January 1907.
69 *Düsseldorfer Zeitung*, 14 June 1909; STAD III 3577, Schulfeste: letter of
    Gotter, 22 July 1911; Kohlmann, op. cit., pp. 82–3.
70 STAD III 3629, Die gewerbliche Fortbildungsschule: *Jahresbericht 1909–
    10*, p. 20; *Jahresbericht 1911–12*, p. 23; STAD III 3613, Schulzucht bei
    der Fortbildungsschule 1908–16: letter by Gotter to the lord mayor, 30
    September 1910, concerning revocation of licenses.
71 STAD III 3611, Die gewerbliche Fortbildungsschule: *Das Rheinische
    Handwerk*, 25 November 1911, pp. 2–4. The quote appears on p. 3.
    At the time the school was under consideration in 1900, the United
    Guilds had requested permission to participate in the deliberations,
    but the committee had primarily consulted the Chamber of Handi-
    crafts. See STAD III 3705, Einführung der obligatorischen Fortbil-
    dungsschule: #275, letter of 16 June 1900 to the city from the
    Innungs Ausschuss der vereinigten Innungen zu D. As the Prussian
    government began considering the new law, the national Bund der
    Handwerker also issued a pamphlet entitled, "Das Fortbildungsschule
    als Gefahr für Industrie und Handwerk." On this, see Kohlmann, op.
    cit., pp. 1–2.
72 STAD III 3611, Die gewerbliche Fortbildungsschule: #72–4, Gotter's
    reply to the United Guilds, 9 February 1912, including the comment
    that it was not surprising that most apprentices could not write, given
    the abilities of most craftsmen. #105, *Jahresbericht 1912–13*, Schlusswort.
    For sentiments on the nature of *Mittelstandpolitik* similar to Gotter's ex-
    pressed by Kerschensteiner in the Reichstag, see Greinert, op. cit.,
    pp. 82–3. Kerschensteiner went so far as to assert that, not social pro-
    tectionism, but the "continuation school is the best *Mittelstandspolitik*."
73 Greinert, op. cit., p. 74.
74 *Verwaltungsbericht der Stadt Düsseldorf 1910–11*, p. 63; STAD III 3629,
    Die gewerbliche Fortbildungsschule: #102, *Jahresbericht 1911–12*,
    p. 24.
75 *Jahresbericht der königliche-preussischen Regierungs- und Gewerberäthe und
    Bergbchörde 1902*, p. 324.
76 Friedrich Frölich, "Das Lehrlingswesen in der Industrie," *Technik und
    Wirtschaft*, 2, no. 9 (September, 1911), pp. 598–602.
77 STAD III 3662, Die kaufmännische Fortbildungsschule: #37–8, letters
    of Karl Jaeger, 23 May and 15 June 1912.
78 *Prussia Landtag: Haus der Abgeordneten, Stenographische Berichte über die
    Vehandlungen*, session 59, vol. 4 (Berlin, 1911), pp. 5265–6.
79 On the role of businessmen in Düsseldorf's city government, see Fred-
    erick C. Howe, *European Cities at Work* (New York, 1913), pp. 243–51.
    Greinert, op. cit., pp. 67, 110–11, accuses large industry of having been
    passive on questions of the continuation schools and vocational schools
    until the 1920s. But it was only when the municipal three-class electoral

system was abolished that they needed to organize more openly in defense of their interests.

80 *Prussia Landtag.* For Trade Minister von Sydow's defense of the bill, see pp. 5205–11; for the fiscal concerns of the National Liberals, see pp. 5235–6; for the need to meet the needs of industry, see p. 5239; for the Progressive position, see pp. 5244–7; for the SPD, see the comments by Hirsch on pp. 5259–60. The need for religious instruction was passionately defended by the Conservative spokesman, Hammer (pp. 5214–15), and the Center spokesman, Schmedding of Münster (pp. 5223–6), among others, whereas the most passionate denunciation of proposals for mandatory religious instruction, which the Trade Ministry opposed, came from Schepp of the Progressives (pp. 5278–9). The Free Conservative Vorster took up the cudgels on behalf of the textile industry and against placing instruction during working hours (pp. 5271–2).

81 "Fortbildungsschule, Religionsunterricht und Handwerk," *Düsseldorfer Tageblatt*, 8 June 1911. After considerable controversy with the school, priests finally obtained the right to introduce voluntary religious instruction for Catholic students in 1908. See STAD III 3629, Die gewerbliche Fortbildungsschule: *Jahresbericht 1907–8*, p. 25.

82 Kühne, op. cit., pp. 16, 40–1; Greinert, op. cit., pp. 40–1; Harney, op. cit., pp. 110–16.

83 On general questions of religious instruction, see Pache, "Ueber Gründung," pp. 50–54. See also *Prussia Landtag*, pp. 5227–30, for von Sydow's objections to religious instruction. First, he thought imposing such instruction by force would be counterproductive; second, confessional instruction would carry over religious differences into areas where they were not appropriate.

84 See Johannes Tews, *Sozialdemokratie und öffentliches Bildungswesen* (Langensalza, 1919), pp. 51–2.

85 Oskar Pache, "Die aus den Forderungen der Gegenwart," pp. 4–5; STAD III 3602, Die gewerbliche Fortbildungsschule 1905–7: #113, letter of Kuypers to the board, 8 February 1906.

86 Quoted in Greinert, op. cit., p. 85.

87 Heinrich Schulz, *Gehörst du zu uns?* (Berlin, 1911), p. 12; *Metallarbeiterzeitung*, 8 August 1908, p. 249; *Arbeiter-Jugend*, 17 July 1909, p. 147. See the attacks on the standard Prussian civics text by the socialist deputy Hirsch in *Prussia Landtag*, p. 5261.

88 Sadler, "German Continuation Schools," in Sadler, ed., op. cit., p. 524. Sadler's entire book was a plea for industrial continuation schools in England. Shadwell, op. cit. See Viscount Haldane's Introduction to Kerschensteiner, *The Schools and the Nation*, pp. xv–xxiv; E. J. T. Brennan, ed., *Education for National Efficiency: The Contribution of Sidney and Beatrice Webb* (London, 1975), pp. 119–20; D. M. Thoms, "The Emergence and Failure of the Day Continuation School Experiment," *History of Education*, 4, no. 1 (Spring 1975), pp. 36–49, esp. pp. 39–40 for the German influence and the quote from the *Morning Post*.

89 See, for example, the assessment by Günther Dehn, *Grossstadtjugend*, 2nd ed. (Berlin, 1922), p. 12.

Chapter 5, pp. 98–117

1 For clerical responses to the continuation schools, see, for example, August Pieper, "Die Thätigkeit der katholischen Vereine in der Fürsorge für die schulentlassene männliche gewerbsthätige Jugend," in *Die Fürsorge für die schulentlassene gewerbliche männliche Jugend: Vorberichte und Verhandlungen der X Konferenz vom 6. und 7. Mai 1901: Schriften der Centralstelle für Arbeiterwohlfahrtseinrichtungen*, no. 21 (Berlin, 1901), pp. 107–8; Günther Dehn, *Grossstadtjugend*, 2nd ed. (Berlin, 1922), p. 12.

2 John R. Gillis, *Youth and History: Tradition and Change in European Age Relations 1770 to the Present* (New York, 1974), p. 149; Michael Mitterauer, *Sozialgeschichte der Jugend* (Frankfurt am Main, 1986), p. 219; C. Fritsch, "Die Thätigkeit der Inneren Mission auf dem Gebiete der Fürsorge für die heranwachsende gewerbliche männliche Jugend," in *Schriften der Centralstelle*, no. 21, pp. 71–2.

3 Karl Kupisch, *Der deutsche CVJM* (Kassel, 1958), pp. 22–36.

4 Fritsch, op. cit., pp. 83, 86–9, 97–105.

5 Ibid., pp. 72, 88–92. In 1900 regional associations like the West German Youth Federation and South German Youth Federation united to form the loose national Organization of German National Committees.

6 Quoted in ibid., p. 71. See also pp. 72–4.

7 *Der Leuchtturm*, 6 March 1904; 29 January 1911. Copies are to be found in the CVJM archive in Wuppertal.

8 Fritsch, op. cit., pp. 74–5.

9 Ibid., pp. 79–81. Pp. 80–1 give full programs for a number of the family fests sponsored by youth associations. The one commemorating Kaiser Wilhelm I was divided into four parts, each treating a different phase of his life: his youth, the initial period of German unification between 1861 and 1870, the final year of unification, 1871, and his rule as kaiser of the new Reich, each with hymns, recitals, and poems.

10 Ibid., pp. 76–8.

11 Walter Stursberg, *Glauben, Wagen, Handeln* (Wuppertal, 1977), p. 138; "Referat über das königlichen Konsitoriums betr. Jugendpflege," *Protokoll über die Verhandlungen des Kreis Synode Düsseldorf*, 26 June 1912, p. 51.

12 Pastor Haarbeck, *Was können und müssen die kirchlichen Organe für ein tatkräftige Pflege und Erziehung der konfirmierten Jugend tun?* (Moers, 1911), p. 11.

13 See Fritsch, op. cit., p. 72, for the figures in 1900, and Hildegard Böhme, "Zentral-Organisationen und Organe," in *Handbuch für Jugendpflege* (Langensalza, 1913), p. 528, for 1912.

14 *Die Verhandlungen des elften Evangelisch-sozialen Kongresses abgehalten zu Karlsruhe, 7–8 Juni 1900* (Göttingen, 1900), pp. 16–17.

15 Rector Christmann, "Welche Aufgabe stellt die in der Gegenwart besonders rege beteiligende Bewegung für Jugendpflege den Geistlichen und Gemeindeorganen?" *Protokoll über die Verhandlungen der Kreis Synode Düsseldorf*, 26 June 1912, pp. 8–12.

16 STAE Rep. 102 IX 377a, Fürsorge für die schulentlassene männliche

Jugend, 1912–13: "Das Jahrhundert der Jugend: Jahrbuch des West-deutschen Jugendbundes," pp. 36–7. Throughout the Rhine–Ruhr region, the West German Youth Federation had 13,468 members between the ages of fourteen and twenty-five, of which half were under seventeen. Of these, almost 5,000 were blue-collar workers, 5,000 were craft workers, over 2,000 were commercial employees, 472 were officials, and the rest was diverse.

17 "Referat über das königlichen Konsistoriums betr. Jugendpflege," pp. 49–65.

18 Ibid., p. 67; *Düsseldorfer Volkszeitung*, 25 March 1913.

19 *Protokoll über die Verhandlungen der Kreis Synode Düsseldorf*, 18 June 1913, pp. 45–6.

20 Dehn, op. cit., pp. 52–7. The first quote below appears on p. 53; the lengthier one, on p. 56.

21 Walther Classen, *Vom Lehrjungen zum Staatsbürger* (Hamburg, 1909); Clemens Schulz, *Gessamelte Schriften eines Jugendpflegers* (Berlin, 1918), for accounts of their work, tribulations, and opposition within the church. See also Jürgen Reulecke, "Bürgerliche Sozialreformer und Arbeiterjugend im Kaiserreich," *Archiv für Sozialgeschichte* 22 (1982), pp. 321–3; Detlev Peukert, *Grenzen der Sozialdisziplinierung* (Cologne, 1986), p. 112.

22 STAE Rep. 102 IX 377a, Fürsorge für die schulentlassense männliche Jugend 1910–12: "Das Jahrhundert der Jugend," pp. 36–9, for statistics on membership and social composition.

23 For Weigle's life and work, see Walther Börner, *Wilhelm Weigle: Leben und Wirken 1862–1932* (Gladbeck, 1974), pp. 8–27, 49–57. The book is an encomium.

24 The following account is based on Wilhelm Weigle, "Nützliches und Schädliches auf dem Arbeitsgebiet der Jugendvereine," *Stein zum Bau*, 1, no. 2 (1907), pp. 6–14.

25 For the activities of the Essen group, see "Geschichte des Evangel.-Jugendvereine Essen/Ruhr" (1913?), pp. 33–6, found in the STAE and STAE Rep. 102 IX 377a, Fürsorge für die schulentlassense männliche Jugend: "Bericht des evangelischen Jugendvereins Essen/Ruhr 1907," pp. 1–14. The entire youth association was supposed to take communion together on Lent Sunday, but this religious observance was attended by only three hundred youths, whereas over eight hundred participated in the summer war games.

26 For the role of the Krupps in Essen, see Emil Kromberg, *Politische Strömungen und Wahlen in der Stadt und Landkreis Essen von der November Revolution bis zur Reichtagswahl von Dezember 1924* (Bonn, dissertation, 1968), p. 16. For urban statistics and the denominational division, see *Statistisches Jahrbuch der Stadt Essen 1907*, p. 8.

27 HAEK Gen. Tit. XXIII, Generalsekretariat der Jugendvereine 1908–1919: letter from Karl Mosterts to Archbishop Dr. Felix Hartmann, 30 April 1913.

28 For an overview of the *Kulturkampf* and its effects on the political and organizational life of German Catholics, see Karl-Egon Lönne, *Politischer Katholizismus im 19. und 20. Jahrhundert* (Frankfurt, 1986), pp. 151–80.

29 For the case of Düsseldorf, see Mary Nolan, *Social Democracy and Society: Working-class Radicalism in Düsseldorf 1890–1920* (Cambridge, 1981), pp. 28–30.

30 These divisions are treated extensively in Ronald J. Ross, *Beleaguered Tower* (Notre Dame, 1976), pp. 134–9. For the *Volksverein*, see Horstwalter Heitzer, *Der Volksverein für das katholische Deutschland im Kaiserreich 1890–1918* (Mainz, 1979). For a more recent, more complex and extensive treatment of the political and social divisions within the Center party and their effects on party policy, see Wilifried Loth, *Katholiken im Kaiserreich* (Düsseldorf, 1984). See also Eric Dorn Brose, *Christian Labor and the Politics of Frustration in Imperial Germany* (Washington, D.C., 1985), 253–84.

31 For the early history of Catholic youth work, see Pieper, op. cit., p. 109. For the Kolpingsvereine and effects of early youth sodalities, see Jonathan Sperber, *Popular Catholicism in Nineteenth Century Germany* (Princeton, 1984), pp. 85–92; Brose, op. cit., pp. 25–7.

32 For Drammer, see Karl Brüls, *Geschichte des Volksvereins*, vol. I, 1890–1914 (Münster, 1960), p. 17. For the process of centralization, see HAEK Gen. Tit. XXIII, Generalsekretariat der Jugendvereine 1908–1919: Karl Mosterts, "Die Verbandzentrale der katholischen Junglingvereinigunen Deutschlands 1908–1918," p. 1. Further, Karl Mosterts, "Verband der katholischen Junglingsvereinigunen Deutschlands," in Herta Siemering, ed., *Die deutschen Jugendpflegeverbände* (Berlin, 1918), pp. 134–46. See Pieper, op. cit., pp. 110–12, for the 1899 statistics, and Siemering for the 1908 statistics. If Catholic associations for journeymen and commercial clerks were included in 1899, Catholic youth membership figures would reach 234,000.

33 See August Pieper, *Jugendfürsorge und Jugendvereine* (Mönchen-Gladbach, 1908), pp. 47–50, for the early history of Catholic youth work.

34 HAEK Gen. Tit. XXIII, Generalsekretariat der Jugendvereine 1908–1919: letter from Karl Mosterts to Archbishop Dr. Hartmann, 30 April 1913.

35 The above account of the various Catholic parish youth associations in Düsseldorf are based on the annual reports found in HSTAD (Kalkum) 33031, Jugendpflege 1915.

36 Karl Mosterts, *Die seelsorgische Vorbereitung auf die Schulentlassung* (Düsseldorf, 1916), pp. 15–16; Mosterts, "Verband," pp. 150–1; Pieper, *Jugendfürsorge*, p. 62.

37 Mosterts, "Verband," pp. 149–50. Ludwig Nieder, "Wie erziehe ich die heranwachsende gewerbliche Jugend zu Glaubensverteidigung und Apostelsinn?" in Karl Mosterts, ed., *Jünglingsseelsorge* (Freiburg, 1920), pp. 55–6. This contribution was originally delivered as a lecture in Düsseldorf during the war.

38 Pieper, *Jugendfürsorge*, pp. 65, 129–30; Mosterts, "Verband," p. 161. Mosterts denied any direct dependency of the Center party but wrote of the congruency of outlook on religious issues.

39 HSTAD (Kalkum) 33031, Jugendpflege 1915: "Jahresbericht des Junglingsvereins 'Aloysianisches Bundnis' St. Rochus."

40 For the content of the lectures that follow, see Volksverein für das kath-

olische Deutschland, ed *Die Jugend: Vorträge für Jugendvereine* (Mönchen-Gladbach, 1909), pp. 97–115. A comprehensive account of Catholic critiques of socialism in the nineteenth and earlier twentieth centuries, including those of August Pieper and the Volksverein, is Walter Friedberger, *Die Geschichte der Sozialismusmkritik im katholischen Deutschland zwischen 1830 und 1914* (Frankfurt am Main, 1978), pp. 155–64.

41 "Krieg oder Frieden?" *Die Wacht*, 1 July 1910; "Wer will unter die Soldaten?" *Die Wacht*, 1 September 1910; "Von Rechten des Staatsbürger" and "Jugendschutz durch die Gewerbeordnung," *Die Wacht*, 1 August 1911. For a celebration of the kaiser, see the issue commemorating his twenty-fifth jubilee and the one hundredth anniversary of the War of Liberation, *Die Wacht*, no. 6, June 1913.

42 For recreational activities of youth groups, see Karl Mosterts, ed., *Handbuch für die Katholiken Düsseldorfs* (Düsseldorf, 1909), p. 147. HAEK Gen. Tit. XXIII, Generalsekretariat der Jugendvereine: meeting of 1 December 1915 in Kaiserwerth. On the Catholic attitude toward plays in youth associations, see Pieper, *Jugendfürsorge*, p. 257.

43 HAEK Gen. Tit. XXIII, Generalsekretariat der Jugendvereine: resolution passed in Essen, 6 July 1910.

44 "Sport und Roheit," *Die Wacht*, 15 September 1910. During the war apparently some priests urged young members to quit sports clubs. See the letter of complaint from the Association of Düsseldorf Gymnasts, 16 August 1916, in HAEK XXIII Generalsekretariat der Jugendvereine.

45 Pieper, "Thätigkeit," pp. 113–14, 120–7, 137–47.

46 For a full discussion of the *Gewerkschaftstreit*, see Michael Schneider, *Die Christlichen Gewerkschaften* (Bonn, 1982), pp. 172–211. See also Loth, op. cit., pp. 232–77.

47 Heizer, op. cit., pp. 95–9; Pieper, *Jugendfürsorge*, pp. 30–1.

48 Pieper, "Thätigkeit," p. 124. See "Ein Wort an die Eltern zur Schulentlassung ihrer Kinder!" reprinted in Mosterts, *Handbuch*, pp. 125–7, for the actual list of occupations; Mosterts, *Vorbereitung*, pp. 30, 36–8, on attitudes toward different occupations and the neglect of the interests of young industrial workers in socially mixed associations.

49 Such an association of artisan and artist was part and parcel of a neo-humanist critique of a utilitarian approach to work common in Germany from the early nineteenth century. See Klaus Harney, *Die preussische Fortbiludingsschule: Eine Studie zum Problem der Hierarchisierung beruflicher Schultypen im 19. Jahrhundert* (Weinheim, 1980), pp. 103–4.

50 Pieper, "Thätigkeit," pp. 118–20; HAEK Gen. Tit. XXIII, Generalsekretariat der Jugendvereine: conference of 1 December 1915 in Kaiserwerth, where Mosterts spoke of job-related courses for artisans and clerks; HSTAD (Kalkum) 33031, Jugendpflege 1915: "Jahresbericht des Junglingsvereins 'Aloysianisches Bundnis' St. Rochus." This latter case suggests that it was only the wealthier parishes that were able to afford sufficiently developed youth programs to include further education.

51 Pieper, *Jugendfürsorge*, p. 173; "Korrespondenzblatt für die Präsides der katholischen Jugend-Vereinigungen," November 1911; HAEK Gen. Tit. XXIII, Generalsekretariat der Jugendvereine: "Denkschrift betr. Seelsorge und Organisation der uber 17 Jahre alten männliche Jugend," 22

November 1912. For membership statistics for the archdiocese of Cologne, see "Fragen der Zeit," *Die Wacht,* 1 November 1910.

52 Pieper, "Thätigkeit," pp. 113–45.

53 HAEK Gen. Tit. XXIII, Generalsekretariat der Jugendvereine: report of 29 December 1910 from Friedrich Schweizer to Cardinal Felix von Hartmann. For the Catholic worker associations, see Pieper, *Jugendfürsorge,* p. 216.

54 *Die Wacht,* 1 May 1911, 15 July 1911, and 1 August 1911, for violations of protection laws; "Die Ziele und Aufgabe der christlichen Gewerkschaften," *Die Wacht,* 1 October 1911, on the purely economic function of trade unions; "Gelb," *Die Wacht,* 15 May 1913, on company unions. For supposed Socialist terrorism against young Catholic workers, *Düsseldorfer Tageblatt,* 24 March 1911.

55 Jürgen Reulecke, "Bürgerliche Sozialreformer und Arbeiterjugend im Kaiserreich," *Archiv für Sozialgeschichte,* 22 (1982), p. 319.

56 HSTAD (Kalkum) 42813, Sammelberichte zu den Terminalberichte: 1 September 1912, #20, 24, 25; HSTAD (Kalkum) 42781, Sammelberichte zu den Terminalberichte: 1 September 1910.

57 HAEK Gen. Tit. XXIII, Generalsekretariat der Jugendvereine: letter from Mosterts to Cardinal Kopp, 28 September 1910. For the powerful, arch-conservative, and irascible Cardinal Kopp, see Ross, op. cit., pp. 47, 106–7.

58 For the controversial article "Gelb," see *Die Wacht,* 15 May 1913. HAEK Gen. Tit. XXIII, Generalsekretariat der Jugendvereine: letter of 11 October 1913 to Cardinal von Hartmann.

59 STAD III 2178, Jugendpflege 1915–18: #256, Gotter, "Auszug aus dem Verhandlungsbericht der Ortstruppe Jungdeutschlandbund."

60 HAEK Gen. Tit. XXIII, Generalsekretariat der Jugendvereine: Undated letter probably written in 1913 from Mosterts to Cardinal von Hartmann.

61 HAEK Gen. Tit. XXIII, Generalsekretariat der Jugendvereine: letter of 30 April 1913 written on behalf of kath. Jugendpflege Deutschland.

62 On religious indifference among workers after confirmation, see Dehn, op. cit., p. 39; see also Ludwig Heitmann, *Grossstadt und Religion,* vol. 2 (Hamburg, 1925), pp. 220–1.

63 Pieper, "Thätigkeit," p. 130, on youthful *Leichtsinn.*

64 There were some differences between Protestant and Catholic clergy, both in terms of social backgrounds and in education. More Protestant clergy by far were the offspring of government officials and the new middle class. Over a quarter enrolled in Protestant theological faculties were sons of ministers. Catholic clergy were more likely to have backgrounds in the old middle class of artisans, small farmers, and tradesmen and supposedly remained closer "to the people" in mental outlook and habits of life. Students with rural and small-town backgrounds were overrepresented among students in both Protestant and Catholic faculties. See Konrad H. Jarausch, *Students, Society and Politics in Imperial Germany* (Princeton, 1982), pp. 135–41. Given that many clergy were upwardly mobile, whereas their profession was losing status due to secularization, one would expect some status anxiety as well.

Chapter 6, pp. 118–38

1 Dieter Fricke, *Die deutsche Arbeiterbewegung 1869–1914* (East Berlin, 1976), p. 23. The Prussian law, which banned students, youth, and women from political activity, went into effect in March 1850.

2 Guenther Roth, *The Social Democrats in Imperial Germany: A Study in Working Class Isolation and National Integration* (Totowa, 1963), pp. 201, 216–20; Barrington Moore, *Injustice: Social Origins of Obedience and Revolt* (White Plains, 1978), pp. 205–16. Moore relies heavily on Adolf Levenstein's *Die Arbeiterfrage* (Munich, 1912).

3 Detlef Hoffmann, Doris Pokorny, and Werner Albrecht, eds., *Arbeiterjugendbewegung in Frankfurt 1904–1945* (Giessen, 1978), pp. 123–4.

4 Horst Ueberhorst, *Frisch, frei, stark und treu: Die Arbeitersportbewegung in Deutschland 1893–1933* (Düsseldorf, 1973), pp. 18–19.

5 Ibid., pp. 32–3; HSTAD (Kalkum) 42809, Terminalberichte über die Sozialdemokratie 1912–14: report on Essen of 5 November 1912.

6 Victor Schmidtchen, "Arbeitersport – Erziehung zum sozialistischen Menschen?" in Jürgen Reulecke and W. Weber, eds. *Fabrik, Familie, Feierabend* (Wuppertal, 1978), pp. 355–6. Apparently the education minister had issued a similar circular the previous year; see Reinhard Höhn, *Sozialismus und Heer:* vol. 2, *Der Kampf des Heeres gegen die Sozialdemokratie* (Bad Harzburg, 1969), p. 464.

7 HSTAD (Kalkum) 16002, Sozialdemokratische Turn- und Radfahrer Vereine: #58, letter from Heinrich Rahn to the District Governor, 15 November 1905, #87, letter from the lord mayor's office in Düsseldorf to the district governor, 17 April 1906; letter from the district governor to the Free Gymnasts, 23 May 1906.

8 Höhn, op. cit., p. 466.

9 Ueberhorst, op. cit., pp. 31–2; Schmidtchen, op. cit., p. 356; Höhn, op. cit., pp. 467–8.

10 STAD III 2178 Jugendpflege: #255, Gotter's reply to critics of the Jungdeutschlandbund, 19 June 1913.

11 See, for example, the highly characteristic comments by the Hamburg Evangelical minister and youth saver Walther Classen in *Zucht und Freiheit: Ein Wegweiser für die deutsche Jugendpflege* (Munich, 1914), pp. 36–8, where he speaks of the early assemblies of youthful agitators as an "unpleasant appearance" and writes, "This youth movement is fundamentally immoral."

12 The following account of the early years of the labor youth movement is largely based on Karl Korn, *Die Arbeiterjugendbewegung* (Berlin, 1922), pp. 6, 36–75. Although Korn, the first editor of *Arbeiter-Jugend*, consistently defends SPD policy, the liveliness of his book and the insider's perspective more than compensate for the outdated polemics. The only other comprehensive study is the East German one produced by the authors' collective headed by Karl Heinz Jahnke, *Geschichte der deutschen Arbeiterjugendbewegung 1904–1945* (Dortmund, 1973). Although adding detail, it is often tendentious. For example, Frank and other reformists who played key roles in the early years are barely mentioned, whereas

Luxemburg and Lenin, who were either peripheral to or utterly inconsequential for the movement, are treated in detail. For the early history,
I have consulted pp. 11–14 of the latter work.

13 For alcohol use and abuse in the German working class in the nineteenth
and twentieth centuries and for Socialist debates on the "drink question,"
see James S. Roberts, *Drink, Temperance and the Working Class in Nineteenth
Century Germany* (Boston, 1984), pp. 85–8, 109–27.

14 For an examination of these links, see Frolinde Balser, *Sozialdemokratie
1848/49–1863* (Stuttgart, 1962).

15 For intraparty developments on the youth issue, see Carl E. Schorske,
German Social Democracy 1905–1917 (New York, 1972), pp. 99–102.

16 STAS F-3-24 Bd. III spec., Politische Vereine und Versammlungen:
police report of 6 August 1906.

17 STAS (Höhscheid) F-3-2 Bd. II gen., Landesvisitationen und Massregeln
gegen staatsgefährliche Bestrebungen 1886–1912: report on meeting of
7 July 1907.

18 HSTAD (Kalkum) 42789, Sozialdemokratische Frauenbewegung: #113,
report on the social democratic youth organization by the Essen police,
20 July 1907, to the district governor.

19 For the provisions of the Imperial Association Law, see O. Pönsgen,
"Vereins- und Versammlungsrecht," in *Handbuch für Jugendpflege* (Langensalza, 1913), pp. 179–80. For the debates over the bill, see Karl Erich
Born, *Staat und Sozialpolitik seit Bismarcks Sturz*, vol. 1 (Wiesbaden, 1957),
pp. 217–22.

20 Höhn, op. cit., pp. 482–3. For debates over the Association Law, see also
Heinrich Muth, "Jugendpflege und Politik," in *Geschichte in Wissenschaft
und Unterricht*, 12, no. 10 (October 1961), p. 604. Actually the representatives of the southern states had requested restrictions on youth political
activity that Bethmann Hollweg rejected, but Conservatives in the Reichstag, indispensable for holding together the Bülow bloc, compelled him
to reverse this position and include such a restrictive clause.

21 *Protokoll der Verhandlungen der 6. Kongresses der Gewerkschaften Deutschlands,
Hamburg 22–27 June 1908*, pp. 320–35.

22 Schorske, op. cit., pp. 106–8; Fricke, op. cit., pp. 347–9.

23 HSTAD (Kalkum) 9058, Sammelberichte zu den Terminalberichte
1895–1907: #291, report from the Düsseldorf police commissioner to
the district governor, 1 September 1906, in which the work of women
with children and youth is discussed. See Richard J. Evans, *Sozialdemokratie und Frauenemanzipation im deutschen Kaiserreich* (Berlin, 1979),
pp. 259–60, on work with children.

24 The leaders in Düsseldorf, Lore Agnes, a key figure in the local women's
movement, Peter Winnen of the regional press bureau, and Emil Müller
were quite typical. HSTAD (Kalkum) 42781, Sammelberichte zu den
Terminalberichte 1910: 1 September 1910 for Lore Agnes; HSTAD
(Kalkum) 42813, Sammelberichte zu den Terminalberichte 1912: 1 September 1912 for Müller and Winnen. For the German Abstinent Workers' League and some of the key figures active in both it and the youth
movement, for example, Wilhelm Sollmann and Simon Katzenstein, see
Roberts, op. cit., pp. 88–93.

25 HSTAD (Kalkum) 42781, Sammelberichte zu den Terminalberichte 1910: report of the Düsseldorf police commissioner, 1 September 1910, on the educational committee meeting of 1 June 1910; *Düsseldorfer Volkszeitung*, 13 June 1910.

26 *Jahresbericht: Zentrallstelle für die arbeitende Jugend Deutschlands Juli 1910– Juni 1911*, pp. 3–11.

27 HSTAD (Kalkum) 42781, Sammelberichte zu den Terminalberichte 1910: report of 1 September 1910.

28 HSTAD (Kalkum) 42813, Sammelberichte zu den Terminalberichte: clipping from the *Freie Presse* of Elberfeld, 12 February 1912, "Bericht des Jugend Auschusses über seine Tätigkeit im Jahre 1911."

29 *Arbeiter-Jugend*, no. 17, 15 August 1914, p. 262.

30 HSTAD (Kalkum) 42813, Sammelberichte zu den Terminalberichte: #13, report of the Düsseldorf police administration to the district governor, 1 September 1912. See also Rudolf Wissel, "Zur Jugendorganisation," *Metallarbeiterzeitung*, no. 12, 19 March 1910, pp. 90–1; "Gewerkschaften und Jugendwanderungen," *Metallarbeiterzeitung*, 1 June 1912, p. 176. Nonetheless, only slightly more than 16,000 young workers belonged to the Metalworkers' Union in 1912 nationwide, about 3 percent of the 515,000 members. *Metallarbeiterzeitung*, no. 13, 30 March 1912, p. 97. Despite discussions of specific youth problems in the Free Trade Unions from 1908, apart from the metalworkers, unions generally waited until 1912 or 1913 before founding special youth sections. See Rotraud Tilsner-Gröll, *Die Jugendbildungsarbeit in den freien Gewerkschaften 1919–1933* (Frankfurt am Main, 1982), pp. 17–20.

31 HSTAD (Kalkum) 42809, Terminalberichte über die Sozialdemokratie: #77, 5 November 1912.

32 "Correspondenzblatt der Gewerkschaften Deutschlands," 11 December 1909, p. 778; Wolfgang Emmerich, ed., *Proletarische Lebensläufe*, vol. 2 (Reinbeck, 1975), pp. 69–70.

33 "Jugendgenossinnen," *Düsseldorfer Volkszeitung* (12 April 1913).

34 HSTAD (Kalkum) 16005, Sozialdemokratische Agitation unter der Jugend: speech by Gerlach on 14 April 1913; HSTAD (Kalkum) 42809 Terminalberichte über die Sozialdemokratie, 8 December 1913.

35 "An die Arbeitereltern," *Düsseldorfer Volkszeitung*, 19 March 1910.

36 "An die schulentlassene Jugend," *Düsseldorfer Volkszeitung*, 2 April 1912. See also STAD III 2178, Jugendpflege: #231, "An die jungen Arbeiter und Arbeiterinnen," April 1913.

37 "Anlage B: Referat über das königlichen Konsistoriums betr. Jugendpflege," *Protokoll über die Verhandlungen des Kreis Synode Düsseldorf*, 26 June 1912, pp. 53–4.

38 "Was heisst Sozialismus?" *Arbeiter-Jugend*, no. 1, 1909; Ludwig Frank, "Die Verfassung des deutschen Reichs," *AJ*, 8 May 1909; "Die politischen Parteien: Das Zentrum," *AJ*, 16 July 1909; "Was heisst Liberal?" *AJ*, 15 January 1910; "Die jugendlichen Arbeiter und die Gewebeordnung," *AJ*, 27 March and 10 April 1910.

39 *Arbeiterjugendbewegung in Frankfurt*, pp. 101–2; *Düsseldorfer Volkszeitung* 21 March 1911.

40 *Jahresberichte für die Zeit vom 1 Juli 1910 bis 30 Juni 1911*, Zentralstelle

für die arbeitende Jugend Deutschlands, pp. 3–8. Of 218 localities reporting on youth work, 147 already had a youth home, although 110 of these had only one room and were open only once or twice weekly. But large cities with strong social democratic movements like Berlin, Hamburg, and Elberfeld already had multiroom centers with libraries. The number of youths visiting the centers daily was under fifty in all but seventeen of these centers, and in most of the centers about one-fourth of the youthful visitors were female.

41 Jürgen Reulecke, "Bürgerliche Sozialreformer und Arbeiterjugend im Kaiserreich," *Archiv für Sozialgeschichte,* 22 (1982), p. 323.

42 HSTAD (Kalkum) 16005, Sozialdemokratische Agitation unter der Jugend: reports of 18 December 1912, 21 May 1913, 13 November 1913.

43 Emmerich, op. cit., pp. 69–70.

44 HSTAD (Kalkum) 42813, Sammelberichte zu den Terminalberichte, 1 September 1912.

45 For the reading habits of workers, see Dieter Langewiesche and Klaus Schönhoven, "Arbeiterbibliotheken und Arbeiterlektüre in wilhelminischen Deutschland," *Archiv für Sozialgeschichte,* 16 (1977); Jochen Loreck, *Wie man früher Sozialdemokrat würde* (Bonn, 1977), pp. 13–39, 95–99, 178–84, explores the relation between oral and written communication in the SPD.

46 HSTAD (Kalkum) 16005, Sozialdemokratische Agitation unter der Jugend: report of 26 March 1913. The speech by Peter Winnen contains a parable about a ruler who could not endure the sun and whose officials all wore black and white livery, that is, the Prussian colors. The Easter speech by Eduard Adler contains a mock history of Kings Schalke I, II, and III, each king greater and more heroic than the last.

47 HSTAD (Kalkum) 42809, Terminalberichte über die Sozialdemokratie: #33, 18 December 1913; "Jugendbewegung," *Düsseldorfer Volkszeitung,* 25 January 1913. For the social travelogue, see the article on Sven Hedin's Tibet journey in *AJ,* 12 February 1910. For science, see the notice in the *Düsseldorfer Zeitung* of 2 April 1909 on Sollmann's planned lecture on Darwin. See also "Charles Darwin und seine Lehre," *AJ,* 12 February 1910; "Vom Urtier zum Mensch," *AJ,* 28 August 1909; the article on Neanderthal man, *AJ,* 15 July 1911. For comparisons with the early Christians, see "Die Pfingsten Fahrt der Arbeiterjugend," *Düsseldorfer Volkszeitung,* 31 May 1912. For an anthropological perspective on religion, see "Das Fest des Geistes," *AJ,* 22 May 1909. For the problem of coherence in the educational programs of the socialist movement, see Vernon L. Lidtke, *The Alternative Culture: Socialist Labor in Imperial Germany* (New York, 1985), pp. 176–80.

48 Emmerich, op. cit., p. 69; *Arbeiterjugendbewegung in Frankfurt,* pp. 43, 10; HSTAD (Kalkum) 42813 Sammelberichte: zu den Terminalberichte clipping from the Elberfeld *Freie Presse* of 12 February 1912 on youth work mentioned one Goethe evening. In 1910 *AJ* carried articles on both Heine and Freilgrath. Some of the recent literature on the socialist subculture, for example, Georg Fülberth, *Proletarische Partei und bürgerliche Literatur* (Neuwied, 1978), has criticized the SPD for adopting middle-class literary values and cultural standards. Such a critique depends on

some notional possibility of an autochthonous proletarian culture and also underestimates the politically selective character of the SPD's cultural appropriation. For a full discussion of the uses of poetry in the socialist movement, see Lidtke, op. cit., pp. 145–8.

49 *AJ*, 11 February 1911, on the dissolution of a youth meeting in Düsseldorf for recitations of Heine's "Die Schlesische Weber" and Freilgrath's "Die Toten an den Lebenden." Ueberhorst, op. cit., p. 31, points out that the Imperial Association Law defined political affairs as "those that include the constitution, administration, and legislation of the state, the civil rights of subjects, and the international relations of states."

50 Korn, op. cit., p. 40. For an example of this sort of combined biographical and doctrinal approach, see "Bebel als Vorbild," *AJ*, 12 February 1910. For the lecture on historical materialism, see HSTAD (Kalkum) 42809, Terminalberichte über die Sozialdemokratie: 18 December 1913.

51 HSTAD (Kalkum) 42813, Sammelberichte zu den Terminalberichte: 24 September 1912, report from the Elberfeld police administration to the district president on a Socialist fest for departing draftees held on 31 August 1912; HSTAD (Kalkum) 9041, Terminalberichte über die Sozialdemokratische Bewegung: report from the district governor to the interior minister, 23 December 1906, discussed trade union–sponsored departure evenings for draftees. Although the district governor stated there was no evidence that the draftees were enlightened on "their rights as soldiers," he suspected that they were informed of their rights to issue complaints through secretly distributed leaflets and mouth-to-mouth agitation.

52 HSTAD (Kalkum) 42809, Sammelberichte zu den Terminalberichte: 1 September 1912 for police fears. See the clipping from the Elberfeld *Freie Presse* of 12 February 1912 on the plans of the local youth committee for hiking.

53 *Düsseldorfer Volkszeitung*, 9 August 1910 and 31 May 1912, for an encounter with an Evangelical youth group and a police attempt to seize the red flag; STAD III 2178 Jugendpflege: #231, April 1913, for a worker youth movement leaflet advertising a hike.

54 HSTAD (Kalkum) 42813, Sammelberichte zu den Terminalberichte: #87, clipping from the Elberfeld *Freie Presse*. See also *Arbeiterbewegung in Frankfurt*, pp. 40, 110–11.

55 *Düsseldorfer Volkszeitung* (6 June 1911, 25 March 1913); HSTAD (Kalkum) 16005, Sozialdemokratische Agitation unter der Jugend: report of 14 April 1914.

56 *Düsseldorfer Volkszeitung*, 31 May 1912, 2 June 1914; HSTAD (Kalkum) 16005, Sozialdemokratische Agitation unter der Jugend: report of 31 May 1914.

57 HSTAD (Kalkum) 42813, Sammelberichte zu den Terminalberichte: report of 1 September 1912. For caution at its most craven, see "Sind wir antimilitarisch?" *AJ*, 17 June 1911, p. 177, which claimed that accusations of antimilitarism were an insult to the leaders of the youth movement and that the apoliticism of the movement was a necessity, not simply because of the association law, but because youth had nothing to do with politics!

58 See *Düsseldorfer Volkszeitung*, 5 April 1911, for a cat-and-mouse game with the police. The police recognized that repression sometimes risked reviving interest in the movement. See HSTAD (Kalkum) 16005, Sozialdemokratische Agitation unter der Jugend: report of 13 November 1913.

59 See Sollmann's speech, reprinted in *Düsseldorfer Volkszeitung*, 14 April 1911.

60 Korn, op. cit., p. 226.

61 *Düsseldorfer Volkszeitung*, 21 March 1911.

62 *Düsseldorfer Volkszeitung*, 5 April 1911, 31 August 1911.

63 HSTAD (Kalkum) 16005, Sozialdemokratische Agitation unter der Jugend: letter of the Düsseldorf police administration to the lord mayor's office, 11 April 1913.

64 HSTAD (Kalkum) 16005, Sozialdemokratische Agitation unter der Jugend: report of 13 June 1913.

65 HSTAD (Kalkum) 16005, Sozialdemokratische Agitation unter der Jugend: letter of November 1913 from the Landrat of the Solingen Landkreis to the district governor; letter of the Essen police administration to the district governor, of 30 November 1913.

66 HSTAD (Kalkum) 16005, Sozialdemokratische Agitation unter der Jugend: report of 13 April 1914 by Police Commissioner Gauer; *Düsseldorfer Volkszeitung*, 14 April 1914. For the events of the following week, see the letter of the political section of the Düsseldorf police to the royal government, 23 April 1914.

67 *Düsseldorfer Volkszeitung*, 2 June 1914; HSTAD (Kalkum) 16005, Sozialdemokratische Agitation unter der Jugend: 31 May 1914 contains the text of Zietz's speech, with its references to the Christian meaning of Pentecost.

68 HSTAD (Kalkum) 16005, Sozialdemokratische Agitation unter der Jugend: report of the Düsseldorf police administration, 13 November 1913. According to the report, "[T]he best means to wreck the Social Democratic youth movement with the best prospects for permanent success should be seen in the continued expansion of national youth cultivation." Writing on 30 November 1913, the police commissioner of Essen agreed, although he also thought it important to take prompt action against violations of the association law. STAS F-3-66 Bd. I spec., Sozialdemokratische Jugendbewegung 1914–21: letter from the lord mayor of Solingen to the district governor, 27 April 1914, contrasted the five hundred to six hundred youths who had attended the kaiser's birthday celebration at the industrial continuation school with the approximately one hundred sixty youths who belonged to the Socialist youth movement.

69 HSTAD (Kalkum) 42809, Terminalberichte über die Sozialdemokratie: quoted in the report of the district governor to the interior minister, 18 December 1913, pp. 27–8 (307–8).

70 *Protokoll über die Verhandlungen der Parteitages der Sozialdemokratische Partei Deutschland* (Jena, 1913), pp. 244–5.

71 Quoted in Schorske, op. cit., p. 273.

Chapter 7, pp. 139–64

1 STAD III 2177, Jugendpflege 1914–15: #247, "Erlass des Ministers der Geistlichen, Unterrichts und Medizinal Angelegenheiten betreffend Jugendpflege," pp. 3–10. For the symbolic significance of the date, see the *Düsseldorfer Volkszeitung*, 4 February 1911. For the shift from *Jugendfürsorge* at the turn of the century to *Jugendpflege* in 1911 to *Jugendbewegung* after the war, see Kommission für Zeitgeschichte (Bonn), 1/13, Jugendbewegung und Jugendpflege, (Jacob Clemens), (1921), p. 1; Heinrich Muth, "Jugendpflege und Politik," *Geschichte in Wissenschaft und Unterricht*, 12, no. 10 (October 1961), pp. 599–600.

2 Klaus Saul, "Der Kampf um die Jugend zwischen Volksschule und Kaserne: Ein Beitrag zur 'Jugendpflege' im wilhelminischen Reich 1890–1914." *Militärgeschichtliche Mitteilungen*, no. 1 (1971), pp. 104–5.

3 See note 1 supra for the Jugendpflege Erlass. The quotes below come from nos. 1 and 2 of the "Grundsätze und Ratschläge für Jugendpflege" that concluded the document, p. 10.

4 "Zur Frage der Fürsorge für die schulentlassene Jugend," *Düsseldorfer Tageblatt*, 4 February 1911, p. 2. On responses from the churches and such, see Saul, op. cit., p. 114. For the Socialist response to the edict, see *Düsseldorfer Volkszeitung*, 4 February 1911.

5 HSTAD (Kalkum) Reg. Düsseldorf Präs. 28: #109, Verwaltungsbericht, 24 July 1911.

6 STAS V-C-22, Protokollbuch der Jugendfürsorge Ohligs, 20 February 1911.

7 *Düsseldorfer Volkszeitung*, 28 May 1913. Transcript of the City Council meeting of May 27.

8 *Düsseldorfer Volkszeitung*, 5 June 1914, suppl. no. 129.

9 HSTAD (Kalkum) Reg. Düsseldorf Präs. 28: Dr. Graf Adelmann, "Jugendpflege auf Grund des Ministerialerlasses vom 18 Januar 1911 im Regierungsbezirk Düsseldorf," in "Gründung des Bezirks-Ausschusses für Jugendpflege im Regierungsbezirk Düsseldorf," 2 April 1912.

10 STAD III 2177, Jugendpflege 1914–15: *Mitteilungen des Bezirksausschusses für Jugendpflege im Regierungsbezirk Düsseldorf*, 2, no. 1, 5 March 1914; HSTAD (Kalkum) 33085, Orts-Kreis Ausschüsse: letter from the lord mayor's office in Düsseldorf to the district governor, 16 October 1911, recommending personnel for the regional committee.

11 For Marie Baum's work in the Düsseldorf district, see her autobiography, *Rückblick auf mein Leben* (Heidelberg, 1950), pp. 135–56.

12 *Düsseldorfer Volkszeitung*, 5 June 1914. On the financing of *Jugendpflege* and conflicts for funding among youth groups, see also Muth, op. cit., pp. 607–8. By 1914 the amount available for *Jugendpflege* in Prussia had risen to four million marks.

13 STAD III 2177, Jugendpflege 1914–15: #69, 70, 73, 77, *Mitteilungen des Bezirksausschusses für Jugendpflege im Regierungsbezirk Düsseldorf*, 2, no. 5 (March 1914). The evaluation of the funding of various types of organizations is based on an analysis of the requests for grants and action on these requests contained in HSTAD (Kalkum) 33031, Jugendpflege

1915. The entire file consists of grant applications from Düsseldorf youth groups.

14   HSTAD (Kalkum) 32998, Leibsübungen für Schulentlassene 1910–13: Circular from the Ministry of Education, 1 April 1911. According to the *Düsseldorfer Volkszeitung,* 5 June 1914, suppl. no. 129, 321,000 marks had been spent on training youth workers in the Düsseldorf governmental district alone since 1911.

15   Walther F. Classen, *Vom Lehrjungen zum Staatsbürger* (Hamburg, 1909), pp. 9–13. For the hopes of a new feminine career, see HSTAD (Kalkum) 33094, Kreisjugendpflegerinnen 1914–17: letter to the district governor from the Central Agency for Popular Welfare, 22 December 1913.

16   For a complete report on the training week and a summary of the presentations, see STAD III 2177, Jugendpflege 1914–15: *Mitteilungen des Bezirksausschusses für Jugendpflege im Regierungsbezirk Düsseldorf,* 1 December 1913.

17   Saul, op. cit., p. 114.

18   STAD III 2176, Jugendpflege 1911–13: #289, Dr. Markus, "Jugendpflege in Düsseldorf," January 1913. For the growth of secular sports clubs, STAD III 2169, Schüler Verbände: #186–8; STAD III 2178, Jugendpflege 1915–18: #25.

19   *Wohlfahrtseinrichtungen der Gussstahlfabrik von Fried. Krupp zu Essen a.d. Ruhr,* no. 1 (1902), p. 114; STAE Rep. 102 IX 377, Fürsorge für die schulentlassene männliche Jugend: #61–4, returned questionnaire of 27 April 1909 on the organization of those released from school at the Gussstahlfabrik.

20   STAE Rep. 102 IX 377a, Fürsorge für die schulentlassene männliche Jugend: #207, letter from the Kruppsches Bildungsverein.

21   The rest of the material on the development of the Krupp youth cultivation program is taken from WA Krupp HA Krupp WA IV 1566 Kruppsche Jugendpflege: "Die Kruppsche Jugendpflege, Oktober 1910–June 1911," on the committee, the reconstitution of the youth sections, lectures, and activities; "Krupp Jugendpflege, 1 Juli 1911–30 Juni 1912 Jahresbericht," #3, p. 1, for the *Wandervogel,* pp. 2–12 on organization, lectures, and activities; "Krupp Jugendpflege, 1913–14," #17–18 on military chest, Krupp youth in denominational associations, and avoidance of competition with Weigle.

22   For several other examples of industrial youth cultivation, see Hans Weicker, "Bildung und Erziehung ausserhalb der Schule," *Die Jugendlichen Arbeiter in Deutschland: Schriften der Gesellschaft für Sozialreform,* vol. 4, no. 4 (Jena, 1911), pp. 18–19. For traditions of paternalism among large Ruhr firms and the social functions of this paternalism, see Elaine Spencer, *Management and Labor in Imperial Germany* (New Brunswick, 1984), pp. 71–9.

23   "Ein halbe Million für ein städtisches Jugendheim im Düsseldorf," *Düsseldorfer Volkszeitung,* 26 May 1913. For the council meeting that approved this project, see the transcript reprinted in *Düsseldorfer Volkszeitung,* 28 May 1913. On the wartime halt in construction, see *Verwaltungsbericht der Stadt Düsseldorf 1914–19,* p. 125.

24   STAD III 2178, Jugendpflege 1915–18: #255, Gotter's reply to critics

of the Young Germany League, 19 June 1913. Already by the end of 1911 over 650,000 youth were encompassed by *Jugendpflege* nationwide; see Saul, op. cit., p. 115.

25 STAD III 2178, Jugendpflege 1915–18: #8, letter from lord mayor's office to the district governor, 14 October 1911; HSTAD (Kalkum) 33085, Orts-Kreis Ausschüsse 1911–14: lord mayor to district governor, 13 November 1911. Wolf-Dietrich Greinert's contention that the continuation schools lost their central position in state youth cultivation as a result of the 1911 edict seems to me completely false. See his *Schule als Instrument sozialer Kontrolle und Objekt privater Interessen: Die Beitrag der Berufsschile zur politischen Erziehung der Unterschichten* (Hannover, 1975), p. 76.

26 STAD III 3629, Die gewerbliche Fortbildungsschule: #102, *Jahresbericht 1911–12*, pp. 31–2.

27 On the proartisanal activities of the continuation school, see STAD III 3629, Die gewerbliche Fortbildungsschule: #102, *Jahresbericht 1911–12*, pp. 28, 32; #105, *Jahresbericht 1912–13*, p. 49. This may in part have been an attempt to defuse the gathering opposition of artisan and *Mittelstand* organizations to the government in the prewar period, opposition that peaked in the Cartel of Productive Estates. See Geoff Eley, *Reshaping the German Right* (New Haven, 1980), pp. 317–21.

28 Gotter, "Bedeutung des Handfertigkeit," *Mitteilungen des Bezirksausschusses für Jugendpflege*, 1 December 1913; Classen, op. cit., pp. 94–5.

29 STAD III 3629, Die gewerbliche Fortbildungsschule: *Jahresbericht 1911–12*, p. 34; *Jahresbericht 1912–13*, pp. 45–50.

30 STAD III 3629, Die gewerbliche Fortbildungsschule: *Jahresbericht 1911–12*, pp. 27–8, 35–6; *Jahresbericht 1912–13*, pp. 41–3, 51.

31 STAD III 3629, Die gewerbliche Fortbildungsschule: *Jahresbericht 1911–12*, pp. 26, 36–7; *Jahresbericht 1912–13*, p. 43; *Jahresbericht 1913–15*, p. 45; STAD III 2176, Jugendpflege: #5, *Amtliches Schulblatt für den Regierungsbezirk Düsseldorf*, 1 December 1912, p. 208.

32 STAD III 2178, Jugendpflege 1915–18: *Monatsblätter*, no. 3, February 1912, p. 45, for the quote below. STAD III 3629, Die gewerbliche Fortbildungsschule: *Jahresbericht 1913–14*, p. 46.

33 STAD III 3629, Die gewerbliche Fortbildungsschule: *Jahresbericht 1911–12*, p. 29. On *Feierabend* and the failure of *Werden*, see STAD III 2177, Jugendpflege 1914–15: letter from Gotter to the district governor, 30 June 1914; HSTAD (Kalkum) 33311, Zeitschriften für Jugendpflege: letter from the Regional Committee for Youth Cultivation to the district governor, rejecting the introduction of *Werden*.

34 STAD III 3629, Die gewerbliche Fortbildungsschule: *Jahresbericht 1910–11*, p. 24; *Jahresbericht 1911–12*, pp. 30–1, 35; *Jahresbericht 1912–13*, pp. 45–6, 53.

35 On von Schenckendorff and the sports movement, see Muth, op. cit., pp. 600–3.

36 See "Auszüge aus dem gemeinsamen Immediatbericht des preussischen Kultus- und Kriegsministers, 28.9.1906," reprinted in Saul, op. cit., pp. 127–30. The following discussion of the paramilitary preparation of youth relies heavily on Saul's documentary article.

37   Ibid., pp. 107–8. The document is reproduced on pp. 130–1. For a local
      response to this *Erlass*, see the protocol of the meeting of the Kuratorium
      of the continuation school in Essen in STAE Rep. 102 IX 377, Fürsorge
      für die schulentlassene männliche Jugend, 31 October 1910: #181, 183.
      They were attempting to arrange for continuation school students to
      attend military exercises of the 159th infantry regiment stationed in
      Müllheim an der Ruhr.
38   Saul, op. cit., pp. 117–18. The statement reproduced appears on p. 117.
39   For the origins of the *Jungdeutschlandbund* and von der Goltz's views, see
      ibid., pp. 118–19; Martin Kitchen, *The German Officer Corps 1890–1914*
      (Oxford, 1968), p. 140; *Düsseldorfer Volkszeitung*, 10 June 1914. Ironically
      von der Goltz may have derived some of his notions of premilitary
      training from Gambetta's attempt to put together a new mass army after
      the Sedan defeat in the Franco-Prussian War. See Muth, op. cit., p. 609.
40   Reinhard Höhn, *Sozialismus und Heer*, vol. 3 (Bad Harzburg, 1969),
      pp. 523–4.
41   Saul, op. cit., pp. 119–21.
42   STAD III 2176, Jugendpflege 1911–13: letter by Gotter, 13 December
      1911.
43   STAD III 2178, Jugendpflege 1915–18: #250 "Auszug aus dem Ver-
      handlungsbericht   der   Ortstruppe   Jungdeutschlandbund   1913,"
      pp. 259–61. For the charity ball, see *Düsseldorfer Volkszeitung*, 26 October
      1912. For an example of the ads placed in local newspapers, see *Düs-
      seldorfer Tageblatt* (1 May 1912).
44   STAD III 3629, Die gewerbliche Fortbildungsschule: *Jahresbericht 1912–
      13*, pp. 46–8.
45   Hans-Ulrich Wehler, *Das deutsche Kaiserreich 1871–1918*, 3rd ed. (Göt-
      tingen, 1977), pp. 158–65.
46   STAE Rep. 102 IX 377, Fürsorge für die schulentlassene männliche
      Jugend: Dr. jur. Reimers, "Das Kriegspiel im Dienst der Jugendpflege,"
      Ratgeber für Jugendvereinigungen (Zentralstelle für Volkswohlfahrt, 5, nos.
      2/3 (August 1911), pp. 31–3; STAD III 3629, Die gewerbliche Fortbil-
      dungsschule: *Jahresbericht 1912–13*, pp. 47–8. For the German Boy Scout
      movement, see Karl Seidelmann, *Die Pfadfinder in der deutschen Jugend-
      geschichte* (Hannover, 1977), pp. 26–8. In 1913 it moved close to the
      Jungdeutschlandbund.
47   For national figures, see Saul, op. cit., pp. 121–3. For Düsseldorf, see
      STAD III 2178, Jugendpflege 1915–18: #254, Gotter's reply to critics
      of the Young Germany League, 19 June 1913, and note 41 supra.
48   "Nationale Jugendpflege," *Düsseldorfer Volkszeitung* (11 December 1912);
      HAEK Gen. Tit. XXIII, Generalsekretariat der Jugendvereine, Band 1:
      printed sheet dated March 1913 for the Catholic accusations of coercion.
      See Muth, op. cit., pp. 610–11, about von der Goltz's repeated warnings
      to local *Jungdeutschlandbund* representatives about the use of unfair tactics
      in recruiting.
49   STAD III 2178, Jugendpflege 1915–18: #254 Gotter's reply, 19 June
      1913.
50   *Protokoll über die Verhandlungen der Kreis Synode Düsseldorf*, 26 June 1912,

pp. 52–3. See also Muth, op. cit., pp. 611–12, for Protestant criticisms of the "religious neutrality" of the league.

51 HAEK Gen. Tit. XXIII, Generalsekretariat der Jugendvereine: letter of complaint from the Association of Düsseldorf Gymnasts, 16 August 1916, on raw physicality; "Bericht über die Stellung der kath. Jugendvereine gegenüber dem Jungdeutschlandbund," March 1913, pp. 1–4.

52 HAEK Gen. Tit. XXIII, Generalsekretariat der Jugendvereine: conference report, 26 March 1913.

53 "Jugendpflege und Krieg," *Die Wacht,* October 1913, p. 123.

54 STAD III 2178, Jugendpflege 1915–18: #250, 29 April 1913. For continued tensions between the Catholic Church and government-sponsored *Jugendpflege* in the overwhelmingly Catholic Trier districts, see, however, Muth, op. cit., pp. 614–18. The church was probably somewhat more aggressive in areas with weak Socialist presence.

55 Höhn, op. cit., p. 548.

56 *Düsseldorfer Volkszeitung,* 1 April 1912.

57 *Düsseldorfer Volkszeitung,* 4 May 1912; "Wie Jungdeutschland gegründet wird," *Arbeiter-Jugend,* 11 May 1912.

58 *Düsseldorfer Volkszeitung,* 26 October 1912.

59 HSTAD (Kalkum) 42813, Sammelberichte soz. Bewegung: Report of 1 September 1912.

60 *Düsseldorfer Volkszeitung,* 20 May 1912.

61 "Der Kampf um die Jugend," *Düsseldorfer Volkszeitung,* 2 July 1913.

62 Wolfgang J. Mommsen, "The Topos of Inevitable War in Germany in the Decade Before 1914," in Volker R. Berghahn and Martin Kitchen, eds., *Germany in the Age of Total War* (Totowa, N.J., 1981), pp. 23–45.

63 For the use of this formulation when discussing the compulsory military training of young males in 1914 by the war minister, see Saul, op. cit., p. 125.

64 STAD III 2178, Jugendpflege 1915–18: #255–6, Gotter's reply to critics of the *Jungdeutschlandbund,* 19 July 1913. On the characterizations of Young Germany as a kind of model society, see STAD III 3629, Die gewerbliche Fortbildungsschule: *Jahresbericht 1912–13,* pp. 46–7; Höhn, op. cit., p. 524.

65 See lists of those recommended to the district governor for commendations as a result of their work in youth cultivation in HSTAD (Kalkum) 33093, Kino für Jugendliche 1908–27. Weigle has already been mentioned as a recipient of the Red Eagle Order fourth class for his *Jugendpflege* work.

Chapter 8, pp. 165–85

1 The complete text of the edict can be found in Deutschen Zentrale für Jugendfürsorge, ed., *Handbuch für Jugendpflege* (Langensalza, 1913), pp. 862–4. This quote and the one following occur on pp. 862 and 862–3, respectively.

2 Anna Heinen, "Jugendpflegearbeit des Vereins katholischer deutscher

Lehrerinnen," in Hertha Siemering, ed., *Die deutschen Jugendpflegverbände* (Berlin, 1918), pp. 334–9; Martha Gennrich, "Jugendpflege in den Ortsgruppen des Landesvereins preussischer Volkschullehrerinnen," in the same volume, pp. 325–34.

3 Alwine Reinald, "Warum ist Jugendpflege für die Mädchen geboten?" in Hauptausschuss für Jugendpflege in Charlottenburg, ed., *Zur Pflege der weiblichen Jugend*, 3rd ed. (Jena, 1913), pp. 2–3.

4 Elisabeth Gnauck-Kühne, "Die Allgemeine Bedeutung und Notwendigkeit des Ausbaus der weiblichen Jugendpflege," in *Pflege der schulentlassenen weiblichen Jugend, Schriften der Zentralstelle für Volkswohlfahrt,* pamphlet 9, new edition. (Berlin, 1913), p. 186. [Hereafter cited as *SZV* 9.] For Gnauck-Kühne, see Alfred Kall, *Katholische Frauenbewegung in Deutschland* (Paderborn, 1983), pp. 268–73. The highly influential Gnauck-Kühne, one of the first university-educated women in Germany, had studied with Gustav Schmoller and then worked briefly in a factory in order to understand the situation of working women. She was active in the Christian social movement around Stöcker and Naumann and addressed the Protestant Social Congress on the social position of women in 1895. A founder of the Evangelical Social Women's Group, after her conversion to Catholicism she was also instrumental in launching the Catholic German Women's Association. As a Christian feminist, she tended to view the two genders as embodying different principles and belonging to different spheres.

5 Max Stritter, "Der Süddeutsche Verband katholischer weiblicher Jugendvereine," in Siemering, op. cit., pp. 203–5. The quote appears on p. 203.

6 For an account of the formation and activities of the *Patronagen,* as well as criticisms of these organizations, see Kall, op. cit., pp. 209–13.

7 Generalpräses Pfarrer von Haehling, "Zentralverband der katholischen Jungfrauenvereinigungen," in Siemering, op. cit., pp. 190–203. For the membership of young working women in the Cologne district, see O. Michalke, "Die katholische Berufsvereine," in *SZV* 9, pp. 121–2. This figure came from a survey conducted in 1906 and probably understates the membership immediately before the war.

8 Kall, op. cit., pp. 92–3.

9 Pastor Kruchen, "Die Jungfrauen-Kongregation und die Mädchenfortbildungsschule in Hochneukirch," in *Handbuch für Jugendpflege,* pp. 306–14. In nearby Neuss, there were socially segregated Marian sodalities for "better-off girls" and factory girls. Such socially distinct sodalities were apparently common in the Rhineland. See Kall, op. cit., p. 92.

10 Pastor Hüfner, "Der Verband katholischer Dienstmädchenvereine," in Siemering, op. cit., pp. 214–21, esp. pp. 216–17 on avoidance of trade union–type organizations and class struggle. A. von Schalscha-Ehrenfeld, "Die Jugendorganizationen des Verbandes katholischer Vereine erwerbstätiger Frauen und Mädchen Deutschlands," in the same volume, pp. 269–73.

11 Pastor Thiele, "Evangelischer Verband zur Pflege der weiblichen Jugend Deutschlands," in Siemering, op. cit., pp. 60–4. For Bodelschwingh, see p. 61.

12   For membership and its geographic concentration, see Pastor Lahde, "Die evangelischen Jungfrauenvereine," in *SZV* 9, pp. 93–4. For problems of narrow social recruitment, see Thiele, op. cit., p. 66.

13   Theodora Reineck, "Die deutsche Bahnhofsmission," in Siemering, op. cit., pp. 84–93. See also Adelheid Semm, "Geschichte, Organisation und Arbeitsziele des Vereins der Freundinnen junger Mädchen," in the same volume, pp. 75–84, for a related and precursor organization that was originally founded to save from prostitution and other forms of moral ruin girls who left their Swiss homes.

14   W. Krapf, "Der Verein Wohlfahrt der weiblichen Jugend," in *SZV* 9, pp. 99–104. For the dormitory, see Mathilde Kirchner, "Das Arbeiterinnenheim Alt-Moabit 39 in Berlin," in *Handbuch für Jugendpflege*, pp. 315–23.

15   H. Caspari, "Die Jugendpflege der Farbenfabriken vorm. Friedr. Bayer & Co., Leverkusen bei Cöln," in *Handbuch für Jugendpflege*, pp. 382–6. Bayer also had a girls' choir and a librarian who served as an adviser to and a mediator in disputes among young female employees. See also O. Michalke, "Einrichtungen von Arbeitgebern," in *SZV* 9, pp. 140–4. For earlier Catholic work in this area, which dated back to the 1850s, see Kall, op. cit., pp. 139–55.

16   Quoted in Alice Profé, "Die körperliche Erziehung unserer schulentlassenen weiblichen Jugend," *Zur Pflege der weiblichen Jugend*, p. 95, from Kaup's "Sozialhygienische Vorschläge zur Ertüchtigung unserer Jugendlichen."

17   Quoted in ibid., p. 95.

18   On commercial continuation schools for young female clerks, see Carole E. Adams, *Women Clerks in Wilhelmine Germany* (New York, 1988), pp. 103–4.

19   For a discussion of continuation schools for young women, see Alfred Kühne, "Die Fortbildungsschule," vol. 6, *Die jugendlichen Arbeiter in Deutschland, Schriften der Gesellschaft für Soziale Reform* (Jena, 1912), pp. 45–9.

20   See Margarete Schecker, *Die Entwicklung der Mädchenberufsschule* (Weinheim, 1963), pp. 63–9; Margarete Henschke, *Ulrike Henschke: Ein Lebensbild aus der deutschen Frauenbewegung* (Berlin, 1931), pp. 113–42.

21   For the institutions for female youth cultivation in Charlottenburg, see *SZV* 9, pp. 147–50. The information had been gathered by Elise Deutsch, the director of the local continuation school for young women. Charlottenburg probably had the most active youth welfare programs for young women prior to the edict of 1913.

22   Ibid., pp. 144–60. Barmen and Elberfeld claimed anomalously high degrees of organization of young women, with approximately 30 and 80 percent, respectively, belonging to religious or sports clubs.

23   Profé, op. cit., p. 99.

24   See F. Kaup, "Notwendigkeit einer umfassende Judgendpflege," in *SZV* 9, pp. 24–30, 66; Agnes Bluhm, "Weibliche Jugendpflege und Volksgesundheit," in the same volume, p. 208.

25   Kaup, op. cit., p. 29.

26   Ibid., pp. 30–3.

27 Ibid., p. 34.
28 Ibid., pp. 34–40; Bluhm, op. cit., pp. 204–7.
29 Quoted in Profé, op. cit., pp. 97–8.
30 Bluhm, op. cit., pp. 202–4.
31 Kaup, op. cit., pp. 67–9. The quote appears on p. 67. See also Rosa
    Kempf, "Das Leben der jungen Fabrikmädchen in München," *Schriften
    des Vereins für Sozialpolitik,* Bd. 135, Teil 2 (Leipzig, 1911), pp. 148–61,
    esp. p. 155.
32 Kaup, op. cit., pp. 47–9, 51–61; Bluhm, op. cit., pp. 211–15.
33 For the following discussions and a comprehensive discussion of delin-
    quency and welfare education cases among female youth see F. Reimers,
    "Verwahrlosung und Kriminalität," in *SZV* 9, pp. 69–85. See also the
    comments by Pastor Wurm during the discussion at the Danzig confer-
    ence of the Zentralstelle, pp. 239–41 of the same volume. Detlev Peukert
    notes that the discussion of juvenile delinquency and "welfare education"
    in Imperial Germany dealt almost exclusively with young males. To the
    degree that a discourse on the neglect of young women emerged, it was
    concerned with precocious or illicit sexuality. Because of the minor role
    that discussion of young females played in formulating programs for
    disciplining juvenile delinquents, Peukert excludes female delinquents
    from consideration. *Grenzen der Sozialdisziplinierung* (Cologne, 1986),
    p. 29.
34 Rosa Kempf, "Das Grossstadt Mädchen der unteren Klassen," in *Hand-
    buch für Jugendpflege,* pp. 27–9.
35 Gnauck-Kühne, op. cit., p. 187; Elise Deutsch, "Jugendpflege und Fort-
    bildungsschule," *Zur Pflege der weiblichen Jugend,* p. 25; Frau Rat Dr.
    Fleming, "Das junge Mädchen," *Weibliche Jugendpflege: Dritter Führerkurs
    veranstaltet von dem Hamburischen landesverband für Jugendpflege* (Hamburg,
    1917), p. 14.
36 Reinald, op. cit., pp. 10–13; the quote appears on p. 12. Deutsch, op.
    cit., pp. 25–6.
37 Reinald, op. cit., pp. 9–10; Deutsch, op. cit., p. 27. For a more sympa-
    thetic treatment of the clothing of factory girls, see Kempf, *Das Leben
    der jungen Fabrikmädchen,* pp. 164–5.
38 Reinald, op. cit., p. 11.
39 Kempf, *Das Leben der jungen Fabrikmädchen,* p. 100.
40 On the breakdown of the working-class family, see Reinald, op. cit., p. 8.
    For the assiduity of the German housewife, its importance in compen-
    sating for unequal real wages, and its decline, see Arthur Shadwell,
    Industrial Efficiency, 2nd ed. (London, 1913), p. 35; Gnauck-Kühne, op.
    cit., p. 47.
41 Kaup, op. cit., p. 64.
42 For Kamp and the agitation of the late 1880s, see Schecker, op. cit.,
    pp. 116–29; for the debates in the Reichstag, see ibid., pp. 129–32.
43 Ibid., pp. 155–66.
44 Elise Deutsch, "Organisation und Ausbau der Pflegeeinrichtungen na-
    mentlich in Verbindung mit der Fortbildungschule," in *SZV* 9, p. 235.
    These are the points listed in Deutsch's guidelines.
45 Kaup, op. cit., pp. 64–7; Kühne, op. cit., pp. 45–9.
46 See the comments at the conference in Danzig, of Paula Müller, who in

her criticisms of Gnauck-Kühne carefully guarded against being perceived as an advocate of full equality of the sexes in occupational life. Despite her complete antipathy to factory work for women, Gnauck-Kühne, in her speech at the assembly of the Zentralstelle, had quoted the labor expert Heinrich Herkner to the effect that old women occupied the worst and dirtiest jobs and had supported trade education for young women. *SZV* 9, pp. 194–5, for Gnauck-Kühne's comments; ibid., pp. 237–9, for the criticisms of Müller.

47 Hertha Siemering, "Pflege der schulentlassene weibliche Jugend," in *Flugschriften der Zentralstelle für Volkswohlfahrt* (Berlin, 1914), p. 18; Gertrud Zucker, "Berufsberatung und Jugendpflege," in *Zur Pflege der weiblichen Jugend,* p. 77.

48 Deutsch, "Organisation und Ausban," pp. 231–6.

49 Profé, op. cit., p. 96.

50 HSTAD 33001, Forderung der Pflege der weiblichen Schulentlassene 1912–13: report of 2 July 1912 from the Ministry of Religious and Educational Affairs to district governors.

51 HSTAD 33001, Forderung der Pflege der weiblichen Schulentlassene 1912–13: report of 27 July 1912 from the commissioner of Solingen county to the district governor in Düsseldorf.

52 HSTAD 33001, Forderung der Pflege der weiblichen Schulentlassene 1912–13: report of 31 July 1912 from the lord mayor of Elberfeld to the district governor in Düsseldorf.

53 HSTAD 33001, Forderung der Pflege der weiblichen Schulentlassene 1912–13: report of 3 August 1912 from the commissioner of Essen county to the district governor in Düsseldorf.

54 HSTAD 33001, Forderung der Pflege der weiblichen Schulentlassene 1912–13: report of 30 June 1913 from the commissioner of Cleve county to the district governor in Düsseldorf.

55 HSTAD 33001, Forderung der Pflege der weiblichen Schulentlassene 1912–13: report of 1 July 1913 from the commissioner of Solingen county to the district governor in Düsseldorf.

56 STAD III 3670, Fortbildungsschule für Mädchen: #6, Lehrplan; STAD III 3717, Die kaufmännische Fortbildungsschule: statistische Übersicht, p. 68.

57 *Düsseldorfer Zeitung* (28 May 1913) contains a partial transcript of the city council meeting of 27 May, on which the following account is based.

58 Schecker, op. cit., pp. 154–5.

59 Ibid., p. 82.

60 HSTAD 33001, Forderung der Pflege der weiblichen Schulentlassene 1912–13: letter of 4 July 1913 from the lord mayor of Düsseldorf to the district governor in Düsseldorf, signed by Herold.

61 HSTAD 33001, Forderung der Pflege der weiblichen Schulentlassene 1912–13: report of 16 August 1913 from the lord mayor of Düsseldorf to the district governor of Düsseldorf, signed by Herold.

62 HSTAD 33031, Jugendpflege 1915: "Bericht der Auskunftstelle für weibliche Berufe 1915."

63 See *Mitteilungen des Bezirksausschusses für Jugendpflege im Regierungsbezirk Düsseldorf,* 1 December 1913, for a précis of the speeches.

64 Deutsch, "Organisation und Ausbau," pp. 226–7. See also Martha Genn-

rich, "Jugendpflege in den Ortsgruppen des Landesvereins Preussischer Volksschullehrinnen," in Siemering, ed., *Die deutschen Judendpflegeverbände,* p. 325.

65   See Christoph Sachsse, *Mütterlichkeit als Beruf* (Frankfurt am Main, 1986), pp. 114–25. For the relatively low status of primary school teachers, see Douglas Skopp, "Auf der untersten Sprosse: Der Volksschullehrer als Semi-Professional im Deutschland des 19. Jahrhunderts," *Geschichte und Gesellschaft,* 6, no. 3 (1979), pp. 383–402, although he only discusses male teachers.

66   Siemering, op. cit., pp. 20–1, 24. See also the circular of the Zentrale für Volkswohlfahrt on this developing feminine profession, in HSTAD 33094, Kreisjugendpflegerinnen 22 December 1913.

67   Anna von Gierke, "Die Fachausbildung für die Jugendpflege," in *Zur Pflege der weiblichen Jugend,* pp. 124–32. For Anna von Gierke's work with endangered girls in the Charlottenburg *Jugendheim* and her ideas on the professionalization of youth work, see Marie Baum, *Anna von Gierke: Ein Lebensbild* (Weinheim, 1954), pp. 32–66.

68   STAD III 2177, Jugendpflege: *Mitteilungen des Bezirksausschusses für Jugendpflege im Regierungsbezirk Düsseldorf,* 5 March 1914; HSTAD 33087, Jugendpflege 1915: request forms #20–2.

Chapter 9, pp. 186–218

1   Voluntary military exercises will be treated below. For an ironic account of an enthusiastic celebration of the kaiser's birthday in 1915 by industrial continuation school students, see STAE Rep. 102 IX 381, Militärische Vorbereitung der Jugend bei der Fortbildungsschule: #97, clipping from the *Essener Volkszeitung* of 2 February 1915. The Trade Ministry continued to give considerable attention to fostering patriotic commemorations during 1915, such as the centenary of Bismarck's birth. See STAD III 3662, Die kauf. Fortbildungsschule 1911–18: #261, copy of a circular from the Trade Ministry dated 18 March 1915, which also called for a festive graduation ceremony at continuation schools in which a lecture, "The War and Youth," would be held.

2   The literature on the SPD's abandonment of opposition and the relationship of this retreat to the mood of labor at the outset of the war is, of course, so vast as to be practically unsurveyable. Positions have ranged from accusations that the SPD leadership "betrayed" the working class to affirmations that the leadership faithfully reflected the war enthusiasm of the rank and file. Much of the work has derived from Robert Michels and hence has focused on the development of a centrist bureaucracy within the SPD that feared that opposition would precipitate government repression. This bureaucracy, which identified totally with the apparatus, was determined to preserve the organization, come what might. An old study from a Communist perspective, albeit one conditioned by the 1956 de-Stalinization wave, that blames the SPD leadership for betrayal but also admits that the outbreak of the war was greeted with enthusiasm in all classes is Jürgen Kuczynski, *Der Ausbruch*

des ersten Weltkrieges und die deutsche Sozialdemokratie (East Berlin, 1957), pp. 77–99. For the development of a centrist bureaucracy and fear of a state of siege, see Carl E. Schorske, *German Social Democracy 1905–1917* (New York, 1972), pp. 285–94. For an interpretation that emphasizes the negative integration of labor and the labor leadership divided between socialism and patriotism, see Dieter Groh, *Negative Integration und revolutionärer Attentismus* (Frankfurt am Main, 1973), pp. 625–727.

3 August Grünweller, *Der Krieg als Volkserzieher und die Volksschule* (Rheydt, 1915), p. 20. Grünweller was general secretary of the Association of German Evangelical School Teachers.

4 STAD III 3664, Die kaufmännische Fortbildungsschule 1914–20: #84, circular from the Ministry of Trade, 25 September 1915.

5 STAD III 3629, Die gewerbliche Fortbildungsschule: #140–1, "Bericht des Direktors der gewerblichen Fortbildungsschule 1914–15."

6 *Verwaltungsbericht der Stadt Düsseldorf 1914–19*, p. 125. For the importance of apprentices in craft workshops, exemptions from continuation schools, and absenteeism in other cities, see Moritz Liepmann, *Krieg und Kriminalität in Deutschland* (Stuttgart, 1930), p. 84. For absenteeism in Düsseldorf, see STAD III 3629, Die gewerbliche Fortbildungsschule: #142, "Bericht des Direktors der gewerblichen Fortbildungsschule 1914–15."

7 STAD III 3606, Die gewerbliche Fortbildungsschule 1914: circular of the Trade Ministry dated 8 October 1914; STAD III 3710, Die militärische Vorbereitung der Fortbildungsschüler: #75; *Verwaltungsbericht der Stadt Düsseldorf 1914–19*, p. 125.

8 *Verwaltungsbericht der Stadt Düsseldorf 1914–19*, p. 125; STAD III 3629, Die gewerbliche Fortbildungsschule: #142, pp. 134, 137.

9 See the extremely detailed and well documented article by Klaus Saul, "Jugend im Schatten des Krieges," *Militärgeschichtliches Mitteilungen*, no. 2 (1983), pp. 93–5, for prewar plans. I have relied heavily on Saul in discussing premilitary training.

10 *Essener Chronik 1914*, pp. 270–2. For the War Ministry's circular on premilitary training, see STAD III 3662, Die kaufmännische Fortbildungsschule 1911–18: circular of 12 August 1914. On religious support for premilitary training, see ibid., p. 96.

11 STAD III 2177, Jugendpflege 1914–18: #226–27, report of Deputy Mayor Knopp, of 30 September 1914; #233, reply to letter of the district governor, 6 November 1914.

12 Saul, op. cit., pp. 96–7. For Krupp's companies, see STAE Rep. 102 IX 381, Militärische Vorbereitung der Jugend bei der Fortbildungsschule: #90, meeting of the municipal finance commission on 11 June 1915 over division of cost for youth companies between Krupp and the city.

13 For the following, see STAD III 3710, Die militärische Vorbereitung der Fortbildungsschüler: #19, list of officers, September 1914; #2, letter from Major General Kade, supervisor for the military preparation of youth in the Düsseldorf governmental district, printed in *Mitteilungen des Bezirksausschusses für Jugendpflege im Regierungsbezirk Düsseldorf*, 1 May 1918.

14   Saul, op. cit., pp. 99, 104–6. See also the discussion below.
15   Ibid., pp. 97–9.
16   STAE Rep. 102 IX 381, Militärische Vorbereitung der Jugend bei der Fortbildungsschule: #245–6, SPD circular of 5 September 1914; #78, circular of the general commander of the Seventh Army Corps, 28 January 1915.
17   For the committee and its report, see STAE Rep. 102 IX 381, Militärische Vorbereitung der Jugend bei der Fortbildungsschule: report of the meeting of February 1915.
18   STAE Rep. 102 IX 381, Militärische Vorbereitung der Jugend bei der Fortbildungsschule: #98, letter from the Landwehr inspector to the commanding general in Münster.
19   STAE Rep. 102 IX 381, Militärische Vorbereitung der Jugend bei der Fortbildungsschule: #101 report of the Essen committee on military preparation of youth, 18 February 1915.
20   "Eingabe des Zentralvorstandes der katholischen Jünglingsvereinigungen Deutschlands an den preussischen Innenminister, 15.8.1913," document #13, reprinted in Saul, op. cit., pp. 132–4.
21   STAE Rep. 102 IX 381, Militärische Vorbereitung der Jugend bei der Fortbildungsschule: letter of 4 February 1915 from the Essen Landwehr inspector to the deputy general commander in Münster on scheduling Sunday exercises in order to assuage the complaints of the Catholic clergy.
22   STAD III 2178, Jugendpflege 1915–18: letter from the Regional Federation of Catholic Youth Associations to the district president, 14 September 1914.
23   STAD III 2178, Jugendpflege 1915–18: #399, letter signed by representatives of both Catholic and Evangelical representatives of youth groups, 12 February 1918, to the Ortsausschuss für Jugendpflege, protesting exercises at 8:00 A.M. on Sunday; reply of 4 March 1918 from First Lieutenant Lehrhoff on continued attempts to ensure that youth wishing to attend church services were able to do so.
24   HSTAD (Kalkum) 33064, Vorbereitung der Jugend für den Krieg: program of celebration held on 16 January 1916.
25   HAEK Gen. Tit. XXIII, Generalsekretariat der Jugendvereine: letter of 8 February 1918 from the General Command of the Seventh Army Corps in Coblenz.
26   Ibid.: "Verhandlungsbericht der Generalversammlung der Präsides katholischer Junglingsvereinigungen der Erzdiözese Köln, 12 July 1916" (Bonn), esp. the comments of Pastor Bremer on the conduct of youth.
27   For organizational strength of Catholic youth groups in the Düsseldorf region during the war, see ibid.: "Verhandlungsbericht der 21 Generalversammlungen der Präsides katholischer Junglingsvereinigungen der Erzdiözese Köln," 20 July 1917 (Essen). For funding, see the reports contained in HSTAD (Kalkum) 33031, Jugendpflege.
28   "Auszug aus dem Bericht des Konsistoriums der Provinz Westfalen an den Evangelischen Oberkirchrat betr. Stand der Jugendpflege, 16.8.1915," document #14, in Saul, op. cit., p. 134.

29 "Denkschrift des Evangelischen Ober-Kirchenrates betr. die Ausgestalt-
    ung der kirchlichen Jugendpflege" (Berlin, 1917), pp. 9–10. See also
    articles in *Neue Kraft*, the monthly of the German YMCA, such as
    "Jugendliches Verbrechertum," no. 9 (September 1917); "Der Tabak-
    genuss der Jugend," no. 11 (November 1917).

30 Pastor Euler, "Bericht über Jugendpflege," *Protokoll über die Verhand-
    lungen der Kreis Synode Düsseldorf* (21 January 1917), pp. 42–8.

31 Pastors Rose und Euler, "Bericht über Jugendpflege," *Protokoll über die
    Verhandlungen der Kreis Synode Düsseldorf* (28 June 1916), pp. 40–1. For
    articles on the war in *Gruss aus der Heimat*, the youth paper of the West
    German Youth Federation, see "Russische Greuel in Ostpreussen," no.
    7 (1914), "Militarismus," no. 24 (1915).

32 STAE Rep. 102 XXII 174, Fürsorge für die Jugend: report on the
    conference of 28 March 1916 on broadening the work of the youth
    cultivation committee. Among the issues discussed at the conference
    were workplace hazards, housing, and alcohol and tobacco abuse.

33 HSTAD (Kalkum) 33094, Kreisjugendpflegerinnen 1914–17: letter of
    29 July 1916 from the lord mayor of Rheydt to the district governor
    in Düsseldorf.

34 HSTAD (Kalkum) 45269, Konferenzen: "Bericht über die weibliche
    Jugendpflege im Regierungsbezirk Trier gegeben von Referentin Frl.
    Raitz von Trentz am 10.6.1920 zu Düsseldorf." For the activities of
    female youth groups during the war, see also "Die Vaterländische
    Frauenvereine und die weibliche Jugend," in *Nachrichten des Hambur-
    gisches Landesverbändes* (Hamburg, 1916), pp. 201–3; *Weibliche Jugend-
    pflege: Dritter Führerkurs veranstaltet von dem Hamburischen Landesverband
    für Jugendpflege* (Hamburg, 1917).

35 HSTAD (Kalkum) 33086, Orts- und Kreis Ausschüsse für Jugend-
    pflege: circular of 17 May 1916 issued by District Governor Francis
    Kruse to county commissioners and lord mayors. This circular, of
    course, preceded the Auxiliary Service Law.

36 For a complete list of women youth welfare workers in the Düsseldorf
    district, see HSTAD (Kalkum) 33094, Kreisjugenpflegerinnen: list of
    1 May 1918. For the center in Düsseldorf, see the letter of Kruse to
    the Educational Ministry, 22 September 1916, in the same file.

37 For the conference and summaries of the speeches given, see HSTAD
    (Kalkum) 33086, Orts- und Kreis Ausschüsse für Jugendpflege: "Düs-
    seldorfer Woche zur Aus- und Fortbildung von Jugendpflegerinnen,"
    25 September 1916. *Völkisch* speeches like "Die sittliche Reinheit der
    Jugend: Die Kraft und Hoffnung des Vaterlandes" were common.

38 Ibid.: letter from District Governor Kruse to county commissioners and
    lord mayors, 20 December 1916.

39 The following discussion and tables are based on Waldemar Zimmer-
    mann, "Die Veränderungen der Einkommens- und Lebensverhältnisse
    der deutschen Arbeiter durch den Krieg," in Rudolf Meerwarth, Adolf
    Guntner, and Waldemar Zimmerman, eds., *Die Einwirkung des Krieges
    auf Bevölkerungsbewegung, Einkommen und Lebenshaltung in Deutschland:
    Wirtschafts- und Sozialgeschichte des Weltkrieges* (Stuttgart, 1932), pp. 281–
    474. For an overview of changes in the labor force, wages, and con-

ditions as a result of the war, see also Jürgen Kocka, *Facing Total War* (Cambridge, Mass., 1984), pp. 16–26.

40 Hans-Joachim Bieber, *Gewerkschaften in Krieg und Revolution*, vol. 1 (Hamburg, 1981), p. 211.

41 One problem, of course, is that the Occupational Census was taken before the Hindenburg Plan and Auxiliary Service Law. These measures, adopted to double the output of war industries, brought large reservoirs of female labor into the factory work force. Presumably, large numbers of young women who had previously remained home entered heavy industry. On the effects of these measures on female employment, see Gerald D. Feldman, *Army, Industry and Labor in Germany 1914–1918* (Princeton, 1966), pp. 306–7.

42 *Verwaltungsbericht der Stadt Düsseldorf 1914–19*, pp. 126–7.

43 Ibid., p. 118.

44 Ibid.

45 "Teuerungszulagen für Lehrlinge," *Düsseldorfer Volkszeitung*, 10 August 1916.

46 Zimmermann, op. cit., pp. 382–3.

47 Ibid., pp. 392–3.

48 "Metallarbeiter in Düsseldorf," *Metallarbeiterzeitung*, 24 November 1917.

49 Zimmermann, op. cit., pp. 374–5.

50 Ibid., p. 392.

51 "Metallarbeiter in Düsseldorf."

52 Based on the official prices for rationed food listed in the *Düsseldorfer Zeitung*, 29 October 1917.

53 *Düsseldorfer Volkszeitung*, 2 May 1916.

54 "Die Lehrlinge und die jugendlichen Arbeiter in der Metallindustrie," *Metallarbeiterzeitung*, 14 April 1917.

55 Liepmann, op. cit., p. 83.

56 STAD III 3629, Die gewerbliche Fortbildungsschule: "Bericht des Direktors der gewerblichen Fortbildungsschule 1914–15," p. 140; HSTAD (Kalkum) 33104, Jugendfürsorge: Alkohol- und Tanzverbote 1916–22: Report by the lord mayor on the situation of laboring youth in Duisberg, 19 December 1916.

57 Liepmann, op. cit., p. 83. See also p. 89 for increased mortality during the war.

58 *Düsseldorfer Volkszeitung*, 2 May 1916. For the objections by the Free Trade Unions to training practices, see "Die Lehrlingfrage," *Metallarbeiterzeitung*, 7 April 1917; "Die Lehrlinge und die jugendlichen Arbeiter in der Metallindustrie," *Metallarbeiterzeitung*, 14 April 1917.

59 John A. Moses, *Trade Unionism in Germany from Bismarck to Hitler: 1869–1918* (London, 1982), p. 212; Bieber, op. cit., pp. 173–4, 211. The Free Trade Unions did, of course, win official recognition because of their support for the war effort, especially with the passage of the Auxiliary Service Law in December 1916, but it would be hard to dispute Feldman's contention that the government won union support at the "cheapest possible price." Feldman, op. cit., p. 520. That was certainly true in terms of union youth policy during the war. The unions often complained about lack of training, overwork, and so forth, but did little.

60 Saul, op. cit., p. 102. See also Ludwig Preller, *Sozialpolitik in der Weimarer Republik* (Düsseldorf, 1978 ed.), p. 55, for official concerns about the elimination of protective legislation for youth and women.

61 HSTAD (Kalkum) 33104, Jugendfürsorge: report by the lord mayor of Duisberg on the situation of laboring youth, 19 December 1916; Adalbert Oehler, *Düsseldorf im Weltkrieg* (Düsseldorf, 1927), pp. 561–2.

62 STAD III 2142, Bekämpfung des Schmutzes 1911–19: circular from the district governor to county commissioners and mayors, 25 June 1916. Typical of this genre were *Um Deutschlands Ehre* and *Das Eiserne Kreuz*, contained in this file.

63 The number of such complaints multiplied exponentially. See, for example, STAD III 2178, Jugendpflege 1915–18: circular from District Governor Kruse, 20 February 1916, on the situation of youth during the war.

64 See "Zwang und Freiheit in der Jugendpflege," *Düsseldorfer Volkszeitung*, 24 November 1916. This article reports on the recent conference of the Central Agency for Popular Welfare.

65 HSTAD (Kalkum) 30473, Schundliteratur 1915–17: proclamation of General von Geyl of the Seventh Army Corps in Münster, 13 December 1915.

66 STAD III 2178, Jugendpflege 1915–18: circular of 20 February 1916 from District Governor Kruse.

67 STAD III 2142, Bekämpfung des Schmutzes 1911–19. The youth literature association was founded at the behest of the district governor in 1915 in order to coordinate the battle against penny dreadfuls. See #278, "Ueber Schundschriftbekämpfung im rheinisch-westfälisches Industriebezirk von allgemeinen Jugendschriften Vereinigungen-Essen." For Koch's activities, see HSTAD (Kalkum) 30473, Schundliteratur 1915–17: report to the police praesidium, 6 October 1915.

68 STAD III 2142, Bekämpfung des Schmutzes: #255, circular of 25 June 1915 from the district governor; #258, Seventh Army Corps list of proscribed penny dreadfuls and books.

69 HSTAD (Kalkum) 30473, Schundliteratur: letter of 16 December 1916.

70 Detlev J. Peukert, *Grenzen der Sozialdisziplinierung* (Cologne, 1986), pp. 176–7.

71 HAEK Gen. Tit. XXIII, Generalsekretariat der Jugendvereine: "Protokoll über die Sitzung des Zentralkommittees der katholischen Junglingsvereinigungen Deutschlands 31 May 1917"; HAEK Gen Tit. XXIII, Generalsekretariat der Jugendvereine: *Jahresbericht des Generalpräses*, 31 May 1917, pp. 4–5.

72 HSTAD (Kalkum) 46077, Kino: #323, 329, 341, 344, circulars from the Deputy general commander of the Seventh Army Corps, 21 October 1915. See documents #368–9 for lists of banned films.

73 STAD III 2178, Jugendpflege 1915–18: #379–81, letter of the police administration in reply to Regional Committee for Youth Cultivation, 24 August 1916.

74 HAEK Gen Tit. XXIII, Generalsekretariat der Jugendvereine: *Jahresbericht des Generalpräs*, 31 May 1917, p. 4.

75 HSTAD (Kalkum) 33068, Vorbereitung der Jugend für den Krieg:

circular of the deputy general commander of the Eleventh Army Corps in Cassel, 17 August 1916.

76 HSTAD (Kalkum) 33068, Vorbereitung der Jugend für den Krieg: letter of Colonel Herrlich to the General Command of the Seventh Army Corps in Münster.

77 Saul, op. cit., pp. 106–7.

78 HSTAD (Kalkum) 33104, Jugendfürsorge, Alkohol- und Tanzverbote 1916–22: replies from the lord mayors of Düsseldorf (16 December 1916), Duisberg (19 December), Essen (29 December), M. Gladbach (16 December), Hamborn (19 December), and Rheydt (undated).

79 Liepmann, op. cit., pp. 98–102.

80 HSTAD (Kalkum) Reg. Präs. 29, Zeitungsbericht 1914–18 #394, report of 15 November 1917. On lack of potatoes and the citizens blaming municipal governments, see the same report, #389.

81 *Düsseldorfer Tageblatt*, 30 June 1917.

82 *Düsseldorfer Volkszeitung*, 12 June 1917, for this and the following account.

83 HSTAD (Kalkum) Reg. Präs. 29, Zeitungsbericht 1914–18: #390, report of 15 April 1917.

84 Liepmann, op. cit., pp. 119–23, for the following.

85 HSTAD (Kalkum) 16005, Sozialdemokratische Agitation unter der Jugend: typed pamphlet dated 20 June 1916 entitled "Ein Sieg der Jugend in Braunschweig." See also Karl Korn, *Die Arbeiterjugendbewegung* (Berlin, 1922), pp. 299–310.

86 HSTAD (Kalkum) 16005, Sozialdemokratische Agitation unter der Jugend: report of 7 April 1916 from the Düsseldorf police administration to the district governor.

87 *Düsseldorfer Volkszeitung*, 12 June 1917.

88 See, for example, the article by the leading SPD educator Heinrich Schulz, "Die militärische Jugenderziehung," *Metallarbeiterzeitung*, 14 August 1915; HSTAD (Kalkum) 16005, Sozialdemokratische Agitation unter der Jugend: letter of Jacob Koch to Käthe Dunker, 27 April 1916, complaining about the regional youth secretary, the moderate, Wilhelm Enz.

89 HSTAD (Kalkum) 16005, Sozialdemokratische Agitation unter der Jugend: report of 7 April 1916 from the Düsseldorf police administration to the district governor.

90 Ibid.: police report of 13 June 1916 on the secret parley of the pro-Liebknecht group.

91 Ibid.: police report of 6 June 1916 on the meeting held on May 30.

92 Ibid.: report by the Elberfeld police, 6 June 1916, on the annual meeting of the lower Rhine youth committee meeting.

93 Ibid.: police report of 13 June 1916 on the secret parley of the pro-Liebknecht faction.

94 Ibid.: Düsseldorf police report, 17 May 1916.

95 Ibid.: reports of the Düsseldorf police, 20 June and 10 July 1916.

96 *Düsseldorfer Volkszeitung*, 30 May 1917.

97 HSTAD (Kalkum) 16005, Sozialdemokratische Agitation unter der Jugend: Düsseldorf police report, 17 May 1916. This report contains a

copy of "Thesen zur Jugendfrage," which the police characterized as a document of the Liebknecht–Rühle tendency.

98   Hans Mommsen, ed., *Sozialdemokratie zwischen Klassenbewegung und Volks-partei* (Frankfurt am Main, 1974), p. 142; Ludwig Preller, *Sozialpolitik in der Weimarer Republik* (Düsseldorf, reprinted 1978), pp. 22, 29.

99   See, for example, Mary Nolan, *Social Democracy and Society: Working-class Radicalism in Düsseldorf 1890–1920* (Cambridge, 1981), pp. 272–3; Bernd Rabe, *Der sozialdemokratische Charakter* (Frankfurt am Main, 1978), pp. 117–18; Karl Oettinger, "Wie ein Stift die Revolution erlebte," in *Arbeiterjugendbewegung im Frankfurt 1904–1945* (Giessen, 1978), pp. 34–5.

100 See WA Krupp, H A Krupp VIII 1254, Verschiedene Arbeitsangele-genheiten 1913–18, #14, 15, on layoffs of youth; Gussstahlfabrik, 7 November 1918, on worries about youthful tumults if there were sub-stantial layoffs. See Charles S. Maier, *Recasting Bourgeois Europe* (Prince-ton, 1975), pp. 67–8, on the SPD's demobilization policies.

101 HSTAD (Kalkum) 33104, Jugendfürsorge: Alkohol- und Tanzverbote: reports of Rhine–Ruhr cities, 16–29 April 1921.

102 *Verwaltungsbericht der Stadt Düsseldorf 1914–19*, p. 103.

103 Ibid., p. 122.

104 The account of the strike that follows is based on material found in STAE Rep. 102 IX 175, Die Stunden und das Lehrplan der Fortbil-dungsschule. The leaflet "An die ganze Jugend der Arbeiterklasse" is included.

105 Letter of Continuation School Director Kayser to Legal Councillor Rich-ter 22 October 1919.

106 #221 Directive issued by the Ministry of Trade, 15 July 1919, #230, report of Director Kayser, 16 October 1919.

107 Report by a teacher named Mager, 24 October 1919.

108 Summary of the meeting of the school's executive committee, 11 No-vember 1919.

109 Letter of 8 November 1919 from Otto Weinauge of the Metalworkers' Union to the lord mayor of Essen.

110 Report on the visit to the school by Otto Weinauge, 13 February 1920.

111 #239 Letter of Richter to Director Kayser, 22 October 1919, #240, Kayser to Richter, 24 October 1919. The students apparently agreed, on the advice of the anarchosyndicalist union, which many of them preferred to the Metalworkers' Union, to halt the strike for three weeks while negotiations continued.

112 Report on a new student strike on 7 July 1921 over the same issues and a confrontation between the students and the police from the director to the mayor of Essen West, 8 July 1921.

Epilogue and conclusion, pp. 219–34

1   Detlev J. Peukert, *Grenzen der Sozialdisziplinierung* (Cologne, 1986), p. 177. For the youth welfare law, see also pp. 134–9.

2   Hermann Giesecke, *Vom Wandervogel bis zur Hitlerjugend* (Munich, 1981), pp. 162–3.

3   Wolf-Dietrich Greinert, *Schule als Instrument sozialer Kontrolle und Objekt privater Interessen: Die Beitrag der Berufsschule zur politischen Erziehung der Unterschichten* (Hannover, 1975), p. 105.

4   Giesecke, op. cit., pp. 158–62.

5   HSTAD 45269, Konferenzen. For the tasks of such regional conferences as laid out by the Prussian welfare minister Adam Stegerwald in a circular to the district governors of Düsseldorf, Coblenz, Cologne, Trier, and Aachen, see #39, and for the actual transcript of this Rhenish conference, see the "Niederschrift über die Tagung der Jugendpflegedezernaten bei der Regierung der Rheinprovinz im Sitzungssaals der Regierung zu Düsseldorf am 10 Juni 1920," with dozens of representatives from the Ministry of Welfare, the district governments of the Rhineland, and professional welfare and youth workers.

6   HSTAD 45269, Konferenzen: #116–17, "Verzeichnis der Mitglieder des Bezirksausschusses für Jugendpflege 1921." One official of the Metalworkers' Union had been added to the regional committee by 1921.

7   Giesecke, op. cit., pp. 142–3; HSTAD 33120, Jugendpflege Sammelberichte 1915–26: for lists of part-time youth cultivators as of 18 March 1921.

8   Giesecke, op. cit., pp. 143–4. For the shortage of funds, see HSTAD 45269, Konferenzen: "Niederschrift über die Tagung der Jugendpflegedezernaten bei der Regierung der Rheinprovinz 10 Juni 1920," at which Hinze of the Welfare Ministry pointed out that because of the desperate financial straits of the state no increase in funding would be available and that the limited funds that were available would have to be budgeted carefully. For expenditures during the French occupation of the Ruhr, see HSTAD 33107, Jugenpflegerische Notstandmassnahmen, Unterstützungskonto (Ruhrkampf): district governor to the mayor of Hamborn, 4 April 1923, in which he made several million (hyperinflation) marks available for Catholic youth organizations in Hamborn. The file also contains numerous requests for funds from various youth groups throughout the Ruhr.

9   Greinert, op. cit., p. 130. See also pp. 101–12, 129–43, for key developments in *Berufsschulen* during the 1920s.

10   For this and the following, see Margarete Schecker, *Die Entwicklung der Mädchenberufsschule* (Weinheim, 1963), pp. 198–211. STAD III 3671, Fortbildungsschule für Mädchen: #10, decree of 17 April 1919 from the Imperial Ministry for Economic Demobilization, transmitted from District Governor Kruse to the lord mayor of Düsseldorf, on the need for obligatory continuation schools for unemployed young women. See also #13, Verzeichnis der gewerblichen Fortbildungsschulen für Mädchen im Regierungsbezirk Düsseldorf. The number of young women enrolled in such schools increased from two thousand in 1920 to seven thousand in 1924. Programmatic comments on youth cultivation for young women are to be found in HSTAD 45269, Konferenzen: #184–87, "Niederschrift: Sitzung zur Klärung grundsätzlichen Fragen

über die Methoden der Jugendpflege im Regierungsbezirk Düsseldorf,"
9 March 1922. See also Giesecke, op. cit., pp. 149–50.

11   Giesecke, op. cit., pp. 140–1.

12   See the comments by Government Councillor Rodewald in "Organisation
      und Stand der Jugendpflege im Regierungsbezirk Köln," in HSTAD
      45269, Konferenzen: #95–6, "Niederschrift über die Tagung der Ju-
      gendpflegedezernaten bei der Regierungen der Rheinprovinz am 10
      Juni 1920," on the need for physical strength if Germany was not to be
      insulted and attacked by weak and inferior neighbors. These comments
      were reinforced by Hinze, #48, at the same conference, when he pro-
      claimed that "substitutes for lost military service must be created in youth
      cultivation. It should not be spoken of much in public so that the Entente
      does not make difficulties." For the claims of gymnastic instructors, see
      #31, "Denkschrift der Turnaufsichtsbeamen westdeutschen Städte über
      die zukunftige Ausgestaltung körperliche Erziehung," Barmen, 2 De-
      cember 1919; #28, "Neugestaltung des städtischen Turn- und Sportwe-
      sens." For a critique of the one-sided emphasis on physical training and
      the disruptions that paramilitary groups like the Jungdeutschlandbund
      had caused for youth cultivation, as well as negative comments about
      the attempts by the Reichsausschuss für Leibesübungen to separate phys-
      ical training from other youth activities, see #46–7, comments of Hintze
      of the Welfare Ministry at the Rhenish conference of 10 June 1920. For
      Father Jahn, see the opening remarks of Government Councillor Hecker
      at the Reichsjugendwettkampf in Geldern in 1926 in HSTAD 33282,
      Jugendpflege 1926.

13   Giesecke, op. cit., pp. 146–9; HSTAD 33123, Verwahrlosung von Ju-
      gend: See the circular of 20 November 1920 from Welfare Minister
      Stegerwald to district governors, noting that he had received countless
      complaints about dance crazes and alcohol abuse of youth and requesting
      local reports and recommendations. See also the recommendations to
      the welfare minister from the district governor, 15 February 1922, on
      the need for restrictions on youthful smoking, bar visits, and aimless
      wandering about. According to the district governor, "[T]he cigarette in
      the mouth of a twelve- to sixteen-year-old lad has become an intentionally
      and obtrusively demonstrated symbol of new freedom, a sign of his
      complete unconcern for authority and discipline." For local reports on
      dance crazes, alcohol abuse, and general wildness, see HSTAD 33104,
      Jugendfürsorge: Alkohol- und Tanzverbote. The county welfare officer
      of Kempen county called the pleasure seeking of youth a "temporary
      mental illness." The report from the district school office in Essen of 29
      April 1921 deplored youthful pleasure seeking but pointed out that
      moral policing had largely failed during the war, when the situation was
      more propitious for such measures, and added that only positive mea-
      sures could lead to some success. The county commissioner of Essen
      Landkreis, in his report of 29 April 1921, saw high wages of youth as
      the most serious problem and urged passage of forced savings. As evi-
      denced by the letter of the mayor of Duisberg to the district governor
      and Prussian Welfare Ministry of 8 December 1922, compulsory savings

for youth were under consideration there. In a letter to the Welfare Ministry of 13 February 1923 the district governor observed that a compulsory savings scheme would have to be national in scope; otherwise, youth would leave any district where such a scheme was in effect. He advised voluntary savings, given the tense political situation.

14 HSTAD 33093a, Kino für Jugendliche: report on cinema visits of youth from the police chief in Essen to the district governor, 3 April 1923; report of 4 December 1923 from the lord mayor and Local Committee on Youth Cultivation in Düsseldorf on control of cinema visits.

15 Detlev J. Peukert, *Jugend zwischen Krieg und Krise* (Cologne, 1987), pp. 271–84. Although much of this is concerned with the depression years of the early 1930s, the statistics on pp. 282–3 make clear that delinquency peaked in the early 1920s, especially during the hyperinflation. On youthful vagabondism, see also *Die Jugendwohlfahrtspflege der Stadt Düsseldorf mit besonder Berüchsichtigung der gesundheitlichen Fürsorge* (Düsseldorf, 1926), p. 9.

16 On the inclusion of representatives of Socialist-affiliated youth groups at the local level, see HSTAD 33278, Jugendpflege 1922–4: letter from the district governor to the county commissioner in Wesel, 6 October 1922. The district governor stated that "labor youth groups in the entire district belong without further ado in youth cultivation organizations. . . ." When the issue still was not settled the following spring, he cited the decree of the minister for science, art, and popular education of 17 December 1918 for his decision: letter of the district governor to the county commissioner of Wesel, 14 March 1923. For examples of hostility between representatives of bourgeois and Socialist youth organizations, see HSTAD 45269, Konferenzen: #102, "Organisation und Stand der Jugendpflege im Regierungsbezirk Aachen"; HSTAD 33278, Jugendpflege 1922–4: letter of county commissioner of Essen Landkreis to the mayor of Rotthausen on the protests of the Socialist representative on the youth cultivation board about the underrepresentation of labor; HSTAD 33282, Jugendpflege 1926: "Sitzung des Ortsausschusses für Jugendpflege," 5 November 1926, Ohligs, where the nonparticipation of the Workers' Sports Cartel in the county youth festival was ascribed to "unbridgeable differences in world views." For initial hesitancy on the part of the Socialists to become involved in official youth cultivation committees, see HSTAD 45269, Konferenzen: #7, "Rundschreiben des Hauptvorstands der Arbeiterjugendvereine Deutschlands, 'Hinein in die staatlichen Jugendpflege Ausschüsse!' " December 1919.

17 HSTAD 45629, Konferenzen: #126, "Protokoll: Bezirksausschuss für Jugendpflege 27 Juni 1921," for the comments of Oberrealschule Direktor Neuendorf of Müllheim–Ruhr on the need for nonparty and supraparty nationalism that could overcome the antagonism between left and right among youth, and the comments of the district governor on the cultivation of good national consciousness while excluding party politics from youth cultivation. See also Giesecke, op. cit., pp. 147–8.

18 For questions about admitting Communists to official youth cultivation boards, see HSTAD 33278, Jugendpflege 1922–4: letter of 1 June 1922 from the government assessor in Moers to the district governor in Düs-

seldorf and the letter of the district governor in Düsseldorf to the county commissioner in Moers, 15 June 1922, in which he urged the local committee to investigate thoroughly whether only party politics were pursued by Communist youth. He also stated, however, that it would be better to get all youth groups to cooperate, rather than excluding some.

19 HSTAD 45269, Konferenzen: "Protokoll-Bezirksauschuss für Jugendpflege 27 Juni 1921," for the discussion of the relation of youth cultivation to the youth movement and the relation of the prewar *Wandervogel* to postwar youth groups like the Deutschnationale Jugendbund, which the speaker supported. For activities in accordance with middle-class cultural norms, see HSTAD 33120, Jugendpflege Sammelberichte: Veranstaltungen des Ausschusses für Jugendpflege Hamborn am Rhein, 17 October 1925. In this coal-mining city, the committee had spent 10,800 marks from the city for youth concerts and plays. Among the six concerts were one of Mozart and several of Romantic composers. For the uses of folk dance, see HSTAD 45266, Jugendpflege Sammelberichte: letter of M. Schnick of the Elberfeld Trade School to Government Councillor Hecker, 3 November 1926, inviting him to a folk-dance festival that would include members of the youth movement "from the extreme left to the extreme right." For the need for rooms for small *Wandervogel*-like groups to meet and for the organization of hikes with songs, lute, and guitar playing, see HSTAD 33261, Jahresbericht des Kreisjugendpfleger und Jugendpflegerin: "Bericht des Gewerbeoberlehrers Holz über seine ehrenamtliche Tätigkeit als Kreisjugendpflegers im Stadtkreis Düsseldorf."

20 Giesecke, op. cit., pp. 156–7. See the comments of Government Assessor Bertram deploring the moral and ecological dangers arising from leaderless hikes and urging that financial support be made available only when hikes were accompanied by an older leader and that leaderless groups be excluded from youth hostels. HSTAD 45269, Konferenzen: #151, "Niederschrift über die Konferenz der Kreisjugendpfleger und Kreisjugendpflegerinnen," 17 September 1921.

21 See, for example, David Blackbourn and Geoff Eley, *The Peculiarities of German History* (Oxford, 1984), pp. 147, 275–85. They concentrate, however, almost exclusively on the political side of this watershed decade.

22 For an English justification of making continuation schools mandatory, based on fears about the future unemployability of young males entering dead-end unskilled positions, see Michael Sadler, "Should Attendance at Continuation Schools Be Mandatory?" in M. E. Sadler, ed., *Continuation Schools in England and Elsewhere* (Manchester, 1907), pp. 699–702, 709–10.

23 Richard J. Evans, "The Sociological Interpretation of German Labour History," in Richard J. Evans, ed., *The German Working Class; The Politics of Everyday Life 1888–1933* (London, 1982), pp. 34–46.

24 Vernon L. Lidtke, *The Alternative Culture: Socialist Labor in Imperial Germany* (New York, 1985), pp. 6–13. Lidtke's conceptual framework of segmentation, coercion, and conflict finds considerable support in the history of the youth salvation campaign as well.

25 Michael Mitterauer, *Sozialgeschichte der Jugend* (Frankfurt am Main, 1986), p. 220.

26 The view that the decision for war was a last desperate gamble by embattled elites is argued most vigorously by Hans-Ulrich Wehler, *The German Empire 1871–1918* (Leamington Spa, 1985), pp. 193–201. For a critique of this interpretation, see David E. Kaiser, "Germany and the Origins of the First World War," *Journal of Modern History* (September 1983), pp. 442–74.

27 Peter Stachura, *Nazi Youth in the Weimar Republic* (Santa Barbara, 1975), p. 245.

28 "Satzungen des Jugendbundes der Nat.-Soz. Arbeiter Partei (März 1922)," reprinted in Hans-Christian Brandenburg, *Die Geschichte der HJ* (Cologne, 1968), pp. 239–40.

29 Richard Grunberger, *The 12-Year Reich* (New York, 1971), pp. 267–74; Fritz Petrick, *Zur sozialen Lage der Arbeiterjugend in Deutschland 1933–1939* (East Berlin, 1974), pp. 88–95.

30 Detlev J. Peukert, *Inside Nazi Germany* (New Haven, 1987), pp. 145–66.

Bibliography

State archives

Hauptstaatsarchiv Düsseldorf – Zweig Kalkum (HSTAD)

Akten der Regierung zu Aachen

17055 A14	Feste, Veranstaltungen der Jugendverbände 1923–9
17056 A14	Verfassungsfeier und Jugendwettkämpfe 1929
17058 A14	JugendpflegeVerschiedenes, Bd. 1, 1925–9
17064 A14	Zusammenarbeit der Landesjugendämter und Regierungen, Bd. 1, 1925–7
17065 A14	Errichtung von Jugendämtern, Bd. 1, 1924–7
17066 A14	Jugendpflege Verschiedenes 1929–33
17069 A14	Berichte über die Jugendpflegearbeit durch die Kreisjugendpfleger und die Behörden
17070 A14	Reichsjugendwohlfahrtsgesetz, Bd. 1, 1920–3
17071 A14	Reichsjugendwohlfahrtsgesetz, Bd. 1, 1921–8
17072 A14	Desgl. Bd. 2, 1928–9
17073 A14	Desgl. Bd. 3, 1929–33
17075 A14	Die im Interesse der Jugendpflege empfohlenen Schriften und Bücher, Bd. 5, 1921–30
17078 A14	Schundbekämpfung 1925–9
17969 A14	Kreisjugendpfleger 1924–30
17970 A14	Kreisjugendpfleger 1928–35
17971 A14	Kreisjugendpflegerkonferenzen 1929–31
17972 A14	Bezirksjugendpfleger, Bd. 1, 1922–9
17973 A14	Orts-, Kreis-, Bezirksausschusse
17974 A14	Sitzung des Bezirksausschusses für Jugendpflege 1921–7
17976 A14	Allgemeine Bestimmungen über Bezirksjugendpfleger und Kreisjugendpfleger, Bd. 1, 1922–9
17977 A14	Kreisjugendpfleger, Bd. 2, 1917–27
18506 A14	Statistik der Jugendpflegeorganisationen 1932

Akten der Regierung zu Düsseldorf

8920–1	Verzeichnis politische Zeit- und Flugschriften
9004	Kino

9039–41	Terminalberichte über die sozialdemokratische Bewegung 1895–1907
9058	Sammelberichte zu den Terminalberichte 1895–1907
15984–5	Spezial- und Sammelberichte zu generellen Angelegenheiten über die sozialdemokratische Bewegung
16002	Sozialdemokratische Turn- und Radfahrer Vereine
16005	Sozialdemokratische Agitation unter der Jugend
24653–4	Schutz von jugendlichen Arbeiter
24656–7	Schutz von jugendlichen Arbeiter
30411–12	Ueberwachung der Arbeiterbewegung 1903–15
30423	Reichsvereingesetz 1908–11
30473	Schundliteratur 1915–17
30480	Kino
32994	Jugendpflege: Druckschriften 1910–16
32998	Leibsübungen für Schulentlassene 1912–13
33001	Forderung der Pflege der weiblichen Schulentlassene 1912–13
33031	Jugendpflege 1915
33064–5	Vorbereitung der Jugend für den Krieg
33081	Jugendpflege-Bezirksausschüsse
33082	Bezirks- und Kreisausschüsse für Jugendpflege, Bd. 2, 1918–20
33083	Mitteilungen des Bezirksauschüsses für Jugendpflege, Bd. 4, 1926–8
33085–6	Orts- und Kreis Ausschüsse für Jugendpflege
33087	Jugendpflege
33093	Kino für Jugendliche 1908–27
33093a	desgl.
33094	Kreisjugendpflegerinnen 1914–17
33095	Bildstelle des Bezirksausschüsses für Jugendpflege 1922–7
33097	Pflege der schulentlassenen Jugend-Fortbildungskurse, Bd. 1, 1917–21
33097a	Kreisjugenpfleger
33099	Kreisjugendpflegerinnen 1920–5
33100	desgl. 1923–7
33102	Statistik der Jugendpflegeorganisation 1920–2
33104	Jugendfürsorge: Alkohol- und Tanzverbote 1916–22
33105	Jugendheime, Turnhalle, Sportplätze, Bd. 1, 1921–3
33106	desgl. Bd. 2, 1923–5
33107	Jugendpflegerische Notstandsmassnahmen, Unterstützungskonto (Ruhrkampf) 1923
33109	Lehrgänge für Jugendpfleger, Bd. 4, 1918–20
33110	Staatsbehilfen, Bd. 2, 1916–20
33111	desgl. Bd. 3, 1920–1
33112	desgl. Bd. 4, 1921
33120	Jugendpflege Sammelberichte 1915–26
33122	Berufsberatung und Lehrstellenvermittlung 1914–19

33123	Verwahrlosung der Jugend – Reichsjugendwohlfahrts-gesetz
33151	Gefährdetenfürsorge, Polizeifürsorgestellen, Bd. 1, 1925–7
33237	Beratungsstelle für Jugendpflege
33240	Beratungsstelle für Jugendpflege
33241	Berichte der Kreisjugendpfleger 1927
33253	Veranstaltungen für Jugendpflege 1926
33261	Jahresbericht des Kreisjugendpfleger und Jugendpflegerin 1925
33278	Jugendpflege 1922–4
33282	Jugendpflege 1926
33299	Berichte der Kreisjugendpfleger 1922–4
33299a	Jugendpflege Sonderberichte, Bd. 4, 1917–23
33311	Zeitschriften für Jugendpflege
33313	Orts- und Kreisausschüsse für Jugendpflege 1924–6
33320	Rheinische Jugend
33326	Ortsausschüsse für Jugendpflege 1925
33505	Schutz von jugendlichen Arbeiter
33512	Schutz von jugendlichen Arbeiter
33520	Lehrling: Fabrik 1877–1931
42781	Sammelberichte zu den Terminalberichte 1910
42789	Sozialdemokratische Frauenbewegung
42809	Terminalberichte über die Sozialdemokratie 1912–14
42813	Sammelberichte zu den Terminalberichte 1912–14
43033	Jugendspiele 1911
45266	Jugendpfleger Sammelberichte 1915–26
45269	Konferenzen
46077	Kino

Akten der Regierung zu Düsseldorf Präsidialburo

28	Zeitungsberichte 1911–14
29	Zeitungsberichte 1914–18

Municipal archives

Stadtarchiv Düsseldorf (STAD)

III 2134–36	Jugendspiel 1888–
III 2142	Bekämpfung des Schmutzes
III 2169	Schüler Verbände
III 2175	Fürsorge für die schulentlassene Jugend 1907–13
III 2176–78	Jugendpflege 1911–18
III 3577	Schulfeste
III 3595–3607a	Die gewerbliche Fortbildungsschule
III 3609	Lehrpläne

III 3611	Die gewerbliche Fortbildungsschule
III 3613	Schulzucht bei der Fortbildungsschule 1908–16
III 3617–22	Die Organisation der Fortbildungschule
III 3627–8	Statistische Uebersichten der Gewerbeschulen
III 3629	Die gewerbliche Fortbildungsschule
III 3641	Lehr- und Lernmittel bei der Fortbildungsschule
III 3642–4	Bücherei, Lehr- und Lernmittel
III 3645–6	Staatszuschüsse der Gewerbeschulen
III 3660–4	Die kaufmännische Fortbildungschule 1888–1920
III 3670–1	Fortbildungsschule für Mädchen
III 3672–4	Schulbesuch in der Mädchenberufsschule
III 3675	Jugendfürsorge in der Fortbildungsschule für Mädchen
III 3695–3704	Das Arbeitsschulseminar
III 3705	Einführung der obligatorischen Fortbildungsschule
III 3710	Die militärische Vorbereitung der Fortbildungsschüler
III 3711–12	Die nebenamtlich beschäftigten Lehrer bei der Fortbildungsschule
III 3717	Die kaufmännische Fortbildungsschule
III 3744	Die Fortbildungsschule-Charlottestrasse

Stadtarchiv Essen (STAE)

Rep. 102 IX	81	Die Stadtauschuss für Jugendpflege
	87	Die bei den Volksschulen während des Krieges getroffenen Massnahmen
	91	Vermittlung von Lehrstellen für schulentlassene Kinder
	166	Die Fortbildungsschule
	172	Das Statut der Fortbildungsschule und die Wahl des Kuratoriums
	175	Die Stunden und das Lehrplan der Fortbildungsschule
	178	Einführung der obligatorischen Fortbildungsschule
	188	Förderung der Jugendpflege bei der hiesigen Fortbildungsschule
	191	Nachweisung derjenige Schüler die voraussichtlich zur Besuch der kaufmännische Fortbildungsschule sind
	202	Fortbildungsschule-Kriegsmassnahmen
	373	Beschaffung der Bilder der Kaiser und Kaiserinnen
	374	Kaisers Geburtstagfeier
	377–7a	Fürsorge für die schulentlassene männliche Jugend
	378	Anträge Jugendpflege 1912–18
	379	Förderung der Jugend- und Volksspiel 1911–19
	381	Militärische Vorbereitung der Jugend bei der Fortbildungsschule

Rep. 102 XXII   174   Fürsorge für die Jugend
               175   Kurse zur Ausbildung in der Jugendpflege

Stadtarchiv Solingen (STAS)

F-3-2	Bd. II gen.	Sozialdemokratische Frauenbewegung
F-3-24	Bd. III spec.	Politische Vereine und Versammlungen
F-3-66	Bd. I spec.	Sozialdemokratische Jugendbewegung 1914–21
G-1-106	Bd. I	Arbeitsverhältnisse, Beschäftigung jugendlichen Arbeiter und kaufmännischen Angestellten
G-1-107	Bd. I gen.	Die Ausführung der Gewerbeordnung
G-1-113	Bd. I spec.	Kinderarbeit in gewerblichen Betrieben
J-5-1		Sonntags- und Fortbildungsschule 1836–88
V-C-22		Protokollbuch der Jugendfürsorge Ohligs
V-D-17		Protokollbuch der Ortsausschusses für Jugendpflege Wald
V-D-18		Protokollbuch der Vereine Jugendschutz Wald

Religious and church archives

Historisches Archiv des Erzbistums Köln (HAEK)

XXIII   Generalsekretariat der Jugendvereine 1908–19

Kommission für Zeitgeschichte (Bonn)

1/11	Mosterts
1/21	Mosterts
1/13	Jugendbewegung und Jugendpflege (Jacob Clemens)

Industrial archives

Historisches Archiv der Fried Krupp Gmbh., Essen

WA 41	73–265	Fortbildungsschule Essen
	73–266	Fortbildungsschule Altendorf
	73–273	Gewerbliche Fortbildungsschule für Mädchen
	73–301	Ev. Kirchengemeinde Jugendpfarrer Amt
WA IV	128	Zirkular #8, 1884
	1254	Verschiedene Arbeitsangelegenheiten 1913–18
	1354	Unterlagen, Bd. 14, Wohlfahrtspflege
	1408	Lehrlingswesen
	1566	Kruppsche Jugendpflege
	1966	Lehrlingswesen
WA VII		Errinerungen
	2	Heiken
	64	Hausmann
	85	Kollenberg

	116	von Werden
	127	Heiken
	128	Heinrich
	134	G. Heinrich
WA Xa3	28	Wohlfahrtseinrichtung
	37	Jugendpflege
	114	(s. 165) Zirkular #14, 1912
	114	(s. 169) Zirkular #16, 1912
	117	(s. 35) Zirkular Lehrlingsausbildung
	124	(s. 26) Bericht-Einweihung
WA XII	52	Jugendpflege Riemers
WA XIX	42	Berufsbildung

Newspapers and other periodicals

Arbeiter-Jugend
Düsseldorfer General Anzeiger
Düsseldorfer Tageblatt
Düsseldorfer Volksblatt
Düsseldorfer Volkszeitung
Düsseldorfer Zeitung
Essener Chronik
Gruss aus der Heimat
Handbuch des deutschen Fortbildungsschulwesens
Jünglings-Bote
Der Leuchtturm
Metallarbeiterzeitung
Technik und Wirtschaft
Die Wacht

Protocols, reports, and official documents

Erwerbslose Grossstadtjugend. Düsseldorf, 1925.
Essener Bürgerbuch. Essen, 1912.
Essener Chronik 1911.
Jahresberichte der königlich-preussischen Regierungs- und Gewerberäthe und Berg-behörde. 1902, 1903, 1906.
Jahresberichte des Vereins Jugendschutz. Solingen, 1911, 1912, 1916.
Jahresberichte: Zentralstelle für die arbeitende Jugend Deutschlands.
Die Jugendwohlfahrtspflege der Stadt Düsseldorf mit besonder Berüchsichtigung der gesundheitlichen Fürsorge. Düsseldorf, 1926.
Mitteilungen des Bezirksausschusses für Jugendpflege im Regierungsbezirk Düsseldorf.
Protokoll über die Verhandlungen der Kreis Synode Düsseldorf. 26 June 1912; 18 June 1913; 21 January 1917.
Protokoll der Verhandlungen der 6 Kongresses der Gewerkschaften Deutschlands. 1908.
Protokoll über die Verhandlungen der Parteitages der Sozialdemokratischen Partei Deutschlands. 1908, 1913.

Prussia Landtag: Haus der Abgeordneten, Stenographische Berichte über die Verhandlungen, 59 Sitz, Bd. 4. Berlin, 1911.
Rheinische Provincial Fürsorge-Erziehungsanstalten Rheindahlen und Solingen. 1906.
Schriften der Centralstelle für Arbeiterwohlfahrtseinrichtungen. 1900, 1901, 1904.
Schriften der Gesellschaft für Soziale Reform. 1912.
Schriften des Vereins für Sozialpolitik 15, 62–70, 134.
Schriften der Zentralstelle für Volkswohlfahrt. 1909, 1912, 1913, 1916.
Statistik des deutschen Reiches.
Statistisches Jahrbuch deutscher Städte, 20 Jg. Breslau, 1914.
Statistisches Jahrbuch der Stadt Berlin, 32 Jg. Berlin, 1913.
Statistisches Jahrbuch der Stadt Essen. 1907.
Die Verhandlungen des elften Evangelisch-sozialen Kongresses abgehalten zu Karlsruhe 7–8 Juni 1900.
Verhandlungen über die Wirksamkeit des Fürsorgeerziehungsgesetzes: Konferenz der Centralstelle für Jugendfürsorge in Berlin am 15. und 16. Juni 1906. Berlin, 1906.
Verwaltungsbericht der Stadt Düsseldorf (Bericht über die Verwaltung und den Stand der Gemeinde Angelegenheiten der Stadt Düsseldorf).
Vierteljahrhefte zur Statistik des deutschen Reiches. 1895, 1900, 1906, 1907, 1908, 1912, 1913.
Weibliche Jugendpflege: Dritter Führerkurs veranstaltet von dem Hamburischen Landesverband für Jugendpflege. Hamburg, 1917.
Zur Pflege der weiblichen Jugend, edited by Hauptausschuss für Jugendpflege in Charlottenburg. Jena, 1913.

Books, articles, and other published sources appearing before 1945

Baedecker, Diedrich. *Alfred Krupp und die Entwicklung der Gussstahlfabrik zu Essen*, 2nd ed. Essen, 1912.
Baum, Marie. *Wohnweise kinderreicher Familien in Düsseldorf Stadt und Land*. Berlin, 1917.
Baumgarten, Otto, et al. *Geistige und Sittliche Wirkungen des Krieges in Deutschland*. Stuttgart, 1927.
Beiträge der Industrie zu den Kosten der Handwerksausbildung und Handwerkswohlfahrtspflege. Bearbeitet von der Handelskammer zu Düsseldorf. Düsseldorf, 1908.
"Die Bekämpfung der Schundliteratur." *Flugschriften der Zentralstelle für Volkswohlfahrt*, Heft 5. Berlin, 1911.
Bernhard, Ernst. *Höhere Arbeitsintensität bei kurzerer Arbeitszeit*. Leipzig, 1909.
Bertram, Adolf. *Jugendpflege im Lichte der katholische Lebensauffassung*. Düsseldorf, 1912(?).
Blitz, Hugo. *Die Allgemein geistig-sittliche Fortbildung unserer schulentlassenen männlichen Volksjugend in obligatorischen Jugendvereine*. Lüneberg, 1901.
Bloehm, Walter. *Der Paragraphenlehrling*. Berlin, 1907.
Brake, Ludwig. *Werkzeugsmaschinen und Arbeitszerlegung*. Berlin, 1911.

Brandt, Otto. *Studien zur Wirtschafts- und Verwaltungsgeschichte der Stadt Düsseldorf im 19. Jahrhundert.* Düsseldorf, 1900.

Bray, Reginald. *Boy Labour and Apprenticeship.* London, 1912.

Calwer, Richard. *Das Kost- und Logiswesen im Handwerk.* Berlin, 1908.

Christliche Gewerkschaften und Arbeiterjugend. Generalsekretariat der christlichen Gewerkschaften. Cologne, 1910.

Classen, Walther. *Vom Lehrjungen zum Staatsbürger.* Hamburg, 1909.

———. *Zucht und Freiheit: Ein Wegweiser für die deutsche Jugendpflege.* Munich, 1914.

"Correspondenzblatt der Gerkschaften Deutschlands," 11 December 1909.

Dawson, William H. *The German Workman.* New York, 1906.

———. *Municipal Life and Government in Germany.* London, 1914.

Dehn, Günther. *Grossstadtjugend.* Berlin, 1919; 2nd ed., 1922.

"Denkschrift des Evangelischen Ober-Kirchenrate betr. die Ausgestaltung der kirchlichen Jugendpflege." Berlin, 1917.

Denkschrift über die Grundsteinlegung des Evangelisches Jugendhauses. Essen, 1911.

Deutsche Zentrale für Jugendpflege, ed. *Handbuch für Jugendpflege.* Langensalza, 1913.

Fest-Nummer des Vereins Anzeiger des Evangelisches Jugendvereins Essen. Essen, 1912.

Flitner, Wilhelm. "Der Krieg und die Jugend." In *Geistige und Sittliche Wirkungen,* edited by Otto Baumgarten. Stuttgart, 1927, pp. 217–356.

50 Jahre Jugendarbeit 1875–1925. CVJM Solingen. Solingen, 1925.

Gerok, Otto. "Der Handwerkslehrling." In *Die Entwicklungsjahre,* Heft 5. Leipzig, 1913.

Geschichte des Evangelischen-Jugendvereins Essen an der Ruhr. Essen, 1913(?).

Grünweller, August. *Der Krieg als Volkserzieher und die Volksschule.* Rheydt, 1915.

Haarbeck, Pastor. *Was können und müssen die kirchlichen Organe für ein tatkräftige Pflege und Erziehung der Konfirmierten Jugend tun?* Moers, 1911.

Hassell, Ulrich von. *Wer trägt die Schuld?* Stuttgart, 1907.

"Hauswirtschaftliche Unterweisung für die gesamte weibliche Jugend." *Flugschriften der Zentralstelle für Volkswohlfahrt,* Heft 2. 1909.

Heinen, Anton. *Mein Leben als Volksbildner: Worum es mir ging.* Unpublished manuscript. Stadtarchiv Mönchen-Gladbach.

Heitmann, Ludwig. *Grossstadt und Religion,* vol. 2. Hamburg, 1925.

Howe, Frederick C. *European Cities at Work.* New York, 1913.

Ilgenstein, Wilhelm. *Die Gedankenwelt der modernen Arbeiterjugend.* Berlin, 1912.

Jeidels, Otto. *Die Methoden der Arbeiterentlöhnung in der rheinisch-westfälischen Eisenindustrie.* Berlin, 1907.

Kanitz, Otto Felix. *Das proletarische Kind in der bürgerliche Gesellschaft.* Jena, 1925.

Die katholische Jugend Deutschlands. Düsseldorf, 1925.

Kautz, Heinrich. *Um die Seele des Industriekindes,* 2nd ed. Donauwörth, 1929.

Kempf, Rosa. "Das Leben der jungen Fabrikmädchen in München." *Schriften des Vereins für Sozialpolitik,* vol. 135, no. 2. Leipzig, 1911.

Kerschensteiner, Georg. *Berufsbildung und Berufsschule: Ausgewählte Pädagogische Schriften,* vol. 1. Paderborn, 1966.

————. *The Schools and the Nation.* London, 1914.

Kipper, Joseph. *Die sozialistische Jugendbewegung in Deutschland.* Mönchen-Gladbach, 1912.

Kohlmann, Curt. *Fabrikschulen.* Berlin, 1911.

Korn, Karl. *Die bürgerliche Jugendbewegung.* Berlin, 1910.

————. *Die Arbeiterjugendbewegung.* Berlin, 1922.

Lande, Dora. "Arbeits- und Lohn Verhältnisse in der Berliner Maschinenindustrie zu Beginn des 20. Jahrhunderts." *Schriften des Vereins für Sozialpolitik,* vol. 134. Leipzig, 1910.

Landsberg, J. F. "Das Jugendgericht." *Einführung in das lebende Recht,* Heft 3. Hannover, 1912.

————. "Die öffentliche Erziehung gefährdeten Jugend." *Einführung in das lebende Recht,* Heft 8. Hannover, 1913.

Lazarsfeld, Paul F., ed. *Jugend und Beruf.* Jena, 1931.

Leinert, Martin. *Die Sozialgeschichte der Grossstadt.* Hamburg, 1925.

Liepmann, Moritz. *Die Kriminalität der Jugendlichen und ihre Bekämpfung.* Tübingen, 1909.

Levenstein, Adolf. *Die Arbeiterfrage.* Munich, 1912.

Lippart, G. "Die Ausbildung des Lehrlings in der Werkstätte." *Technik und Wirtschaft,* 5, no. 8 (August 1912), pp. 501–18.

Matschoss, Conrad. *Ein Jahrhundert deutscher Maschinenbau von der mechanischen Werkstälte bis zur deutschen Maschinenfabrik 1819–1919.* Berlin, 1919.

Mosterts, Carl, ed. *Handbuch für die Katholiken Düsseldorfs.* Düsseldorf, 1909.

————. *Die seelsorgische Vorbereitung auf die Schulentlassung.* Düsseldorf, 1916.

————. *Der Religionsunterricht in der Fortbildungsschule.* Düsseldorf, 1916(?).

————. "Verband der katholischen Jünglingsvereinigungen Deutschlands." in *Jugendpflegeverbände,* edited by Hertha Siemering, Berlin, 1918, pp. 32–66.

————. *Die Verbandzentrale der katholischen Jünglingsvereinigungen Deutschlands in ihren ersten zehn Jahren.* Düsseldorf, 1918.

————. *Jünglingsseelsorge.* Freiburg, 1920.

————. *Krieg und Kriminalität in Deutschland.* Stuttgart, 1930.

Nachrichten des Hamburgisches Landesverbändes. Hamburg, 1916.

Oehler, Adalbert. *Düsseldorf im Weltkrieg.* Düsseldorf, 1927.

Pieper, August. *Jugendfürsorge und Jugendvereine.* Mönchen-Gladbach, 1908.

Potts, K. *Die Entstehung und Entwicklung der Arbeit an der evangelischen männlichen Jugend in Düsseldorf.* Düsseldorf, 1920.

Rieppel, A. von. "Lehrlingsausbildung und Fabrikschulen," *Technik und Wirtschaft,* 4, no. 3 (March 1911), pp. 146–54.

Rühle, Otto. *Das proletarische Kind.* Munich, 1911.

Sadler, M. E., ed. *Continuation Schools in England and Elsewhere.* Manchester, 1907.

Schmedes, Hella. *Das Lehrlingswesen in der deutschen Eisen- und Stahlindustrie.* Münster, 1930.

Schultz, Clemens. *Gesammelte Schriften eines Jugendpflegers.* Berlin, 1918.

————. "Die Halbstarken." In *Die Entwicklungsjahre,* Heft 2. Leipzig, 1912.

Schulz, Heinrich. *Gehörst du zu uns?* Berlin, 1912.

Shadwell, Arthur. *Industrial Efficiency,* 2nd ed. London, 1913.

Siemering, Hertha. "Pflege der schulentlassene weibliche Jugend." *Flugschriften der Zentralstelle für Volkswohlfahrt.* Berlin, 1914.
———. *Die deutschen Jugendpflegeverbände.* Berlin, 1918.
———. *Die weibliche Jugend Preussens in Wirtschaft und Beruf.* Berlin, 1930.
Sörgel, H. T. "Zwei Nürnberger Metallgewerbe." *Untersuchungen über die Lage des Handwerks in Deutschland,* vol. 3, Süddeutschland. *Schriften des Vereins für Sozialpolitik,* 62. Leipzig, 1895.
"Die städtische Arbeitslosen – Beschäftigung im Winter 1901–2." *Mitteilungen der Statistik der Stadt Dusseldorf,* p. 4.
Tews, Johannes. *Sozialdemokratie und öffentliches Bildungswesen.* Langensalza, 1919.
Timm, Paul. *Was kann die Volksschule zur Förderung der Jugendpflege beitragen?* Potsdam, 1912.
Tollkühn, Gertrud. *Die planmässige Ausbildung des gewerblichen Fabriklehrlings in der metall- und holzverarbeitende Industrie.* Jena, 1926.
Urwick, E. J., *Studies of Boy Life in Our Cities.* London, 1904.
Voigt, Theodor P. *Berufswahl für Knaben.* Berlin, n.d.
Volksverein für das katholische Deutschland, ed. *Die Jugend: Vorträge für Jugendvereine.* Mönchen-Gladbach, 1909.
Wegeleben, Fritz. *Die Rationalisierung im deutschen Werkzeugmaschinenbau.* Berlin, 1924.
Weigle, Wilhelm. "Der Einfluss der Jugendvereine auf der sittliche und religiöse Entwicklung der männliche Jugend." Elberfeld, 1902.
———. "Nützliches und Schädliches auf dem Arbeitsgebiet der Jugendvereine." *Stein zum Bau,* 1, no. 2 (1907).
———. *Die Pflege der konfirmierten Jugend in unseren Vereine.* Barmen, 1907.
———. "Die moderne Jugendbewegung." *Stein zum Bau,* 2, no. 2 (1908).
Westhaus, Wilhelm. "Das Düsseldorfer Schlachtergewerbe." *Untersuchungen über die Lage des Handwerks in Deutschland,* Bd. 1., *Schriften des Vereins für Sozialpolitik,* 62 Leipzig, 1895.
Wilden, Josef. "Aufgaben der Innungen zur Pflege des Lehrlingswesens." *Flugschriften der Zentralstelle für Volkswohlfahrt.* 1913.
Wohlfahrtseinrichtungen der Gusstahlfabrik von Fried. Krupp, Bd. 1–3. Essen, 1902.
Wolgast, Heinrich. *Das Elend unserer Jugendliteratur.* Hamburg, 1896.
Zimmermann, Waldemar. "Die Veränderungen der Einkommens- und Lebensverhältnise der deutschen Arbeiter durch den Krieg." In *Die Einwirkung des Krieges auf Bevölkerungsbewegung, Einkommen und Lebenshaltung in Deutschland: Wirtschafts- und Sozialgeschichte des Weltkrieges,* edited by Rudolf Meerwarth, Adolf Guntner, and Waldemar Zimmermann. Stuttgart, 1934, pp. 281–474.

Books, articles, and other printed sources since 1945

Adams, Carole E. *Women Clerks in Wilhelmine Germany.* New York, 1988.
Albisetti, James C. *Secondary School Reform in Imperial Germany.* Princeton, 1983.

Bader, Josef. *Jugend in der Industriekultur.* Munich, 1962.

Bäthge, Martin. *Ausbildung und Herrschaft: Unternehmerinteressen in der Bildungspolitik.* Frankfurt am Main, 1970.

Balkenol, Bernd. *Armut und Arbeitslosigkeit in der Industrialisierung dargestellt am Beispiel Düsseldorfs.* Düsseldorf, 1976.

Balser, Frolinde. *Sozialdemokratie 1848/49–1863.* Stuttgart, 1962.

Barkin, Kenneth P. *The Controversy over German Industrialisation 1890–1902.* Chicago, 1970.

Barth, Ernst. *Entwicklunglinien der deutschen Maschinenbauindustrie von 1870 bis 1914.* East Berlin, 1973.

Baum, Marie. *Anna von Gierke: Ein Lebensbild.* Weinheim, 1954.

———. *Rückblick auf mein Leben.* Heidelberg, 1950.

Bausinger, Hermann, et al. *Grundzüge der Volkskunde.* Darmstadt, 1978.

Becker, Howard S. *Social Problems: A Modern Approach.* New York, 1966.

Bendele, Ulrich. *Sozialdemokratische Schulpolitik und Pädagogik im wilhelminischen Deutschland.* Frankfurt am Main, 1979.

Berg, Christa. *Die Okkupation der Schule.* Heidelberg, 1973.

Bergmann, Klaus. *Agrarromantik und Grossstadtfeindschaft.* Marburg, 1970.

Bernstein, Basil. *Class Codes and Control.* vol. 3, *Towards a Theory of Educational Transmissions.* London, 1975.

Bers, Günther, ed. *Arbeiterjugend im Rheinland.* Hamburg, 1978.

Bertlein, Hermann. *Jugendleben und soziales Bildungsschicksal.* Hannover, 1966.

Bieber, Hans Joachim. *Gewerkschaften in Krieg und Revolution* (2 vols.). Hamburg, 1981.

Blackbourn, David. *Class, Religion and Local Politics in Wilhelmine Germany.* Wiesbaden, 1980.

——— and Eley, Geoff. *The Peculiarities of German History.* Oxford, 1984.

Blankertz, Herwig. *Bildung im Zeitalter der grossen Industrie.* Hannover, 1969.

Bölling, Rainer. *Volksschullehrer und Politik: Der deutsche Lehrerverein 1918–33.* Göttingen, 1978.

Börner, Walter. *Wilhelm Weigle: Leben und Wirken 1862–1932.* Gladbeck, 1974.

Bollenbeck, Georg. *Zur Theorie und Geschichte der frühen Arbeiterlebenserrinerungen.* Siegen, 1976.

Borcherding, Karl. *Wege und Ziele politischer Bildung in Deutschland.* Munich, 1965.

Bordieu, Pierre, and Passeron, Jean Claude. *Reproduction in Education, Society and Culture.* London, 1970.

Born, Karl Erich. *Staat und Sozialpolitik seit Bismarcks Sturz,* vols. 1–2. Wiesbaden, 1957.

———. "Structural Changes in German Social and Economic Development at the End of the Nineteenth Century." In James Sheehan, ed., *Imperial Germany,* New York, 1976, pp. 16–38.

Brady, Robert A. *The Rationalization Movement in Germany,* 2nd ed. New York, 1972.

Brandenburg, Hans-Christian. *Die Geschichte der HJ.* Cologne, 1968.

Brennan, E. J. T., ed. *Education for National Efficiency: The Contribution of Sidney and Beatrice Webb.* London, 1975.

Brose, Eric Dorn. *Christian Labor and the Politics of Frustration in Imperial Germany.* Washington, D.C., 1985.

Brüls, Karl. *Geschichte des Volksvereins.* Teil 1, 1890–1914. Münster, 1960.

Bry, Gerhard. *Wages in Germany 1871–1945.* Princeton, 1960.

Christ, Karl. *Sozialdemokratie und Volkserziehung.* Frankfurt am Main, 1975.

Clarke, John, ed. *Jugendkultur als Widerstand.* Frankfurt am Main, 1979.

Conze, Werner, and Engelhardt, Ulrich, eds. *Arbeiter im Industrialisierungsprozess.* Stuttgart, 1979.

Crew, David. *Town in the Ruhr.* New York, 1979.

Croon, Helmut. "Die Einwirkungen der Industrialisierung auf die gesellschaftlichen Schichtung der Bevölkerung im rheinisch-westfälischen Industriegebiet." *Rheinische Vierteljahrblätter,* 1955.

Ditt, Karl. "Technologischer Wandel und Strukturveränderung der Fabrikarbeiterschaft in Bielefeld 1890–1914." In *Arbeiter im Industrialisierungsprozess,* edited by Werner Conze and Ulrich Engelhardt. 1979, pp. 237–61.

Dyos, H. J., ed. *The Study of Urban History.* London, 1968.

Eisenstadt, S. N. *From Generation to Generation.* New York, 1956.

Elder, Glen H., Jr. *Children of the Great Depression.* Chicago, 1974.

Eley, Geoff. *Reshaping the German Right.* New Haven, 1980.

———. "Labor History, Social History, *Alltagsgeschichte:* Experience, Culture and the Politics of Everyday Life – A New Direction for German Social History? *Journal of Modern History,* 61 (June 1989), pp. 297–343.

Emmerich, Wolfgang, ed. *Proletarische Lebensläüfe,* vols. 1–2. Reinbeck, 1974.

Esler, Anthony. *Generations in History: An Introduction to the Concept.* 1982.

Evans, Richard J. *Sozialdemokratie und Frauenemanzipation im deutschen Kaiserreich.* Berlin, 1976.

———. *Society and Politics in Wilhelmine Germany.* London, 1978.

———, ed. *The German Working Class: The Politics of Everyday Life 1888–1933.* London, 1982.

———, and Lee, W. R., eds. *The German Family.* London, 1981.

Farrell, Ronald, and Swigert, Victoria. *Deviance and Social Control.* Glenview, 1982.

Feldman, Gerald D. *Army, Industry and Labor in Germany 1914–1918.* Princeton, 1966.

Fischer, Fritz. *Bündnis der Eliten.* Düsseldorf, 1979.

Fishman, Sterling. *The Struggle for German Youth.* New York. 1976.

Flora, Peter. "Die Bildungsentwicklung im Prozess der Staaten- und Nationalbildung: Ein vergleichende Analyse." In *Soziologie und Sozialgeschichte,* edited by Peter Christian Ludz Opladen, 1972.

Fogt, Helmut. *Politische Generationen.* Opladen, 1982.

Foucault, Michel. *Discipline and Punish: The Birth of the Prison.* New York, 1979.

———. *Power/Knowledge.* New York, 1980.

Franzoi, Barbara. "Domestic Industry." In John C. Fout, ed. *German Women in the Nineteenth Century.* New York, 1984.

———. *At the Very Least She Pays the Rent: Women and German Industrialization 1871–1914.* Westport, Conn., 1985.

Fricke, Dieter. *Die deutsche Arbeiterbewegung 1869–1914.* East Berlin, 1976.

Friedberger, Walter. *Die Geschichte der Sozialismuskritik im katholischen Deutschland zwischen 1830 und 1914.* Frankfurt am Main, 1978.

Fülberth, Georg. *Proletarische Partei und bürgerliche Literatur.* Neuwied, 1978.
Gestrich, Andreas. *Traditionelle Jugendkultur und Industrialisierung.* Göttingen, 1986.
Giesecke, Hermann. *Vom Wandervogel bis zur Hitlerjugend.* Munich, 1981.
Gillis, John R. *Youth and History: Tradition and Change in European Age Relations 1770 to the Present.* New York, 1974.
Goslin, D. A., ed. *Handbook of Socialization.* Chicago, 1973.
Grebing, Helga. *History of the German Labour Movement.* Leamington Spa, 1985.
Greinert, Wolf-Dietrich. *Schule als Instrument sozialer Kontrolle und Objekt privater Interessen: Der Beitrag der Berufsschule zur politischen Erziehung der Unterschichten.* Hannover, 1975.
Griese, Hartmut M. *Sozialwissenschaftliche Jugendtheorie.* Weinheim, 1977.
Groh, Dieter. *Negative Integration und revolutionärer Attentismus.* Frankfurt am Main, 1973.
———. "A research project on base processes." *Social History,* 4, no. 2 (May 1979), pp. 265–83.
Grote, Heiner. *Sozialdemokratie und Religion 1863–75.* Tübingen, 1968.
Grunberger, Richard. *The 12-Year Reich.* New York, 1971.
Gusfield, Joseph R. *Symbolic Crusade.* Chicago, 1963.
Hall, Alex. "Youth in Rebellion: The Beginnings of the Socialist Youth Movement 1904–14." In *Society and Politics in Wilhelmine Germany,* edited by Richard J. Evans. London, 1978, pp. 241–66.
Harney, Klaus. *Die preussische Fortbildungsschule: Eine Studie zum Problem der Hierarchisierung beruflicher Schultypen im 19. Jahrhundert.* Weinheim, 1980.
Hasenclever, Christa. *Jugendhilfe und Jugendgesetzgebung seit 1900.* Göttingen, 1978.
Heckart, Beverly. *From Bassermann to Bebel.* New Haven, 1974.
Heitzer, Horstwalter. *Der Volksverein für das katholische Deutschland im Kaiserreich 1890–1918.* Mainz, 1979.
Henschke, Margarete. *Ulrike Henschke: Ein Lebensbild aus der deutschen Frauebewegung.* Berlin, 1931.
Hentschel, Volker. *Wirtschaft und Wirtschaftpolitik im wilhelminischen Deutschland.* Stuttgart, 1978.
Höhn, Reinhard. *Sozialismus und Heer,* vols. 2, 3. *Der Kampf des Heeres gegen die Sozialdemokratie.* Bad Harzburg, 1969.
Hoffmann, Detlef. Pokorny, Doris, and Albrecht, Werner, eds. *Arbeiterjugendbewegung in Frankfurt: Material zu einer verschüteten Kulturgeschichte.* Giessen, 1978.
Homburg, Heidrun. "Anfänge des Taylorsystems in Deutschland vor dem ersten Weltkrieg." *Geschichte und Gesellschaft,* 4, no. 2 (1978).
Horhorst, G., et al. *Sozialgeschichtliches Arbeitsbuch II: Materialien zur Statistik des Kaiserreiches 1870–1914.* Munich, 1978.
Humphries, Stephen. *Hooligans or Rebels? An Oral History of Working Class Childhood and Youth 1889–1939.* Oxford, 1981.
Jahnke, Karl Heinz, et al. *Geschichte der deutschen Arbeiterjugendbewegung 1904–1945.* Dortmund, 1973.
Jarausch, Konrad H. *Students, Society and Politics in Imperial Germany.* Princeton, 1982.

Johnson, Eric A., and McHale, Vincent E. "Socioeconomic Aspects of Delinquency Rate in Imperial Germany." *Journal of Social History* (Spring 1980), pp. 384–402.

Kaiser, David E. "Germany and the Origins of the First World War." *Journal of Modern History* (September 1983).

Kall, Alfred. *Katholische Frauenbewegung in Deutschland.* Paderborn, 1983.

Kitchen, Martin. *The German Officer Corps 1890–1914.* Oxford, 1968.

Knopp, Gisbert. *Die Preussische Verwaltung des Regierungsbezirks Düsseldorf 1899–1919.* Cologne, 1974.

Kocka, Jürgen. *Klassengesellschaft im Krieg 1914–1918.* Göttingen, 1973. (Translated as *Facing Total War.* Cambridge, Mass., 1984.)

Krafeld, Franz-Josef. *Geschichte der Jugendarbeit.* Weinheim, 1984.

Kratzsch, Gerhard. *Kunstwart und Dürerbund.* Göttingen, 1969.

Kromberg, Emil. *Politische Strömungen und Wahlen in der Stadt und Landkreis Essen von der November Revolution bis zur Reichtagswahl von Dezember 1924.* Bonn, dissertation, 1968.

Kruse, Wilfred. *Die Qualifikation der Arbeiterjugend.* Frankfurt am Main, 1976.

Kuczynski, Jürgen. *Der Ausbruch des ersten Weltkrieges und die deutsche Sozialdemokratie.* East Berlin, 1957.

———. *Die Geschichte der Lage der Arbeiter unter dem Kapitalismus,* Teil I, Band 4, *Darstellung der Lage der Arbeiter in Deutschland von 1900–1917/18.* East Berlin, 1967.

Kupisch, Karl. *Der deutsche CVJM.* Kassel, 1958.

Langewiesche, Dieter, and Schönhoven, Klaus. "Arbeiterbibliotheken und Arbeiterlektüre im wilhelminischen Deutschland." *Archiv für Sozialgeschichte* 16 (1976), pp. 135–204.

———. "Wanderungsbewegungen in der Hochindustrialisierungsperiode." *Vierteljahrschrift für Sozial- und Wirtschaftsgeschichte,* 64 (1977), pp. 1–40.

Laqueur, Walter. *Young Germany: A History of the German Youth Movement,* 2nd ed. New Brunswick, 1984.

Lees, Andrew. *Cities Perceived.* New York, 1985.

Lepsius, M. Rainer. "Parteisystem und Sozialstruktur." In *Deutsche Parteien vor 1918,* edited by Gerhard A. Ritter. Cologne, 1973, pp. 56–80.

Lessing, Helmut. *Jugendpflege oder Selbsttätigkeit?* Cologne, 1976.

———, and Liebel, Manfred. *Jugend in der Klassengesellschaft.* Munich, 1974.

Lidtke, Vernon L. *The Alternative Culture: Socialist Labor in Imperial Germany.* New York, 1985.

Liebersohn, Harry. "Religion and Industrial Society: The Protestant Social Congress in Wilhelmine Germany." *Transactions of the American Philosophical Society,* 76, no. 6 (1986).

Linton, Derek S. *Imperializing Laboring Youth.* Unpublished dissertation, Princeton, 1983.

———. "Between School and Marriage, Workshop and Household: Young Working Women as a Social Problem in Late Imperial Germany." *European History Quarterly* 18, no. 4 (1988), pp. 387–408.

Lönne, Egon. *Politischer Katholizismus im 19, und 20, Jahrhundert.* Frankfurt, 1986.

Loreck, Jochen. *Wie man früher Sozialdemokrat würde.* Bonn, 1977.

Loth, Wilfried. *Katholiken im Kaiserreich.* Düsseldorf, 1984.

Lukas, Erhard. *Zwei Formen von Radikalismus in der deutschen Arbeiterbewegung.* Frankfurt, 1976.

Lüdtke, Alf. "Alltagswirklichkeit, Lebensweise und Bedürnisartikulationen." *Gesellschaft: Beiträge zur Marxischen Theorie* (Frankfurt am Main), 11 (1978), pp. 311–50.

Lundgreen, Peter. "Die Eingliederung der Unterschichten in die bürgerliche Gesellschaft durch das Bildungswesen im 19. Jahrhundert." *Internationales Archiv für Sozialgeschichte der deutschen Literatur,* 3 (1978), pp. 87–107.

Maier, Charles S. *Recasting Bourgeois Europe.* Princeton, 1975.

Mannheim, Karl. *Essays on the Sociology of Knowledge.* New York, 1952.

Mattheier, Klaus. *Die Gelben Gewerkschaften.* Düsseldorf, 1973.

Matull, Wilhelm. *Der Freiheit einer Gasse.* Bonn, 1980.

Mayer, Arno. "Domestic Causes of the First World War." In *The Responsibility of Power,* edited by Leonard Krieger and Fritz Stern. New York, 1969.

Meyer, Folkert. *Schule der Untertanen.* Hamburg, 1976.

Merquior, J. G. *Foucault.* Berkeley, 1985.

Mielke, Siegfried. *Der Hansa-Bund für Gewerbe, Handel und Industrie 1909–14.* Göttingen, 1976.

Mitterauer, Michael. *Sozialgeschichte der Jugend.* Frankfurt am Main, 1986.

Mommsen, Hans, ed. *Sozialdemokratie zwischen Klassenbewegung und Volkspartei.* Frankfurt am Main, 1974.

Mommsen, Wolfgang J. "The Topos of Inevitable War in Germany in the Decade Before 1914." In *Germany in the Age of Total War,* edited by Volker R. Berghahn and Martin Kitchen. Totowa, N.J., 1981, pp. 24–41.

Moore, Barrington. *Injustice: Social Origins of Obedience and Revolt.* White Plains, 1978.

More, Charles. *Skill and the English Working Class.* London, 1980.

Morgan, David M. *The Socialist Left and the German Revolution.* Ithaca, N.Y., 1975.

Moses, John A. *Trade Unionism in Germany from Bismarck to Hitler.* vol. 1, *1869–1918.* London, 1982.

Mosse, George. *The Crisis of German Ideology.* New York, 1964.

Musgrove, Frank. *Youth and the Social Order.* Bloomington, Ind., 1965.

Muth, Heinrich. "Jugendpflege und Politik." *Geschichte in Wissenschaft und Unterricht,* 12, no. 10 (October 1961), pp. 597–619.

Nipperdey, Thomas. "Wehlers 'Kaiserreich': Eine kritische Auseinandersetzung," *Geschichte und Gesellschaft,* 1 (1975), pp. 539–60.

Nolan, Mary. *Social Democracy and Society: Working-class Radicalism in Dusseldorf 1890–1920.* Cambridge, 1981.

Oberschall, Anthony. *Empirical Social Research in Germany 1848–1914.* Paris, 1965.

Orthmann, Rosemary. "Labor Force Participation, Life Cycle and Expenditure Patterns: The Case of Unmarried Female Factory Workers in Berlin (1902)." In *German Women in the Eighteenth and Nineteenth Centuries,* edited by Ruth-Ellen Joeres and Mary J. Maynes. Bloomington, Ind., 1986.

Otto, Christian F. "Modern Environment and Historical Continuity: The Heimatschutz Discourse in Germany." *Art Journal,* 43, no. 2 (Summer 1983), pp. 148–54.

Pascal, Roy. *From Naturalism to Expressionism.* New York, 1973.

Petrick, Fritz. *Zur sozialen Lage der Arbeiterjugend in Deutschland 1933–1939.* East Berlin, 1974.

Peukert, Detlev J. *Grenzen der Sozialdisziplinierung.* Cologne, 1986.

———. *Inside Nazi Germany.* New Haven, 1987.

———. *Jugend zwischen Krieg und Krise.* Cologne, 1987.

Preller, Ludwig. *Sozialpolitik in der Weimarer Republik.* Düsseldorf, 1978.

Rabe, Bernd. *Der sozialdemokratische Charakter.* Frankfurt am Main, 1978.

Ratz, Ursula. *Sozialreform und Arbeiterschaft.* Berlin, 1980.

Reulecke, Jürgen, ed. *Arbeiterbewegung am Rhein und Ruhr.* Wuppertal, 1974.

———, ed. *Die deutsche Stadt im Industriezeitalter,* 2nd ed. Wuppertal, 1980.

———. "Bürgerliche Sozialreformer und Arbeiterjugend im Kaiserreich." *Archiv für Sozialgeschichte* 22 (1982), pp. 299–329.

———, and Weber, W., eds. *Fabrik, Familie, Feierabend.* Wuppertal, 1978.

Ritter, Emil. *Die Katholisch-Sozial Bewegung Deutschlands im neunzehnten Jahrhundert und der Volksverein.* Cologne, 1954.

Ritter, Gerhard A. *Die Arbeiterbewegung im wilhelminischen Reich,* 2nd ed. Berlin, 1969.

Roberts, James S. *Drink, Temperance and the Working Class in Nineteenth Century Germany,* Boston, 1984.

Rosenberg, Hans. *Grosse Depression und Bismarckzeit.* Berlin, 1967.

Roth, Guenther. *The Social Democrats in Imperial Germany: A Study in Working Class Isolation and National Integration.* Totowa, N.J., 1963.

Roth, Lutz. *Die Erfindung des Jugendlichen.* Munich, 1983.

Sachsse, Christoph. *Mütterlichkeit als Beruf.* Frankfurt am Main, 1986.

Samuel, R. H., and Thomas, R. H. *Education and Society in Modern Germany.* New York, 1971.

Saul, Klaus. "Der Kampf um die Jugend zwischen Volksschule und Kaserne: Ein Beitrag zur 'Jugendpflege' im wilhelminischen Reich 1890–1914." *Militärgeschichtliche Mitteilungen,* no. 1 (1971), pp. 97–142.

———. *Staat, Industrie und Arbeiterbewegung im Kaiserreich.* Düsseldorf, 1974.

———. "Jugend im Schatten des Krieges." *Militärgeschichtliche Mitteilungen,* no. 2 (1983), pp. 91–184.

Schecker, Margarete. *Die Entwicklung der Mädchenberufsschule.* Weinheim, 1963.

Schieder, Theodor. *Das deutsche Kaiserreich von 1871 als Nationalstaat.* Cologne, 1961.

Schenda, Rudolf. *Volk ohne Buch.* Frankfurt am Main, 1970.

Schneider, Michael. "Kirche und Soziale Frage im 19. und 20. Jahrhundert." *Archiv für Sozialgeschichte* 21 (1981), pp. 533–54.

———. *Die Christlichen Gewerkschaften.* Bonn, 1982.

Schomerus, Heilwig. *Die Arbeiter der Maschinenfabrik Esslingen.* Stuttgart, 1977.

Schorske, Carl E. *German Social Democracy 1905–1917.* New York, reprinted 1972.

Schröder, Wilhelm Heinz. *Arbeitergeschichte und Arbeiterbewegung.* Frankfurt am Main, 1978.

Schult, Johannes. *Aufbruch einer Jugend.* Bonn, 1956.

Schumann, Ingeborg, Korff, Hans-Jürgen, and Schumann, Michael. *Sozialisation in Schule und Fabrik.* Berlin, 1976.

Schwerdtfeger, René. "Von Kinematographen-Zelt zum Burgtheater: Geschichte des Kinos im Kempen." Kempen, 1967.

Seidelmann, Karl. *Die Pfadfinder in der deutschen Jugendgeschichte.* Hannover, 1977.

Sheehan, James J. *German Liberalism in the Nineteenth Century.* Chicago, 1978.

———. *The Career of Lujo Brentano.* Chicago, 1966.

Simons, Diane. *Georg Kerschensteiner.* London, 1966.

Skopp, Douglas. "Auf der untersten Sprosse. Der Volksschullehrer als Semi-Professional im Deutschland des 19. Jahrhunderts." *Geschichte und Gesellschaft,* 6, no. 3 (1979), pp. 383–402.

Spencer, Elaine. *Management and Labor in Imperial Germany.* New Brunswick, 1984.

Sperber, Jonathan. *Popular Catholicism in Nineteenth Century Germany.* Princeton, 1984.

Spree, Reinhard. *Wachstumstrends und Konjuncturcyklen in der deutschen Wirtschaft von 1820 bis 1913.* Göttingen, 1978.

Springhall, John. *Youth, Empire and Society.* London, 1977.

Stachura, Peter. *The German Youth Movement 1900–1945.* New York, 1981.

———. *Nazi Youth in the Weimar Republic.* Santa Barbara, 1975.

Stearns, Peter. *Lives of Labor.* London, 1975.

Stursberg, Walter. *Glauben, Wagen, Handeln.* Wuppertal, 1977.

Tenfelde, Klaus. "Grossstadtjugend in Deutschland vor 1914: Ein historisch-demographische Annäherung." *Vierteljahrschrift fur Sozial- und Wirtschaftsgeschichte,* 69 (1982), pp. 182–218.

Tenorth, Heinz-Elmar. "Jugend und Generationen im historischen Prozess." *Internationales Archiv für Sozialgeschichte der deutschen Literatur,* 13 (1988), pp. 107–39.

Thoms, D. M. "The Emergence and Failure of the Day Continuation School Experiment." *History of Education,* 4, no. 1 (Spring 1975), pp. 36–51.

Thyssen, Simon. *Die Berufsschule in Idee und Gestaltung.* Essen, 1954.

Tilly, Louise, and Scott, Joan. *Women, Work and Family.* New York, 1978.

Tilsner-Gröll, Rotraud. *Die Jugendbildungsarbeit in den freien Gewerkschaften 1919–1933.* Frankfurt am Main, 1982.

Titze, Hartmut. *Die Politisierung der Erziehung.* Frankfurt am Main, 1973.

Trotha, Trutz von. "Zur Entstehung von Jugend." *Kölner Zeitschrift für Soziologie und Sozialpsychologie,* 34, no. 2 (1982), pp. 254–77.

Ueberhorst, Horst. *Frisch, frei, stark und treu: Die Arbeitersportbewegung in Deutschland 1893–1933.* Düsseldorf, 1973.

Volkov, Shulamit. *The Rise of Popular Antimodernism in Germany.* Princeton, 1978.

Vondung, Klaus, ed. *Das wilhelminische Bildungsbürgertum.* Göttingen, 1976.

Wehler, Hans Ulrich. *Krisenherde des Kaiserreiches.* Göttingen, 1970.

———. *Das deutsche Kaiserreich 1871–1918,* 3rd ed. Göttingen, 1977.

———. *Preussen ist wieder chic...: Politik und Polemik.* Frankfurt am Main, 1983.

———. *The German Empire 1871–1918.* Leamington Spa, 1985.

Wierling, Dorothee. *Mädchen für alles: Arbeitsalltag und Lebensgeschichite Städtischer Dienstmädchen um die Jahrhundertwende.* Bonn, 1987.

Wernet, Wilhelm. *Handwerkpolitik*. Göttingen, 1952.
Willis, Paul. *Learning to Labour*. Westmead, 1977.
Witt, Peter Christian. *Die Finanzpolitik des deutschen Reiches von 1903–13*. Lübeck, 1970.

Index